Praise for *Magic Wor*

MW00851491

"[A]n impressive work. . . . The 'take away' I had from this book has less to do with the amusing words and their definitions, and more to do with a thoughtful consideration of the role of the magic word in my own work."
　　—Brad Henderson, *MAGIC, The Magazine for Magicians*

"I am in awe of the volume and variety of the usages and references discussed: the research seems monumental. . . . Yes, it will not only give you the importance of magic words, the kinds of magic words used under what circumstances, what the public (as expressed through references in literature) thinks about magic words and what are magic words, it will help you understand magic and your relationship to it. Recommended as a very useful resource for those who think and care."
　　—Phil Willmarth, *Linking Ring Magazine*

"No matter how you approach it, Conley has given us a delightful resource that entertains, informs, and inspires. If only more books, especially those for magicians, offered as much."
　　—Gordon Meyer, author of *Smart Home Hacks*

"Recommended!"
　　—Eugene Burger, author of *Mastering the Art of Magic*

"Truly words of magic about magic words!"
　　—Bill Wisch, creator of "The Magic Word" program

"This is a great book. Loads of fun to browse through and stimulate understandings and possibilities . . . fascinating information that is stimulating for the creation of either tricks or presentations, being quite difficult to let go of."
　　—Robert Neale, author of *The Magic Mirror*

"Too often we forget the real Magic in our lives. Craig Conley is a student of Wonder, and like all true Wonder Experiencers, he is moved to share that. Mr. Conley reminds us to open our eyes, minds, ears and hearts to the Wonder within and without. Those of us who travel along such paths are ever grateful for Those Few who travel with us in spirit. Craig Conley is one of Those Few."

—Kenton Knepper (The Mystic of Magic), author of *Wonder Words*

"Extremely good, and shows an astounding amount of research. . . . Wonderful and fascinating."

—Stephen Minch, author of *Mind and Matter*

"A fascinating piece of scholarship, and an invitation to wonder."

—Bernie DeKoven, author of *The Well Played Game*

"Useful . . . entertaining."

—Taylor Ellwood, author of *Pop Culture Magick*

"A Magic Masterpiece!"

—Magic-Al Garber, creator of "It's a Magic-Al World!"

"Contains notes on everything from the fractal magic word abacaba-dabacaba to the typographically charged zxcvbnm, and a few more besides."

—Science Fiction and Fantasy Writers of America

"We must return to the magic. We must open our minds."

—Marilyn Jenett, prosperity counsellor

"Wonderful."

—Graham P. Collins, editor of *Scientific American*

"Particularly interesting."

—Professor Hex, "scholar of the strange and mysterious"

"A wealth of information for the aspiring magician."

—*SpookyLibrarians.com*

To: Fuge

MAGIC
WORDS

"And above all, watch with glittering eyes
the whole world around you because the
greatest secrets are always hidden in the
most unlikely places. Those who don't
believe in magic will never find it."
                              - Roald Dahl

Enjoy!

Gale and
Gordon

MAGIC WORDS

A Dictionary

CRAIG CONLEY

WEISERBOOKS
San Francisco, CA / Newburyport, MA

First published in 2008 by
Red Wheel/Weiser, LLC
With offices at:
500 Third Street, Suite 230
San Francisco, CA 94107
www.redwheelweiser.com

Copyright © 2008 by Craig Conley.
All rights reserved. No part of this publication may be reproduced or transmitted in any form or by
any means, electronic or mechanical, including photocopying, recording, or by any information storage and retrieval system, without permission in writing from Red Wheel/Weiser, LLC. Reviewers may
quote brief passages.

ISBN: 978-1-57863-434-7
Library of Congress Cataloging-in-Publication Data available upon request.

Cover and text design by Donna Linden.
Typeset in Baskerville, Dalliance, and Felix Titling.
Cover photograph © Emrah Turudu/iStockphoto.com.

Printed in Canada
TCP
10 9 8 7 6 5 4 3 2 1

The paper used in this publication meets the minimum requirements of the American National Standard for Information Sciences—Permanence of Paper for Printed Library Materials Z39.48-1992
(R1997).

For June and Allan

For Michael

For Jonathan

I . . . used magic words to wake the magic arts.
—Ovid, *The Metamorphoses*, translated by Horace Gregory

The magic word, the mystic fire.
—Sri Aurobindo, *Savitri: A Legend and a Symbol* (1995)

Magical words . . . are a prism of the universe; they reflect,
decompose, and recombine all its wonders. The sounds imitate colours,
the colours merge into harmony. The rhyme, rich or strange, swift or lingering, is inspired by poetic insight, that supreme beauty of art and triumph of
genius which discovers in nature all secrets close to the human heart.
—Madame de Staël, *Corinne, or Italy* (1807),
translated by Sylvia Raphael (1998)

Say a magic word if you have one.
—Bart King, *The Big Book of Boy Stuff* (2004)

Magic words give you another means of taking control of your performance.
—Jeff Galloway, *Galloway's Book on Running* (2002)

Across the land came a magic word
When the earth was bare and lonely,
And I sit and sing of the joyous spring,
For 'twas I who heard, I only!
—Fay Inchfawn, "The Thrush" (1920)

INTRODUCTION

A Tip of the Hat

It may be a magic spell in the dictionary, but in the mind of man all the world over it signifies the respect and consideration paid to great powers and noble qualities.
—*Blackwood's Edinburgh Magazine* (1898)

A moment of epiphany inspired this book—a moment as dazzling, in its way, as a conjuror's most triumphant revelations. One Sunday evening, I had the privilege of witnessing a marvelous performance of the famous "die box" effect, at Hollywood's Magic Castle. Although the presentation of this classic trick was nothing short of expert, the performance seemed somehow to be lacking something. In the art of magic, nothing is more crucial than the level of involvement of the audience. And on this memorable occasion, it was the level of involvement of one particular audience member which triggered my insight into precisely what was missing from an otherwise flawless display.

At the climax of the trick, the magician began to open the doors of his wooden box to reveal that the spectacularly oversized die inside had, evidently, vanished into thin air. Suddenly, a voice from the audience rang out across the hushed tension of the theatre. A heckler? No, not exactly—though one could perhaps brand her a "kibitzer." What, then, was the content of her momentous interjection? It was merely one word: *Voilà!*

"Voilà!" My fellow spectator called the word out in a loud whisper, like an efficient script girl prompting a delinquent stage actor's lines from behind the curtain. "Voilà!" she repeated, perhaps with a hint more insistence, when the magician failed to take her cue.

One can certainly sympathize with the professional entertainer who has trained himself to ignore distractions, criticism, insults, flirtation, and motherly advice from the audience, lest his rhythm falter or his control waver. What magician could be at once so humble (a trait not generally associated with magicians) and so self-confident as to let a "Voilà!" pass his lips, after an audience member has attempted to spoon-feed it to him? No, it should not surprise us that the performer ignored our heroine and simply continued with his routine.

But the spectator was expressing a genuine desperation, rooted in a legitimate expectation. She awaited, she desired, she *needed* something that the magician was not providing: a *magic word* to trigger the effect's finale. Her point was crystal clear—a wondrous effect demands to be marked and activated by a magic word, a word that bespeaks the history of the craft, the requisite secret knowledge, the focused intent of the performer . . . and, above all, humanity's deep-rooted reverence for the creative power of language. *Voilà:* behold! As the lady's unheeded request lingered awkwardly in the room, the sheer vibrancy and urgency of magic words was dramatically revealed.[1] And it was revealed with a power and resonance that eclipsed even that of the onstage illusion.

Our current fascination with magic words stems from a general revival of interest in the arts of close-up magic and grand illusions. This began in the late twentieth-century and has continued into the twenty-first, fueled by the work of such performers as Criss Angel, Lance Burton, David Copperfield, Siegfried & Roy, David Blaine, and Jeff McBride. But magic words are, as one might guess,

---

1   As Stephen L. Carter succinctly puts it, "Words are magic. We conjure with them" (*Civility* [1998]). The reason for this is equally simple: "Words and magic were in the beginning one and the same thing" (Sigmund Freud, *A General Introduction to Psychoanalysis* [1917]).

as old as conjuring itself.[2] Their presence, as echoes of the rhythm and vibration of creative power, has always gone hand-in-hand with sleight-of-hand.

Professional magician Jeff McBride considers the very first magicians to have been storytellers: "They told a story with words. Words are powerful tools."[3] Indeed, "One of the most powerful ways of specifying your magical or mystical intent is through the use of words."[4] Any magician, like any storyteller, uses many of the same words as the population at large. But then there are those special words, those that are the hallmark of his art: the "magic" ones. The heft of these words cannot be denied. They convey import and influence, whether one regards them as embodying a supernatural significance and origin; or, instead, as the original creations of human culture, the trappings of superstition and showbiz. Where they fail to produce awe, they instead invite a linguistic fascination. If they're not really "magic," thinks the skeptical scholar, then let us explore why and how we have evolved and perpetuated these particular words.

A great many magic words have stood the test of time, passed on from master to apprentice, generation through generation, to find expression on the modern stage and street. These ancient, musical, poetic incantations have a profound—but not necessarily unfathomable—mystique. From the familiar but oft-perplexing classics like *abracadabra*, *alakazam*, *hocus pocus*, *presto-chango*, *shazam*, and *sim sala bim*, to whimsical modern inventions like *izzy wizzy let's get busy*, to lesser known gems like the tongue-twisting *tirratarratorratarratirratarratum*, these venerable magic words and phrases warrant a serious, scholarly tribute.

These potent and glorious words, long prized by shamen, conjurors, and illusionists, have earned the right to the ultimate linguistic honor—enshrinement in their own special dictionary. The volume you are holding explores the most intriguing magic words and phrases from around the world, from a vast assortment of periods and civilizations. The entries touch upon each term's special aura of mystery, its meaning or meanings, and its origin and history. We will also encounter popular variations, amusing trivia, and some fascinating examples of usage from both literature and popular culture.[5] Sources—by which I mean

---

2   One of Japan's earliest chronicles of history and mythology, *Holy Nihongi* (720 CE), traces the first use of magic incantations to the year 660 BCE.

3   "Spiritual Strength and Introspection," *The Secret Art* (2001)

4   Jason Augustus Newcomb, *New Hermetics* (2004)

5   As literary theorist Samuel C. Wheeler III has noted, "[T]here are no magical words which interpret themselves . . . The meaning of a word can be given only in other words" (*Literary Theory After Davidson*, edited by Reed Way Dasenbrock [1993]). One might say the same of all words, of course—hence the notorious circularity of dictionaries.

those remarkable practitioners of magic, throughout the ages, who have been documented as using these words—range from prominent modern magicians to their distant ancestors: the hierophants of ancient Egypt; the high priests, medicine men, sorcerers, and alchemists of the Middle Ages; and the workers of wonders and miracles throughout history—all performers of their day, seeking "to mystify, to enchant, to entertain."[6] Nor have we neglected their prominent, if fictitious, cousins—the necromancers and wizards of legend and fairy tale.

Open sesame, one of the most celebrated magic phrases, held enough power for Ali Baba to shift boulders and open a passage into the unknown. This colorful, centuries-old fable points to a literal truth about the power and importance of magic words:

> We know that words cannot move mountains, but they can move the multitude. . . . Words shape thought, stir feeling, and beget action; they kill and revive, corrupt and cure. The "men of words"—priests, prophets, intellectuals—have played a more decisive role in history than military leaders, statesmen, and businessmen.
>
> Words and magic are particularly crucial in time of crisis when old forms of life are in dissolution and man must grapple with the unknown. Normal motives and incentives lose then their efficacy. Man does not plunge into the unknown in search of the prosaic and matter-of-fact. His soul has to be stretched by reaching out for the fabulous and unprecedented. He needs the nurse of magic and breath-taking fairy tales to lure him on and sustain him in his faltering first steps. Even modern science and technology were not in the beginning a sober pursuit of facts and knowledge. Here, too, the magicians—alchemists, astrologers, visionaries—were the pioneers.[7]

From ideology to science, from spiritualism to cultural revolutions, words open passages into the unknown. And anyone, whether leader or follower, for whom discourse serves as a first step to unexplored territory, is an Ali Baba, a personal pioneer.

---

6   Ralph A. Hefner, *The Atlanta Society of Magicians, Twenty-fifth Anniversary Souvenir Program* (1949)

7   Eric Hoffer, *The Ordeal of Change* (1976)

Modern magicians continue to pioneer, constantly redefining "the fabulous and unprecedented." Uttering a magic word, they wave a collective wand over the scientific spirit of our times, to reveal "soul-stirring myths and illusions."[8] Their effect on us recalls a rapturous passage in the work of novelist Angela Thirkell, which one may read as a kind of tribute to the *open sesame* effect: "Oh, word of magic, of freedom, of bliss, of old life forgotten, new life begun."[9]

Jim Butcher, author of mystery novels set in a magic-enabled world, posits that words aren't so much magical in themselves as they are containers that hold the magic. "They give [magic] a shape and a form, they make it useful, describe the images within." One might imagine a magician's enchanted silk as such a container, giving shape and form to the invisible magic force that animates it. Or one might picture the age-old cup-and-ball tumbler, or the magician's signature top hat, as delineating a space within which marvels occur.

Butcher adds that a few particular words are so magical "they resound in the heart and mind, they live long after the sounds of them have died away, they echo in the heart and the soul. They have power, and that power is very real."[10] Even professional magicians, intimately familiar as they are with the mechanics of illusion, long to enjoy that heart-, mind-, and soul-wrenching amazement along with their spectators. We must remember, after all, that a craving for wonder is universal. Moreover, it stands to reason that this craving might be especially intense in the psyches of those individuals who pursue magic as a career or avocation. As a budding magician's skill in understanding and contriving illusions develops, there is no reason to suppose that his hunger for wonder accordingly diminishes. Perhaps this is why magic catalogs so often promise that the magician will be equally amazed by an illusion. For example, magician Jim Cellini's "Lord of the Rings" routine vows: "You will stand in front of a mirror and amaze even yourself when you perform these moves."[11] Likewise, magician Lubor Fiedler's "Blue Crystal" trick promises it "allows you to experience the astonishment yourself, when the crystal surface that you just touched allows coins and cards to sink inside. The visual effect will cause you to question your own eyes."[12] Knowledge of procedures may be beguiling to a point, but

---

8   *Ibid.*

9   *August Folly* (1936)

10   *Grave Peril* (2001). Similarly, D.A. Carson notes: "There is nothing magical in the words themselves. But when you actually *mean* the words you say, they are life changing" (*Sunsets: Reflections For Life's Final Journey* [2005]).

11   Denny Haney, *DennyMagic.com* (2005)

12   Misdirections Magic Shop, *Misdirections.com* (2005)

the very sounds of "magical words, sacred references, and metaphors" can prove "irresistible."[13] Everyone can share that primal amazement, gloriously augmented by the reverberations of the right magic words.

What is the source of primal amazement? Language has the power to re-awaken vestiges of humankind's earliest communication—our ancient ances-tors' savage cries of anger or love. All such cries were commands, "originally bound up with the act" and indeed inseparable to the primitive mind. Much in the way that a small child learns to conjure up a parent from the unseen void of an adjoining room, simply by employing a magic word like "Mama," we can reflect that "The savage called his friend's name, and saw his friend turn and answer; what more natural to conclude than that the name itself in some way *compelled* an answer?"[14]

Eons later, words are still magic:

Dipped in the wisdom
Of our ancestors
Words pluck strings reaching far through time[15]

The word, "having originally formed part of the act, is able to evoke all the concrete emotional contents of the act. Love cries, for instance, which lead up to the sexual act are obviously among the most primitive words; hencefor-ward these and all other words alluding to the act retain a definite emotional charge."[16] One needn't look far to observe that those words which reference "the act" are indeed remarkable in their power to arouse, titillate, shock, offend, and even amuse.

This primitive vestige is alive in a magician's magic words as well. The audience has an instinctive understanding (inherited from humanity's earliest ancestors) that one's commands and actions are mysteriously bound together into what Arthur Koestler calls "an almost indivisible unity"[17]—notwithstand-ing the claim of Shakespearean spell-casters that they are engaging in a "deed

---

13   Martín Prechtel, *Long Life, Honey in the Heart* (1999). Scholar Thomas Seifrid notes that "every word is in principle a metaphor" (*The Word Made Self: Russian Writings On Language, 1860–1930* [2005]).

14   Joy Davidman, *Smoke on the Mountain* (1953)

15   Blain Bovee, *The Sabian Symbols & Astrological Analysis* (2004)

16   Jean Piaget, *Language and Thought of the Child* (1926)

17   *The Act of Creation* (1964)

without a name."[18] Every audience brings its own emotional component to this mystery. "That same feeling of awe is still manifest in children's eyes when they listen to a magician's *abracadabra*."[19] This sort of emotion is priceless to the art of conjuring: "Sartre used the word 'magic' to describe the way in which . . . emotions completely overrule logic, until the world is seen through a sort of distorting mirror."[20]

Manipulating the audience through language, the magician can do even more than distort logic and obscure reality: he can "replace it altogether."[21] He accomplishes some of this with ordinary language, complementing his leger-demain with a patter calculated to shape our perceptions and expectations, mis-direct our attention, and obfuscate our sensory cues. But at the critical moment, it is not ordinary language on which the magician traditionally relies.

It is the intention of this dictionary to showcase those powerful words that give shape and form to a magician's ungraspable feats, much like his piece of silk, or that construct a puzzling new reality, like his landscape of smoke and mirrors. Whether you are a professional illusionist, an amateur at sleight-of-hand, or simply a word lover intrigued by the power of language, may this dictionary enlighten and inspire you to create pure wonder and awe whenever you speak. *Voilà!*

Hocus Pocus Is No "Mumbo Jumbo"

Magic words may be even more meaningful than ordinary ones.
—Tore Janson, *A Natural History of Latin* (2004)

The root of the word "grammar" is "grimoire" . . . Language is a book of spells.
—William A. Covino, *Magic, Rhetoric, and Literacy* (1994)

Magic words, to use the colorful phraseology of diarist Anaïs Nin, are like fugi-tives from a subtle world of fairy tales and dreams, "beyond the law of gravity [and] chaos." They comprise a mysterious language "which is shadowy and full of reverberations" and deep in meaning. They catch the essence of "what we pursue in the night dream, and which eludes us, the incident which evaporates

---

18   *Macbeth*, IV.i.49

19   Marcel Danesi, *Of Cigarettes, High Heels, and Other Interesting Things: An Introduction to Semiotics* (1999)

20   Colin Wilson, *The Mammoth Book of True Crime* (1973)

21   Neil Postman, *Conscientious Objections* (1988)

as we awake."[22] They establish a sacred space where miracles can occur. And of course they trigger transformations. "'Magic words' . . . immediately lead to action and transform reality."[23]

Medieval conjurors first began using exotic words to "give their performances an air of authentic secret knowledge."[24] Whether they employed pseudo-Latin phrases, nonsense syllables, or esoteric terms from religious antiquity, these magicians were doing far more than merely adding a bit of enigmatic audio to their visuals.[25] They were enhancing their specific illusions with a universal mystery: language as an instrument of creation.

Ancient-sounding words project an aura of tradition, of "'old wisdom' handed down through generations."[26] It's little wonder that the archetypical depiction of a magician involves the utterance of antiquated words, in addition to the grand gestures that impart a larger-than-life dimension to his activities.[27] And because archaic magic words necessarily predate a magician's own life, they point to the existence of a "transcendent" realm[28] beyond the logic and laws of our ordinary world.

The world of the past is always mysterious to those too young to recall it. We can also assume that people are more likely to accept the amazing if it is associated with a context other than their own. It is no accident that fantastic tales are often introduced as having happened "once upon a time" or "long ago and far away." "[I]t does not matter whether this archaism is genuine or fake" as long as members of the audience experience themselves "as participating in something extended far beyond their own life."[29] "Knowledge of such special words and languages enables the magician to communicate with [and activate] elements belonging to [sacred] space."[30] And when the magician intones such words he transforms any parlor, theatre, municipal arena—or even the whiskey-stained surface of a rickety card table—into a sacred space primed for the extraordinary.

---

22   Anaïs Nin, *Fire: From 'A Journal of Love': The Unexpurgated Diary of Anaïs Nin, 1934–1937* (1995)

23   Anthony Olszewski, "When Baraka Blows His Horn" (2004)

24   Paul Kriwaczek, *In Search of Zarathustra: The First Prophet and the Ideas That Changed the World* (2003)

25   Needless to say, a magician's patter can serve to distract, for "We get mesmerized by magic words" (Dale Mathers, *An Introduction to Meaning and Purpose in Analytical Psychology* [2002]).

26   Jesper Sorensen, *Magical Rituals and Conceptual Blending*

27   *HiddenRealms.net* (2002)

28   Jesper Sorensen, *Magical Rituals and Conceptual Blending*

29   *Ibid.*

30   *Ibid.*

There are profound truths in that old cliché of a magician pulling a rabbit out of an empty hat with the magic word *abracadabra*. Almost everyone recognizes the image. But what relatively few people know is that our stereotypical magician is speaking an ancient Hebrew phrase that means "I will create with words."[31] He is making something out of nothing, echoing that famous line from *Genesis:* "Let there be light, and there was light." Only in this case, the magician's venue being already equipped with light, the magic is applied toward the creation of rabbits—and perhaps a sensational flash of supplementary illumination, in the form of fire.

The magic word, whether it be *abracadabra* or another at the magician's disposal, resonates with the audience because there is an instinctive understanding that words are powerful, creative forces. "The word has always held an ancient enchantment for humans," says scholar Ted Andrews. "It hints of journeys into unseen and unmapped domains."[32] No wonder it has been said that "all magic is in a word."[33]

The inherent enchantment of the word is of course what gives literature its magical influence. In 1865, scholar Thomas Babington Macaulay examined what makes the poetry of Milton so magical, and his conclusions are most appropriate to magic words in general:

> His poetry acts like an incantation. Its merit lies less in its obvious meaning than in its occult power.

Moving from the sublime to the sublimely ridiculous, one could perhaps make an analogous argument regarding the evocative nonsense of Lewis Carroll's "Jabberwocky"—the words of which are as compelling as they are meaningless. But Macaulay goes on:

> There would seem, at first sight, to be no more in his words than in other words. But they are words of enchantment. No sooner are they pronounced than the past is present and the distant near. New forms

---

31   David Aaron, *Endless Light: The Ancient Path of Kabbalah* (1998). See the entry on *abracadabra* for additional interpretations.

32   *Simplified Qabala Magic* (2003)

33   Alphonse Louis Constant (Eliphas Levi), *The Key of the Mysteries* (1861)

of beauty start at once into existence, and all the burial-places of the
memory give up their dead.[34]

Throughout the various discussions of magic words in this dictionary, we will
explore exactly how and why they conjure the mystique and romance of the
past and the glittering promises of the future.

There is a marvelous discussion of sacred language in the Pulitzer Prize–
winning novel *House Made of Dawn* (1966) by N. Scott Momaday, in which words
are equated with sleight-of-hand. Momaday speaks of his Kiowa Indian grandmother teaching him how to "listen and delight" through her storytelling. With
her words, she took him "directly into the presence of her mind and spirit." As
he explains, "[S]he was taking hold of my imagination, giving me to share in
the great fortune of her wonder and delight. She was asking me to go with her
to the confrontation of something that was sacred and eternal. It was a timeless,
timeless thing." For his grandmother, "words were medicine; they were magic
and invisible. They came from nothing into sound and meaning." As in *Genesis*,
the Kiowa creation story begins with something happening in the nothingness.
"There was a voice, a sound, a word—and everything began."

Let us apply Momaday's discussion directly to the art of a magician by positing a few questions:

- *Does not a magician want his audience to "listen and delight" in his performance?*
- *Does not a magician want to draw an entire audience into his presence?*
- *Does not a magician wish to take hold of people's imaginations and help them to share in the awe and wonderment?*
- *Does not a magician wish to present a timeless mystery?*

By speaking a magic word, a magician most certainly encourages his audience
to "listen and delight" as he encompasses them in his presence, takes hold of
their collective imagination, and allows them to share in the "wonder." By uttering his magic word, a magician invites the audience to accompany him in
confronting something "sacred and eternal . . . a timeless thing," as Momaday

---

34   *Critical and Historical Essays*, quoted in *Nets of Awareness: Urdu Poetry and Its Critics* by Frances W.
      Pritchett (1994)

puts it. And when he produces the magic syllables for all to hear, a magician makes every member of the audience an active participant in the miracle. For "in the world of magic, the Word creates."[35]

---

35 Gahl Sasson, *A Wish Can Change Your Life: How to Use the Ancient Wisdom of Kabbalah to Make Your Dreams Come True* (2003). Howard Rheingold writes that "We create the world every day when we utter words. Yet we are rarely aware of this awesome act. The power of words is woven so tightly into our daily lives that we hardly ever take time to marvel at it. Our ancestors knew, though: It is no accident that many of the world's religious scriptures assert that the universe was created by a word" *(They Have a Word for It* [2000]). Migene Gonzalez-Wippler provides an example: "The Kabbalah has a fascinating story to tell on the creation of the world by sound. It says that when God decided to create the universe He was uncertain as to which letter he would use to begin creation. All the letters of the Hebrew alphabet came to God in one long line and each pleaded with Him to use it, naming and vastly exaggerating all its wonderful qualities. God listened to all of them thoughtfully, and finally decided on the letter *Beth*, which means house or container. With the power of the letter *Beth* God 'contained' the unmanifested universe and created the entire cosmos" (*The Complete Book of Spells, Ceremonies and Magic* [1978]).

DEEP ASPECTS OF MAGIC WORDS

A Special Reverence for the Mystery

Every word is magic, a story achieved through will.
—Rochelle Lynn Holt, "Take Nothing for Granted," *Bless the Day* (1998)

If intoned in the proper spirit, any word can be a magic word. In *The Re-enchantment of Everyday Life* (1997), Thomas Moore notes that "we may evoke the magic in words by their placement, . . . rhyme, assonance, intonation, emphasis, and, as [mythologist James] Hillman suggests, historical context." Even the mundane connotations of the words we use depend frequently on the many details of their packaging. The more essential the responsibilities we intend for a given word, the more we depend on the magic of its presentation. A "key" word should enjoy a flourish as it is revealed. We should draw it forth like a prestidigitator who, with great drama, produces an egg from his mouth.

"Historical context" may seem like a peculiar attribute to group with the elements of pronunciation and the techniques of poetry. But historical context is a fundamental property of any word, and can be a heavy determinant of its potential impact. As Thomas Armstrong explains, "In a sense each word in the English language rides upon the waves of history. It represents the outcome of an evolutionary process that has its origins in archaic languages and at each step in history underwent a refining process in its spelling, pronunciation, and meaning until it reached its present status in the dictionary (which is still 'in progress.')"[36]

Commonplace Words with Magical Connotations

A great many "commonplace" words—i.e. words that the editor of a dictionary of *magic* words respectfully regrets that he will be unable to include—come standard with a special spark of their own. Literature, folklore, and even advertising are replete with examples of commonplace words that are rich with "magical" connotations. Take for example the word *Paris*. For many people who reside outside the City of Lights but within the sphere of Western culture, *Paris* instantly conjures images of romance. "The magic word *Paris* drew them on," writes Barbara W. Tuchman.[37] Similarly, the old name for China, *Cathay*, conjures up an exotic, faraway land of spices and silks, while *the Riviera* is "full of aspirations of elegance [and] excitement."[38] For author M.M. Kaye, "Zanzibar is one of those names that possess a peculiar, singing magic in every syllable; like Samarkand or Rajasthan, or Kilimanjaro."[39] In *The Story of Mankind* (1921), Hendrik Willem Van Loon speaks of people "forever under the spell of this magic word 'Rome.'"

Place names are indeed among the words most often imbued with primal, powerful connotations. (For no matter how sophisticated the implied glamour of the word *Paris*, our attraction to this magic word is the product of primitive emotions.) But this magic is by no means limited to place names, and we have only to toss out a few choice words like *birthday* and *romance* and *home* to demonstrate this. Discussing the songs of Hoagy Carmichael (and his collaborating lyricists), author William Zinsser identifies what he calls "magical words" with powerful connotations:

- *moonlight*
- *Wabash*
- *sycamore*

---

36   *Seven Kinds of Smart* (1993)

37   *Guns of August* (1962)

38   Barrie Kerper, *Provence* (2001)

39   *Death in Zanzibar* (1959)

- *'possum*
- *oleander*
- *rhubarb*
- *veranda*
- *buttermilk*
- *old mill*
- *watermelon*

Zinsser explains: "They reach us not only through the eye, ear and nose but through two even more powerful transmitters: memory and yearning for the simplicities of yesterday."[40] The effect of the magic words on this short list comes from a symbiosis of sense and sound. And, not surprisingly, every one of them has a musical cadence. Even without their ready-made nostalgia, the syllables are fun to say.

Evocative song lyrics are known for their power to inspire sentiment, singing along, out-of-context quotation and even parody . . . but words don't have to be associated with songs to similarly intoxicate. Author Amy Hirshberg Lederman confesses, "As a little girl I would whisper words to myself just to hear the sounds of them; magical words like *canopy, arithmetic* and *Ethiopia*."[41]

Stephen King recounts his personal story of two powerful words and a litany of historical figures that capture a child's imagination:

> [T]wo magic words [were] glittering and glowing like a beautiful neon sign; two words of almost incredible power and grace; and these two words were PIONEER SPIRIT. I and my fellow kids grew up secure in this knowledge of America's PIONEER SPIRIT—a knowledge that could be summed up in a litany of names learned by rote in the classroom. Eli Whitney. Samuel Morse. Alexander Graham Bell. Henry Ford. Robert Goddard. Wilbur and Orville Wright. Robert Oppenheimer.[42]

In one way or another, these American pioneers all embodied the spirit of a world-shaking word that encompasses a plethora of possibilities: *revolution*.

---

40   *Easy to Remember* (2000)

41   *To Life!* (2004). Novelist Pete Hamill has his own mesmerizing list: "Magic words. *Europe. Steeples. The Vatican. Japan. Horses. Hallways. Pigeons. Jeeps*" (*Snow in August* [1998]). So, too, does Audre Lorde: "Carriacou, a magic name like cinnamon, nutmeg, mace" (*Zami* [1982]).

42   *Danse Macabre* (1981)

"The magic word 'revolution' made people hopeful, happy, and ready to embrace each other."[43] In its political sense, the call of *revolution* draws on a desire for freedom that is in some ways analogous to the beckoning horizons that infuse pioneers with their own revolutionary aspirations (be they spatial, technological, or intellectual).

Freedom and its synonym *liberty* provide further examples of words that have massive clout in both political and other arenas. "Liberty! A magic word, a word full of feeling, a sentiment for which millions have laid down their lives."[44] A concept deemed to be worth dying for is, by the lights of an underlying ideology, recognized as accordingly life-enhancing. And the concept's power to rally and inspire always depends on the words that succinctly and evocatively package this ideology. For example, at the risk of his own life, Pope John Paul II visited Soviet-occupied Czestochowa, Poland, where he defiantly "validated the magic word that he used over and over again: SOLIDARITY!"[45]

Magicians' Exalted Words

A magician's entire patter could no doubt be described as "magic words." But in this book we dedicate attention to those words spoken with a special reverence for the Mystery—those enigmatic words and phrases, not usually employed in everyday discourse or conversation, which invoke the powers of creation and destruction when something is to appear out of thin air or to disappear back into the great void. Too often dismissed as "meaningless gibberish," such magic words are, on the contrary, rich in meaning for those initiated into their significance. And unlike computer-generated gibberish, for example—which typically prompts nothing deeper than shoulder-shrugging or hair-tearing—the sacred vocabulary of mystery-makers has always affected listeners in profound (if indescribable) ways.

The key to this paradoxical resonance of mysterious words among the uninitiated—those, that is, to whom their meanings are not understood—may be that the words' meanings, though obscure to the listener, possess an implicit profundity that is transmitted through its sounds and cadences. "People are

---

43   Edward P. Gazur, *The March of Time* (2004)

44   Dale Carnegie, *How to Develop Self-Confidence and Influence People by Public Speaking* (1991)

45   Virgilio Levi, *John Paul II: A Tribute in Words and Pictures* (1999). On the opposite end of the revolutionary spectrum is the concept of meekness: "Humility—that is the magic word" (Ben Hogan, *Five Lessons: The Modern Fundamentals of Golf* [1985]).

struck by something and yet they don't really seem to know what it is," music critic Robert Shelton observes. "That's always been the case with the most acute and exalted poetry. There are lines of Shakespeare like this, in which you don't have to [understand] . . . to be struck by the magic of words."[46]

Every magician knows that even young children are deeply moved by magic words. This makes sense, when we consider how attuned they are to the magic of words in general: writing teacher Deena Metzger describes a three-year-old pupil who "knew the magic of words; she knew that words could create magic, that they were magic. She knew that they could create worlds, could describe worlds, explore worlds, and also be the bridge between one world and another."[47]

If magic words can inspire awe even among those who do not understand them, then why has a classic, time-tested magic word like *abracadabra* become "a very tired cliché" to such professional magicians as David Pogue, author of *Magic for Dummies*?[48] Composer and philosopher David Rothenberg suggests a convincing answer: whenever words are tossed out without the proper feeling, they "[take] revenge by becoming hokey as hell."[49] Consider this advice from scholar Phillip Cooper:

> If words are going to be used, they should be meant. Words of power work because the person puts feeling, belief, and imagination into those words. Nonmagic words—the vocabulary of the human race—hinder real communication. . . . Magic words emanate from the heart.[50]

The rich heritage of magic words need not fade away,[51] and certainly no magician should cringe over the terms of his art, much less turn a deaf ear to his sonorous legacy. This book seeks to reach deep into the glimmering treasure-chest of magic words and reinstate dignity to a dusty, subsidiary treasury—the little jewel box full of terms that have lost their sparkle over the years. It also seeks to

---

46   *No Direction Home: The Life and Music of Bob Dylan* (1986)

47   Quoted in *Awakening at Midlife* by Kathleen A. Brehony (1997)

48   Pogue claims "You could probably think of something funnier and more entertaining [than *abracadabra*] without even trying" (*Magic for Dummies* [1998]).

49   *The Book of Music and Nature: An Anthology of Sounds, Words, Thoughts* (2001)

50   *Esoteric Magic and the Cabala* (2002)

51   As Roland Barthes has said, "These words, whose magic is dead for us, can be renewed" (*The Rustle of Language* [1986]).

celebrate and codify the new magic words that magicians are, with a wave of a wand or the tip of a hat, adding to the lexicon every day. Just as the Russian poet Andrei Bely "enthused over nothing less than the literal magic of words and urged that the force of primitive incantations be recreated"[52] in poetry, this dictionary is testament to the magic of words and urges magicians to reinvest their incantations with that primitive power everyone remembers at the deepest level.

The Vocabulary of Ritual

Adults have lost touch with the mystery and magic of words.
—Thomas Armstrong, *Seven Kinds of Smart* (1999)

As we shall see, the infinite world of magic has room enough for both reverence and self-parody. This dictionary celebrates fun, new forms of magic wordplay, especially those humorous send-ups of the old standards, like ripening *abracadabra* into *have a banana* or dancing *hocus pocus* around to *hokey pokey*. Clever wordplay—a sort of verbal magic wand—keeps the culture of magic rich, vital, and growing . . . and, of course, entertaining. (Remember, a magician is nothing if not a performer.)

Irreverent comical twists serve a legitimate purpose. Nevertheless, the exotic, historical terminology in its authentic form has by no means been rendered useless. Philosopher and law professor William Ian Miller posits that cryptic terms lend an important air of "inaccessibility" to our rituals.[53] A magic show is without question its own form of ritual. And Miller defines a "Big *R* ritual" as one that involves "something that we call, if we do not fear being struck down by some offended power, hocus-pocus" and that can be "distinguished from the small rituals of daily life by a sacred separation." Miller points out that Rituals are often carried out in a language we don't understand:

> as when I pray in Hebrew or Catholics used to pray in Latin, or when Protestants recently used the King James Bible, or when kids have not a clue as to what the words are or mean, though in English, when they sing Christmas carols or the national anthem or say the pledge of allegiance. What of the "forgive us our trespasses" of the Lord's prayer, when it was understood that cutting across Mrs. Keappock's lawn ranked right

---

52   Thomas Seifrid, *The Word Made Self: Russian Writings On Language, 1860–1930* (2005)
53   *Faking It* (2003)

up there with murder in what got God really mad. What eight-year-old knew that "plejallegiance" was or what one nation was "invisible"?[54]

It is this mysterious quality, among other things, that differentiates a Ritual from lower-case rituals like reading the funnies over breakfast or doing the laundry on Sunday.

In the same spirit as those magicians who consider the *abracadabras* of old to be out of touch with modern audiences, religious reform movements "often make the inaccessibility of sacred language to the laity the rallying point of their program," says Miller. "But that seems to miss the point of what defines sacredness: its inaccessibility. So much of the uncanniness of successful Ritual depends precisely on our not understanding what is said, probably because we think Ritual should be dealing with the mysterious, the incomprehensible, the ineffable." Certainly our magic show Rituals are meant to be uncanny, mysterious, incomprehensible, and ineffable. And strange, enchanting words from vanished languages can be instrumental in achieving these goals.

Miller raises a fascinating question: why, he asks, do people feel more urges to get the giggles during Ritualized experiences than in ordinary settings? Miller alludes to settings like religious services, graduation speeches, weddings, and funerals—events at which most of us have probably observed, or worse yet embodied, that perverse manifestation of involuntary physiology that we laughingly call "the giggles." Anyone who has ever been overtaken by the giggles knows that it's no joke, and Miller takes the phenomenon quite seriously. He notes that "The giggles are not brought on by the mere demand to play a role we are not up to playing, for then we would get the giggles every time we feigned interest in a conversation." He suggests that something distinctly different is at work in Ritualized settings, something that leaves us a little spooked or unsettled.

Solemnity virtually dares us not to get the giggles: "More than the willful disobedience in the Garden of Eden, getting the giggles is the profoundest revolt against authority that we have at our disposal, perhaps because it is really not at our disposal but comes unbidden, the very image of unvarnished truth." Also, "Ritual seems to invite us to suffer breaks with total immersion and see the whole pageant as the highly contrived performance it is. The actors for a mere moment are seen as puppets, mechanical, as ciphers, and this vision is loaded with cosmic possibility." And the possibilities are not only cosmic but comic, as

---

54 *Ibid.*

we see when we relate Miller's insights to a growing phenomenon in the modern world of magic—the brilliant melding of humor with illusion.

Why the emergence of the funny magician as a ubiquitous (to say nothing of commercially-successful) contemporary archetype? From stars like Penn and Teller to the guy who does tricks at your local chain restaurant on Wednesday nights, the marriage of comedy and magic is more than good entertainment— it's an expression of the very principles that Miller has identified. For it is in his calculated, controlled undermining of the Ritual's spell, while he continues to carry us along with it, that we recognize the breathtaking brilliance of the skilled comedic magician.

No matter how adept his legerdemain or how expert his delivery of a one-liner, the magician-comedian's most skillful feat of all is to invite the audience to break with the total immersion. He encourages them not to take the tuxedo too seriously, whether it be his own or the garb of his forebears. (In his successful bid to have it both ways, he takes care to wear the tuxedo—and then demystify it—rather than simply appearing in casual attire.) At every turn, he reminds the crowd that the show is a "highly contrived performance" that is yet "loaded with cosmic possibility." He reveals his pageant to be what Miller calls a mechanical puppet show, but lo and behold, the magician-comedian remains the puppet master, pulling the strings of his spectators by encouraging them to get the giggles.

Why is this so important and masterful an accomplishment? Miller notes that "the demand Ritual makes on us to suspend disbelief is at times no easy task," and the urge to get the giggles is testament to that fact. "Part of the way Ritual achieves a feeling of sacred separation from the commonplace is by not letting you forget that the whole thing is staged and then asking you simultaneously to forget you know that it is staged so that you can be transported by it." When we reflect on the tension between the sense of immersion and the sense of unreality, some of the unique properties of the Ritualized experience are thrown into focus. Like an absorbing fantasy novel or a lucid dream, an effective Ritual makes the subject at once a skeptical outsider and a fully-involved participant. Moreover, Miller claims that "There is much comic possibility in the contrasting visions."[55]

---

55   *Ibid.*

Through his individual style of patter, every magician-comedian admits, whether explicitly or by implication, that his act is just a bunch of hocus-pocus. And yet, as his audience giggles complicitly and aloofly on cue, he forces them to suspend their disbelief by manipulating their very laughter. Perhaps some of the funny magician's jokes are just throwaways, designed more to buy time and earn audience appreciation than to cagily lampoon his art. But, even here, any successful attempt to "involve" the audience by engaging them with humor ultimately serves the purpose of the Ritual. And in the hands of a masterful trickster, the amused chuckles of a comedy-magic show's audience and the nervous titters of a Ritual's assembled can flow back and forth as swiftly as the dice he pours from tumbler to tumbler.

Manipulation of the giggles is also intrinsic to the inspired artistry behind another contemporary trend—the "bizarre" magic genre. The shocking bloody finger chops, gross-out illusions, or occult-inspired performances of its practitioners leave their squirming audiences spooked and unsettled, daring anyone not to crack up. Their strange magic words, whether meant to sound uncanny or to produce an uneasy burst of laughter from "thin" air thick with tension, are like insurance policies—incomprehensibility is guaranteed.

Four Archetypes of the Magician; Four Magical Dialects

My words as magic wands. My words, not as a metaphor for power,
but as the thing itself. My words as a synonym for creation.
—asha bandele, *The Prisoner's Wife* (1999)

Professional magician Jeff McBride discusses four primary aspects (or roles) of a magician: Trickster, Sorcerer, Oracle, and Sage. These are four possible personae that an actor-magician may choose to adopt,[56] and of course the facets may overlap or evolve through time. As McBride points out, a magician might even play out all four aspects during the course of a single performance. Each persona naturally comes with its own vocabulary of magic words—its own dialect, if you will.

---

56   Jeff McBride, *Mystery School* (2003)

The Trickster

The Trickster is probably the most common persona of a magician. This persona is epitomized by the close-up sleight-of-hand artist who works with cards, silks, cups and balls—the sort who might effortlessly pull a silver dollar from your ear even as he mischievously loosens your wristwatch. "The trickster's medium is words. A parodist, joker, liar, con-artist, and storyteller, the trickster fabricates believable illusions with words."[57] Before we discuss the Trickster's dog-eared lexicon, a bit of background on the archetype is in order.

Tricksters are mythology's wise fools. Like the mischievous sprites of fairy-lore, they are divine boundary-dwellers who exist outside the laws of the world. Magicians famously defy the law of gravity with levitations and shatter the law of cause-and-effect at every turn. In violating the laws of physical nature, tricksters are simultaneously creators and destroyers, hence a magician's propensity to make things appear—*Voilà!*—and disappear—*Poof!*—at will. It should come as no surprise that the rabbit, the animal classically associated with professional magicians, is a common Trickster figure in folklore.[58] In general, Tricksters are comedians, mocking convention and disrupting order.[59] Tricksters are typically proud and boastful,[60] and thus we see an historical tendency for magicians to title themselves as "The Great" So-and-So or "The Magnificent" Such-and-Such. Tricksters remind their spectators that things are not as they seem, challenging everyone to wake up to the fact that nature is unstable, uncertain, and fluctuating. The "Trickster conveys that our assurances about ourselves and our realities are illusions"[61]—just as a jester challenges the rule of authority and propriety. Jeff McBride describes the Trickster archetype this way:

> The Trickster is fast-talking and quick-thinking. He (or, of course, she) represents the element of Air. Many magicians become interested in magic as children or adolescents. The Trickster teaches us how to use magic to develop our communication skills. Some magicians stay Tricksters and never feel the need to explore the other archetypes. Some modern-day Tricksters have developed this style of magic to a high

---

57 Jeanne Smith, *Writing Tricksters: Mythic Gambols in American Ethnic Literature* (1997)

58 Jeanne Campbell Reesman, *Trickster Lives: Culture and Myth in American Fiction* (2001). Other common Tricksters are the coyote, raven, and spider.

59 Allan Combs, *Synchronicity: Through the Eyes of Science, Myth, and the Trickster* (1996)

60 *Ibid.*

61 *NuanceProject.org*, quoted in *Trickster Tales* by J.P. Briggs (2005)

art. Penn and Teller, Dan Harlan, and Robert Neale are all excellent modern-day examples of performers who exude the Trickster spirit. In the age cycle of the magician, the Trickster represents approximately ages eight to eighteen.[62]

In Native American stories, Tricksters "are said to talk in funny ways."[63] As the supreme joker, the Trickster is apt to use funny-sounding magic words: *Abracadoody, Hocus jokus, Huey fooey chop suey gifeltte fish*. His vocabulary is occasionally crude and invariably irreverent. Sometimes his words are strikingly blunt, imbuing a deceptively anticlimactic element to a trick's climax: *Now you see it, now you don't*.

In reminding his audience that reality is an illusion, the Trickster whisks away even his own mask. In other words, he has to make his craft's hallowed vocabulary ring hollow because magicians themselves are illusory! "You dare not take even my message seriously," the Trickster seems to say, "lest this silk I used to illustrate my point come to replace the wool I just pulled from your eyes."

The Sorcerer

The archetype of the Sorcerer might be likened to the more elaborate stage illusionist, who manipulates grand props and dazzles us with large-scale effects. If for no other reason than budgetary considerations, there are certainly fewer Sorcerer-type magicians than Tricksters within amateur and professional circles alike. But Sorcerers' flashy productions generally make a huge impression. Due to their flair for drama and theatricality, it's the Sorcerers who tend to snag the big television specials. McBride says:

> The Sorcerer is skillful and disciplined and puts considerable time and energy into his magical work. He evokes the element of Fire. The Sorcerer is interested not only in his art but also in honing his skills in stagecraft and the theatrical arts. Modern-day sorcerers include Jonathan Pendragon, Siegfried and Roy, and Lance Burton. Many magicians choose to move into the discipline of the Sorcerer after they've explored the archetype of the Trickster to their satisfaction. In the age

---

62   Jeff McBride, *Mystery School* (2003)

63   Franchot Ballinger, *Living Sideways: Tricksters in American Indian Oral Traditions* (2004)

cycle of the magician, the Sorcerer represents approximately the time of the twenties through the forties.[64]

Unlike the Trickster, who loves pronouncing magic words with tongue planted firmly in cheek, the Sorcerer tends toward the serious in his articulation of magical vocabulary. He favors those weighty and mysterious syllables handed down from Egyptian priests and European wizards: *Abracadabra, Akramma-chamari, Anthropropolagos.* The Sorcerer *means* for his words to sound strange and incomprehensible, for that's part of the mystique, and it makes for sound showmanship and colorful pageantry. Even if he prefers a silent routine, his grand gestures, intricate choreography, exotic costumes, requisite props, and dramatic musical accompaniment serve the same purpose as a mouthful of syllables. Every aspect of the Sorcerer's performance is part of the ritual—a ritual as old as humankind, playing out our primal quest to understand, influence, and control the great powers of the universe.

The Oracle

The archetype of the Oracle is associated with those mesmerizing magicians who specialize in hypnotism and concern themselves with the psychological aspects of magic. As McBride puts it,

> The Oracle is more interested in matters of insight and intuition. The elemental correspondence of the Oracle is Water. The Oracle explores subtle techniques of mentalism and psychology. Exploring the depths of the collective unconscious are modern-day Oracles like Max Maven and Alain Nu. The Oracle represents the middle age in the magician's life cycle, approximately age forty to sixty.[65]

By contrast with a Sorcerer's spectacle, designed to fill the most generous stage and eclipse the grandeur of the most opulent theater, the Oracle's greatest feats never actually take place—except in the minds of the audience. The Oracle's vocabulary contains magic words that instantly mesmerize the spectators, dazzling them from the inside out. Following on our *Akrammachamaris* and suchlike arcana, a surprising example of an Oracle's magic word is *vacation*—a friendly, familiar word that causes people to "momentarily spirit off to their private bit

---

64   Jeff McBride, *Mystery School* (2003)
65   *Ibid.*

of paradise, [and to] disappear to somewhere that exists between fantasy and the world-as-we-know-it."[66] The casual inclusion of the word *vacation* in a magician's patter is a guaranteed distraction. Another example is that deceptively trivial word *now*—which, when employed with a particular intonation, conjures vestiges of that six-year-old child within oneself that still viscerally recalls "the power of Mom's command, and the physical consequences if you disobeyed."[67] The Oracle's use of magic words might be reminiscent of Neuro-Linguistic Programming, but with diabolical simplicity and straightforwardness. The Oracle isn't actually mind-melding or brainwashing anyone—the spectators hypnotize themselves with the subtlest suggestions by the simplest magic words.

The Sage

The Sage is the wise philosopher and venerable teacher of magic, the white-bearded elder of impossible age or, in a more contemporary mythology, a pointy-eared creature who coaches Jedi knights. McBride explains:

> The Sage is the mentor and master of the art, whose work is to pass on a lifetime of distilled wisdom to those who seek it. The Sage represents the element of Earth: patience and power. He is interested in the philosophy and history of magic, and in teaching what he has learned, keeping the art alive. Eugene Burger and Rene Lavand are two of the important Sages in the world today. The Sage represents the later part of a magician's life, from age sixty on.[68]

With a fascination for the long, meandering rivers of history and an attraction to the deep skies of philosophy, the Sage will likely favor magic words from the esoteric scholars: Judaism's Kabbalists, Islam's Sufis, Christianity's Gnostics, Buddhism's Lamas, Hinduism's Gurus, the mystics of all faiths, the alchemists of all centuries. The Sage will chant his incantations—*Ha-ya-ba-ra-la, Kum kunki yali, kum buba tambe, Om yee pesh*—reminding us of an Aboriginal elder, an African witch doctor, or perhaps a Native American shaman as he *open-sesames* invisible portals and guides us to other realities. The Sage's magical words give us "symbolic wings" with which to move from one world to the next with the speed

---

66   Scott Rains, "The Six Knows to Preparing to Travel" (2004)

67   Geoffrey Knight, "Covert Hypnosis" (2002)

68   Jeff McBride, *Mystery School* (2003)

of light.[69] In leading us through the darkness of the unknown toward flashes of insight and marvel, he is the quintessential guide. He is in one sense antithetical to the archetype of the Trickster, who is wholly detached from the lesson on illusion that he illustrates. He is also somewhat unlike the archetype of the Sorcerer, who celebrates the presentation of illusion itself, from his side of the proscenium arch. Nor does his art, like that of the Oracle, depend on manipulating the consciousness of his subjects from a position of control that keeps him outside looking in. Rather, the Sage is a full and willing participant in the drama, sitting in the sweat lodge or around the bonfire alongside everyone else.

Where the modern-day Sorcerer requires a substantial venue (or television studio) to bring off his act, all the world's a stage to the Sage. He's the indefatigable magician who technically never performs. "Why are you looking at me?" he seems to be asking. "Magic is happening all around us!" The Sage's magic word *Behold!* calls upon spectators to "witness and be amazed." He beckons everyone to become mystical "seers" endowed with profound spiritual insight and the power to perceive miracles. In other words, the Sage generously invites everyone to participate in the magic, to suspend their disbelief and be convinced that "seeing is believing." With every word he speaks, this wise spinner of yarns weaves story-magic. His incantation *Once upon a time* opens the floodgates of imagination[70] and calls upon our inner children to never stop believing, to connect with and renew an innate sense of wonder. And his *What if* beckons us to question the rational, think beyond our accepted reality, and expand the limits of what is possible.

Which Archetype Resonates?

Again, as McBride has noted, a magician may play out the roles of Trickster, Sorcerer, Oracle, and Sage throughout the course of his career or within the span of a single performance. Each archetype is crucial to the vast cultural tableau of magic in human history, and no one of these mutually compatible archetypes is better or worse than another. It is therefore appropriate that the magic words collected in this dictionary comprise the vocabularies of all four archetypes. If you are a budding conjuror in search of your performing identity,

---

69   Eva Jansen, *The Book of Hindu Imagery: Gods, Manifestations and Their Meaning* (1993)

70   Dale Carnegie, *The Quick and Easy Way to Effective Speaking* (1990)

noting which words seem especially appealing and intriguing will help you to determine which archetype resonates with you at this point in your life. And identifying which words strike you as effective within the context of particular tricks or illusions may help you bring various archetypes into your service as you shape your routine.

The Power Is in How You Say It

> The sound of a voice, the rhythm of a line, the magic of words.
> —Marcia Landy, *The Historical Film* (2001)

> A magic word—merely pronounced, it creates a turbulence, an agitation. This quick movement of emotions and ideas brings another scene to the fore.
> —Thomas C. Heller, *Reconstructing Individualism* (1986)

It has been said that the "secret" of magic words is this: "It doesn't matter what you say as much as it matters how you say it!"[71] Naturally, each magician must make a magic word his or her own, so that its utterance flows comfortably and seamlessly—though nonetheless impressively and mysteriously—from his or her lips. However, with unfamiliar words, it is generally recommended that you vocalize as much vibration as possible, "as you would any mantra. Emphasis on each syllable, so that you can hear it resonate and feel it vibrate within you, is the key. The sound of any power-word or name seeks and harnesses that power. When this sound is combined with concentration and visualization, you stir the energy and power to which you are heir" as a magician.[72] The very act of "speech is the 'Open Sesame,' the magical power."[73] Note that the *act* of speech is where the magic is. Kabbalah scholar Phillip Cooper reminds us that "No word or statement contains power—power lies within the mind of the person who speaks those words."[74]

Following are several additional pointers to help spark one's oratorical imagination.

---

71   Joseph Max, quoted by Azaz Cythrawl (1999)

72   Eleanor L. Harris, *Ancient Egyptian Divination and Magic* (1998)

73   C. Van Ripper and L. Emerick, quoted in *Everybody Belongs* by Arthur Shapiro (1999). Similarly, "Words are open sesames to secret caves" (Frank Lentricchia, *Introducing Don Delillo* [1991]).

74   *Esoteric Magic and the Cabala* (2002)

Respect Consequences

Speak magic words with all the mystery, wonder, and sense of danger of saying "I love you" for the first time. The lover who is about to make that critical verbal leap speaks with a courage that is, ideally, tempered by a healthy respect for consequences beyond his or her control. Lauri Cabot explains:

> [B]eing in love can remind us of the power of the word. Saying "I love you" to someone for the first time, for example, is an act fraught with mystery, wonder, and danger. How will she take it? Am I saying it too soon? Should I wait? For what? To let him say it first? Saying those three little words is a highly charged act of power. It brings consequences.[75]

Accordingly, a magic word spoken with a vivid awareness of consequences would sound courageous but not haughty, determined but not sanguine, adventurous but not reckless. Perhaps the deliberate introduction of just a hint of hesitation beforehand might dramatically suggest some intriguing inner dialogue: "Am I saying the magic word too soon? Should I wait just another moment? Should I be concerned about unexpected results?" Such a hesitation need not detract from one's air of mastery—for one clearly knows the magic word and how to say it properly—but rather would impart a strong sense of the awesome responsibility inherent in wielding such power.[76] And just as a movie audience becomes wrapped up in the thrill and turmoil of a character who is preparing to say "I love you," the magician's audience will be deeply involved in the performer's arrival at this momentous threshold, if he imparts its significance effectively. In giving voice to the magic word, the expert magician will exude the perfect balance of control and uncertainty, tinging his confidence with the tense energy of mystery and wonder. When a magic word is imbued with these intangible qualities of mystery and wonder, some people might describe it as sounding "spooky," and indeed "This is the magic of words—a touch of the supernatural" that addresses the spirit.[77]

---

75 *Love Magic* (1992)

76 "Words *are* powerful. Being powered projections, spoken words themselves have an aura of power."—W. Ong, *The Presence of the Word* (1967), quoted in *The Taste of Ethnographic Things* by Paul Stoller (1989). "Magic words carry far more than the weight of one word. . . . [T]hey carry immense power."—Jay Conrad Levinson, *Guerrilla Advertising* (1994)

77 Gladys Hunt, *Honey for a Child's Heart* (2002)

Cultivate Reverence

N. Scott Momaday has paid tribute to "the old, sacred respect for sound and silence which makes the magic of words and literatures."[78] To cultivate that age-old respect, speak magic words carefully, artfully, and with reverence, as Thomas Moore recommends: "If we want a real spirit to settle into our . . . words, we could present them with care, art, and magic" (*The Re-enchantment of Everyday Life* [1997]). Proper reverence is important because, as Moore suggests, in works of beauty, "it is impossible to separate art, religion, and magic, for all three work together to make these ordinary acts . . . truly enchanting." Consider also this advice by scholar Molefi Kete Asante: "One must certainly be careful how the word is spoken because when it is spoken it creates an awesome power. We speak and the words are life, they are material and substantive."[79] This is what the poet Emily Dickinson meant when she wrote:

> *A word is dead*
> *When it is said,*
> *Some say.*
> *I say it just*
> *Begins to live*
> *That day.*[80]

"Such a living word permeates everything when it is spoken with power and honesty," Asante suggests. "[A]ll magic is word magic and there is no magic without the word."[81]

Elongate Vowels

Try elongating your vowel sounds to engender a dreamy, otherworldly quality to a word of enchantment, as described in this famous *Esquire* story about a game of nude croquet:

---

78   *The Man Made of Words* (1997)

79   *The Egyptian Philosophers* (2000)

80   *Complete Poems* (1924)

81   *The Egyptian Philosophers* (2000). Similarly, "All magic is word magic, incantation and exorcism, blessing and curse. Through Nommo, the word, man establishes his mastery over things" (Janheinz Jahn, *Muntu: The New African Culture* [1961]).

"Just look at the moonlight!" He pointed through the splintered pane to the sky whose murkiness an occasional lightning flash showed without dispelling.

"It'll be wonderful! We'll be like ghosts in the lightning. *Nude* ghosts." Noo-oo-oo-oode, she said it, lingering dreamily over the vowel of what was for her a magic word. "Nude ghosts."[82]

If you elongate your vowel sounds enough, you'll find yourself singing. "Imagine you are a magician of song and magic sounds," suggests Margo Anand in *The Art of Everyday Ecstasy* (1999). "Take a deep breath and open your mouth and throat wide. Pushing out from your belly, begin to sing." Singing magic words is quite natural, as they have traditionally been sung: "'Magic' and 'song'—especially song like that of birds—are concepts that are frequently expressed by the same term, or closely-related ones. For example, the Germanic word for magic formula is *galdr*, derived from the verb *galen*, 'to sing.'"[83]

Savor Syllables

Savor the magic word as you speak or sing it,[84] as you might savor a morsel of fine chocolate. In this vein, Mort Rosenblum writes about the very term *chocolate,* giving an exquisite taste of the nearly-tangible properties of a rich, potent word:

> Sometimes she would whisper it, like a magic word, as if by saying, she could taste it. It was a word of consonants, a collision of hard and soft sounds. She would utter them slowly, savoring even the tiny silence between the two syllables, and the almost inaudible *t*. Chocolate.[85]

---

82   Leslie A. Fiedler, "Nude Croquet" (1957), *Lust, Violence, Sin, Magic: Sixty Years of Esquire Fiction*

83   Mircea Eliade, *Shamanism* (1951)

84   "They were practicing, tasting the magic words in their mouths." —Deborah J. Archer, "At Fourteen," *Love Shook My Heart 2* (2001). "She said the magic words to herself, out loud, several times, until, tasted and savored and swallowed, she had them by heart." —George P. Garrett, *The Magic Striptease* (1964). "[S]imply to utter that magical word, to savour it on the tongue."—Robertson Davies, *The Rebel Angels* (1981)

85   Mort Rosenblum, *Chocolate: A Bittersweet Saga of Dark and Light* (2005)

This example of savoring the delicious word chocolate can be applied to any magic word.[86] Take, for instance, *hocus pocus,* with its own "collision of hard and soft sounds" (from the long *o* to the short *k*) and its own pregnant silences

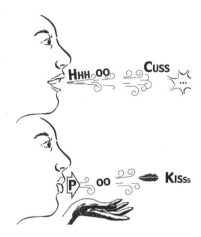

Figure 1. Breathing life into *hocus pocus.*

between syllables and between words. This phrase comes into being on the whirling eddies of one's breath, with the hard *hhh* sound, and is propelled by the plosive *p* of *pocus,* blown like a kiss to a distant lover. Then the softly hissing *s* trails off into the unknown (see Figure 1). One can literally breathe life into words, for "Language . . . is the province of Air, and using . . . speech for magic is a very ancient practice."[87]

Softness, Shape, Innocence

An oft-quoted television commercial once touted whispering as a means of getting a person's attention. And, indeed, words are sometimes more penetrating when spoken softly, "like a feather on the breeze."[88]

---

86 Magician Jared Markowitz uses *chocolate* itself as a magic word during card routines in which he makes a card placed in the middle of the deck suddenly appear at the top.

87 Deborah Lipp, *The Way of Four: Create Elemental Balance in Your Life* (2004)

88 Eric Butterworth, *The Universe is Calling* (1994)

She spoke quietly, but something—the word *magic* seemed almost too ordinary—shimmered in the room.[89]

Aldous Huxley said of such speech: "Soft, soft, but how piercing! boring and drilling into reason, tunnelling through resolution."[90] Say a magic word softly, as if it were a dim, distant memory, as if you were conjuring it from your own depths, where it had been locked away for safekeeping. Author Steve Cash provides an excellent example:

> It had been fourteen years since she'd seen her father's face, and physically he had aged twice that, but she walked over to him and sat on the bed next to him and held his hand in both of hers. "Papa," she said in the softest voice. "Papa," she said again, then again and again as if the word itself had shape and weight and meaning beyond the sound. It was a word to her from another life, another self. It was a word she'd buried in order to survive, but used without speaking it aloud to protect her . . . It was her secret word, her magic word. "Papa" had power. "Papa" was the one word that kept her alive and the one word she never thought she would say again.[91]

As with *Papa* in the passage above, every magic word should be spoken as if it has shape,[92] weight, and "meaning beyond the sound."[93] It should be spoken as a relic from another time, as something once buried for its own survival,[94] as something unspoken that dimly endures in one's memory, as a subtle but vital

---

89   Nora Roberts, *Heaven and Earth* (2001)

90   *Brave New World* (1932).

91   *The Meq* (2005)

92   For example, "The language was unfamiliar to Kim, but every word seemed to hang in the air, clear and sharp as broken crystal. She could almost feel their edges."—Patricia C. Wrede, *Mairelon the Magician* (1991)

93   As sleight-of-hand magician, linguist, naturalist, and philosopher David Abram observes, "Linguistic meaning is not some ideal and bodiless essence that we arbitrarily assign to a physical sound or word and then toss out into the 'external' world. Rather, meaning sprouts in the very depths of the sensory world, in the heat of meeting, encounter, participation" (*The Spell of the Sensuous* [1996]).

94   In relation to buried relics, consider how "the word *Egyptian* has a mysterious sound about it, and calls up visions of thaumaturgists working wonders in crypt, temple, and pyramid" (Henry Ridgely Evans, "Evansoniana," *Magic* [1902]).

energy. Speak a magic word as if you might never utter it again, with all the innocent awe of a child beseeching a parent.

Childhood words are themselves interesting to contemplate. "The first 'words' of a baby are not words at all," suggests professor Selma H. Fraiberg, "but magic incantations, sounds uttered for pleasure and employed indiscriminately to bring about a desired event." A one-year-old baby will discover that "the syllable 'mama,' repeated several times if necessary, will magically cause the appearance of the invaluable woman who ministers to all needs and guards him against all evil. He doesn't know just how this happens, but he attributes this to his own magic powers."[95] This is why Fraiberg contends that "language originates in magic." In addition to embodying magical expectations, a baby's incantations are characterized by surprise and excitement, two crucial qualities for magic words.[96]

Allow Silence

Speak the magic word from your heart. And if, when the magic moment arrives, no sound escapes your lips, then let silence be louder than words.[97] "The delight that we unveil always seems to come down to this: I have a feeling in my heart and now, without any words—abracadabra: You have that feeling in your heart."[98] That's what magic is—a kind of communion, an imparting of a transcendent experience from one who is initiated to those who assemble

---

95 *The Magic Years* (1996)

96 As David Abram explains, "We do not, as children, first enter into language by consciously studying the formalities of syntax and grammar or by memorizing the dictionary definitions of words, but rather by actively making sounds—by crying in pain and laughing in joy, by squealing and babbling and playfully mimicking the surrounding soundscape, gradually entering through such mimicry into the specific melodies of the local language, our resonant bodies slowly coming to echo the inflections and accents common to our locale and community. *We thus learn our native language not mentally but bodily.* We appropriate new words and phrases first through their expressive tonality and texture, through the way they feel in the mouth or roll off the tongue, and it is this direct, felt significance—the *taste* of a word or phrase, the way it influences or modulates the body—that provides the fertile, polyvalent source for all the more refined and rarefied meanings which that term may come to have for us" (*The Spell of the Sensuous* [1996]).

97 As Robert Cormier notes "the other side of words where we find silence. And how silence, too, is precious. Knowing when not to use the words and holding them back, which isn't always easy. And then arriving at the moment to stop" (*I Have Words to Spend* [1991]).

98 George Alistair Sanger, quoted in *The Art of Digital Music: 56 Visionary Artists and Insiders Reveal Their Creative Secrets* by David Battino (2005)

around him. And some of these shared, transcendent experiences are just too magical for words.

A Note About Magic Word Notations

Throughout this dictionary you will find magic words with a history of intriguing depictions. We have said a great deal about how to speak magic words. But let us not forget that ever since the dawn of written culture, the printed word has carried tremendous power. Magic words in printed form can serve as fascinating props in magic routines, adding a touch of mystique by conjuring the artistry of spiritual visionaries from around the world.

Some magic words have traditionally been written in graceful calligraphy on talismans. Others have been ornately embossed on amulets. Still others have been depicted in geometric formation, in "magic squares" and "magic triangles." In every case, these written forms have done more than merely communicate the magic word in question. They have served as circuits, channeling the forces of nature toward specific ends. Consider the following five circuit-like drawings (see Figure 2). One is a Taoist talisman for the protection of women. One is a "sigil" or magical glyph from *The Lesser Key of Solomon* (the famous 17th century treatise on rituals and prayers for summoning spirits). One is a Buddhist mantra of compassion. One is a Vodou *veve* representing the trickster spirit Papa Legba.

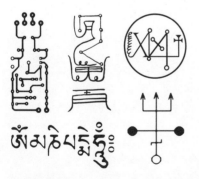

Figure 2. Printed magic words are circuit boards for channeling energy. Top left, a modern wiring diagram for an electrical light bears similarities to ancient magic schematics. Top middle, a Taoist talisman for the protection of women. Top right, a sigil from *The Lesser Key of Solomon*. Bottom left, the Buddhist mantra of compassion, *om mani padme hum*. Bottom right, a Vodou *veve* for the spirit of the crossroads, Papa Legba.

And one depicts the wiring of a modern lighting control device. Can you tell them apart? Their similarity is due to the fact that each is its own kind of schematic to control energy. Spoken magic words channel energy, of course, but their written forms actually diagram the process. If you were to write out a magic word on a piece of parchment, perhaps as a "mystical mind-reading talisman" prop during a mentalism routine, you might consider the rigid lines and sinuous curves of the lettering as forming a circuit board through which magical energy will flow. This is a tangible way to give shape and meaning to magic words.

"Magic squares" and "magic triangles" are also related to circuitry. In such depictions of magic words, letters are stacked upon one another and perhaps repeated to form geometric shapes. These letterforms are found in such diverse places as the magical papyri of Greco-Roman Egypt, fever-curing talismans from Medieval times, and even graffiti unearthed in the ruins of Pompeii. The ancient purpose of such notation might be illuminated by a modern example of a magic triangle depicting the laws of electrical current. In Figure 3, the P symbolizes "power," the V "voltage," and the I "intensity in amps." The rather mystical arrangement of symbols reveals a variety of relationships and meanings to a body of initiated individuals known as electrical engineers. A skilled practitioner uses the triangle by covering up the unknown to reveal a mathematical solution to an algebraic mystery. For example, if P is unknown, one is left with V next to I (multiply V by I). If V is unknown, one is left with P over I (divide P by I). If I is unknown, one is left with P over V (divide P by V). The laws of power are contained within the diagram, just as our ancestors mapped out their own understandings of cosmic processes. Those ancient diagrams have an occult appearance today, but their purpose is less mysterious in light of the magic triangle of our own electrical engineers. The main difference is that today we separate the fields of science and spirituality, whereas our ancestors did not.

Figure 3. The laws of electronic circuits are contained with a "magic triangle."

Even if all the letters are the same within a magic triangle, the arrangement can hold profound meaning. For example, a single letter *A* might symbolize the divine singularity, and a row of two *A*'s above or below it might symbolize duality springing forth. The significance of such a simple magical formula is actually rather vast. In the early 400s BCE, the Pythagoreans (whose "spiritual tradition . . . has been practiced continuously, in one form or another, for at least twenty-six centuries"[99]) formulated a model for understanding the twofold nature of creation. This model is comprised of two principal elements in the universe, which the Pythagoreans called the "Monad" and the "Dyad." The Monad is the male principle of Unity and constancy. It is the "Primordial One," the Logos or "Word," the embodiment of Love, and the ultimate singularity. The Pythagoreans argued that if there were only the Monad, there would by definition be no such thing as "otherness." As a universe without otherness is considered to be both untrue to nature and uninteresting to contemplate, the Pythagoreans conceived of the female Dyad, the indefinite number Two ("where 'Indefinite' must be understood to mean indeterminate, unlimited, boundless, and infinite"[100]), which governs the concept of separation. In separating from the Monad, the Dyad, in the Pythagorean paradigm, creates the dual forces of Love and Strife. By establishing the concept of dimension (as opposed to the oneness of the Monad), she carries the Beginning to the End. The Dyad is our path to the infinite, since she introduces the property of boundlessness, in contrast to the strict limit of the Primordial One. The Pythagoreans called the Dyad "the Goddess of Primordial Matter" because her formless fertility provides the foundation of creation—the generative source of being. She is the pregnant Silence which precedes the Word. Whereas the Monad is "something," the Dyad is "the limitless power to be anything."[101] This power of plurality was also named Rhea ("The Ever-Flowing," hence our word *rhythm*), because through her tension of opposites she governed recurring motion and thus created a fluid, demarcatable presence known as Time out of the Monad's monolithic, immeasurable Eternity. Consider also this explanation from the visionary philosopher Emanuel Swedenborg:

> The Divine Itself is one, yet our finite perception of the Divine requires
> a sense of duality to increase our understanding of it. As with the heat
> and light of the sun, which is from one source, but is distinguished by us

---

99   John Opsopaus, *A Summary of Pythagorean Theology*, 2002

100   *Ibid.*

101   *Ibid.*

into two distinct energies, light and heat, so we perceive the Divine nature as being both Love and Wisdom. The relationship between the two forms a dynamic, since they work towards unity to provide life. From this come the forms of dualism in creation, such as male and female, symmetry, etc., and the internal dualities of good and truth, will and understanding, faith and charity, etc., which are complementary to one another. The essential balance in all life is a manifestation of this.[102]

Magicians, who can be thought of as a tribe of flashy philosophers, constantly demonstrate metaphysical and related dynamics—from the creation and destruction of matter (silk handkerchiefs or whatnot), to the concept of separation (cut ropes and sawed ladies), to the idea of harnessing limitless power through proper language and skillful handiwork. Magic words, written upon anything from a mystic-looking parchment scroll to an ordinary playing card, emblazoned on a t-shirt or appearing on skin rubbed with ash, can serve to represent and even embody the cosmic laws of energy—laws proclaimed and encoded within the very lines, curves, and arrangements of the letters.

The Impact a Single Word Can Make

Words can be magic.
—Lama Surya Das, *Awakening the Buddha Within* (1998)

There's one last step. We have to say the magic words.
Does anyone here know magic words?
—D.K. Smith, *Nothing Disappears* (2004)

Professional magician John W. LeBlanc notes that there are "untold numbers of anecdotes told by professional performers who found that just changing one, single word made an enormous difference in the response of the audience to a performance piece. One word. That's magic."[103] As in the fables of old, "It's in the words that the magic is—'Abracadabra,' 'Open Sesame,' and the rest— but the magic words in one story aren't magical in the next. It seems . . . that

---

102 Quoted by Julian Duckworth in "Presenting Swedenborg: A Roadmap for Readers," Swedenborg Association of Australia (2004)

103 "NLP—Neuro-Linguistic Prodding," *Escamoteurettes.com* (2004)

the real magic is to understand which words work, and when, and for what."[104] Hence this dictionary.

There is an early Germanic word, *lekjaz,* which means "an enchanter, speaking magic words."[105] May every storyteller be a true lekjaz, enchanting his audience with that one magic word that makes all the difference—master storyteller Gustave Flaubert's *mot juste,* or "right word." May every one of us find and use the magic of words to enhance and increase the power and mystery in our own lives.[106] Mr. Magic (a.k.a. Jeff Russ) encourages us to "Say the magic words, and the magic will work every single time, I promise."

---

104 Quoted by Julian Duckworth in "Presenting Swedenborg: A Roadmap for Readers," Swedenborg
       Association of Australia (2004)

105 Ibid.

106 Ibid.

MAGIC
WORDS

A

Aaaa

Mystique: The four aces, so often coaxed from a deck of cards by a magician's skillful fingers, actually spell out an ancient magic word discovered in the "Greek magical papyri." Dating from the second century BCE, these scrolls collected hymns, rituals, magical spells, and mystic formulae from Greco-Roman Egypt.[1] Modern scholars have failed to find a definitive translation of the incantation *aaaa*, but there is no doubt how the word was used: *aaaa* was a sacred word of power, sometimes chanted in conjunction with the name of a deity. The vibratory sound of Egyptian priests chanting vowel sounds was said to be "so euphonious that men listen[ed] to it in place of the flute and lyre."[2]

It's little wonder that *aaaa* sounds like our word *awe*. *Aaaa* is an expression of wordless wonder, when language fails and yet one feels compelled to cry out. *Aaaa* is a magic word that always finds its way into performances of magic, whether intoned by the magician or gasped by the amazed audience.

Meanings:

People soon forget the meaning,
but the impression and the passion remain.
—Edmund Burke,
"A Letter to Richard Burke, Esq." (1793)

Figure 4. The four aces spell the Egyptian magic word *aaaa*, a universal expression of awe in the face of something incomprehensible.

Egyptologists and linguists may be misguided in their quest to interpret cryptic words like *aaaa*. One compelling theory suggests that the ancient wonder-workers who transcribed the magical scrolls were "hymning and naming a deity whose true nature is inexpressible silence," and their "language [broke] out in abstract vowel chanting and glossolalia ['speaking in tongues']."[3]

Facts: The letter *a*, called *alpha* in the Greek alphabet, has historically been symbolic of beginnings. Like the famous Sanskrit mantra *om*, *alpha* "is the sound that brings into being all of creation."[4]

In *The Greek Qabalah* (1999), a study of the alphabetical mysticism and numerology in the ancient world, Kieren Barry explains that *alpha* "appears frequently in Greek and Coptic magical papyri, not only in conjunction with the other vowels, but also by itself as having special power. In a Christian Coptic spell from about 600 CE, it is set out in 'wing' formation" as shown on page 52.

---

1   Hans Dieter Betz, *The Greek Magical Papyri in Translation* (1997)

2   Garth Fowden, *The Egyptian Hermes* (1986), quoted by Laurel Holmstrom in "Self-Identification with Deity and Voces Magicae in Ancient Egyptian and Greek Magic" (2005)

3   Marvin W. Meyer, *Ancient Christian Magic* (1999)

4   David A. Hulse, *New Dimensions for the Cube of Space* (2000)

A A A A A A
A A A A A
A A A A A
A A A A
A A A
A A
A

In *The Gnostic Gospels of Jesus*, Marvin Meyer notes that "In texts of ritual power . . . vowels may be arranged for visual effect" (2005).

The *alpha* state of brainwave activity is that of relaxed awareness, as in daydreaming or meditation.

In Literature: Hans Dieter Betz, *The Greek Magical Papyri in Translation* (1986)

Aalacho

Meanings: The "eleventh hour" is a figure of speech referring to a decisive moment at hand.

Origins: *Aalacho* is a name that appears in the *Lemegeton Clavicula Salomonis or The Lesser Key of Solomon* (17th century). It means the eleventh hour of the night.

Ab

Origins: *Ab* is a divine name associated with Saturn. It appears in Heinrich Cornelius Agrippa's *Of Occult Philosophy, Book II* (1533).

Abab

Origins: *Abab* is a divine name associated with Jupiter. It appears in Heinrich Cornelius Agrippa's *Of Occult Philosophy, Book II* (1533).

Ababaloy

Origins: *Ababaloy* is an angelic name discussed in the *Grimorium Verum* (1880).

Facts: *Ababaloy* is part of an incantation to dispell "all illusion" from a conjuror's quill pen.[5]

Ababra Abrakakraka
(see also *abracadabra*)

Origins: "Sound poetry began with the dawning of language itself," explains Peter Finch. "Tribal chantings, group wailings, rhythmic mumblings in celebration of gods and victories. These were the pre-literate verbalisings that are actually claimed as a common source by all poetries. Through the centuries they became mantras, meditational repetitions, sonic meaninglessness: Try this—*Om Amkhara om om*. Or this—*ababra abrakakraka abrakal abrakal abrakal abraka abra abrabcadarrab era abaracadabara*. Recognise them? Of course you do. In Babylonian times spells like these were installed in the corners of houses as traps for demons. The text was written in the shape of an inward turning spiral. The demon, only ever able to read in one direction, would follow the spell in its irresistible progression and end trapped, hard in the centre. The first ever visual poetry. And one with a purpose. What is poetry for? For catching the dark things at the back of our heads and fixing them for all to see" ("Sound Poetry" [2003]).

----

5 Arthur Edward Waite, *The Book of Black Magic* (1898)

Abacaba-Dabacaba

(see also *abba* and *abracadabra*)

Mystique: Reminiscent of the quintessential magic word *abracadabra* and an equally-rich alternative to it, *Abacaba-Dabacaba* represents a fractal pattern, "one of the fundamental patterns in our universe" that structures such things as our music, art, poetry, and geometry.[6] Fractal diagrams often look like trees, with offshoots branching out progressively. "It's fun to think about how every decision we make leads us in a new direction, as if our lives are an infinite fractal tree," suggests fractal expert Michael Naylor. He explains the pattern inherent in the word *Abacaba-Dabacaba*:

> Instead of using numbers to describe the . . . marks on [an English] ruler, let's call the shortest lengths "a," the next longest "b," then "c," and so on. The pattern then becomes . . . "Abacada-Dabacaba!" This word sounds very much like the magician's phrase "abracadabra," a very apt resemblance given the seemingly magical properties of this pattern. To understand the pattern a little better and see how to continue it, let's see how this pattern grows. Start with an "a." This is the first step, the "tree trunk" if you like:
>
> 1. a
>
> To grow the pattern, add the next letter in the alphabet and then repeat everything that has gone before (which is just the letter "a" in this case.) The next step, then, is "aba," which is like a trunk ("b") with two branches ("a").
>
> 2. aba
>
> Continue by adding the next letter, "c," and repeating the "aba."
>
> 3. abacaba
>
> The fourth step adds the letter "d" and repeats the pattern: abacabadabacaba! The next few steps are shown:
>
> 4. abacabadabacaba
> 5. abacabadabacabaeabacabadabacaba
> 6. abacabadabacabaeabacabadabacaba-fabacabadabacabaeabacabadabacaba
>
> It's fun to see how much you can say aloud. How long would it take to say the word all the way to "z"?[7]

Facts: While *abracadabra* is historically a "shrinking word" (see the entry for *abracadabra*), we have seen in the above quotation that *Abacaba-Dabacaba* is a growing word.

In music, the alternating pattern displayed in the letters of *abacaba* is called a "sonata-rondo"—"'A' stands for the refrain, and the remaining letters, for couplets of differing material."[8] This pattern is also called "chiastic," named after the X-shaped Greek letter *chi*, as its form is "symmetrically organized around a central axis."[9]

---

6   Michael Naylor, "Abacada-Dabacaba!" (2005)

7   "Abacada-Dabacaba!" (2005)

8   William Earl Caplin, *Classical Form* (1998)

9   Calvin R. Stapert, *My Only Comfort* (2000)

In Literature: "Rushes are not straighter, and ermine is not white, sheep are less gentle, eagles less proud, and deer less nimble, than Abacaba." —Voltaire, *The Ingénue* (1767)

Abba

(see also *abracadabra*)

Mystique: The magic word *abba* indicates that a magical effect will occur on the authority or with the assistance of a higher power. This power could be of divine origin, or it could be the forefather who handed down the secret through the generations.

Meanings:

- Divine connection to the creator
  —Peter Terpenning, "Sacred Unity, Giving Birth to the World" (2004)

- Father; parent
  —Wayne A. Meeks, *The HarperCollins Study Bible* (1997)
    "Since 'Abba' refers to the earliest form of a child's address to father, I discuss [Jesus'] appeal to the power of Abba's name in light of Freud's comment in his defense of the 'talking cure' . . . that 'words were originally magic' . . . This statement has bearing on the controversy in contemporary Jesus studies whether the word 'magician' applies to him, and moves this discussion from its exclusively sociological locus to a more psychological one."
  —Diane E. Jonte-Pace, *Teaching Freud* (2003)

- God; holy name
  —Henry Cornelius Agrippa, *Three Books of Occult Philosophy* (1531)

- King
  —Norman Davies, *Europe: A History* (1998)

- Miracle worker
  —Richard Lee Kalmin, *Jewish Culture and Society Under the Christian Roman Empire* (2002)

- Primordial father, supernal father
  —Kala Trobe, *Magic of Qabalah* (2001)
  —Israel Regardie, *The Golden Dawn* (1971)

- Sound of the wind
  —Peter Terpenning, "Sacred Unity, Giving Birth to the World" (2004)

- Term of endearment
  —Zondervan, *Revolution* (2003)

- Unity of all things
  —Peter Terpenning, "Sacred Unity, Giving Birth to the World" (2004)

Origins: *Abba* is of Aramaic origin.

Facts: Some etymologists consider the root *ab*, meaning father, to be the first part of the magic word *abracadabra*, translating that word as a sentence: *Ab, Ben, Ruch a cadasch* (reading as *father, son,* and *holy spirit*).[10]

In the Bible, Jesus uses the word *Abba* to address God, marking what religious scholar Rufus Goodwin calls a "psychological leap" in the sphere of prayer as well as a social reform. The spoken word *Abba* marks "a turning point in time, indeed, of the evolution of consciousness. In prayer, Jesus does not propitiate a tyrant—he is not a slave, but a son. This is a shift in consciousness for humankind, a sign of a new personal, conscientious ego in a personal relation to God."[11] "'Abba' is a very intimate word," explains Abbot Thomas Keating.

---

10 *Llewellyn Encyclopedia* (2002)

11 *Give Us This Day: The Story of Prayer* (1999)

"Apparently, it expressed Christ's consciousness of the Ultimate Mystery, as a paternal-maternal, loving, intimate, and tender presence—all the things that might be summed up when one says 'Poppa' to a very dear earthly father."[12] Jesus' use of the "homely family word" *Abba* in his invocation of God was unprecedented in the immense prayer literature of ancient Judah.[13]

Variations and Incantations:

* Aba
  This is the name of an angel mentioned in a work attributed to Peter de Abano, *Heptameron, or Magical Elements* (13th century).

* Abba Abba Abba Ablanatha Nafla Akrama Chamari Ely Temach Achoocha
  This unusual summoning spell from ancient Egypt conjures the divine power of God's tattoos. On the original Coptic manuscript is "a rather exotic image [showing] the seven holy vowels of the Greek alphabet . . . tattooed across god's chest. We also have forms of the names Ablanathanalba and Akramachamari."
  —Marvin W. Meyer, *Ancient Christian Magic: Coptic Texts of Ritual Power* (1999)

* Abba zabba

* Abba zabba cadabra
  —*Beefheart.com* (2002)

In Literature: "'[I]t's a magic place, just like the forest is magic,' Daffonia said. 'Abba made it that way.'"
—Rosemarie E. Bishop, *Noah's Garden* (2000)

Abbadabba
(see *abba, abba-dabba-ooga-booga-hoojee-goojee-yabba-dabba-doo,* and *abracadabra*)

Ever and ever on an abbadabba.
—Carl Sandburg,
"The Abracadabra Boys" (1970)

Mystique: *Abbadabba* suggests a casual kind of manipulation of life in which one can operate outside the rules or break the rules with a deceptive flourish, leaving even the victim feeling a sort of admiration for the perpetrator's gift.

Meanings:

* Abracadabra
  "[F]rom the gangsters of the 1930s, particularly Dutch Schultz's legendary financial handler, Otto Berman (whose nickname 'Abbadabba' was derived from 'abracadabra'), came a recognition of exactly how the numbers could be manipulated; Abbadabba used quadratic equations and probability formulas to rig his boss's illegal gambling rackets, increasing gross profits by more than 50 percent."
  —Art Kleiner, *The Age of Heretics* (1996)

* Gibberish, incomprehensible language
  —Jim Bouton, *Ball Four*

* I love you
  —Arthur Fields and Walter Donovan, "Aba Daba Honeymoon" (1914)

* Jargon

---

12 *Sundays at the Magic Monastery* (2002)
13 John R.W. Scott, *The Message of the Sermon on the Mount* (1978)

Facts: *Abbadabba* is a palindrome.

Aba daba is monkey chatter for "I love you" in the old ragtime song "Aba Daba Honeymoon" by Arthur Fields and Walter Donovan (1914):

> *"Aba, daba, daba, daba, daba, daba, dab,"*
> *Said the Chimpie to the Monk,*
> *"Baba, daba, daba, daba, daba, daba, dab,"*
> *Said the Monkey to the Chimp.*

Variations and Incantations:

- Aba Daba

- Abba Cadabra

- Abba Dabba

- Abba dabba cadabra
  —*BrothersJudd.com* (2004)

- Abbadabba dabbadabba
  —Jim Bouton, *Ball Four* (1990)

- Abbadazoola
  See *mitchakaboola abbadazoola*

- Abba zabba

In Literature: The magic word *abbadabba* appears in the Carl Sandburg poem "The Abracadabra Boys." The boys in question have been hanging around "the stacks and cloisters" and have "been to a sea of jargons and brought back jargons." They "make pitty pat with each other" in a sort of "private pig Latin." Sandburg asks, "Do they have fun? Sure—their fun is being what they are, like our fun is being what we are—only they are more sorry for us being what we are than we are for them being what they are."[14]

Abba-Dabba-Ooga-Booga-Hoojee-Goojee-Yabba-Dabba-Doo
(see also *abba, abbadabba, abracadabra, ooga-booga,* and *yabba-dabba-doo*)

Mystique: Seemingly nonsensical rhythmic sounds can indicate that the speaker hears his own beat and is in touch with a mysterious and joyous reality unknown to the listener. Scholar of metaphysics Raymond Buckland suggests that all magic words "must be spoken rhythmically. Chants and spells should either rhyme or, at the very least, have a repetitive, heavy, sonorous beat to them. This can, and should, contribute to a gradually rising state of excitement within the magician, adding immeasurably to the amount of power produced."[15]

In Literature: Edward Allen, *Mustang Sally* (1992)

Abbazabba
(see also *abba* and *zabba*)

Facts: *Abba Zabba* appears in a Captain Beefheart song of the same name (1974). The lyrics are a sort of nursery rhyme about childhood rituals and seem to suggest that the primal syllables *abba zabba* are "song before song before song."

Abba Zabba is the name of an old-fashioned peanut butter taffy candy bar.

Variations and Incantations: Abba zabba

In Literature: Tracy Jarobe, *26 Easy and Adorable Alphabet Recipes for Snacktime* (2002)

---

14 *The Complete Poems of Carl Sandburg* (1970)

15 *Ray Buckland's Magic Cauldron: A Potpourri of Matters Metaphysical* (1995)

Abbibibitywhurl

Mystique: *Abbibibitywhurl* is a conglomeration of cultural references, melding the Biblical *abba*, the magic word *bibbity* popularized by Disney's film *Cinderella*, and the wild turning of a carnival tilt-a-whirl ride into a cry of exhilaration and abandon.

In Literature: Anonymous, "The Kids on the Net Spellbook" (1998)

Abdubia

In Literature: "I met Jundugio in my first tour of the interior provinces of Panama. He was not a great magician but he had a couple of effects he could sell very well. One of these was the stunt of eating a drinking glass which he did to the accompaniment of a weird dance while he shouted 'Abdubia!' his own magic word which he used in all his effects instead of the more common 'Abracadabra' or 'Hocus Pocus.'"
—Marko, "Jundugio and the Runaway Girl," *The Learned Pig Magic eZine* (2000)

Abecedarian

Meanings:

- Arranged alphabetically

- Elementary

- Novice

Origins: The late Latin root word *abecedarius* (meaning "alphabetical") is the origin of *abecedarian*.

In Literature: "The magician spoke the word 'abecedarian' and pulled the rabbit out of his hat."
—*GotApex.com* (2004)

Ablanathanalba Sisopetron

Origins: *Ablanathanalba sisopetron* is a "widespread magical charm"[16] appearing in a group of Cypriot magical curses. The first word, *Ablanathanalba*, "is usually conceded to be derived from the Hebrew (Aramaic), meaning 'Thou art our father.'"[17] The second word presumably means "rock-shaker"[18] (see *open sesame*, perhaps the most famous rock-shaker).

Facts: "The magic word 'Ablanathanalba,' which reads in Greek the same backward as forward, also occurs in the Abraxas-stones as well as in the magic papyri."[19] (See *Abraxas*.)

In an ancient Egyptian invocation, Ablanathanalba is identified as a "'griffin of the shrine of the god which stands today.' (A griffin is a mythical animal with the body and mane of a lion, the head and face of an eagle, two front lion-legs with talons, and the wings of an eagle.)"[20]

Variations and Incantations: Iao barbathiaoth ablanathanalba

"Taking up the rhythm from the twig and the previous words of power, Garric and the old woman cried together, 'Iao barbathiaoth ablanathanalba!'"
—David Drake, *Lord of the Isles* (1997)

---

16   Kieren Barry, *The Greek Qabalah: Alphabetical Mysticism and Numerology in the Ancient World* (1999)

17   Ludwig Blau, "Abraxas," *JewishEncyclopedia.com* (2002)

18   E.S. Shaffer, *Comparative Criticism, Volume 9* (1987)

19   Ludwig Blau, "Abraxas," *JewishEncyclopedia.com* (2002)

20   Eleanor L. Harris, *Ancient Egyptian Divination and Magic* (1998)

Aborizah

Meanings:

- "A bargain is a bargain (and you must accept the outcome)"
  —David Tufte, "Lost Tribe Found?" (2004)

- Magic word, "as in an old folktale, like 'shazam' or 'abracadabra'"
  —Hillel Halkin, *Across the Sabbath River* (2002)

- O God the creator
  —Hillel Halkin, *Across the Sabbath River* (2002)

- "The End"
  —Hillel Halkin, *Across the Sabbath River* (2002)

Origins: *Aborizah* is purportedly a corruption of the Hebrew words *ha-borey Yah*, an ending to a prayer.[21]

Abra

(see also *abracadabra*)

Meanings:

- Become

- Create

- Transform

Facts: *Abra* is the first part of the famous magic word *abracadabra* and is sometimes treated as a separate word (when *abracadabra* is written as the phrase "Abra Cadabra").

Abra, "the female form of Abraham, was most widely used [as a girl's name] in seventeenth-century England, making a later appearance in the John Steinbeck novel and James Dean movie *East of Eden*. But while the name itself has a good deal of creative charm, a girl named Abra could easily tire of it being followed by 'Cadabra.'"[22]

In the Pokemon card game, the character Abra evolves into Kadabra and finally into Alakazam, who has strong psychic powers.

Variations and Incantations:

- Abra and cadabra
  —Steven L. Case, *The Book of Uncommon Prayer* (2002)

- Abra-dee, abra-do, with a hay and a ho and a nonny nonny no!
  These magic words to grant a wish are featured in an episode of the television series *Today's Special* (1982)

- Abra without the cadabra
  —Stephen A. Devaux, *Total Project Control* (1999)

- Abre
  This Spanish word, meaning "it opens," is used as a magic word in the animated television series *Dora the Explorer* (2001).

In Literature:

- "I need a real drink. Mama looks at Caro and says, Abra! Caro winks at her and says, Cadabra! Then Caro guns the car in the direction of Davis Street, which means the Abracadabra Liquor store."
  —Rebecca Wells, *Little Altars Everywhere* (1996)

- "I pointed out that Victor had named the barn cats Abra and Cadabra, after I had wanted to call them Emily and Lavinia."
  —Maxine Kumin, "Mutts," *Dog is my Co-Pilot* (2003)

---

21   Hillel Halkin, *Across the Sabbath River* (2002)

22   Linda Rosenkrantz, *Baby Names Now* (1995)

- "[H]e pulled the dollar bill out of his pocket and examined it. It had been face down under the blotter. He now studied it and found the words *Arbadac Arba* written across George Washington's forehead on the front of the bill. 'Abra Cadabra,' he said, reading each word backwards. He thought there was a good chance that the words were a user name and password . . ."
—Michael Connelly, *Chasing the Dime* (2002)

- "The two most potent magic words are not abra and cadabra."
—Steven L. Case, *The Book of Uncommon Prayer* (2002)

Abracadabra

As your head honcho said,
there is nothing that matches abracadabra.
—Joseph Brodsky, "Vertumnus,"
Collected Poems in English (2000)

Mystique:

He gave us story-oceans
and abracadabras.
—Salman Rushdie,
The Moor's Last Sigh (1997)

It's that spine-tingling thing that gives you goose bumps.[23] It's the instant of a wish coming true. It's opening your eyes and seeing that the workaday world has transformed into something holy.[24] It's that moment of clarity when everything suddenly "clicks," and you see that the whole is greater than the sum of its parts. These clicks and ticks can trigger a resounding chime, signaling the fullness of time. And yet it is that very same chime of the clock that can disintegrate a dream ("At the stroke of midnight, you know, abracadabra."[25]). Energy builds and builds to a breaking point: "Abracadabra. Something flipped in my head."[26] Then it diminishes. This is the cosmic process of creation and destruction, of waxing and waning, reflected by *abracadabra*.

"The link between language and ritual reaches far back into the origin of human culture when certain words were felt to have awesome magical powers. That same feeling of awe is still manifest in children's eyes when they listen to a magician's *abracadabra*."[27] Arguably the best-known and best-loved magic word in history, *abracadabra* is pure dazzle, and it has never lost its spark over the centuries. "When a magician says the word 'abracadabra,' wonderful things happen. A rabbit hops out of a hat, the ace floats to the top of the deck, and the comely young assistant vanishes in a puff of smoke."[28] Though some magicians now consider it a cliché due to its sheer ubiquity, *abracadabra* remains *the* word

---

23 "Amid a blinding cloud of smoke, a cadaverous voice cries aloud, 'Abra-cadabra.'"—*Variety* review of the television program "The Magic Horseshoe" (1953). "'Abracadabra.' The sound had cold fingers squeezing Luke's spine."—Nora Roberts, *Honest Illusions* (1992)

24 "The custom of closing or covering the eyes while saying the blessing enacts the transformation of the world, since, when you reopen your eyes *Abracadabra!* the weekday, workaday world is special, holy, and Shabbat."—Anita Diamant, *How to Be a Jewish Parent: A Practical Handbook for Family Life* (2000)

25 Alan Furst, *Dark Voyage* (2004), referencing the fairy tale of Cinderella

26 Carolyn S. Kortge, *The Spirited Walker: Fitness Walking For Clarity, Balance, and Spiritual Connection* (1998)

27 Marcel Danesi, *Of Cigarettes, High Heels, and Other Interesting Things* (1999)

28 Martin Fry (1991)

```
ABRACADABRA
ABRACADABR
ABRACADAB
ABRACADA
ABRACAD
ABRACA
ABRAC
ABRA
ABR
AB
A
```

Figure 5. Abracadabra written as a "shrinking" word.

associated with conjuring,[29] and such is its power that it is virtually impossible to speak the syllables without some vestige of reverence or at least respect. "'Magic words,' be they as commonly known as Abracadabra, or as deeply secret as the Unknowable Name of God, have always carried great power."[30] As novelist Terry Kay points out, "Illusions [are] made of words, like a magician's singsong of abracadabra secrets."[31]

We'll likely never know who first coined or uttered the word *abracadabra*, but it was passed along to us by way of the ancient Jewish mystics and was no doubt antiquated even in their time. Sustained over generations by its undeniable profundity, today the word pops up virtually any time someone wants to describe a magical moment in life. It's so versatile that it appears as every part of speech, from noun to adjective to verb, and it is instantly poetic: "[D]ewdrops perched on tall blades of grass became small prisms in the abracadabra

light of sunrise," writes poet Diane Ackerman.[32] Indeed, *abracadabra* captures that wavelength of light that scintillates and makes rainbows. It's also the mystery of shadows, as poet Barbara Smith describes:

> *[W]ait while darkness*
> *pronounces its abracadabra,*
> *and the moon rises*
> *from the tips of trees.*[33]

It's a building block, a blueprint: "I was getting back to simple abracadabra," writes novelist Henry Miller, "the straw that makes bricks, the crude sketch, the temple which must take on flesh and blood and make itself manifest to all the world."[34]

It is said that when *abracadabra* was originally chanted, it was reduced letter by letter until only the final "A" remained.[35] Likewise, it was written on paper as in Figure 5. Such a notation signified a totality gradually shrinking away to nothing.[36] Similar to sawing a lady in half, "Dismemberment of language produces enigma; but at the same time a performative act is being brought about. Language is simultaneously ruined and employed."[37]

For all its syllables, *abracadabra* is one of those "one-piece words" that "seem complete in themselves."[38] Not easily divided into smaller linguistic pieces (morphemes), *abracadabra* has a dynamism to it, something that carries the speaker smoothly through the syllables. It's like a handful of other long yet unified words that roll off the

29   "'Please is a good magic word,' I said, 'but the magic word for magicians is 'abracadabra.'"—Ace Starry, *The Magic Life: A Novel Philosophy* (2003)

30   Deborah Lipp, *The Way of Four: Create Elemental Balance in Your Life* (2004)

31   *The Valley of Light* (2003)

32   *Deep Play* (2000)

33   *Wild Sweet Notes: Fifty Years of West Virginia Poetry 1950–1999* (2000)

34   *Sexus* (1962)

35   Gustav Davidson, *Dictionary of Angels: Including the Fallen Angels* (1994)

36   Richard Cavendish, *The Black Arts* (1968)

37   E.S. Shaffer, *Comparative Criticism, Volume 9* (1987)

38   Richard Coates, *Word Structure* (1999)

tongue: *didgeridoo, mulligatawny, millennium, rhododendron*.[39] It's as if there's a sonic "glue" holding the syllables together, and that gives the word strength.

Meanings:

The virtues of Abracadabra are well known; though the meaning of the word has puzzled some of the best critics of the last age.
—Tobias Smollett,
The Adventures of an Atom (1748)

• A (the letter)
"By the father of physic, thought I, this study of medicine is not the pleasant task I anticipated—rather arduous in the long run for the stomach, I should judge, to swallow and digest all the medicines, from Abracadabra to Zinzibar."
—Henry Clay Lewis, *The Swamp Doctor's Adventures* (1858)

• Alphabet
"'Abra cadabra,' that famous saying that everyone learned, is actually a very good ancient magical formula. It just takes the alphabet, supplies some extra vowel sounds, and you turn it into a very spooky sounding word, at least from a Greek perspective."
—L. Michael White, "Magic, Miracles, and the Gospel" (1998)

• Antiquated knowledge or wisdom
"On the blackboard the futile abracadabra which the future citizens of the republic would have to spend their lives forgetting."
—Henry Miller, *Tropic of Cancer* (1961)

• Assyrian deity
"Today we know that Abracadabra was the supreme deity of the Assyrians."
—H.E. Dudeney, *The Canterbury Puzzles* (1907)

• Changing or transforming; the cause of change
"[S]ort out the jigsaw pieces of problems, then abracadabra them into brilliant solutions."
—Linda Goodman, *Linda Goodman's Star Signs* (1988)

• Creating
"There was magic in sketching. She heard Joel at the door, turned around, and said, Abracadabra, I create as I sketch."
—Pearl Abraham, *The Seventh Beggar* (2005)

• Cryptic language
"[T]he facts tumbling out of the coding machines in Navy abracadabra."
—Herman Wouk, *War and Remembrance* (2002)
"He saw—waking or dream, he still couldn't say—a ghost mumbling all sorts of Biblical abracadabra in a dead tongue, Chaldean perhaps or Hittite."
—Amos Oz, *A Perfect Peace* (1993)

• Devil's name
"'There, you see? The devil's name, Abracadabra!' He frowned for a few seconds. 'The writer claims Abracadabra can be raised to this world by invoking his name above the Grail.'"
—Bernard Cornwell, *Vagabond* (2003)

• Diagram
"Right now, unnoticed by the pilot of the big plane, Allard's hand was building a complicated pyramid of letters that looked like a mystic abracadabra. Zigzagging lines between those letters, he gave potential meanings to dots and dashes in the body of Zanigew's message."
—Maxwell Grant, *Shadow Over Alcatraz* (1938)

• Diminishing, causing to disappear
—Laura Lippman, *By A Spider's Thread* (2004)
"[R]oughly translated from a Chaldean word [abracadabra] means 'to diminish.'"
—Patricia Telesco, *How to be a Wicked Witch* (2001)

- Divine utterance
"[A] puff of smoke and a holy abracadabra."
—Lisa Samson, *The Church Ladies* (2001)

- Exotic, otherworldly
"[H]e longed to clear a way for himself into unknown territories, the abracadabra realms we feel inside which nobody dares to touch."
—David Grossman, *See Under: LOVE* (2002)

"Unaware of their cage unless they try to leave it, the objects seem to float in the abracadabra realm of flying carpets."
—Diane Ackerman, *A Natural History of the Senses* (1990)

- Gibberish
"The effect [of James Joyce's literary methods] at times is astounding, but the price paid is the entire dissolution of the very foundation of literary diction, the entire decomposition of literary method itself; for the lay reader the text has been turned into abracadabra."
—Sergei Eisenstein, *Film Forum: Essays in Film Theory* (1969)

"If the encryption only yields abracadabra, something along the transmission path has gone wrong . . . The difference between messages that make sense and abracadabra might be subjective."
—M.H.M. Schellekens, *Electronic Signatures Volume 5* (2004)

- "Host of the winged ones" (i.e., angels)
This is an interpretation of the word *Abrakad*, from a prayer attributed to Rabbi Nehunya ban harKanah (Philip Schaff, *The New Schaff-Herzog Encyclopedia of Religious Knowledge, Vol. I*).

- "I bless the dead"
—*A Dictionary of Angels* (1997)

- Inspired
"[N]o abracadabra insights, just plain old hard work."

—Joseph J. Luciani, *Self-Coaching: How to Heal Anxiety and Depression* (2001)

- Instantly
"We'll have you some heat in here before you can say abracadabra, and you can put your money on it."
—Mark Edward Hall, *Holocaust Opera* (2004)

"Reality is like a magic act, and magic by definition contradicts what we expected. But life's magic acts don't always have us applauding. Before you can say 'abracadabra' many of us discover we're the dumb bunnies pulled from a top hat and blinking blindly into the lights only to again disappear as wondrously as we first appeared. We are no sooner here than we disappear."
—Noah benShea, "Life is a Contradiction in Terms" (2003)

- Key to unlock or open
"Tibetans have been reported to lift stones through the use of certain combinations of sound frequencies. Perhaps the Arab word 'Abracadabra' pronounced correctly really did cause something to open."
—Paul Von Ward, *Gods, Genes, and Consciousness* (2004)

"He thought 'CIA' was a kind of abracadabra that would magically open all the important doors in Washington."
—Robert Baer, *See No Evil* (2003)

"The safe hummed once, then clicked. 'Abracadabra,' Roarke stated, and opened it."
—J.D. Robb, *Purity in Death* (2002)

"No amount of intellectual authority, arrogant confidence, name dropping, or ego and ambition pounding on the door demanding to be admitted will allow us passage. Beyond a certain point, faith is the magic lamp and humility the abracadabra."
—Gregg Michael Levoy, *Callings: Finding and Following an Authentic Life* (1998)

- Keyword or buzzword
"The abracadabras of a champion job search."
—Jay A. Block, *2500 Keywords to Get You Hired* (2002)

- Lingo
"He was certain that if he sailed a hundred years on the *Caine* he would understand such abracadabra no better than he did at that moment."
—Herman Wouk, *The Caine Mutiny* (1951)

"[T]he abracadabra of the philosophers."
—Christa Wolf and Jan Van Heurch, *Cassandra: A Novel and Four Essays* (1988)

- Magic
"Change is magical, like . . . Abracadabra."
—Angeles Arrien, *The Tarot Handbook: Practical Applications of Ancient Visual Symbols* (1997)

"There were abracadabra spells for protection on journeys."
—Paul M. Johnson, *A History of the Jews* (1988)

"Lacking an abracadabra wand, you're stuck with people."
—Rose Rosetree, *The Power of Face Reading* (2001)

"[I]t worked like abracadabra."
—Lynn Hightower, *The Debt Collector* (2001)

"One word from me and, abracadabra!, reality was transformed."
—Eva Luna, quoted in *Conversations with Isabel Allende* by Isabel Allende (1999)

- Magician
"That mausoleum right there [is] the permanent home of the Great Abra Cadabra—one of the greatest magicians that ever lived."
—Deborah Gregory, *The Cheetah Girls: Growl Power* (2000)

- Magic word
"I can't touch it without an abracadabra either from her or from Grandpappy."
—*Robert A. Heinlein, Time Enough for Love* (1973)

"[T]he right abracadabra to select the winning lottery number . . ."
—Stephen Jay Gould, *I Have Landed: The End of a Beginning in Natural History* (2003)

"[T]he appropriate abracadabra may be . . ."
—Andrew Tobias, *Extraordinary Popular Delusions & the Madness of Crowds* (1995)

"[H]oping to acquire an abracadabra or open sesame . . ."
—Helen Valentine, *Better Than Beauty: A Guide to Charm* (2002)

"The magician says 'Abracadabra,' and the genie comes out of the bottle."
—Charles Hartshorne, *Omnipotence and Other Theological Mistakes* (1984)

- Mantra
"[B]reathe in—*abra*, breathe out—*cadabra*, abra, cadabra*. If you can do this successfully in a quiet place, with near total relaxation, you will achieve a particularly satisfying state of mind. Some would call it a religious experience."
—Bill Greene, *Think Like a Tycoon* (1980)

- Meaningless
"The word *good*, when applied to [God], becomes meaningless: like abracadabra."
—C.S. Lewis, *A Grief Observed* (1961)

- Moment in time
"The cooking of the dish is nearly as quick as abracadabra."
—Pierre Franey, *The New York Times 60-Minute Gourmet* (2000)

"She'd have me in a cell before I could say abracadabra."
—Jim Butcher, *Fool Moon* (2001)

"Before one could say abracadabra, they had moved to a corner of the lawn . . ."
—James Duffy, *Dog Bites Man: City Shocked* (2001)

- Momentousness
"[W]ith an abracadabra tone in his voice . . ." —Stuart Ewen, *PR!* (1998)

- Mumbo-jumbo
—Richard Cavendish, *The Black Arts* (1968)
"Mumbo jumbo and abracadabra, all of it."
—Lesley Blanch, *The Wilder Shores of Love: The Exotic True-Life Stories of Isabel Burton, Aimee Dubucq de Rivery, Jane Digby, and Isabelle Eberhardt* (2002)
"I was growing stupid listening to nothing but statistical abracadabra."
—Henry Miller, *Plexus* (1963)
"By the time Lucien, hunted down and on the run, had brought himself to read this abracadabra, he had received notice that a judgment had been obtained against him."
—Honoré de Balzac, *Lost Illusions*, translated by Kathleen Raine (1951)

- Music
"Music is planetary fire, an irreducible which is all sufficient; it is the slate-writing of the gods, the abracadabra which the learned and the ignorant alike muff because the axle has been unhooked."
—Henry Miller, *Tropic of Capricorn* (1961)

- Mystic importance
Judge Benjamin Kaplan wrote of the "oddity of accepting . . . an enlargement of copyright while yet intoning the abracadabra of idea and expression" (quoted in *Free Culture: How Big Media Uses Technology and the Law to Lock Down Culture and Control Creativity* by Lawrence Lessig [2004]).

- Mystique
"The costuming, pageantry, and general abracadabra had attracted him to the Masonic ritual in the first place, just as the theatricalism of the conjurer's art had lured him to the money-digging of his youth."
—Fawn M. Brodie, *No Man Knows My History: The Life of Joseph Smith* (1995)

- Nonsensical babble
"The Egyptologists make nothing out of it but abracadabra."
—Patrick Geryl, *The Orion Prophecy: Will the World Be Destroyed in 2012* (2002)
"[U]nintelligible 'abracadabras.'"
—John R. Donahue, *The Gospel of Mark* (2002)

- Out of the blue
—Tom Spanbauer, *In the City of Shy Hunters* (2001)

- Prayer
"'Abracadabra, great Siva,' prayed Gottfried."
—Erich Maria Remarque, *Three Comrades* (1998)

- Ritualistic utterance
"Ritualistic utterances . . . whether made up of words that had symbolic significance at other times, of words in foreign or obsolete tongues, or of meaningless syllables, may be regarded as consisting in large part of presymbolic uses of language: that is, accustomed sets of noises which convey no information, but to which feelings . . . are attached. Such utterances rarely make sense to anyone not a member of the group. The abracadabra of a lodge meeting is absurd to anyone not a member of the lodge. When language becomes ritual, its effect becomes, to a considerable extent, independent of whatever signification the words once possessed."
—S.I. Hayakawa, *Language in Thought and Action: Fifth Edition* (1991)

"[A]ll they really wanted was to do the abracadabra and get the hell out."
—Yvonne Navarro, *Shattered Twilight* (2004)

- Secret
"[H]e practiced the abracadabra of calling dogs."
—Beryl Markham, *West with the Night* (1982)

- Spiritual connection
"If you make abracadabra with spirits you can get money from them."
—Wole Soyinka, *The Road* (1965)

- "Superstition"
—Susan Albers, *Eating Mindfully* (2003)

    "The United States retains, unusually for an advanced industrial society, about the same per capita level of religious superstition as Bangladesh. What one of Jimmy Carter's aides once referred to as the 'abracadabra vote' is ample."
—Francis Wheen, *Idiot Proof: Deluded Celebrities, Irrational Power Brokers, Media Morons, and the Erosion of Common Sense* (2004)

- Talisman
"The next morning a sorcerer's talisman in the form of a small, oddly shaped shell filled with evil smelling ashes and bound with dried sinews was found tied to his door. Well aware that the eyes of the entire village were watching his every action, he took the token and with a great show of contempt tied it to the tail of a large hog. All that day the swine snouted and grubbed for food in the usual noisy way of such an animal, quite unaware of the abracadabra at its rump but in the evening it died."
—John Farrow, *Damien the Leper* (1954)

- Transform
"You belong in any position or career that allows you to sort out the jigsaw pieces of problems, then abracadabra them into bril-liant solutions—and permits you to play marbles with jelly beans on your lunch break."
—Linda Goodman, *Linda Goodman's Star Signs* (1987)

- Unity, totality
"All is one! Life is a unity! *Abracadabra!*"
—Bruce Duffy, *The World As I Found It* (1987)

Origins:

"It sounds like we need some kind of ancient word of wisdom?" "Abracadabra?"
    Teabing ventured, his eyes twinkling.
—Dan Brown, *The DaVinci Code* (2003)

Because *abracadabra* has been adopted in so many languages without translation, there is speculation that it predates the Biblical story of the confusion of languages at the Tower of Babel.[40] In spite of exhaustive inquiry, "the origin of Abracadabra is unknown, and most of the attempts made to translate or explain it are not impressive."[41] Some scholars have suggested that the word originated with the Chaldeans of the old Babylonian period.[42] The so-called "Abracadabra texts" of Babylonia contain mysterious incantations, some derived from other languages such as Old Elamite and subsequently incomprehensible.[43]

Frequently cited as a possible source is the name Abraxis, the supreme being in Gnosticism, "the source of divine emanations from which all things were created."[44] Stones inscribed with *abracadabra* are called "abraxis stones."[45] One scholar of Greek Qabalah, Kieren Barry, suggests that

---

40   *RecipeLand.com*

41   Richard Cavendish, *The Black Arts* (1968)

42   Herman Slater, *A Book of Pagan Rituals* (1978)

43   Wolfram Von Soden, *The Ancient Orient* (1994)

44   Constance Victoria Briggs, *The Encyclopedia of God: An A–Z Guide to Thoughts, Ideas, and Beliefs About God* (2003)

45   Bob Brier, *Ancient Egyptian Magic* (1999)

abracadabra is derived from the word *Akrankanarba* from Greek magical papyri dating from the second century BCE to the fifth century CE.[46] Other scholars claim the word is a corruption of the name *Abu Abdullah abu Jafar Muhammad ibn Musa al-Khwarizmi*, a ninth century Arabian mathematician who pioneered algebraic formulae.[47]

In 1822, Samson Arnold Mackey suggested that *abracadabra* is actually a sentence formulated by ancient astronomers to describe the constellation of the bull, meaning literally "the Bull, the only Bull": "The ancient sentence split into its component parts stands thus: Ab'r-achad-ab'ra, *i.e.*, Ab'r, the Bull; achad, the only—Achad is one of the names of the Sun, given him in consequence of his Shining *alone*,—and he is the *only* Star to be seen when he is seen—the remaining ab'ra, makes the whole to be, The Bull, the only Bull."[48]

More popularly, *abracadabra* is associated with a Hebrew-Aramaic expression, variously transliterated: *ibra k'dibra* ("I create through my speech"[49]), *abhadda kedkabhra* ("disappear like this word"[50]), *Abra kadavra* ("I will create with words"[51]), *ha brachah dabarah* ("speak the blessing"[52]), *abreq ad habra* ("hurl your thunderbolt even unto death"[53]), *abraq ad habra* ("I will create as I speak"[54]), *Avra c'dabrah* ("it came to pass as it was spoken"[55]), and *Ab, Ben, Ruch a cadasch* (the words for *father, son*, and *holy spirit*[56]). Scholar William Isaacs explains it this way: "*Abra* comes from the Aramaic verb *bra* meaning to create. *Ca* translates to 'as.' *Dabra* is the first person of the verb *daber*, 'to speak.' In other words, *abracadabra* literally means 'I create as I speak.' Magic!"[57]

Ultimately, the meaning of *abracadabra* doesn't matter: "The true magic 'word' or spell is untranslatable, because its power resides only partially in that outward sense which is apprehended by the reason, but chiefly in the rhythm, which is addressed to the subliminal mind."[58]

Facts: Scholar Joshua Trachtenberg notes that certain words take on occult virtues through the tradition that has developed around them "or because of their fancied descent from potent charms of ancient times or foreign peoples." He notes that magic is the most conservative of disciplines: "like the law it clings to archaic forms long after they have lost currency." (Many prominent figures in professional magic are certainly wary of what they consider old clichés, like the icons of the tuxedo, top hat, white rabbit, and words like 'abracadabra,' urging their fellow performers to adopt styles more current with the times.) But Trachtenberg points out that magic's conservatism "is not inspired by intellectual inertia. The very nature of magic demands a strict adherence to the original form of the magical name or word, for its potency lies hidden within its syllables, within its very consonants and vowels—the slight-

46   *The Greek Qabalah: Alphabetical Mysticism and Numerology in the Ancient World* (1999)

47   Daniel Hillis, *Pattern on the Stone* (1999)

48   *'Mythological' Astronomy of the Ancients Demonstrated*, quoted in *The Secret Teachings of All Ages* by Manly Palmer Hall (1928)

49   Estelle Frankel, *Sacred Therapy: Jewish Spiritual Teachings on Emotional Healing and Inner Wholeness* (2004)

50   David Colbert, *The Magical Worlds of Harry Potter: A Treasury of Myths, Legends, and Fascinating Facts* (2004)

51   David Aaron, *Endless Light: The Ancient Path of Kabbalah* (1998)

52   Gustav Davidson, *Dictionary of Angels: Including the Fallen Angels* (1994)

53   J.E. Cirlot, *A Dictionary of Symbols* (2002)

54   Susan G. Woolridge, *Poemcrazy: Freeing Your Life with Words* (1997)

55   Alan Lew, *This is Real and You are Completely Unprepared* (2003)

56   *Llewellyn Encyclopedia* (2002)

57   *Dialogue: The Art Of Thinking Together* (1999)

58   Evelyn Underhill, *Mysticism* (1911)

est alteration may empty the word of all its magic content." Naturally, words undergo changes over time, transmitted as they are through inaudible whispers or all-too-fallible scribes, and eventually they become so corrupted as to be "altogether exotic and meaningless," offering few if any clues to their original sense and tongue, and essentially "unintelligible to the heirs of the tradition." Ironically, a mystery offers its own a kind of potency, and magic words came to be considered efficacious to the degree that they *were* strange and incomprehensible: "Rashi, in the eleventh century, proved his familiarity with this phenomenon when he wrote: 'The sorcerer whispers his charms, and doesn't understand what they are or what they mean, but . . . the desired effect is produced only by such incantations.'" Trachtenberg notes that the Cherokee medicine men, aborigines in India, and Tibetan and Chinese Buddhists all hold in high regard archaic, unintelligible expressions "that have conveyed no meaning for centuries," considering them "more potent than their own. The 'abracadabra' of the modern stage magician reflects a phenomenon familiar to us all."[59]

A very early written record of *abracadabra* dates back to 208 CE, as "part of a folkloric cure for a fever."[60] The record is actually an incomplete poem on medicine by the Roman doctor Serenus Quintus Sammonicus, "containing curious lore, ancient remedies, and magical formulae—such as the Abracadabra charm—and was much used in the Middle Ages."[61]

Abracadabra was commonly used as a conjuring word by the Middle Ages.[62]

As a talisman against disease, *abracadabra* was inscribed on parchment and worn around the neck.[63] In the late 1600s, John Aubrey transcribed instructions for creating such a charm in *Miscellanies Upon Various Subjects:*

> *Abracadabra, strange mysterious word,*
> *In order writ, can wond'rous cures afford.*
> *This be the rule:-a strip of parchment take,*
> *Cut like a pyramid revers'd in make.*
> *Abracadabra, first at length you name,*
> *Line under line, repeating still the same:*
> *Cut at its end, each line, one letter less,*
> *Must then its predecessor line express;*
> *'Till less'ning by degrees the charm descends*
> *With conic form, and in a letter ends.*
> *Round the sick neck the finish'd wonder tie,*
> *And pale disease must from the patient fly.*

In *Journal of the Plague Year* (1722), Daniel Defoe reported that many people attributed the Black Death to possession by an evil spirit and believed the Abracadabra charm could ward it off.

In popular culture, the word *abracadabra* is most often associated with awakening the genie in a magic lamp (to grant a wish) and pulling a rabbit out of a hat.

Dogura-Magura is a Japanese equivalent to *abracadabra*.

"Abner Kadabra" is the title of an episode of the television series *Bewitched* (1965).

When a little girl asked professional magician David Greene, "Why does a magic word like abracadabra work?" his reply was "It works because you believe in it."[64]

Abra Kadabra is a villainous stage magician who first appears in the comic book *Flash #128*

---

59   Joshua Trachtenberg, *Jewish Magic and Superstition* (1939)

60   Tom Ogden, *The Complete Idiot's Guide to Magic Tricks* (1998)

61   Donald Tyson's annotation to works of Henry Cornelius Agrippa, *Three Books of Occult Philosophy* (1993)

62   Tom Ogden, *The Complete Idiot's Guide to Magic Tricks* (1998)

63   Gustav Davidson, *Dictionary of Angels: Including the Fallen Angels* (1994)

64   "Magician David Greene Launches Lower School Book Fair with Demonstration of the 'Magic of Reading,'" Christ Church Episcopal School newsletter (2003)

(1962): "Abra Kadabra hails from the 64th Century, an era in which science is sufficiently advanced to be indistinguishable from magic, and the art of stage magic is dead. Obsessed with a need for applause, and championing the cause of the individual in an era of mechanical precision, he traveled back in time to torment the second Flash."[65]

"Debra Kadabra" is the title of a song by Frank Zappa (1975), concerning a "witch goddess" whose full name is "Debra Algebra Ebneezra Kadabra" or "Debra Fauntleroy Magnesium Kadabra."

Abra Cadabra is a legendary old wise woman and oracle in the novel *Jonah* by Dana Redfield (2000).

In the Bugs Bunny cartoon "Transylvania 6-5000" (1963), Bugs the Magician uses *abracadabra* to turn the menacing vampire Count Bloodcount into a "bumbling bat." "Always enchanted by wretched excess, Bugs experiments with ever-weirder abracadabras, resulting in ever-more-extravagant vampiric incarnations."[66]

"Lady Abracadabra" is the name of a fairy "in no humor to be turned into a toad," in *The Hope of the Katzekopfs* (1844) by William Churne of Straffordshire.[67]

"Abracadabra Day" is "the best holiday of all," listed "in no almanac and printed in no calendar." It is explained in *Mr. Mysterious & Company* (1962) by Sid Fleischman: "The secret was this: No matter how bad you were on Abracadabra Day or no matter what pranks you pulled, you would not be spanked or punished. . . . There was only one rule about Abracadabra Day. You must not tell anybody the day you had chosen to be bad. . . . It was like magic to do something naughty and not get punished."

Common Magician's Applications: Production, vanishing, transformation. Jeff McBride says *abracadabra* in the finale of his torn and restored bill routine entitled "The Greatest Illusion Ever Created—Money," featured in his DVD *The Magic of Jeff McBride* (2003).

Historically a "shrinking word,"[68] *Abracadabra* is especially appropriate for vanishing illusions.

Variations and Incantations:

- Abachugaba
  —Jimmy Akin (2005)

- Abaracadabara
  "[M]ist streaming over the ridge, snatching trees and boulders from view then magically revealing them once more. Abaracadabara! Spring has appeared in the forest."
  —Ric Soulen, "Thundersnow" (2003)

- Abaracadabara Allakazam Hocus-Pocus Walla Walla Washington
  —*Vanguardsoh.com* (2005)

- Abarcadera
  This is a magic incantation used by Taoist monks in the film *Shaolin vs. Evil Dead* (2004).

- Abba-cadabra
  "'Abba-cadabra,' chants Twinkie, suddenly taking off her shorts."
  —Deborah Gregory, *Cheetah Girls Livin' Large* (2003)

- Abbykadabby
  —Professional magician Steve Charney, *Hocus Jokus: 50 Funny Magic Tricks Complete with Jokes* (2003)

---

65   Kelson Vibber, "The Flash: Those Who Ride the Lightning" (2005)

66   Steven Jay Schneider, *Horror Film and Psychoanalysis* (2004)

67   Peter Hunt, *Children's Literature: An Anthology 1801–1902* (2001)

68   Richard Cavendish, *The Black Arts* (1968)

- Abra-abra-cadabra
This is a lyric from a song by the Steve Miller Band.

- Abra and cadabra
—Steven L. Case, *The Book of Uncommon Prayer* (2002)

- Abra Cababra Alla Kazamm
—*Tales to Astonish #58* (1964)

- Abracababra wackity wack
—"Kids on the Net" (1998)

- Abracabooger
—Professional magician Steve Charney, *Hocus Jokus: 50 Funny Magic Tricks Complete with Jokes* (2003)

- Abracabra
"Abracabra, alakazee."
—*Substratum.org* (2004)

- Abraca-chicken
"The magician places a chicken bone into a magic box. He says *abracadabra* but nothing happens. He considers for a moment (consults his magic puppet or assistant if he has one) and realizes he should have said *Alaka-chicken*. He places the bone into the box again. He reminds the audience to help him remember the correct magic word. He waves his magic wand over the box and says *Abraca-chicken*! Oh no! (either the assistant or the magic puppet or the audience can point out that he's used the wrong magic word again). What can it mean? What happened? The magician looks nervous and tells the audience that *Abraca-chicken* is a very advanced magic word . . . he wasn't ready for magic that advanced."
—*KidZone.ws* (2005)

- Abra Ca Dabra
"This time instead of passing the quarter to your other hand, you're going to say the magic words, 'abra ca dabra,' make this coin leave the room now!"
—*Indianchild.com* (2004)
"When you stop the music, the lucky player holding the box must say 'Abra Ca Dabra.'"
—Professional magician Ken Scott (2001)

- Abra Cadabra
"Daddy . . . will you tell me the story of old Abra Cadabra again?"
—Dana Redfield, *Jonah* (2000)

- Abracadabra, abracaboo
—Angela Johnson, *When Mules Flew on Magnolia Street* (2000)

- Abracadabra, abracadee
—Joan Novelli, *40 Sensational Sight Word Games: Grades K–2* (2002)

- Abra cadabra Abra cazoom
—Homer Public Library (2005)

- Abra Cadabra Ala Ca Zear
"He saved the best trick for last. He waved his magic wand over the table three times and said, 'Abra Cadabra Ala Ca Zear—Make a wonderful snack appear!' He jerked his cape up and under it was a bowl of popcorn!"
—Peter Keiniger, "The Babysitter" (2004)

- Abra-ca-dab-bra ala-ka-zam
—Ken Stejbach, "Marceau is Exeter's Magician," *The Exeter News-Letter* (2000)

- Abracadabra alacazam
"His feet like magic wands. Abracadabra alacazam! Another opposition defense was sawn in half."
—Harry Pearson, *The Far Corner* (2000)

- Abracadabra, Ala-Kazam
—Tadahiko Nagao, *Kokology: The Game of Self-Discovery* (2000)

- Abracadabra Alakazam
"Abracadabra! Alakazam! He gives his wand a shake. Bees fly out of the Abbot's sleeve, and daisies sprout from a cake!"
—Brian Jacques, *A Redwall Winter's Tale* (2001)

- Abracadabra Alakazam Hocus Pocus Addaboombam
These magic words are from a riddle: "Abracadabra, alakazam. Hocus, pocus, addaboombam. Take just a second with each magic word. Tell me the substance these words conjured." The secret to finding the answer lies in the phrase "just take a second." Take the second letter of each magic word to form the "substance" in question (*Able2Know.com* [2004]).

- Abracadabra Alakazam Hocus Pocus Sim-Sala-Bim
"Wave your wand . . . 'Abracadabra! Alakazam! Hocus Pocus! Sim-Sala-Bim!' And just like magic . . . you become the magician!"
—Levite Jewish Community Center (2005)

- Abracadabra Allacazoo
"[F]irst I must say the magic words. Abracadabra! Allacazoo!"
—*Caillou's Corner* (2002)

- Abracadabra! Allakazam! Mahendralal! Praphullachandra! Jagadishchandra!
"My photocopied stage was peopled by paper actors with names impossible for my tongue to wrap around. Muttering an archaic incantation: 'Abracadabra! Allakazam! Mahendralal! Praphullachandra! Jagadishchandra!' I conjured from my bed like a genie from a magic lantern."
—Leslie Forbes, *Fish, Blood, and Bone* (2001)

- Abra, Kadabra. Alakazam, Watashiwa, Wakama Walla Walla bing bang! Tsukina Hikaiwa Ino Message!
"Now, with these words . . . Abra, Kadabra. Alakazam, Watashiwa, Wakama Walla Walla bing bang! Tsukina Hikaiwa Ino Message! And . . . There was a flash of light and a puff of smoke as she pulled away the black cloth that hid the hat."
—"The Sixth Column Fanfiction Group," *Yahoo.com* (1999)

- Abracadabra, allez-oop
—Edward Eager, *Knight's Castle* (1999)

- Abracadabra, bibbledeebee
—Gertrude Chandler Warner, *The Pizza Mystery* (1993)

- Abracadabra, Bridget Bardo
—Henry Miller, "Genesis: What Really Happened Or What Those Repressed Little Bespectacled Female Spinster Sunday School Teachers Refused to Tell You"

- Abra-cadabra, buzz, buzz bil-i-ous, Buzz, buzz, bob bob-a-loo.
—Ralph Allen, *The Best Burlesque Sketches* (1995)

- Abracadabra Cadabra Cadeen
—Prof. Henry Bessette

- Abra Cadabra Candelabra
—Michael Valeur (2005)

- Abra cadabra capoosh
—Natalie Babbitt (2005)

- Abra-cadabra dev and chort
—James Mallory, *Merlin: The Old Magic* (1999)

- Abracadabra dum dum dum
"Here is the cloak: when you want to go traveling on it, say 'Abracadabra, dum, dum, dum'; when you want to come back again, say 'Abracadabra, tum tum ti.'"
—Maria Dinah Mulock Craik, *The Little Lame Prince* (1875)

- Abra Cadabra Fiddle-de-fee
—Jenepher Lingelbach, *Hands-On Nature* (2000)

- Abracadabra! Hocus pocus
"'Abracadabra! Hocus pocus!' says the magician, and something happens. A pack of cards is turned into a pigeon."
—Joseph Hillis Miller, *Others* (2001)

- Abracadabra, hocus pocus, alakazam
"'Abracadabra, hocus pocus, alakazam,' said Kevin. 'And presto, this clump of dirt is now a diamond.' Kevin opened his palm to reveal a small blue diamond that sparkled coolly in the sun."
—Neal Shusterman, *The Eyes of King Midas* (1992)

- Abracadabra, hocus-pocus, sim salabim, OPEN SESAME!
—Allan Pred, "Re-Presenting the Extended Moment of Danger: A Meditation on Hypermodernity, Identity and the Montage Form," *Space and Social Theory: Interpreting Modernity and Postmodernity* (1997)

- Abracadabra Kazam
—Mike Thaler, *The Teacher from the Black Lagoon* (1989), in which the magic words are followed by a flash of light, a puff of smoke, and someone changing into a frog.
"[A] once-and-for-all, abracadabra-kazam kind of . . . experience."
—Peter J. Gomes, *Strength for the Journey* (2004)

- Abracadabra, Now you see it, now you don't
—Jodi Picoult, *Keeping the Faith* (1999)

- Abracadabra! Oooga booga!
—David Brin, *The Practice Effect* (1984)

- Abracadabra, please and thank you
—Laurell K. Hamilton, *Bite* (2004)

- Abracadabra Pon
This is the magic phrase of transformation that the character Chibi-Usa (also known as Rini) uses in the *Sailor Moon* manga stories (1992).

- Abracadabra, presto
—John Altman, *The Watchmen* (2004)

- Abracadabra presto-change
"A little mysterious hoeing and manuring was all the *abra cadabra presto-change*, that I used . . ."
—Henry David Thoreau, *Collected Essays and Poems* (2001)

- Abracadabra! Presto chango! Hocus pocus! Alakazam!
"She waved her arms around, sprinkled some glittery dust, and said, 'Abracadabra! Presto chango! Hocus pocus! Alakazam!' Nothing. More glittery dust. 'Abracadabra! Presto chango! Hocus pocus! Alakazam!' Nothing. 'Ahem. Maybe you didn't hear me. I *said*, 'Abracadabra! Presto chango! Hocus pocus! And AlakaZAM! ARE YOU DEAF OR WHAT?' And then . . . there appeared . . . *a ghost.*"
—Michele Torrey, *The Case of the Graveyard Ghost* (2002)

- Abracadabra. Presto change-o. Open Shazaam. Voilà
"I'd like to wave a magic wand . . . Clap my hands. *Abracadabra. Presto change-o. Open Shazaam. Voilà!*"
—Milena McGraw, *After Dinkirk* (1998)

- Abracadabra shalakazam
—Marek Kohn, "Sir Teo's Quest" (2000)

- Abracadabra! Shazam!
"Remember, you're releasing yourself from the handcuffs and need to say the magic words, 'Abracadabra! Shazam!' to transport yourself."
—Elena Bates, *I Am Diva!* (2003)

- Abracadabra-simsalabim
—Susanne Friedrich (2001)

- Abra Cadabra, skiggily, scoo
"She waved her wand in the air and said, 'Abra Cadabra, skiggily, scoo—good table manners just for you.'"
—Linda Hagler, *Good Citizenship Counts* (2003)

- Abracadabra tum tum ti
—Maria Dinah Mulock Craik, *The Little Lame Prince* (1875)

- Abracadabra-zimmity-ZAM
—Ray Bradbury, *Dandelion Wine* (1946)

- Abracadabra zip tumblo
—Peter Lerangis, *Whoa! Amusement Park Gone Wild!* (2003)

- Abracadabra Zot Beeble
"'I shall now make this bill vanish by saying the magic words *abracadabra . . . zot . . . beeble!*' Max made a fist with his left hand and shoved the bill into it. Then he opened his fist . . . and the five-dollar bill was gone."
—Peter Lerangis, *Presto! Magic Treasure* (2002)

- Abracadabry, hocus-poo
"Jack fixed her with a trancelike gaze and chanted in the wizard's elderly irritable voice: 'Abracadabry, hocus-poo, Roger Skunk, how do you do, Roses, boses, pull an ear, Roger Skunk, you never fear: *Bingo!*'"
—John Updike, "Should Wizard Hit Mommy?" *The Early Stories: 1953–1975* (2003)

- Abra-Cadaver
"He just waved his hands over the body three times while chanting the magic words: Abra-Cadaver."
—*National Lampoon* (2002)
    In an episode of the cartoon series *Powerpuff Girls* (1998), magician Al Lusion returns from the dead as the evil magical zombie Abracadaver.

- Abra-Ca-Dazzle
—Professional magician Larry White (1982)

- Abracadebra
—Professional magician Steve Charney, *Hocus Jokus: 50 Funny Magic Tricks Complete with Jokes* (2003)

- Abracadiddle
—Professional magician Nicholas J. Johnson (2003)

- Abracadoody
—Professional magician Steve Charney, *Hocus Jokus: 50 Funny Magic Tricks Complete with Jokes* (2003)

- Abra-ca-pocus
This magic word for transformation is from the Bugs Bunny cartoon "Transylvania 6-5000" (1963).

- Abracapocus
—Professional magician Steve Charney, *Hocus Jokus: 50 Funny Magic Tricks Complete with Jokes* (2003)

- Abra-Ca-Whoops
—Professional magician John Pizzi (1982)

- Abracazebra
—Professional magician Steve Charney, *Hocus Jokus: 50 Funny Magic Tricks Complete with Jokes* (2003)

- AbraCowDabra
This is the title of an art installation by Julie Alexander for the Texas Children's Cancer Center: "This is sheer magic! You never know what this clever bovine will pull out of its hat. She wears a cape bearing the magic incantation—AbraCowDabra! The viewer discovers familiar magical transformations— a rabbit in a hat, doves flying from a cap, card tricks, knotted scarves, and a flower surprise. But who is the magician here? The rabbit carries the magic wand. Doves pull

scarves from one pocket and flowers from another. Is the magician the big purple cow dressed in formal attire and magic cape, or could it be the rabbit, or the doves? The real magic is in the eyes of the beholder."
—*Houston.cowparade.net* (2001)

- Abra Ca Drab Ra
—Barbara LaBarbera (2003)

- Abrahadabra
This is the spelling coined by occult philosopher Aleister Crowley. "[Abrahadabra] means by translation Abraha Deber, the Voice of the Chief Seer" (Israel Regardie, *777 and Other Qabalistic Writings of Aleister Crowley* [1986]). It also symbolizes "the union of Macrocosm and Microcosm" (Christopher S. Hyatt, *Taboo: Sex, Religion & Magick* [2001]).
   "Words do change reality. Abrahadabra!"
—Denny Sargent, *Your Guardian Angel and You* (2004)

- Abrakadabra
This is the magic word in the computer adventure game "The Caves," used to exit the game.

- Abrakadabra hokuspokus filiokus simsalabim
—Jens Vigen (2003)

- Abra Kadabra Shazam
—Debra Susan Antin, "Meshoogie's Poem On Breast Cancer Round Two" (2004)

- Abrakhadabra
—*TheMagicCafe.com*

- Abraqcadabra
—Memphis Shelby County Public Library and Information Center

- Abrasadabra
This is a Greek spelling of the word.

- Abra without the cadabra
—Stephen A. Devaux, *Total Project Control* (1999)

- Abra-Zabra
—Henry Boltinoff, "The Magic Genie," *House of Secrets #78* (1966)

- Alakapocus
—Professional magician Steve Charney, *Hocus Jokus: 50 Funny Magic Tricks Complete with Jokes* (2003)

- Alley-Kat-Abra
This is a cape-wearing, wand-wielding feline superhero who practices magic in the comic book *Captain Carrot and His Amazing Zoo Crew* (1982). She can create solid objects out of thin air.

- Avada Kedavra
—J.K. Rowling, *Harry Potter* series

- CadabraAbra
—Professional magician Charles Kraus ("Charles the Magician") (2005)

- Epplekedepple
—Professional magician Steve Charney, *Hocus Jokus: 50 Funny Magic Tricks Complete with Jokes* (2003)

- Have a banana
—Professional magician Steve Charney, *Hocus Jokus: 50 Funny Magic Tricks Complete with Jokes* (2003)
   "'What's your favorite magic word?' professional magician Magic-Al (Alan Garber) will ask during a kids' show. Someone inevitably yells out 'Abracadabra.' Magic-Al says he loves to respond 'What? I look like your Grandma?' They say, 'No, abracadabra.' I respond, 'No, I'm not from Alabama.' They yell 'Abracadabra!' and I say, 'Oh, Have a Banana!' As I say this I make a banana appear. Then I proceed to make

several bananas appear to the laughter of the audience."[69]

- Rabbit-Cadabra
  Rabbit-Cadabra is the title of a picture book for children, featuring a vampire rabbit and characters from the *Bunnicula* series of books by James Howe (1993).

- Sabbra Cadabra
  —Black Sabbath's album *Sabbath Bloody Sabbath* (1973)

In Literature:

- "One of the most fantastic words going is 'abracadabra.'"
  —John-Roger, *Psychic Protection* (1976)

- "Abracadabra. Fee Fo Fi Bloody Fum. And just when everyone thinks you're going to produce the most ludicrously faked bit of cheese-cloth ectoplasm, or a phoney rap on the table, it comes. Clear as a bell. Quite unexpected. The voice of truth!"
  —John Mortimer, *Rumpole of the Bailey* (1978)

- "We came around the peak of a high hill and there in front and to the right of us (and far, far below stretched miles of soft-colored sands and in the distance, much further out than I had dreamed) was the traditional castle, ethereal and unreal as though it had just risen from the sea, like an 'Arabian Nights' castle, exactly as if someone had just wished it there: 'Abracadabra!'"
  —Anne Morrow Lindbergh, *Bring Me a Unicorn: Diaries and Letters* (1971)

- "And I, her daughter, listening wide-eyed to her charming apocrypha, with tales of Mithras and Baldur the Beautiful and Osiris and Quetzalcoatl all interwoven with stories of flying chocolates and flying carpets and the Triple Goddess and Aladdin's crystal cave of wonders and the cave from which Jesus rose after three days, amen, abracadabra, amen."
  —Joanne Harris, *Chocolat* (2000)

- "'You think you're the only magician in the family? I'm going to make an old eyesore disappear. And in its place . . . abracadabra. A brand new town.' 'Nobody says abracadabra anymore.' He laughed. 'They will now.'"
  —D.K. Smith, *Nothing Disappears* (2004)

- "'Abracadabra,' Charlene murmured to herself as she crossed against the traffic in the rain, 'that's an exotic word.' Somewhere in the distance a bomb exploded softly."
  —Kate Atkinson, *Not the End of the World* (2003)

- From Jamrach Holobom, quoted in *The Devil's Dictionary* by Ambrose Bierce (1911):

By Abracadabra *we signify*
    An infinite number of things.
'Tis the answer to What? and How? and Why?
And Whence? and Whither?—a word whereby
    The Truth (with the comfort it brings)
Is open to all who grope in night,
Crying for Wisdom's holy light.

Whether the word is a verb or a noun
    Is knowledge beyond my reach.
I only know that 'tis handed down.
      From sage to sage,
      From age to age—
An immortal part of speech!

Of an ancient man the tale is told
That he lived to be ten centuries old,
    In a cave on a mountain side.
    (True, he finally died.)
The fame of his wisdom filled the land,

---

69   Personal correspondence (2005), *Magic-Al.com.*

For his head was bald, and you'll understand
His beard was long and white
And his eyes uncommonly bright.

Philosophers gathered from far and near
To sit at his feat and hear and hear,
Though he never was heard
To utter a word
But "Abracadabra, abracadab,
Abracada, abracad,
Abraca, abrac, abra, ab!"
'Twas all he had,
'Twas all they wanted to hear, and each
Made copious notes of the mystical speech,
Which they published next—
A trickle of text
In the meadow of commentary.
Mighty big books were these,
In a number, as leaves of trees;
In learning, remarkably—very!

He's dead,
As I said,
And the books of the sages have perished,
But his wisdom is sacredly cherished.
In Abracadabra it solemnly rings,
Like an ancient bell that forever swings.
O, I love to hear
That word make clear
Humanity's General Sense of Things.

- "Geoffrey pulled up his sleeve, cleared his throat again, and tried once more. '*Arzemy barzemy yangelo igg lom,*' he intoned. Quickly, he added, '*Abra cadabra.*' Turning to Kate, he whispered, 'That sometimes helps.' At that moment, the cooking pot quivered slightly. It slid toward the rim of the barrel. Then, with a slight crackling sound, it slowly lifted into the air, hovering a few inches above the barrel. 'You did it,' said Kate in wonderment."
—T.A. Barron, *The Merlin Effect* (1994)

- "'Whatever.' A single word. A single, everyday word. Who would expect it to be as powerful as 'Abracadabra.' Full of enough magic and monstrosity to stir the Something Ugly that had been sleeping between them for a long time. Two people who need each other always have one—an Ugly—bewitched by mutual agreement, a stone neither person turns, a door neither one opens for the common good. To turn, to open, doesn't just rock the relationship boat, it upends it. And for all either person knows, that boat might not ever, ever float again."
—Karyn Langhorne, *A Personal Matter* (2004)

- "Like a reverse abracadabra, the desire would be wiped away, stuffed down, and stomped."
—Diane Conway, *What Would You Do If You Had No Fear? Living Your Dreams While Quakin' in Your Boots* (2004)

- "'Perhaps it's waiting for the magic word?' After all, the mule was just an animal, like me or the cat, only bigger. And I knew what motivated the cat and me. 'Magic word? Yes, perhaps that would work. Now let me think, magic words . . . all right. *Abracadabra.*'"
—Peggy Christian, *The Bookstore Mouse* (2002)

- "Couldn't he have just said the divine equivalent of abracadabra, and all would be well?"
—Robert Lewis, *The Church of Irresistible Influence* (2003)

- "[O]ur world burned up to ashes because someone somewhere said 'Abracadabra' the wrong way."
—Holly Lisle, *Memory of Fire* (2002)

- "Think of a [story's] premise as the abracadabra that puts the rabbit into the hat."
—James N. Frey, *How to Write a Damn Good Novel* (1987)

- "[T]he Baltic president of an abracadabra-stan that didn't exist until three weeks ago." —Linda Fairstein, *Likely to Die* (1998)

- "The owl's name was Abracadabra. He was so big and important that he thought the toy shop belonged to him." —Rumer Godden, "The Story of Holly and Ivy," *Hey! Listen to This: Stories to Read Aloud* (1992)

- "I didn't move my gaze off the coffin except once, to turn the page in the order of the service; and when I looked back it had vanished—gone clean through the red plush curtains from which the rollers protruded. *Abracadabra!* and my father had dematerialized, like a knotted handkerchief or a white dove." —Jonathan Raban, *Passage to Juneau: A Sea and Its Meanings* (2000)

- "'Abracadabra!' Liane shouted, as the crowd sucked in its breath." —David Drake, *Master of the Cauldron* (2004)

- "Abracadabra, thus we learn / The more you create, the less you earn." —Ogden Nash

- "There is an element of abracadabra as the very last seam is stitched [in the quilt], because what you see in one single pieced triangular segment is not what you get in the multiplied sum." —Paula Nadelstern, *Kaleidoscopes & Quilts* (1996)

- "Gingerly he lifted up a corner of the handkerchief. Several cogs and some pieces of glass rolled across the table. Mr. Curry let out a roar of wrath. 'I think I forgot to say "abracadabra,"' faltered Paddington. 'Abracadabra!' shouted Mr. Curry, beside himself with rage. 'Abracadabra!' He held up the remains of his watch. 'Twenty years I've had this watch, and now look at it!'" —Michael Bond, *A Bear Called Paddington* (1958)

- "'Abr-abr-abr,' [the baby] gurgled happily when she was settled in her cradle. 'She is trying to say abracadabra,' said Little Witch Girl." —Eleanor Estes, *The Witch Family* (2000)

- From Peter Fallon, "Spring Song," *The Penguin Book of Contemporary Irish Poetry* (1991):

  It was as if
  someone only had to say
  Abracadabra
  to set alight
  the chestnut
  candelabra.

- "The abracadabra boys—. . . They know postures from impostures." —Carl Sandburg, "The Abracadabra Boys," *The Complete Poems of Carl Sandburg* (1969)

- From Cole Porter, "I Always Knew" (1942):

  Since that lovely evening
  In the twilight's blur,
  When the Fates cried "abracadabra,"
  And there you were.

- "You're right, ABRACADABRA is a magic word to make things appear or disappear." —Monalisa DeGross, *Donavan's Word Jar* (1998)

- "Abracadabra from nowhere, with lightning and thunder, you entered life, you stepped on life's giant stage." —Sorana Salomeia, "Simsalabim" (2004)

- "'Abracadabra' swings. If you don't believe me, pronounce it slowly, out loud, one syllable at a time, and tap your feet and snap your fingers while you say it. Crazy, man." —Brian Fleury, "Ardara Town" (2002)

- "I remember being about seven years old and sent by my teacher to fetch a tube of glue from another class which was full. I walked in and received the object. 'Kevin, what's the magic word?' I was asked upon receiving it. I had never heard of this saying before and replied straight-faced 'Abracadabra.' The whole class erupted in hysterical and loud laughter. The teacher glared angrily at me obviously thinking I was trying to be smart. I was asked again and I said, 'It works.'"
—Kevin Phillips, quoted in *Loving Mr. Spock* by Barbara Jacobs (2003)

- "'You know the magic words?' Vili asked. Rori looked at his mother. 'Not magic words,' Vili whispered. 'Magician's words.' 'Abracadabra?' 'Shssh . . . ,' Vili said. 'Our secret, remember?'"
—Anna Porter, *The Storyteller* (2000)

- "'[N]ow I will say a few magic words, and my assistants will disappear!' Rapping on Julian's cabinet I shouted, 'Abracadabra!' which was the only thing that came into my head. I might lose points with the Great Chamberlain for lacking imagination, but if the trick worked, it wouldn't matter."
—Joan Lowery Nixon, *A Deadly Game of Magic* (1983)

- "'Let's get the Ingoldsby Legends. There's a thing about Abra-cadabra there,' said Cyril, yawning. 'We may as well play at magic. Let's be Knights Templars. They were awfully gone on magic. They used to work spells or something with a goat and a goose. Father says so.'"
—Edith Nesbit, *The Phoenix and the Carpet* (1904)

- "We had a delightful custom in nursery days, devised by my mother, that on festival occasions, such as birthdays or at Christmas, our presents were given us in the evening by a fairy called Abracadabra. The first time the fairy appeared, we heard, after tea, in the hall, the hoarse notes of a horn. We rushed out in amazement. Down in the hall, talking to an aunt of mine who was staying in the house, stood a veritable fairy, in a scarlet dress, carrying a wand and a scarlet bag, and wearing a high pointed scarlet hat, of the shape of an extinguisher. My aunt called us down; and we saw that the fairy had the face of a great ape, dark-brown, spectacled, of a good-natured aspect, with a broad grin, and a curious crop of white hair, hanging down behind and on each side. Unfortunately my eldest brother, a very clever and imaginative child, was seized with a panic so insupportable at the sight of the face, that his present had to be given him hurriedly, and he was led away, blanched and shuddering, to the nursery. After that, the fairy never appeared except when he was at school: but long after, when I was looking in a lumber-room with my brother for some mislaid toys, I found in a box the mask of Abracadabra and the horn. I put it hurriedly on, and blew a blast on the horn, which seemed to be of tortoiseshell with metal fittings. To my amazement, he turned perfectly white, covered his face with his hands, and burst out with the most dreadful moans. I thought at first that he was making believe to be frightened, but I saw in a minute or two that he had quite lost control of himself, and the things were hurriedly put away. At the time I thought it a silly kind of affectation. But I perceive now that he had had a real shock the first time he had seen the mask; and though he was then a big schoolboy, the terror was indelible. Who can say of what old inheritance of fear that horror of the great ape-like countenance was the sign? He had no associations of fear with apes, but it must have been, I

think, some dim old primeval terror, dating from some ancestral encounter with a forest monster. In no other way can I explain it."
—Arthur Christopher Benson, *Where No Fear Was* (1914)

- "Say abracadabra, but mean it." —Armand Okur, *Pandora's Box* (2002)

- "A flawless sapphire, star-bright, a cosmic abracadabra . . ."
  —Lisa Rosenblatt, "Rivke: The Last Proletariat" (2004)

- "The whole thing seemed the stuff of abracadabra."
  —Jack Dann, *Dreaming Down-Under* (2002)

Abra-dee, Abra-do, with a Hay and a Ho and a Nonny Nonny No

(see also *abra*)

Mystique: The sing-song rhythm of this phrase lends a playful and non-dramatic tone.

Facts: *Abra-dee, abra-do, with a hay and a ho and a nonny nonny no* are magic words to grant a wish, featured in an episode of the television series *Today's Special* (1982).

Similar to *hey diddle diddle* and *hey derry down*, *hey nonny nonny* are nonsense words to English folk songs dating back to the Elizabethan era. Such songs were typically performed by dancing jesters. Nonsense phrases were often used by troubadours in Renaissance song lyrics as substitutes for words considered risqué.[70]

---

70   Bill Markwick, *Classical 96 FM Music Dictionary* (2001)

Abraxas

Abraxas, the perfect word.
—Louise Erdrich, "Hydra,"
Baptism of Desire: Poems (1989)

Mystique: Have you ever been mesmerized while waiting for the sunrise? As you watch the horizon for that first burst of light, you get swept up in the eternal present moment. With baited breath, your sense of time is suspended, and you're primed for a miracle. This is the "liminal zone," the threshold between night and day, between here and there, between this and that. It's the crossroads where anything is possible. And then the dawn breaks through, like a sudden burst of inspiration, like an act of creation: "Let there be light." That is the magic of *Abraxas*, a word that has perhaps always been closely associated with the power of the sun. This "strange, mysterious name"[71] captures that magical, suspended, timeless moment: "all of time as an eternal instant."[72] *Abraxas* is the power of infinity—the promise of endless possibilities, the "cosmos" itself.[73] The word suggests a power that is not properly ours but rather a gift from another world.

Abraxas represents "a mystery, an enigma."[74] It is the "maker of effect"[75] that governs "deceitful reality,"[76] as celebrated through the conjurer's art of illusion. *Abraxas* is the great power of sleight-of-hand, great "because man does not

---

71   Annemarie Schimmel, *The Mystery of Numbers* (1993)

72   Gene Wolfe, *Shadow and Claw* (1994)

73   Carl Jung, the third sermon of the *Seven Sermons to the Dead* (1917)

74   Ellen Hart, *Immaculate Midnight* (2003)

75   Marvin Spiegelman, *Reich, Jung, Regardie & Me* (1992)

76   Carl Jung, the third sermon of the *Seven Sermons to the Dead* (1917)

Figure 6. Abraxas as depicted in a gnostic gem, from Charles W. King's *The Gnostics and Their Remains* (1887).

perceive it at all."[77] *Abraxas* is "fullness uniting itself with emptiness,"[78] and therefore is muse to magic involving vanishing. *Abraxas* is "love and the murder of love,"[79] a cosmic drama played out every time a magician plunges a sword through the lady in the basket.

Meanings:

- Absolute nothingness
  —Maurice Nicoll, *Psychological Commentaries on the Teaching of Gurdjieff and Ouspensky, Volume 3* (1996)

- Blessed name
  "Abraxas. The adorable, blessed name—the unutterable word."
  —Moses W. Redding, The Illustrated History of Freemasonry (2004)

- Gemstone engraved with "a mystical word used as a symbol of divinity"
  —Gotthold Ephraim Lessing, *Laocoon: An Essay on the Limits of Painting and Poetry* (1766), translated by Edward Allen McCormick (1962)
    "I should like someday to find and secure an abraxas."
  —Judith Tarr, *Pride of Kings* (2001)

- God of the Egyptians, Romans, and Gnostics, knowledge of whom resurfaced through the writings of Carl Jung and Hermann Hesse
  —Ellen Hart, *Immaculate Midnight* (2003)

- Holy word
  —Ludwig Blau, "Abraxas," *JewishEncyclopedia.com* (2002)

- Ineffable name
  —Ludwig Blau, "Abraxas," *JewishEncyclopedia.com* (2002)

- Infinity
  —Maurice Nicoll, *Psychological Commentaries on the Teaching of Gurdjieff and Ouspensky, Volume 3* (1996)

- Master key
  "From the papyri and the magic gems it is certain that the word refers to the use of the Ineffable Name as a master-key with which the powers of all the upper and the nether world are locked or unlocked, bound or loosened."
  —Ludwig Blau, "Abraxas," *JewishEncyclopedia.com* (2002)

- Number three-hundred-sixty-five
  "The magic word 'Abrasax' or 'Abraxas' signifies the Aeon. It was intended to express the numerical value 365 in one word."
  —Joseph Campbell, *The Mysteries: Papers from the Eranos Yearbooks* (1955)

- Pure thought; language taken to the "nth power"
    Philosopher Gilles Deleuze suggests that *abraxas* is an immobilized "pure thought" and the "highest finality of sense," like a seemingly-nonsensical one-word simile, the paradoxical conclusion of an infinite regression of propositions (a is like b, and b is like c, and c is like d, and so on forever). "There is only one kind of word which expresses

---

77 *Ibid.*

78 *Ibid.*

79 *Ibid.*

both itself and its sense—precisely the nonsense word: abraxas" (*Difference and Repetition* [1995]).

Origins: It is likely, as an etymologist posited in 1891, that *abraxas* belongs "to no known speech" but rather some "mystic dialect," perhaps taking its origin "from some supposed divine inspiration."[80] Yet scholars, of course, search for a root. There are speculatory shreds of evidence which suggest that *Abraxas* is a combination of two Egyptian words, *abrak* and *sax*, meaning "the honorable and hallowed word" or "the word is adorable."[81] *Abrak* is "found in the Bible as a salutation to Joseph by the Egyptians upon his accession to royal power."[82] *Abraxas* appears in "an Egyptian invocation to the Godhead, meaning 'hurt me not.'"[83] Other scholars suggest a Hebrew origin of the word, positing "a Grecized form of *ha-berakhah*, '*the blessing*,'"[84] while still others speculate a derivation from the Greek *habros* and *sac*, "the beautiful, the glorious Savior."[85] The name has appeared in the ancient Hebrew/Aramaic mystical treatises *The Book of Raziel* and *The Sword of Moses*, and in post-Talmudic Jewish incantation texts,[86] as well as in Persian mythology.[87]

An interesting occurrence of *Abraxas* is found in a papyrus from late antiquity (perhaps from Hellenized Egypt, though its exact origin is unknown). The papyrus contains "magical recipes, invocations, and incantations," and tells of a baboon disembarking the Sun boat and proclaiming: "Thou art the number of the year ABRAXAS." This statement causes God to laugh seven times, and with the first laugh the "splendor [of light] shone through the whole universe."[88]

The Basilideans, a Gnostic sect founded in the second century CE by Basilides of Alexandria, worshipped Abraxas as the "supreme and primordial creator"[89] deity, "with all the infinite emanations."[90] The god Abraxas unites the opposites, including good and evil,[91] the one and the many.[92] He is "symbolized as a composite creature, with the body of a human being and the head of a rooster, and with each of his legs ending in a serpent."[93] His name is actually a mathematical formula: in Greek, the letters add up to 365, the days of the year[94] and the number of eons[95] (cycles of creation).

"That a name so sacredly guarded, so potent in its influence, should be preserved by mystic societies through the many ages . . . is significant,"[96] notes Moses W. Redding, a scholar of secret societies. Redding suggests that only in

80　Harnaek, *Ueber dal gnostische Buch Pistil-Sophia*, quoted in Philip Schaff, *The New Schaff-Herzog Encyclopedia of Religious Knowledge, Vol. I*

81　Philip Schaff, *The New Schaff-Herzog Encyclopedia of Religious Knowledge, Vol. I*

82　Moses W. Redding, *The Illustrated History of Freemasonry* (2004)

83　Philip Schaff, *The New Schaff-Herzog Encyclopedia of Religious Knowledge, Vol. I*

84　*Ibid.*

85　*Ibid.*

86　Moshe Idel, *Jewish Magic and Superstition: A Study in Folk Religion* (2004)

87　Constance Victoria Briggs, *The Encyclopedia of God* (2003)

88　Marie-Louise Von Franz, *Creation Myths* (1972)

89　Zecharia Sitchin, *The Cosmic Code* (1998)

90　Gustave Flaubert, *The Temptation of Saint Anthony* (1874), translated by Lafcadio Hearn

91　Tracy R. Twyman, *The Merovingian Mythos and the Mystery of Rennes-le-Chateau* (2004)

92　Marc Ian Barasch, *Healing Dreams* (2001)

93　Manly Palmer Hall, *The Secret Teachings of All Ages* (1928)

94　John Michael Greer, *The New Encyclopedia of the Occult* (2003)

95　Carl Lindahl, *Medieval Folklore: A Guide to Myths, Legends, Tales, Beliefs, and Customs* (2002)

96　*The Illustrated History of Freemasonry* (2004)

Freemasonry has this "Divine Word" been "held in due reverence."[97]

Facts: The psychologist Carl Jung discussed the deity Abraxas in such works as *The Seven Sermons to the Dead* (1917).

In mythology, Abraxas is the name of a celestial horse that draws the dawn goddess Aurora across the sky.[98]

The word *abraxas* was a favorite inscription on Mediterranean amulets and magical papyri dating back to the first century BCE.[99]

Abraxas is used as an oath in the nineteenth-century Swedish classic *The Queen's Tiara* by Carl Jonas Love Almqvist.

Common Magician's Applications: Vanishing. For example: "With his free hand, the magician removed his top hat and held it out before him. '*Abraxas!*' he intoned dramatically. One by one, the doves took wing and disappeared into the seemingly infinite depths of the black silk topper."[100]

Variations and Incantations:

- Abracax
  —*Occultopedia* (2005)

- Abraksas
  "I conjure thee, prince whose name is Abraksas."
  —*The Sword of Moses* (c. 10th century), translated by M. Gaster (1896)

- Abrasax
  —Kurt Rudolph, *Gnosis: The Nature and History of Gnosticism* (1987)

- Abraxis
  —Constance Victoria Briggs, *The Encyclopedia of God* (2003)

In Literature:

- "The bird fights its way out of the egg. The egg is the world. Who would be born must first destroy a world. The bird flies to God. That God's name is Abraxas."
  —Hermann Hesse, *Demian* (1925)

- From Jean-Paul Sartre, *The Flies* (1943), translated by Stuart Gilbert (1946):

  ZEUS: By the way, if those flies bother you, here's a way of getting rid of them. You see that swarm buzzing round your head? Right. Now watch! I flick my wrist—so—and wave my arm once, and then I say: Abraxas, galla, galla, tsay, tsay. See! They're falling down and starting to crawl on the ground like caterpillars.
  ORESTES: By Jove!
  ZEUS: Oh, that's nothing. Just a parlor trick. I'm a fly charmer in my leisure hours.

- "Other magic words in the history of the world had never had any effect on her: 'open sesame,' 'abracadabra,' 'abraxas,' 'please,' 'I love you.' But times had changed. The old alchemical incantations had been replaced by the modern buzzwords of mental chemistry."
  —William Kowalski, *The Good Neighbor* (2004)

- "I need to be a new kind of Magician, one who not only flows through and around and quickly, but one who can change and mold and effect these creatures. I must be an Abraxas of change, a maker of effect."
  —Marvin Spiegelman, *Reich, Jung, Regardie & Me* (1992)

- "Suddenly a severe and vibrant voice like a bell immobilized him with the words: 'Abraxas is a cock and the cock crows before dawn.' A kind of chorus replied in a deep refrain. The young man, astonished and excited, thought

97 *Ibid.*
98 Anna Franklin, *Midsummer: Magical Celebrations of the Summer Solstice* (2002)
99 Richard Kieckhefer, *Magic in the Middle Ages* (2000)
100 Greg Cox, "Sideshow Slayer" (2004)

that it resembled a response from the Earth to the call of Heaven. He turned his attention to the meaning of the sentence, but he had scarcely begun to do so when something like a sack enveloped him from head to foot, and a powerful blow to the head hurled him into the black pit of unconsciousness."
—Jorge A. Livraga, *The Alchemist* (1999)

- "The abraxas, the phalangeal rhythm, the multicolored wobbly notes which nevertheless bind the hair of the lover, whom he has yet to glow."
  —Hugh Knox, *The Paving Stones of Xanadu* (2004)

- "Chanting the name ABRAXAS, I finished inscribing the circle into the moist sand, and carefully replaced the stone at the Eastern point. Just then the wind blew a sudden gust into the cave, echoing deep within the mountain like some great haunted drum."
  —Douglas Monroe, *The 21 Lessons of Merlyn: A Study in Druid Magic and Lore* (1992)

Abulafia

Origins: Jewish scholar Abraham Abulafia (1240–c.1292) was a writer of treatises on practical mysticism. Denounced and branded as a heretic, he is now recognized as "one of the great Kabbalists."[101]

In Literature: "Even the sound of Abulafia's name sets off music in her head. A-bu-la-fi-a. It's magic, the open sesame that unblocked the path to her father and then to language itself."
—Myla Goldberg, *Bee Season* (2000)

Aburadan
(see *perciphedron*)

Acba

Origins: *Acba* may be derived from the Arabic word *akbar*, "most great."

Facts: This magic word is featured in the role-playing game "I Blame Society." It is recommended for use with "marbles of transformation": "These small glass or marble balls appear to be ordinary marbles, but are actually a bizarre mystical transmutation of a common object such as a length of rope. . . . The marble will transform into the original object, in perfect condition, when the character mentally wills it to do so and says the magic word 'Acba' three times."[102]

Variations and Incantations: Allah acba
—John A. Topping, *Runaway* (2000)

Accio

Origins: *Accio* is from a Latin word meaning "I summon."

In Literature: *Accio* is used to call objects toward the caster in *Harry Potter and the Goblet of Fire* by J.K. Rowling (2000).

101 Myla Goldberg, *Bee Season* (2000)

102 C.J. Gardiner, *IBlameSociety.ca* (2005)

Acka Shazam

(see *alakazam* and *shazam*)

In Literature: "Now, Acka Shazam!"
—Justin Martin, *150 Totally Terrific Writing Prompts* (1999)

Ada Ada Io Ada Dia

The word of power of a magician
does not necessarily have to be a single one.
—Migene Gonzalez-Wippler,
*The Complete Book of Spells,
Ceremonies and Magic* (1978)

Facts: These are magic words spoken by Welsh Romany Gypsies as they tell fortunes with dice. "The phrase sounds rather like 'Oh dear, oh dear, I owe, oh dear, dear.'"[103] "Exactly what it means is now lost in the mist of time, but it is a traditional divination rune or formula of words of power, probably Celtic in origin."[104]

Adadadoodi Skippadoodi

Origins: *Adadadoodi skippadoodi* appears in a fable from India.

Common Magician's Applications: Transformations.

In Literature: "Mrs. KindFairy waved her wand and said the magic word 'Adadadoodi Skippadoodi.' In the blink of an eyelid she became a tiny worm."
—*Dimdima.com*, "Omni Learns a Lesson" (2004)

---

103 Gillian Kemp, *The Fortune Telling Book* (2000)
104 Myla Goldberg, *Bee Season* (2000)

Adarakadabara

In Literature: "Magus waved his hooves and spoke the ancient magic word, 'Adarakadabara!'"
—Clever Clover, "Magical Pony Girl Enchantment," *My Little Pony Monthly* (2002)

Adi, Edi, Idi, Odi, Udi, Oo-i-oo Idu, Ido, Idi, Ide, Ida, Woo

Common Magician's Applications: Dove production.

In Literature: "He came out of his throne to stand before the Shaggy Man, and then he waved his hands, palms downward, in seven semicircles over his victim's head, saying in a low but clear tone of voice the magic wugwa: '*Adi, edi, idi, odi, udi, oo-i-oo! Idu, ido, idi, ide, ida, woo!*' The effect of this well-known sorcery was instantaneous. Instead of the Shaggy Man, a pretty dove lay fluttering upon the floor, its wings confined by tiny cords wound around them."
—L. Frank Baum, *Tik-Tok of Oz* (1914)

Adiatmoaamvpmsciccajfz

In Literature: "I have no idea how long it takes to summon the devils. I have no grimoire, no magic textbook. I have only my purity of soul and my one magic word, the word that calls all demons. The villagers have told me that I will see horrible sights. Everyone seems to be an expert on devils. Everyone but me. Nevertheless, I know I am prepared. I whisper. 'Adiatmoaamvpmsciccajfz.' I expect to whisper many times. But before

my tongue can relax from the sibilance of the final *z*, a face appears before me."
—Donna Jo Napoli, *The Magic Circle* (1993)

Aeeiouo

(see also *ye ye ye woopy a e i o u bang bang fling flang*)

Mystique: The Egyptians believed in "the power of language to affect the world. Words, spoken or written, were not just symbols, but realities in themselves."[105] "In [Egyptian] magical texts, the word, like the name of the divinity, is the true active instrument to obtain certain effects."[106] The musical quality of vowel sounds has long been believed to "have a profound spiritual effect"[107] and to "put the practitioner into union (resonance) with the celestial songs."[108]

Meanings: The meaning of *aeeiouo* remains shrouded in the mists of time. Modern scholars consider it "untranslatable" or "incomprehensible."[109] However, in the context of the magical papyri, *aeeiouo* is clearly a word of primal power.

Origins: Incantations of long strings of vowels appear in Greek-Egyptian magical papyri dating back to the second century BCE. "In certain Gnostic writings and in the magical papyri . . .

sequences of vowels . . . are used to invoke gods and concentrate divine powers."[110]

Facts: Vowel invocations in the magical papyri are transcribed in "wing formation" thusly:

$$A\ E\ E\ I\ O\ U\ O$$
$$E\ E\ I\ O\ U$$
$$E\ I\ O$$
$$I\ O$$
$$I$$

Aeeiouo is comprised of "the seven 'holy vowels' of the Greek alphabet: Alpha, Episilon, Eta, Iota, Omicron, Upsilon, and Omega."[111]
Aeeiouo is the shape of "the self-begotten soul" according to the *Nag Hammadi Library*, a collection of fifty ancient papyrus texts on the mystical meanings of the letters of the alphabet and their relation to divinity and the human soul.

Variations and Incantations: Aeeioyo

Aemaer

(see also *aemaet*)

Meanings:

- Friend
  "'A friend?' Ashtaroth swung back his left hand and shot it forward in a wicked pitch that sent a stream of fiery energy crashing into the statue. 'AEMAER! Friend you are and friend you shall be, emblazoned now for all to see!' As the arcane smoke cleared, Loew

105 Laurel Holmstrom, "Self-Identification with Deity and Voces Magicae in Ancient Egyptian and Greek Magic" (2005)
106 Jan N. Nremmer and Jan R. Veenstra, *The Metamorphosis of Magic from Late Antiquity to the Early Modern Period* (2002)
107 Shulamit Elson, *Kabbalah of Prayer: Sacred Sounds and the Soul's Journey* (2004)
108 Patricia Telesco and Don Two Eagles Waterhawk, *Sacred Beat: From the Heart of the Drum Circle* (2003)
109 *Ibid.*
110 Guy L. Neck, *Sonic Theology: Hinduism and Sacred Sound* (1993)
111 Marvin W. Meyer and Richard Smith, *Ancient Christian Magic: Coptic Tests of Ritual Power* (1999)

edged in to examine the demon's handiwork. The golem leaned back against its dolly, as impassive as before, but there was a change. Carved into its wide flat forehead were the letters F-R-I-E-N-D."
—Deborah Van Fossen, "Gone with the Golem" (2006)

- Protection, forgiveness, life
"I don't know why, but I took an eyeliner pencil, and I wrote the word 'AEMAER' on his forehead. I meant it only as a last gesture— my own goodbye. I knew the word from my Pop Pop's books, a magic word meant to give life, to grant protection. I in no way imagined that it would act as anything more than a symbol—a mark of forgiveness that would fade away all too quickly as I stuffed John's body into the crematorium oven."
—Christopher Michael Davis, "Cosmetics," *Little Knives: Twelve Tales of Horror and the Supernatural* (2004)

Origins: Kabbalic lore. *Aemaer* is likely a variation of *Aemaet*.

Aemaet
(see also *aemaer*)

Meanings:

- Confidence
—Richard Riesen, "Jean 14/6: Je suis la vérité" (2001)

- Fidelity
—Richard Riesen, "Jean 14/6: Je suis la vérité" (2001)

- God
—Michael Koenig, "The Golem (1920)," *Film Monthly* (1999)

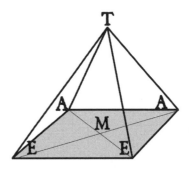

Figure 7. *Aemaet* is depicted here following the structure of sacred geometry, giving the word shape and weight.

- Sincerity
—Richard Riesen, "Jean 14/6: Je suis la vérité" (2001)

- Truth
Aemaet is the Hebrew word for *truth* (Shelomo Morag, *A History of the Hebrew Language* [1996]).

Origins: Kabbalic lore.

Facts: *Aemaet* appears as a magic word written in smoke in the film *The Golem* (1920). Critic Michael Koenig describes a scene from *The Golem*: "Through prayer, a circle of fire rises to engulf Rabbi Loew and in this trance-like state he is told that if he places the magic word 'Aemaet' . . . in an amulet and then puts it upon the Golem's chest, the creature will come to life. If the amulet is removed, the creature becomes inanimate again."[112]

The word *aemaet* is written in Psalm 25:10, usually translated as *truth*.[113]

---

112 Michael Koenig, "The Golem (1920)," *Film Monthly* (1999)
113 Richard Riesen, "Jean 14/6: Je suis la vérité" (2001)

Afa Afca Nostra

Origins: *Afa Afca Nostra* was found written in "an Elizabethan manuscript in the British Museum."[114] The words are part of an incantation for banishing sickness attributed to Albertus Magnus (St. Albert the Great) in the thirteenth century.

Facts: These words are purportedly part of a chant to prolong orgasm and were cited in evidence against alleged witches and warlocks in a sixteenth-century tribunal.

In Literature: Peggy Christian, *The Bookstore Mouse* (2002)

- -

Agimagilataragi

Origins: This word is of Farsi origin.

Facts: *Agimagilataragi* is equivalent to *Abracadabra*, used to indicate any sort of magical occurrence.

- -

Agla

"Agla!" a name of great potency.
—Katherine Kurtz,
Two Crowns for America (1997)

Meanings:

- Angelic name
  —Migene Gonzalez-Wippler, *The Complete Book of Spells, Ceremonies and Magic* (1988)

- Divine name
  —Donald Tyson, *Enochian Magic for Beginners* (1997)

  "[In the Old Testament,] Agla is a name of God that Joseph invoked when he was delivered from his brothers."
  —Gustav Davidson, *Dictionary of Angels: Including the Fallen Angels* (1994)

  "[B]y the name of God Agla, which Lot heard and was saved with his family . . ."
  —*The Lesser Key of Solomon*, quoted by Mitch Henson, *Lemegeton* (1999)

- Earth element
  —Amber Wolfe, *In the Shadow of the Shaman* (2004)

- Eternal power; "Thou Art Mighty Forever, O Lord"
  "AGLA is written all in capital letters since it is an acronym composed of the first letters from the Hebrew words *Ateh Gibor Le-olam Adonai* that translate 'Thou art mighty forever, O Lord.'"
  —Donald Tyson, *The Magician's Workbook* (2003)

- Fruitful principle of nature
  —Alphonse Louis Constant (Eliphas Levi), *The Key of the Mysteries* (1861)

- Incommunicable name
  "[O]bedient to him who knows how to pronounce duly the incommunicable name of Agla . . ."
  —Alphonse Louis Constant (Eliphas Levi), *History of Magic* (1913)

- Magical letters
  —Malcolm Jones, *The Secret Middle Ages* (2002)

- Magical word
  —Paul Foster Case, *True and Invisible Rosicrucian Order* (1981)

---

114 Migene Gonzalez-Wippler, *The Complete Book of Spells, Ceremonies and Magic* (1988)

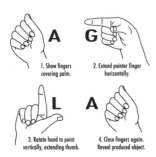

1. Show fingers covering palm.

2. Extend pointer finger horizontally.

3. Rotate hand to point vertically, extending thumb.

4. Close fingers again. Reveal produced object.

Figure 8. A slight-of-hand performer can use sign language to fingerspell a magic word (such as Agla, shown above) before producing an object out of thin air.

- Mysterious name
  —Manly Palmer Hall, *The Secret Teachings of All Ages* (1928)

- Perfect word
  —Nigel Pennick, *Magical Alphabets* (1992)

- Primal nature of God, fountain of truth
  —Nigel Pennick, *Magical Alphabets* (1992)

- Protective word
  —Harald S. Naess, *A History of Norwegian Literature* (1993)

- Strength
  "Now meditate on the name AGLA. This is the name that is related to the Strengths."
  —Aryeh Kaplan, *Meditation and Kabbalah* (1982)

- The number thirty-five
  "Thirty-five is . . . the number of the magical word Agla (AGLA), found on many magical talismans and seals."
  —Paul Foster Case, *True and Invisible Rosicrucian Order* (1981)

- Unity leading back to unity
  "Agla represents unity, symbolized by the first Aleph, leading back to unity, represented by the final Aleph."
  —Nigel Pennick, *Magical Alphabets* (1992)

Origins: This "famous magical word,"[115] of Hebrew origin, is found on magical talismans and seals from the fifteenth to seventeenth centuries.

Facts: "In the Middle Ages, AGLA was one of the names of God used in exorcisms, healing magic, and divination."[116]

Agla is actually an acronym, made up of the initials of the sentence *Atah gebur le-olahm Adonai*, meaning "Thine is the power throughout endless ages, O Lord."[117]

Agla is a magic word for conjuring Sylphs in *The Queen Pedauque* (1893) by Anatole France.

Variations and Incantations:

- Agla, Aglai, Aglata, Aglatai
  These words are part of an incantation from *The Key of Solomon* (as translated by S. Liddell MacGregor Mathers).

- Admai Aday Eloy Agla
  —Arturo Perez-Reverte, *The Club Dumas* (1996)

In Literature:

- "Old Coignard has been warned by the Rosicrucian not to pronounce the word

---

115 David Ovason, *The Secrets of Nostradamus* (2002)

116 Deborah E. Harkness, *John Dee's Conversations with Angels: Cabala, Alchemy, and the End of Nature* (1999)

117 Paul Foster Case, *True and Invisible Rosicrucian Order* (1981)

Figure 9. The magic amulet *Agla* of medieval times.

Agla, and the moment he does so, a wheel comes off his carriage."
—Aleister Crowley, *Diary of a Drug Fiend* (1922)

- "'My name is Agla,' she said. 'My mother was Agla, and her mother was, also. It is the name for a healer, although some of the barbarians believe that I am a witch.'"
—Ben Bova, *Orion* (1984)

- "'You request me?' replied the cabalist. 'Well, then, know that whenever you want the assistance of a Sylph, you have but to pronounce the simple word *Agla*, and the sons of the air will at once come to you. But understand, M. Abbe, that the word must be spoken by the heart as well as by the lips, and that faith alone gives it its virtue. Without faith it is nothing but a useless murmur. Pronounce it as I do at this moment, putting in it neither soul nor wish, it has, even in my own mouth, but a very slight power, and at the utmost some of the children of light, if they have heard it, glide into this room, the light shadows of light. I've divined rather than seen them on yonder curtain, and they have vanished when hardly visible. Neither you nor your pupil has suspected their presence. But had I pronounced that magic word with real fervour you would have seen them appear in all their splendour. They are of a charming beauty. Now, sir, I have entrusted you with a

grand and useful secret. Let me say again, do not divulge it imprudently. And do not sneer at the example of the Abbe de Villars, who, for having revealed their secrets, was murdered by the Sylphs, on the road to Lyons.'"
—Anatole France, *The Queen Pedauque* (1893)

Ah

Mystique: "The 'AH' sound is a sacred seed syllable. It is found in most of the God and Goddess names on the planet (Tara, Buddha, Krishna, Yah, Astara), as well as many of the sacred words (Amen, Alleluia, Aum). Most mystical traditions worldwide also find it to be the sound of the heart chakra. Yet, as a vowel sound, it defies denomination or description as a mantra and is acceptable by everyone."[118]

Meanings:

- Egyptian moon god
"By the magic of thy name of Ah (moon god)."
—Donald Mackenzie, *Egyptian Myth and Legend* (1907)

- Mantra of compassion
"The 'AH' sound is almost universally regarded in different traditions as a heart sound—a sound for resonating the heart center and embodying compassion and love."
—Jonathan Goldman, "World Sound Healing Day" (2004)

- Waking consciousness
"Allegorically, the initial A[h sound] of [the sacred Hindu syllable] AUM is said to represent the field and state of Waking Consciousness, where objects are of 'gross matter' . . .

---

118 Jonathan Goldman, "The 'AH' Sound to Generate Peace and Compassion" (2004)

and are separate both from each other and from the consciousness beholding them."
—Joseph Campbell, *The Mythic Image* (1974)

ruled by men. These women gained the popular appellation Superwomen or Wonder women.

Aim

You said the magic word—*aim.*
—*LittleBlackDog.com* (2002)

Mystique: The word *aim* has assumed the force of focused intent and is used to invoke emotional, psychological, and physical powers. How-to manuals and self-help gurus alike advise those seeking personal power to activate their *aim.*

Variations and Incantations: Ready, aim, fire

"'Ready, aim, fire' is [a] mantra."
—Howard Kaminsky and Alexandra Penney, *Magic Words at Work* (2004)

In Literature: "When he was a boy, another boy had taught him magic words for hitting a bird with a stone: 'Aim, aim, got my aim—if I miss you I'm not to blame.'"
—Gabriel Garcia Marquez, *Love in the Time of Cholera* (1988)

Airolg Meniets

Fact: These are the magic words that Marie Osmond spoke on *The Donnie and Marie Show* (late 1970s) to transform into Wonder Woman. The words are the name of the feminist leader Gloria Steinem spelled backward. For many people of the 1960s and the 1970s, former Playboy Bunny and feminist activist Gloria Steinem embodied the virtues and powers of a cult of women who were able to use intellectual ability, physical beauty, and financial savvy to gain dominance in a culture previously

----

Akos Pakos
(see also *hocus pocus*)

Origins: In a fifteenth-century German-Jewish manuscript, a magical formula of mystical names is spelled out. "One of the incantations in it . . . contains the names 'Akos Pakos,' the earliest literary occurrence of the terms which, with slight orthographic variations, have become the hallmark of pseudo-magic in a dozen European tongues—our Hocus Pocus."[119]

Akrakanarba
(see also *abracadabra*)

Meanings: This ancient magical charm is generally considered to be gibberish,[120] its letters most likely having a numerological significance.

Origins: The word *Akrakanarba* is found in the magical papyri of Graeco-Roman ritual magic[121] dating from the second century BCE to the fifth century CE.[122]

119 Joshua Trachtenberg, *Jewish Magic and Superstition* (1939)

120 Kieren Barry, *The Greek Qabalah: Alphabetical Mysticism and Numerology in the Ancient World* (1999)

121 E.S. Shaffer, *Comparative Criticism, Volume 9* (1987)

122 Kieren Barry, *The Greek Qabalah: Alphabetical Mysticism and Numerology in the Ancient World* (1999)

```
AKRAKANARBA
 KANARBA
  ANARBA
   NARBA
    ARBA
     RBA
      BA
       A
```

Figure 10. Akrakanarba as a dissolving spell.

Facts: Like *abracadabra*, *akrakanarba* was written and spoken as a "dissolving"-type spell. "This is followed by an injunction: 'Utter the entire name . . . in the shape of a wing.' . . . One editor leaped to the conclusion that *lege*, 'utter' was a mistake for *graphe*, 'write.' But this is quite mistaken. The spell is to be uttered 'wing-like,' which refers simultaneously to the graphic form and to the Homeric cliché for effective speaking, 'winged words.' Unlike concrete poetry, these shapes are not clever linguistic games but attempts to change the world. Dismemberment of language produces enigma; but at the same time a performative act is being brought about. Language is simultaneously ruined and employed."[123]

Akrakanarba is one possible origin of the magic word *abracadabra*.[124]

- -

Akrammachamari

Everything seemed bewitched with the
inarticulate mumbling of old,
forgotten words . . . old magic words.
—Feodor Sologub, *The White Dog* (1915)

Origins: This word is found "in a list of magical words ('Ephesia grammata') on a curse-tablet from Hadrumetum in North Africa," as well as in "magical papyri, sometimes in amulets to ward off ill, sometimes in spells to achieve some object."[125] The word is believed to be an imperative, "uproot the spells," to conclude an invocation.[126]

Variations and Incantations:

- Anoch ai akrammachamari
  "Dipping the boxwood twig toward the writing at each syllable, she said, '*Anoch ai akrammachamari.*'"
  —David Drake, *Lord of the Isles* (1997)

- Akramachamari
  —Marvin W. Meyer, *Ancient Christian Magic: Coptic Texts of Ritual Power* (1999)

- -

Ala

Some thought he's said *Allah*, others that he's
spoken some magical word . . .
—Clive Barker,
The Essential Clive Barker (1999)

Meanings: The sound of the magic word *ala* can represent different meanings simultaneously. It can mean "à la," as in the French expression meaning "according to" or "from," thereby communicating that a magical effect will happen in accordance to the proper syllables of esoteric knowledge or that the magic word has been handed down through the ages from its source. *Ala* can also mean "Allah," as in the divine name of Arabic origin (etymologically related to the Hebrew title for God *Elohim*[127]), thereby commu-

123 E.S. Shaffer, *Comparative Criticism, Volume 9* (1987)
124 *Ibid.*

125 *Ibid.*
126 Morton Smith, *Studies in the Cult of Yahweh* (1996)
127 Penny Warren, "Is the Word Allah Similar to Elohim?" *Plim Report* (1998)

nicating that a magical effect will occur on the authority or with the metaphysical assistance of a higher power.

Facts: *Ala* not only appears in several different magic words (like *alakazam*, *alakazee*, *a-la peanut butter sandwiches*, and *alikazoola*) but also can be a magic word on its own.

Ala is the name of a dangerous demon that envelopes people, mentioned in antiquated Mesopotamian magical texts.[128]

Variations and Incantations:

- À la
  This French spelling, meaning "according to," is followed by the name of a forefather or sage.

- Ala and kazamm
  —Steven L. Case, *The Book of Uncommon Prayer* (2002)

- Ala cadabra kazam
  —*SunSpiritGallery.com* (2002)

- Ala zam kazam zam ala kazam ala zam zam ala
  —"Rapid's Journey," *ThePokemonTower.com* (2004)

- Ali
  —Migene Gonzalez-Wippler, *The Complete Book of Spells, Ceremonies and Magic* (1978)

- Alla

- Allah
  This is the divine name, the higher power called upon to manifest a miracle.

Alacadabra

Facts: This phrase combines the two popular magic words *abracadabra* and *alakazam*.

Common Magician's Applications: Triggering. For example: "Looking to have something special at your next party? Just say the magic word 'Alacadabra' and our magicians will be there."[129]

Variations and Incantations:

- Ala cadabra kazam
  This phrase combines the magic words *ala*, *kazam*, *alakazam*, *cadabra*, and *abracadabra*.
  "I do not know of a magic wand and an 'ala cadabra kazam' formula to snap one out of it."
  —*SunSpiritGallery.com* (2002)

Alakazam
(see also *ala* and *kazam*)

A word I did not understand
It sounded like magic
Like Alakazzam
—Frigid Darkness,
"Alakazzam," *Allpoetry.com* (2003)

Amazing how a few words could change a person's mood in an instant. Alakazam! And not just words, but how a person said them.
—Vaunda Micheaux Nelson,
Possibles (1995)

Mystique: *Alakazam*'s power lies in its mystery. The word is the very definition of *secret*. It's something beyond understanding, something we can

---

128 M.J. Geller, *Forerunners to Udug-hul, Sumerian Exoristic Incantations* (1985)

129 *Bounce-4fun.com* (2005)

never get to the bottom of,[130] something so wondrous it should only be whispered, if uttered at all. *Alakazam* expresses something unobservable, hence its appropriateness for sleight-of-hand. It describes a contradiction—a paradox—hence its appropriateness for illusions demonstrating the impossible. It's an ephemeral word, gone almost before it can be fully spoken: the initial *ala* is a distant echo by the time the *zam* takes a powder. It's also an ethereal word, inherently otherworldly.

Alakazam retains an aura of mystery—and therefore magic—even as most other words have become mundane with usage. Serge Kahili King, scholar of Polynesian philosophy, explains:

> As writing became more popularized, it lost a lot of its mystery, and therefore its magic, though some poets and a very few novelists can still evoke it. But where there is mystery, there is still magic. The less well known a language is, the more magical power it is thought to have. Imagine a powerful magician with a pointy little beard wearing a black cloak with red lining. He raises his arms, lightning flashes from his fingers, and he says in a commanding voice, "Do what I want!" Not too exciting. But if he says "Alakazam!" Wow, impressive![131]

Alakazam reminds us that life itself is a great mystery, and the word expresses a reverence that is already in our hearts.[132] *Alakazam* reveals the extraordinary in the ordinary. Simply put, *alakazam* makes magic.

---

130 Sam Mackintosh, "Mystery and Reverence in Family Ritual" (2001)

131 Serge Kahili King, *Instant Healing* (2004)

132 This statement is inspired by Sam Mackintosh, "Mystery and Reverence in Family Ritual" (2001)

Meanings:

- Conjure, create, as through an act of magic
  "[I]f necessary he will conjure something from nothing—a hare from a hat, wine out of water—whatever—life out of death (that would be nice) . . . if it comes to it he will alakazam a miracle."
  —Bruce Olds, *Raising Holy Hell* (1995)

- Disappear, vanish
  "These humbugs were going to alakazam outa here along with your priceless scroll!"
  —Reneau H. Reneau, *Misanthropology: A Florilegium of Bahumbuggery* (2003)

- Euphemism for God, oath
  "In the name of Allahkazam . . ."
  —*GameReviews.net* (2005)

- Lucky stars
  "They should thank their allah-kazam . . ."
  —*LittleGreenFootballs.com* (2002)

- Magic
  "[A]lakazam, your wound is mended."
  —James Morrow, *Only Begotten Daughter* (1996)

- Magician
  "Based on the fourth book in J.K. Rowling's well thumbed series, players will take the role of adolescent alakazam artist Potter as he competes in an international hocus-pocus competition called the Triwizard Tournament."
  —"New Harry Potter Revealed," *Games Radar.com* (2005)

- Magic word
  "Was there a magic word, something like alakazam? Yeah."
  —Stephen King, *Dreamcatcher* (2001)

  "[M]uch more powerful than 'voila' or 'alakazam' in opening the vaults of love and true friendship . . ."
  —Eric Aronson, *Dash* (2004)

- Midas touch
  "We recorded it with some girl backup singers the next week, and it was alakazam Ricky."
  —Gabrielle Kraft, "One Hit Wonder," *Speaking of Greed* (2001)

- Surprise
  "[T]he alakazam surprise in this world: / Love's miracle never dies in this world."
  —Barbara Little, "Drink, My Love, and Deeply," *Ravishing Disunities* (2000)

- Voilà
  "Supposedly an architect brought his four-year-old daughter in to work one day. Playing with her crayons, the kid produced the kind of picture a child that age will. Squiggles. The drawing got into the production line by accident and *alakazam!* Three days later it rolls off the line, ready to be lived in by some seriously deranged people."
  —John Varley, *The Golden Globe* (1998)

Origins: This word has its roots in an Arabic incantation.[133] A similar-sounding Arabic phrase, *Al Qasam*, means "oath."

Because *Alakazam* is a proper name, it may have originally been used as a magic word invoking the powers of a particular person named Alakazam.[134]

Alakazam has also been traced to a Hindu word meaning "flawless" and a spell intended "to stave off pain while performing some great act of physical endurance."[135]

Facts: The Japanese word for *alakazam* is *foodin,* a reference to the famous professional magician

Harry Houdini or his predecessor Jean Eugène Robert-Houdin.[136]

For forty years, Danish professional magician Henri Alakazam (Henry Hermansen) toured his "Alakazam Magical Theatre" through Denmark, Norway, and Sweden. He passed away in 2001.

"Alakazam the Great" is a character in a Japanese anime film by the same name (1961). Alakazam is a mischievous monkey who becomes monarch after forcing Merlin, the world's greatest magician, to teach him everything about magic. "Alakazam the Great" is also the name of a character by comedian Jonathan Winters.

In an episode of the *Flintstones* cartoon series, Fred borrows a magic kit from magician "Rockstone the Great" and ushers Wilma and Betty into a "disappearing cabinet." "He says the magic words and, alakazam! They're gone. (They found the back exit and snuck out to go along with the gag.)"[137]

In the Pokemon card game, the character Abra evolves into Kadabra and finally into Alakazam, who has strong psychic powers.

Common Magician's Applications: Vanishing, triggering. For example: "Pick up each glass and say, '*Alakazam*, this glass is (Bill's) glass.' If you have a magic wand or want to use a special magic wave, you can then wave over the glass before you put it on the tray."[138]

Variations and Incantations:

- Alabama
  In the Walter Lantz cartoon "100 Pygmies and Andy Panda" (1940), Andy practices magic with a mail-order magician's wand and the special magic word *Alakazam.* He is challenged by a Pygmy witch doctor who is envious of the wand and who manages to

133 John Skoyles and Dorion Saga, *Up From Dragons* (2002)

134 Terry O'Connor, "Word for Word," *PlateauPress .com* (2004)

135 *TheMagicCafe.com* (2005)

136 *Wikipedia.com* (2005)

137 Tom Hill, *TV Land to Go* (2001)

138 Loris Bree, *Kids' Magic Secrets* (2003)

steal it away. But the witch doctor mispronounces the magic word as *Alabama* and thereby transports his tribe smack into the middle of modern civilization.

- A-La-KaZam
"'I have another trick. It's the . . . Chinese Mystery. A-La-Ka-Zam,' he murmured, spinning on his heels."
—Glen Gold, *Carter Beats the Devil* (2002)

- Acka shazam
—Justin Martin, *150 Totally Terrific Writing Prompts* (1999)

- Al-A-Kazzam
"He had borrowed the Al-A-Kazzam! Junior Magic Kit from Eugene and taken it home; over one weekend he had mastered every trick."
—Michael Chabon, *The Amazing Adventures of Kavalier & Clay* (2000)

- Ala and kazamm
—Steven L. Case, *The Book of Uncommon Prayer* (2002)

- Alacazam
"The heavy steel door opened itself with a lethargic electric whir. I mumbled, 'Alacazam.'"
—David Farris, *Lie Still* (2003)
　"I told you, 'Alacazam' was the mystical word / That would bring the magic carpet to life / Or at least it would have had it not been unravelled / To make mitts by some silly old wife"
—Gary Hogg, "The Secret Life of Walter's Mittens" (2002)
　"[Y]ou count to three, all right? Then say the magic word: Alacazam. Got it? Alacazam. Any time you want me to appear, just say the magic word."
—Robert Grossmith, "Company," *Best English Short Stories II* (1990)

- Alakazaam
—Bruce Olds, *Bucking the Tiger* (2001)

- Ala-ka-ZAM
"James opened his hands. 'Ala-ka-ZAM,' he cried. A quarter dropped out of his hand."
—Glen Gold, *Carter Beats the Devil* (2002)

- Ala kazam
—Stewart D. Ferguson, *Organizational Communication* (1987)
　"Ala kazam / How's your wife, Sam? / I am what I am."
—Ira Gershwin, quoted in *Ira Gershwin: The Art of the Lyricist* by Philip Furia (1996)

- Alaka, zam alakazam, alakazam alakazam. Kazam?! Kazam alakazam! Zam alakazam, kazam ala. ALA! KAZAM KAZAM ALAKA? ALAKAZAM KAZAM! Kazam alakazam, alakazam kazam. Alakazam zam
—"Raichi's Pokemon Page," *Expage.com* (2004)

- AlaKazam, AlaKazee
"Sam puts a cloth over a fish bowl full of feathers. 'AlaKazam, AlaKazee!' he says, waving a magic wand, and pulls the cloth off of the bowl. 'And the feathers are gone! Ta-da!'"
—"A Runaway Spell," *Today's Special* (1987)

- AlaKazam, AlaKazoo
"'AlaKazam, AlaKazoo,' and as soon as he says it, the feathers disappear."
—"A Runaway Spell," *Today's Special* (1987)

- Ala-kazam, hocus-pocus
—Paul Beatty, *The White Boy Shuffle* (2001)

- Alakazam kazim kazoo
—Kimberly Foster, *A Dolphin up a Tree* (2002)

- Alakazam kazive kazoy
—Kimberly Foster, *A Dolphin up a Tree* (2002)

- Alakazam-kazoo
"As fast as you can say 'Alakazam-kazoo,' your fairy godmother arrives in a swirl of sparkles and pastels."
—Valerie Wells, *The Joy of Visualization* (1990)

- Alakazam kazoo kazive
—Kimberly Foster, *A Dolphin up a Tree* (2002)

- Alakazam, Open Sesame
"Is there some magic phrase, *alakazam, Open Sesame* that would bring back the moment . . ."
—John Edgar Wideman, *Two Cities: A Love Story* (1998)

- Alakazam-wabadadingdong
—*NZmusic.com* (2005)

- Alakazot
—"The Wizard of Id" comic strip

- Alakazzam

- Ala zam kazam zam ala kazam ala zam zam ala
—"Rapid's Journey," *ThePokemonTower.com* (2004)

- Alia Kazam
—Gilbert Sorrentino, *The Orangery* (1978)

- Alikazam
—Robert Lamb, *Atlanta Blues* (2002)

- Ali-kazam
—Jack Dann, *Dreaming Down-Under* (2004)

- Alla gazam
—John Scarne, *Scarne on Card Tricks* (1950)

- Alla Ka-Zam, Alla Ka-Zook
—Denise Anton Wright, "A Witch's Winter Kitchen," *One-Person Puppet Plays* (1990)

- Alla-kazooey, alla-kazammy, hey presto
"[H]e waved the wand over the cloth-covered cage several times, 'Alla-kazooey, alla-kazammy, hey . . . presto!' He tapped the cage sharply with his wand, whipped the black cloth away with a flourish, and turned to the audience."
—Elaine Clark McCarthy, "Maximillian's Magic" (2000)

- Allah-kazam
"A very low-key ritual dance began with a peck of a kiss followed by certain wigglings and allah-kazam, they were in the missionary posture."
—Leon Uris, *A God in Ruins* (1999)

- Allah Kazam
"The Fairy moved the wand. 'Allah Kazam!' The princess shook her foot. It was no longer made of stone."
—Jane Yolen, *Sleeping Ugly* (1981)

- Alla Kazam
—Clyde Edgerton, *Floatplane Notebooks* (1989)

- Alla Kazamm
—*Tales to Astonish #58* (1964)

- Alla kazam shazam
—Robert Asprin, *Another Fine Myth* (1978)

- Allakazam
Professional magician Mark Wilson used this word in his show *The Magic Land of Allakazam*, the first network television magic series.[139]

- Allakazoo allakazam
—Salman Rushdie, *The Satanic Verses* (1988)

- Allakazoot
—Peter Lerangis, *Presto! Magic Treasure* (2002)

- A-Lla Kazzim-a-lla-kazzam
—Etgar Keret, *Jetlag* (1998)

- AllaKhazam
Founded in 1999, "AllaKhazam's Magical Realm" is the name of a website dedicated

---

139 Mark Wilson, *Mark Wilson's Complete Course in Magic* (1975)

to covering "Massive Multiplayer Online Role Playing Games."

- Alley shazam
  —Nevada Barr, *Track of the Cat* (1993)

- Ally-Kazam
  —Peter Fredson, "Genesis For Beginners" (2004)

- Bam wham ham flam jamb cram alla kazam slam!
  —Linda Varsell Smith, *The Rainbow Redemption* (2003)

- Bim bam alakazam
  —Ruth I. Dowell, *Move Over Mother Goose* (1987)

- Bip, bomp, bam alakazam
  —Frankie Smith, "Double Dutch Bus"

- Flash Bam Alakazam!
  —Will Friedwald, *Jazz Singing* (1990)

- Shallakazam
  —Charles Harrington Elster, *Tooth and Nail* (1994)

- Slam Bam Alacazam
  —Mel Torme, *Drummin' Men* (1990)

- Uguh Buguh Alacazam
  —Brian Hill, *Cisco: The Complete Reference* (2002)

- Wam! Bam! Alakazam!
  —Penn Jilette, *Penn & Teller's How to Play in Traffic* (1997)

- Wham bam Alacazam
  "Wham, bam, alacazam we got a new head monkey running the country and old Sam has got him in his pocket."
  —John Sayles, *Los Gusanos* (1991)

- Wham! Bam! Alakazam!
  "Wham! Bam! AlakaZam! The old gal was her old self again."
  —Dave Galey, *The Joys of Busing* (1996)
  "That's when it hit her—wham bam alakazam."
  —Nancy Moser, *Time Lottery* (2002)

- Wham bam allakazam
  —Marjorie Dorfman, *A Taste of Funny* (2002)

- Wham bang alikazam!
  —Tom Murphy, *Conversations on a Homecoming* (1985)

- Zam-zam alacazam
  —Harvey Milkman, *Craving for Ecstasy* (1987)

In Literature:

- "Bill and his wife came to enjoy the illusion of control. 'It'd be like a guy standing by Old Faithful and every hour saying "Alakazam!" and up pops the geyser. But the guy isn't controlling anything; he just knows how the geyser works so it seems like he's making the geyser spout.'"
  —Stephanie Brown, *The Family Recovery Guide* (2000)

- "*Alakazam*. Hell, I'd even twitch my nose if I thought it would work."
  —Kim Harrison, *Every Which Way But Dead* (2005)

- "To tell the truth, I didn't at first take her seriously; the whole thing suddenly seemed the stuff of abracadabra and ali-kazam, with Templeton the wizard who would vanish on our waking."
  —Jack Dann, *Dreaming Down-Under* (2002)

- "It was as if I had said the magic words, Alakazam!—and her face went blank, her

mouth closed, her arms went slack, and she backed out of the room, stunned, as if she were blowing away like a small brown leaf, thin, brittle, lifeless."
—Amy Tan, *Joy Luck Club* (1989)

- "Moncrief was playing with a loop of string, creating cat's-cradles and the like and defying Cooner to predict the outcome of each, the wager being ten dinkets, which Cooner consistently won. Thus, he was emboldened when Moncrief handed him a sharp knife and, holding the loop stretched between his hands, defied Cooner to cut the string, so as to break the loop into a simple length of line. Cooner was assured that he could easily do so, and when Moncrief offered to bet him ten sols to five, he readily placed down his money and cut one of the taut strands Moncrief held between his hands. Moncrief called out: 'Alakazam! Let the string be whole!' When Cooner took the string, the loop was unbroken. Moncrief thereupon took up the five sols. Cooner stamped his feet and tore his hair, to no avail. He still carries the loop of string which he examines from time to time, hoping to find where he made the cut."
—Jack Vance, *Ports of Call* (1998)

- "He held his hands up. He waved them in strange gestures above the kitchen table. 'Alaka*zam*,' he said, and the cooler and the bag of groceries from the back of the car appeared."
—Nina Kiriki Hoffman, *Past the Size of Dreaming* (2001)

- "[H]is mouth and tongue did things to hers that made words meaningless. Surrendering, she whispered 'Alakazam' against his lips."
—Patricia Rice, *Carolina Girl* (2004).

- "Then there is the colored smoke—mustard yellow, candy-cane pink—coughed out across the river by flares, from which in one shot Willard's boat emerges like something produced by a demented sideshow conjuror with an 'alakazam.'"
—Ryan Gilbey, *It Don't Worry Me: The Revolutionary American Films of the Seventies* (2003)

- "[S]ay the magic word: Alacazam. Got it? Alacazam. Any time you want me to appear, just say the magic word."
—Robert Grossmith, "Company," *Best English Short Stories 2* (1990)

- "[T]he room has already darkened and the wall screen is lit with the profuse greens of a Florida swamp. 'This is Fakahatchee,' Bill says. The word sounds magical to Cora, like *abracadabra* or *alacazam*."
—Pamela Ditchoff, *Seven Days and Seven Sins* (2003)

- "Alakazam! You now have $200,000 in the bank!"
—Steve Ross, *Happy Yoga: 7 Reasons Why There's Nothing to Worry About* (2003)

Alakazee
(see also *ala* and *alakazam*)

Facts: *Alakazee* is featured in the episode "A Runaway Spell" of the television series *Today's Special* (1987).

Variations and Incantations:

- Ala-ka-zee, Ala-ka-zam
"Ala-ka-zee, Ala-ka-zam, Let me be who I am."
—Elyse F. Aronson, "Ms. Goose and Her Wonderful Rhymes" (1999)

- Alakazee, Alakazore
  —Jasper C. Coligny, *Factory4.org* (2004)

- Alakazy
  This is part of an incantation for making a serpent hiccup in the novel *The Key to the Land of Dogs* by Gareth M. Wilson (2004).

In Literature: Hazel Hutchins, *Casey Webber the Great* (1988)

Alakazoo
(see also *ala*, *alakazam* and *allekazu*)

"Alakazoo," he said,
and rubbed his hands together.
—Justin Cronin, *The Summer Guest* (2003)

Variations and Incantations:

- AlaKazam, AlaKazoo
  —"A Runaway Spell," *Today's Special* (1987)

- Alakazoo, four-leaf clover
  "Alakazoo, four-leaf clover, back we fly, your turn is over."
  —Deborah Hautzig, *Little Witch's Big Night* (1984)

- Alakazoo, alakazam, son of a bitch, goddam
  —Richard Lederer, "Fight Song," *The Cunning Linguist* (2003)

- Alakazoom
  —Craig Smith, *Narrative Therapies With Children and Adolescents* (1997)

- Allacazoo
  —*Caillou's Corner* (2002)
  "I am the weather wizard; I can tell weather with a feather. Tomorrow there will be a storm of laughter, followed by clearing smiles. In Allacazoo, the weather will turn blue."
  —The Weather Classroom's "Sky Journal" (2005)

- Allakazoo
  —Patrick Drazen, "Return to the Realm: Ten Years Later" (2005)

- Allakazoo allakazam
  —Salman Rushdie, *The Satanic Verses* (1988)

- Allekazu
  —Sorana Salomeia, "Simsalabim" (2004)

A-la Peanut Butter Sandwiches
(see also *ala*)

I watched with glee as his
magic tricks always began with
"a la peanut butter sandwiches."
—Antoinette C. Nwandu,
Fifteen Minutes (2000)

Facts: These are the Amazing Mumford's magic words on the *Sesame Street* television series.
The magic phrase appears in a "Rugrats" comic strip (1999).

Variations and Incantations:

- Ala peanut butter sandwiches
  "Ala peanut-butter sandwiches! According to these magicians [The Amazing Gregory (aka Greg Stringer), John Riggs, John Chaney], the tricks themselves aren't nearly as fun as playing into the psychology of the audience."
  —Mike Gibson, "Being a Working Magician Ain't Easy," *Weekly Wire* (1997)

- Alla peanut butter sandwiches
  "All Munkar has to do is get the warriors into his castle and say 'Alla Peanut Butter Sandwiches!' and turn them into farm animals!"
  —*BadMoviePlanet.com* (2005)

- Allah peanut butter sandwiches "Knock-knock. Who's there? Allah. Allah who? Allah peanut butter sandwiches!" —Ben Guaraldi (2002)

- Presto Chango! Ala Peanut Butter Sandwiches! Alakazaam! —David E. Bell (2001)

In Literature:

- "The Amazing Mumford knew what he was doing when he chose peanut butter as the trigger words for his magic tricks. I never cared if his tricks turned out the proper results, which was lucky for him since they never did! All he had to do was say 'peanut-butter sandwiches' and I believed, with all my four-year-old body and soul, that he could do anything! But now I know better. Mumford's tricks would have been more successful—and actually magical—had he added the words 'and jelly' to his mantra. After all, featuring peanut butter without its sweet, sticky, and slurpy sidekick is like launching Superman without his cape— it just doesn't fly!" —P.J. Tanz, "The Beat on the Street: A-La-Peanut-Butter-Sandwiches," *Sesame Street Beat Newsletter* (1999)

- "To uncover the sandwich's origins, we said those magic words 'A la, peanut butter sandwiches!'" —*Ask.Yahoo.com* (2002)

Ala Tule Paha Kakku Tuke Hyva Kakku

Meanings: One might translate this Finnish phrase as "Down with the bad cake; let's hear it for the good cake." *Ala* means "down(wards),"[140] *tule* means "come,"[141] *paha* means "evil,"[142] *kakku* means "cake,"[143] *tuke* means "support,"[144] *hyva* means "good,"[145] and *kakku* again means "cake."

Origins: *Ala tule paha kakku tuke hyva kakku* is of Finnish origin.

Facts: This is a spell for clairvoyance in the Balanced Alternative Technologies Multi-User Dimension.[146]

Albóndigas

Origins: *Albóndigas* is a Spanish word meaning meatballs.

In Literature: "I wanted to shout something that sounded like a magic word. But all my frozen brain could come up with was, '¡*Albóndigas!*'" —David Lubar, *Wizards of the Game* (2003)

Algol, Almach, Elnath, Alpheratz, Hamal, Mirfak, Antares, Caph

(see also *Betelgeuse*)

Origin: This incantation names stars in the night sky.

140 Lauri Hakulinen, *The Structure and Development of the Finnish Language* (1997)

141 *Ibid.*

142 *Ibid.*

143 Taimi Previdi, *The Best of Finnish Cooking* (1996)

144 Lauri Hakulinen, *The Structure and Development of the Finnish Language* (1997)

145 Judith Geller, *Titanic: Women and Children First* (1998)

146 *Bat.org* (1996)

In Literature: From Alan Watts, "Incantation of the Stars" (1971), *Cloud-hidden, Whereabouts Unknown* (1974):

> *O Algol, Almach, Elnath, and Alpheratz,*
> *Hamal, Mirfak, Antares, and Caph—*
> *with the music of your far-out names*
> *the magician casts a spell upon the sky.*

Alia

Meaning: Elephant

> We had just finished a pint bottle of cherry brandy when I felt a gentle touch upon my shoulder, and our look-out man whispered in my ear the magic word 'alia' (elephant), at the same time pointing in the direction of the tank.
> —Sir Samuel White Baker, *The Rifle and The Hound in Ceylon* (1853)

Origin: *Alia* is a Latin word meaning "other."

Ali-Baba-Cadabra
(see also *abracadabra, ala, cadabra, open sesame*)

Meanings: *Ali* is an Arabic word meaning "by the most high." *Ali'i* is a Hawaiian word meaning "chief."

Facts: Ali Baba is the title character in the story "Ali Baba and the Forty Thieves" from the *Arabian Nights* by Antoine Galland (18th century).

Ali-Baba-Cadabra, echoing *abracadabra*, is an alternative to *open sesame*, as it can be read to mean "Ali Baba's magic word" or "Ali Baba's *abracadabra*."

"Ali-Baba-Cadabra" is the name of a musical composition by Paul Amrod.

Alikazoola Mitchikaboola Bibbidy-Bobbidy-Boo
(see also *alakazoo, bibbidy-bobbidi-boo, mitchakaboola abbadazoola*)

In Literature: Edward G. Rozycki, *America: An Education Strategy: The Artifact of a Society Past* (1999)

Ali-Sis-Koombah
(see also *ala* and *sis sis siscumbah*)

Facts: This magic phrase is featured in a skit by the U.S. Scouting Service Project Team entitled "The Yellow Bandana" (1997).

Alithe Zamadon

Mystique: These are ancient words of power whose very echoes make the syllables more distinct. They are "not the speech of human beings" but rather, "the language of the demiurges who could adjust the powers on which the cosmos turned."[147]

Alizam
(see also *ala* and *shazam*)

Origins: *Alizam* is derived from the Arabic *al-a'zam*, "grand" or "supreme."

Facts: The comic book character Hoppy the Marvel Bunny (1942) was an extension of the Captain Marvel franchise, but with a change

----

147 David Drake, *Master of the Cauldron* (2004)

in ownership (1954), his name was changed to Hoppy the Magic Bunny and his magic word was changed from *Shazam* to *Alizam*.[148]

Alizebu

Meanings: The word *zebu* comes from the Tibetan *ceba*, meaning "hump."[149] *Zebu* is a breed of hump-backed Indian ox. With the Arabic *Ali* ("by the most high") in front, *Alizebu* could be translated as "holy cow."

Zebu is reminiscent of the legendary Canaanite god Baal-Zebub ("Lord of the Flies"), who became the demon Beelzebub.

Facts: *Alizebu* is a magic word for revealing secret passages in the computer game "King's Quest 6" (1992).

Alka-Seltz

Facts: This is a mispronunciation of *alakazam*, reminiscent of the name of a popular antacid medication.

In Literature: "'[T]his time you count to three, all right? Then say the magic word: Alacazam. Got it? Alacazam. Any time you want me to appear, just say the magic word.' She counted with ponderous deliberation. 'Alka-seltz!'"
—Robert Grossmith, "Company," *Best English Short Stories 2* (1990)

Alla
(see *ala*)

Variations and Incantations: Alla Voom —Marlene Karkoska, "The Knight and the Wizard" (2005)

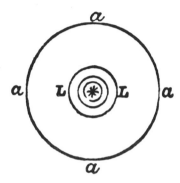

Figure 11. The magic word *Alla* is encoded in this 1893 diagram of a "Catadioptric Holophote," in which spherical mirrors focus the rays of a central flame.

Allah-hu-Akbar
(see also *ala*)

Meaning: God is great

Origin: *Allah-hu-akbar* is of Arabic origin.

Variations and Incantations:

- Allah Akbar
- Allaho Akbar
- Allah Ho Akbar
- Allahu Akbar
- Allah-u Akbar
- Allahuakhbar

---

148 Donald D. Markstein, *Toonopedia* (2004)
149 Erie Zoological Society, "Miniature Zebu" (2004)

In Literature: "When he got to the top of the mountain [the stag] asked the eagle, 'Excuse me, could you tell me what the magic words are?' 'Allah-hu-Akbar,' said the eagle."
—Jamil Momand, "The Magic Tree" (2004)

Allekazu
(see also *alakazoo*)

Allekazu, a magic circle around my heart.
—Sorana Salomeia, "Simsalabim" (2004)

Origin: This word is a variation of *alakazam*.

Variations and Incantations:

- Alakazoo
  —Deborah Hautzig, *Little Witch's Big Night* (1984)

- Allakazoo

- Allakazoo allakazam
  —Salman Rushdie, *The Satanic Verses* (1988)

All Will Be Well, and All Will Be Well, and All Manner of Things Will Be Well

Origins: This is a proclamation by the Medieval mystic Lady Julian of Norwich.

Facts: *All will be well, and all will be well, and all manner of things will be well* is used as a mantra in the tradition of Christian meditation.

Variations and Incantations:

- All shall be well, and all shall be well, and all manner of things shall be well

- All will be well, and all will be well, and every kind of thing will be well

- All will be well, and all will be well, and every manner of being will be well

- Shalom, shalom—all will be well
  —Rueben P. Job and Norman Shawchuck, *A Guide to Prayer for Ministers and Other Servants* (1991)

In Literature: In the story "We Who Walk Through Walls" by Jeremy Dyson, the magic words *all will be well, and all will be well, and all manner of things will be well* send a man through a solid wall (*Never Trust a Rabbit* [2000]).

Aloha

Mystique: "Native Hawaiian spirituality is one of humanity's treasures, and contact with its wisdom is always a gift," says spiritual author Marianne Williamson. "The Hawaiian soul is full of depth and magic."[150] The sacred Hawaiian word *Aloha* is a magical chant that opens the heart.[151] This "simple word that is so much more than a word"[152] is the key to the universal spirit, understanding, and fellowship.[153] "Aloha is the ability

---

150 Quoted in *Chicken Soup for the Soul of Hawaii* (2003)
151 Susan Gregg, *The Complete Idiot's Guide to Spiritual Healing* (2000)
152 Jack Canfield and Mark Victor Hansen, *Chicken Soup for the Soul of Hawaii* (2003)
153 Duke Paoa Kahanamoku, quoted in *Chicken Soup for the Soul of Hawaii* (2003)

to put yourself into the mind, heart, and soul of another," explains Kenneth F. Brown.

Meanings:

- Breath of life
  "When you say *aloha* to someone it means 'I recognize the (same) breath of life within you as I have within.'"
  —Kathy Boast (1999)

- Caring

- Compassion

- Fun

- Goodbye

- Good luck

- Hello

- Hope

- Mutual regard

- Sharing

- Unconditional Love
  "'Love' is indeed contagious. It is the key and magic word of Polynesia. Whether it is greeting or farewell, it matters not. It is either *Ofa! Alofa! Aroha! Talofa!* or *Aloha!*"
  —Jane Resture, "Samoa" (2003)

- Welcome

Origins: *Aloha* is of Hawaiian origin.

In Literature: "[A] lei is draped around your neck and, for the first of many times on your visit, you hear the magic word: 'Aloha.'"
—Lee Siegel, "Hawaii," *These United States* (2003)

Alohomora
(see also *aloha*)

Origins: *Alohomora* (also spelled *Alohomoré* [from the Arabic *al-homra*, "red"[154]] is the figure of "The Diviner" in Sikidy, the Madagascar variant of Arabic geomancy. The same figure represents "Illumination" and "Wisdom" in the original Arabic practice.[155] It is sometimes spelled *alahamora*.

In Literature: *Alohomora* is a spell used for unlocking doors and windows in *Harry Potter and the Philosopher's Stone* by J.K. Rowling (1997).

Alpha and Omega

Meanings:

- Beginning and end

- Eternal present
  —Eckhart Tolle, *The Power of Now* (1999)

- First and last

- Ineffable name of God
  —Migene Gonzalez-Wippler, *The Complete Book of Spells, Ceremonies and Magic* (1978)

- Infinite Godhead
  —Nevill Drury, *Everyday Magic* (2001)

- Invisible center-point around which existence revolves
  —Douglas Monroe, *The Lost Books of Merlyn: Druid Magic from the Age of Arthur* (1998)

---

154 *Journal Asiatic* (1905)

155 Serena Powers, "Serena's Gude to Geomancy," *SerenaPowers.com* (2004)

- Magic
  "Alpha and Omega. . . . I want you never to forget this. . . . This is the greatest magic that man will ever come to. . . . The ultimate source of energy. . . . The greatest magic."
  —Barry Targan, *Kingdoms* (1980)

- Primal oneness
  —Printer Bowler, *The Cosmic Laws of Golf (and Everything Else)* (2001)

- Symbol of Christ
  "I am Alpha and Omega, the beginning and the ending, sayeth the Lord, which is, and which was, and which is to come, the Almighty."
  —Revelation 1:8

- Timeless perfection
  —Eckhart Tolle, *The Power of Now* (1999)

- Transcendence; spiritual awareness
  "[T]he circle represents . . . Alpha and Omega, the state of spiritual awareness and transcendence to which the magician aspires."
  —Nevill Drury, *Everyday Magic* (2001)

- Union of opposites
  —Eckhart Tolle, *The Power of Now* (1999)

Origin: *Alpha* and *omega* are the first and last letters of the Greek alphabet.

Facts: *Alpha* and *omega* are words of power commonly included in hymns, prayers, and recitations of ceremonial magic traditions.

The stage magician's dove is a symbol of alpha-omega. In Greek gematria (the study of letter-number correspondence), "the numerical equivalent of [Alpha-Omega] is 801, made up of Alpha's 1 and Omega's 800. . . . The dove['s number is also 801]. Thus, through gematria, the dove symbolizes Alpha and Omega."[156]

---

156 Nigel Pennick, *Magical Alphabets* (1992)

In Literature:

- "Elizabeth cast her mind back to the words with which the Archbishop bespoke his reverence for the sacred things in heaven and earth. 'Alpha and Omega . . .'"
  —Jane Resh Thomas, *The Princess in the Pigpen* (1989)

- From Sri Aurobindo, "The Book of Beginnings, Canto IV: The Secret Knowledge," *Savitri, A Legend and a Symbol* (1995):

  Reconstitute the perfect word, unite
  The Alpha and the Omega in one sound;
  Then shall the Spirit and Nature be at one.

- -

Alpha Beta Gamma

Origin: *Alpha*, *beta*, and *gamma* are the first three letters of the Greek alphabet.

Facts: "The psychologist Eugene Subbotsky showed four-to-six-year-olds a magic box that, he said, turned drawings into real objects if you said the magic words 'alpha beta gamma.' When the experimenter left them alone in the room with the box and a set of drawings, almost all of the children tried the machine out. They put drawings in the box, said "alpha beta gamma.' and looked disappointed when nothing happened" (Paul Bloom, *Decartes' Baby* [2004]).

Figure 12. The incantation *alpha beta gamma* is composed of three Greek letters.

Alu

(see also *rune*)

Meanings:

- Ale, beer
  Though the precise meaning of *alu* is un-clear, "it is evident that as time went on it became increasingly identified with the Germanic terms for 'ale' or 'beer.' The eddic poem *Sigrdrífumál* speaks of *ölrúnar* ('ale-runes'), which may describe rules where *alu* is invoked, while the Old English poem 'Beowulf' describes grief or terror as *ealuscerwen* ('pouring away of *alu*?')."
  —Andy Orchard, *Cassell's Dictionary of Norse Myth and Legend* (1997)

- Ecstatic psychic force
  —Edred Thorsson, *Runelore: A Handbook of Esoteric Runology* (1987)

- Good fortune

- Inspiration
  —Edred Thorsson, *Runelore: A Handbook of Esoteric Runology* (1987)

- Magic
  —Edred Thorsson, *Runelore: A Handbook of Esoteric Runology* (1987)

- Power
  —Nigel Pennick, *Magical Alphabets* (1992)

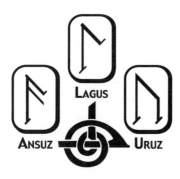

Figure 13. *Alu* is an acronym of three Norse runes.

- Protection
  —Freya Aswynn, *Northern Mysteries and Magick* (1998)

Origins: *Alu* is the "best attested of a range of magic words" found inscribed in Norse runes, evidently invoking luck or the suggestion of protection.

Facts: *Alu* is composed of three runes: Ansuz, Lagus, and Uruz.[157]

Amber

Mystique: "I recalled a magical word. *Amber*. . . . The word was charged with a mighty longing and a massive nostalgia. It had, wrapped up inside it, a sense of forsaken beauty, grand achievement, and a feeling of power that was terrible and almost ultimate."[158] "Since ancient times, amber has been an object of value and mystery. . . . Part of the mystery of amber is its ability to become electrically charged when rubbed with a soft cloth."[159]

Amen

The god Amen, the only god, shall be with thee.
  —E.A. Wallis Budge, *Egyptian Magic* (1901)

> The Liturgie is naught
> With magicke, and Amens
> (god blesse us) fraught.
>   —Sir Thomas Aston (1640)

157 Freya Aswynn, *Northern Mysteries and Magick* (1998)

158 Roger Zelazny, *Nine Princes in Amber* (1970)

159 Charles Reasoner, *The Magic Amber: A Korean Legend* (2002)

Meanings:

- Certainly, truly, always
  —Florence Hayllar, *Notes and Queries* (1864)

- Let it be
  —Brian Murdoch, *German Literature of the Early Middle Ages* (2004)

- Make firm, establish permanently
  —Jane Gordon, *A Companion to African-American Studies* (2006)

- May it be so
  —Kerry Olitzky, *The Complete How To Handbook for Jewish Living* (2004)

- Peace
  —Purushottam Nagesh Oak, *Some Missing Chapters of World History* (1973)

- Reliable
  —Martha Nandorfy, *The Poetics of Apocalypse* (2003)

- Secret, hidden
  —Thomas Milton Stewart, *Symbolism of the Gods of the Egyptians and the Light They Throw on Freemasonry* (1927)

Origins: *Amen* is an affirmation of divine action. It originated as a Hebrew word meaning "truth"[160] and is often translated to mean "let it be so." There is speculation that *amen* originally invoked the Egyptian god Amun, "the Hidden One," who represented the sun in the Mother's belly before dawn.

In Literature:

- "Whenever you're ready, you just say it, the magic word. Amen. And it's showtime."
  —Chuck Palahniuk, *Survivor* (1999)

- "The Witch said Amen, and made the Maid say Amen, and the Spirits said Amen, Amen."
  —Montague Summers, *Witchcraft and Black Magic* (1946)

- "It was a rule in the Eisenhower household that no one was permitted to leave the dinner table until after Ida said, 'Amen.' Dwight usually sat on a stool, champing at the bit to be freed of his symbol of family togetherness. . . . When his mother finally pronounced the magic word, 'he was off and gone like a shot.'"
  —Carlo D'Este, *Eisenhower* (2002)

America

Mystique: "From the point of view of magical symbolism, the letter A is a very powerful figure. It incorporates the idea of beginning, of the number 1, of unfinished work, of the eye of God, and of the Trinity. Part of this significance is transferred to the word AMERICA, which begins and ends with the letter A, and which (from a magical point of view) hints at a hidden meaning in the word, linked with the meanings of the letters at the beginning and end of the word. We see, then, that in terms of magical theory, the word AMERICA may be considered as the base of a triangle, the upper part of which is invisible. The word AMERICA is therefore a form of the truncated pyramid."[161]

In Literature: "America! What magic word. The yearning of the enslaved, the promised land of the oppressed, the goal of all longing for progress. Here man's ideals had found their fulfillment."
—Hippolyte Havel, *Emma Goldman* (1910)

---

160 John Ayto, *Dictionary of Word Origins* (1990)

161 David Ovason, *The Secret Symbols of the Dollar Bill* (2004)

Amichamchou Kai Chochao Cheroei Oueiacho Odou Proseionges

Origins: This phrase is of Egyptian origin, dating back to the 3rd–4th century CE.[162]

Facts: This phrase is part of "a remedy for ascent of the womb"[163] and invokes the names of angels who "sit over the cherubim."

Amore

(see also *love*)

Origins: *Amore* is an Italian word meaning "love."

In Literature:

• "Constantly recurring in the song, as if set there for his ear, he understood the magic word '*amore, amore*' strung like beads down the necklace warm on a girl's bosom."
—Arlo Bates, *The Puritans* (1899)

• "Love, under the name of Eros, is described [in Marsilio Ficino, *De Amore* (1496)] as 'sophist and magician'; it is a sophist because under its influence people easily take what is false for truth, and a magician because it functions through the attractive power of correspondences, which establish the harmony of the universe: 'tota vis magice nin amore consistat' (all magic power is founded on love)."
—Michael Mitchell, *Hidden Mutualities: Faustian Themes of Gnostic Origins to the Postcolonial* (2006)

Anazapta

Mystique: This musical word has an exotic ring to it, with a sizzling *zap* in the middle and a plosive *ta* to mark the impact at the end.[164]

Meanings:

• Magic word
—Eamon Duffy, *The Stripping of the Altars: Traditional Religion in England, 1400–1580* (1992)

• Plea for health
—Rich Cline, *theZreview.co.uk* (2001)

Origins: Anazapata has been traced back to Europe in the 1300s, in talismanic parchments containing exotic-sounding names of God and guaranteeing longevity.[165]

Figure 14. The musical impact of *anazapta*.

----

164 "Plosives . . . involve a momentary stoppage of the air flow and a subsequent, slightly explosive, release."—David Abram, *The Spell of the Sensuous* (1996)

165 Mary R. Lefkowitz, *Women's Lives in Greece and Rome* (1982)

162 Mary R. Lefkowitz, *Women's Lives in Greece and Rome* (1982)

163 *Ibid.*

And a-One! And a-Two! And a-One, Two, Three!

In Literature: "Out of nowhere, Mr. Bundy started reciting a magic spell. 'And a-one! And a-two! And a-one, two, three! Look who's back. Hooray! It's . . . me!' Poof! Mr. Bundy was his old self again."
—Stephanie Calmenson, *The Frog Principal* (2001)

Animovividus Homonivalis

Origins: This pseudo-Latin spell for bringing a snowman to life was coined by Gale Meyer and magician Gordon Meyer. The word *animo* refers to the life force or soul of the snowman, which is conjured to vivify with the word *vividus*. *Nivalis* means "snowy," and *homo* means "man."

Anthropropolagos

Meanings: *Anthro* comes from the Greek and Latin and means "human." *Propo* recalls the French expression *à propos*, meaning "by the way," "naturally," or "connected to what has gone before." *Lagos* is a Greek word meaning *hare*, the trickster of folklore and the classic magician's animal companion. Lagos also recalls the Greek *logos*, meaning "word." Hence, one could translate *anthropropolagos* to mean: "I am human by way of language" or perhaps "Man and rabbit are naturally connected."

Origins: The great magician Harry Houdini invented this magic word "which has an authentic ring."[166]

----

166 Henning Nelms, *Magic and Showmanship: A Handbook for Conjurers* (1969)

In Literature: Henning Nelms, *Magic and Showmanship: A Handbook for Conjurers* (1969)

Aparecium

Origins: *Aparecium* is a Latin word meaning "I appear," from the Latin *appareo*.

In Literature: *Aparecium* is used to make invisible ink reappear in *Harry Potter and the Chamber of Secrets* by J.K. Rowling (1998).

Apokalypto

Meanings:

- Uncover, unveil, reveal
- Unfolding
  —Douglas Connelly, *The Bible for Blockheads* (1999)

Origin: *Apokalypto* is of Greek origin.

Facts: *Apokalypto* is the source of the word *apocalypse*.

In Literature: "He withdrew his wand from a pocket, then waved it in a circular motion in front of the large eye-shaped glyph in the very center of the door. Then, quietly, he spoke the magic word, 'Apokalypto,' and four of the many glyphs glowed golden, forming a word."
—Thalia M. Kendall, "Charms and Curses" (2002)

Arbadacarba

(see also *abracadabra*)

Facts: *Arbadacarba*, the word *abracadabra* spelled backwards, is "the most powerful magic spell extant" according to Jean Hugard and Frederick Braue in *The Royal Road to Card Magic* (1951).

Common Magician's Applications: Reversing an effect.

In Literature:

- "The Magician put a serious expression on his face and raised his cloaked arms. 'Arbadacardba,' he muttered mysteriously."
  —T. S. Ionta, *The Cloak of Dreams* (2003)

- "'Arbadacarba!' he shouted, lowering his hands at the same time, like pulling an invisible curtain over the frustrating magical scene he surveyed."
  —Lloyd H. Whitling, *This World* (2002)

Ariath Dupius Cancyck

In Literature: "'Ariath dupius, cancyck!' chanted the mage, and the trees and thornbushes before him curled out of the way."
—Douglas Niles, *Black Wizards* (2004)

Art

Just pronounce the magic word
'Art', and everything is O.K.
—George Orwell, "Benefit of Clergy:
Some Notes on Salvador Dali,"
Fifty Orwell Essays (1944)

In Literature:

- "And then, too, Madame Chebe no longer believed in her husband, whereas, by virtue of that single magic word, 'Art!' her neighbor never had doubted hers."
  —Alphonse Daudet, *Fromont et Risler* (c. 1874)

- "I wear an amulet, and have a spell of art-magic at my tongue's end, whereby, sir ancient, neither can a ghost see me, nor I see them."
  —Charles Kingsley, *Westward Ho!* (1855)

- "Art! If I had not that magic word before me in the distance I should have died already. But for Art one has need of no one; we depend entirely upon ourselves and if we fail, it is because there was nothing in us, and that we ought to live no longer."
  —Marie Bashkirtseff, *The Journal of a Young Artist* (1889)

Arzemy Barzemy Yangelo Igg Lom

(see also *abracadabra*)

Common Magician's Applications: Levitation.

In Literature: "[H]e set down the book, pointed a long finger at the cooking pot of spices resting on the upturned barrel, and cleared his throat. 'Arzemy barzemy yangelo igg lom,' he chanted."
—T.A. Barron, *The Merlin Effect* (1994)

Asa

Origins: *Asa* is a magic name of Hebrew origin, mentioned in *Magic Spells and Formulae* by Joseph Naveh and Shaul Shaked (1993).

Asdfghjkl

(see *qwertyuiop asdfghjkl zxcvbnm*)

Origins: This magic word comes from the standard typewriter keyboard's second rows of letters.

Ashashalika

In Literature: "Kerry concentrated, gesturing toward the ground, and said, 'Ashashalika,' one of the old words of magic. Rocks shifted, shaking off their dusting of snow. Big ones rolled quickly to the points Kerry had visualized, and smaller ones filled in the spaces between. When they had settled, they spelled out SH in the snow."
—Jeff Mariotte, *Winter* (2005)

Ashi Vanghuhi

Origins: In Zoroastrianism, *Ashi Vanghuhi* is the name of a Beneficent Immortal who presides over blessings.

Asi Nise Masa

Meanings: Film scholar Charles Affron notes that this magic phrase (also spelled *Asa Nisi Masa*) is "apparently meaningless," achieving its affect "by transcending precise meaning." The words "convey . . . the full wonder of . . . childhood perception. Magical, enigmatic, an invitation to meaning, 'Asa Nisi Masa' is susceptible to interpretation."[167] Avant-garde theatre director Arthur Holmberg points out that "The intelligi-

bility of ritual language is not the critical factor. . . . The purpose is to establish contact with the transcendent. . . . Ritual language stresses the sounds of words and heightens language as a sensuous and emotional experience. Often unintelligible, ritual language is associated with the holy and with the authority of divine revelation."[168]

- Anima

- Child-like wonder

- Nonsense

- Soul

Origins: *Asi nise masa* is an Italian phrase, the equivalent of *abracadabra*.

"These words are derived from 'la lingua serpentina' (serpentine language), a children's language game akin to pig Latin that inserts 'sa' and 'si' syllables into existing words—here into 'anima.' 'Anima' has a dual resonance. It means 'soul' in Italian; it is also a key concept in Jungian psychology: the female element lodged within all human beings. . . . The search for meaning leads back to the mysterious symbol of the children's game, the symbol that contains the inexpressible in its ambiguity."[169]

Facts: These magic words are featured in Federico Fellini's film *8½* (1963). "The phrase 'Asi Nise Masa' is the key that unlocks Guido's unconscious. (It can be translated as *anima*, a Jungian term meaning soul or spirit.) For Guido, it is a magical phrase from his childhood, and he goes back there to try to find a solution to his lack of inspiration *through magic*."[170] Critic Mark Abraham suggests that the "child-code foolery" of *Asi*

---

167 Charles Affron, *8½* (1987)

168 *Theatre of Robert Wilson* (1997)

169 Charles Affron, *8½* (1987)

170 Nicholas Proferes, *Film Directing Fundamentals* (2001)

nise masa encapsulates "importance disguised with inanity, erudition breathed through giggling lips, lucidity rearticulated as gibberish. It's also a bridge between the past and present (Fellini has two magicians pull the phrase from an adult Guido's mind as a way to link temporal states in his film); it's a bridge between different spaces; . . . it means that animus 'boy' and anima 'girl' (or any other category) might exist, but none of us exist that simply, animated only as girls or boys (or any other category)."[171]

Variations and Incantations:

- Asa Nisi Masa

- Asanisimasa

- Asi Nisi Masa

Aski Kataski

Meanings: "No convincing interpretation of the words has yet been proposed."[172] *Aski Kataski* begins a larger incantation: *Aski-kataski-haix-tet-rax-damnameneus-aision*, which Athanasius Kircher translated to mean "Darkness, Light, Sun, and Truth."[173]

Origins: The mystic words *Aski Kataski* are part of an ancient Greek magic spell, perhaps of Ephesian origin. They begin the so-called *Ephesia Grammata*, or "Ephesian letters."

Facts: "The most celebrated words of power in the classical world, the Ephesia grammata were used in a wide range of magical applications and even gave rise to a slang term for magic itself. . . . The use of the Ephesia grammata was so widespread that *aski kataski*, a shortened version of the first two words, was used as a slang term for magic in the Greek-speaking world, with much the same connotations that 'hocus pocus' has in modern English."[174]

Plutarch said that priests would recite these words over persons possessed by demons.[175]

Atizoo
(see also *oozita*)

In Literature: In the BBC Puppet Theatre production *Tunnel Trouble* (1976) by Gordon Murray, *Atizoo* is an *Open Sesame*-type magic word:

NARRATOR: Weatherspoon took a deep breath of air–and dust!
WEATHERSPOON: Ah. Atizoo!
NARRATOR: And he sneezed! . . .
RUFUS: (over) Whoops!
NARRATOR: Immediately, the square section of marble floor on which the King was standing, descended, depositing His Majesty into the blackness below. Weatherspoon, still under the black cloth, had his eyes closed, and his mouth open.
WEATHERSPOON: Ah . . . ah . . . Atizoo! . . . NARRATOR: The marble slab rose up, and fitted itself neatly back into place in the checkerboard floor.
WEATHERSPOON: I'm sorry, Your Majesty, but . . . Your Majesty? (puzzled) Where have you gone?

171 "Shining" (Feb. 16, 2007)

172 John Michael Greer, *The New Encyclopedia of the Occult* (2003)

173 Scott J. Osterhage, *Collation of Theosophical Glossaries* (1997)

174 John Michael Greer, *The New Encyclopedia of the Occult* (2003)

175 Scott J. Osterhage, *Collation of Theosophical Glossaries* (1997)

(miffed) We-ell! Fancy rushing off like that! Just because I sneeze! How very petty! . . .

NARRATOR: Weatherspoon started to paint. What a strange character Ampumpo was, he thought. He wore his hat upside down, and his tunic back-to-front! Perhaps he walked backwards too! (almost laughing) And wrote backwards! (sounding more serious) Ooh, then the magic word might be Oozita backwards! Weatherspoon stared at the letters carved into the ancient stone.

WEATHERSPOON: (slowly spelling) A, T, I, 'Zed', O, O. Atizoo! . . .

NARRATOR: (over) The earth shook and the new post box swayed.

WEATHERSPOON: Ooh, dear!

NARRATOR: The ancient stone, with the pillar box on top, had sunk into the ground!

WEATHERSPOON: My new post box!

NARRATOR: Suddenly, two grimy heads appeared from the gaping hole.

WEATHERSPOON: Your Majesty! Lord Chamberlain!

RUFUS: Help me out, Weatherspoon!

WEATHERSPOON: Are you alright, Sire?

RUFUS: Ooh. We had a terrible time down there, Weatherspoon! What happened?

WEATHERSPOON: I sneezed, Sire, and a sneeze sounds just like the magic word!

RUFUS: What is the magic word?

WEATHERSPOON: Atizoo.

Aum
(see also *om*)

Aum is the creative sound whose vibrations build the worlds. . . . He who can pronounce it with the right tone, is able to work wonders.
—Alexandra David-Neel,
With Mystics and Magicians in Tibet (1931)

Mystique: Martial arts expert Dr. Haha Lung writes: "Recall that our voices alone have the power to put another person (or ourselves) into a hypnotic trance. Ancient peoples respected and feared the power of words. Thus we have tales of heroes going in search of magic words that would grant them great power: 'Abracadabra,' 'Open Sesame,' or 'Aum.' Some of these mysterious sounds and words were used to accomplish magic. . . . *The Kama Sutra* speaks of magical verses that have the power of 'fascination' and makes reference to them appearing in ancient Indian texts such as the Indian *Anunga Runga (Kamaledhiplava).* Down through the ages, many 'words to conjure by' were sacred or forbidden. In India, these sacred sounds are known as mantra."[176]

Avada Kedavra
(see also *abracadabra*)

Origins: These magic words are a variation of *abracadabra.*

Facts: *Avada Kedavra* is a killing curse in *Harry Potter and the Philosopher's Stone* by J.K. Rowling (1997).

Avis

Origins: *Avis* is a Latin word meaning "bird."

In Literature: *Avis* is used to make birds fly out of a wand in *Harry Potter and the Goblet of Fire* by J.K. Rowling (2000).

Awake
(see also *sleep*)

Common Magician's Applications: Hypnotism. For example: "After an hour and a half, it's time to wind down and prepare the volunteers to emerge from their trances, a process called 're-vivification.' [Professional hypnotist Steve] Taubman plants a few post-hypnotic suggestions, telling the group how proud and wonderful they'll feel when this is over: well rested, alert, healthy and very much awake. Then he counts backwards from five and pronounces the magic word: 'Awake!'"[177]

Aza

Origins: *Aza* is a magic name of Hebrew origin, mentioned in *Magic Spells and Formulae by* Joseph Naveh and Shaul Shaked (1993).

Meanings: Demon with a forked tongue.
—Marjorie Madelstam Balzer, *Shamanic Worlds* (1997)

----

177 Ruth Horowitz, "Mind Games: Hypnotist Steve Taubman Throws One Hell of a Trance Party" (2004)

Azzara Rhosta Magnah Bhostu! Azzara Rhosta Magnah Bhostum! Abzzada Xszo! Xzso Tintullum!

In Literature: "SETH: Are you the sorcerer who conjures great monstrosities? . . . Let me join my magic with yours, and we will fashion an indestructible demon, for he must be strong enough to challenge the resurrected god. To your dark incantations, add my accomplishments for yeast. Take disillusionment, lost hope, diseases of the mind and of the soul, false truths! Sworn lies of tribes and nations! Supernatural corruption . . . WIZARD: Hold on! Give me time to prepare the proper, eh, preparations! I don't want to miss this opportunity to go beyond the limits of ordinary evil. (WIZARD *puts on crown, cape, and staff; he chants a magic spell.*) Azzara Rhosta Magnah Bhostu! Azzara Rhosta Magnah Bhostum! Abzzada Xszo! Xszo Tintullum!"
—Sterling Houston, *Isis in Nubia* (1993)

B

Baba's Chicken Soup

Meanings: The word *Baba* could refer to a grandmother or to the "Ali Baba" of fable.

Facts: These were the magic words of professional magician Tom Kovnats.

Backwards, Turn Backwards O Time in Thy Flight; Back to the Past with the Speed of Light

Facts: This is a magic spell for reversing time in the *Bewitched* television series.

Variations and Incantations: Night into day and day into night; Back to the past with the speed of light.
—*Bewitched*

Bagabi Laca Bachabe, Lamac Cahi Achababe

Meanings: This magical phrase is "apparently nonsensical."[178]

Origin: This phrase is perhaps of Basque origin.

Common Magician's Applications: Summoning spirits.

In Literature: Gregory Caergill MacHale, *The Coming Man* (2001)

Bagus

Meanings: Very good, wonderful
  "Bagus. This magic word, meaning 'very good' or 'wonderful,' depending on the inflection, served him in every situation."
  —Stewart Wavell, *The Naga King's Daughter* (1965)

Origin: This word is of Malay origin.

Balance Sheet

In Literature: "The balance-sheet! That is the magic word. All through the year we go on and on in the eddying whirl of business. Money comes and goes, circulates, attracts other money, vanishes; and the fortune of the firm, like a slippery, gleaming snake, always in motion, expands, contracts, diminishes, or increases, and it is impossible to know our condition until there comes a moment of rest. Not until the inventory shall we know the truth, and whether the year, which seems to have been prosperous, has really been so."
—Alphonse Daudet, *Fromont et Risler, vol. 2* (c. 1874)

Bam Wham Ham Flam Jamb Cram Alla Kazam Slam

In Literature: Linda Varsell Smith, *The Rainbow Redemption* (2003)

Banana Bones

From bananas to bones. With one . . . spark, the imagination can be set on fire.
—Elizabeth Gilbert, *A Writer's Workbook* (2000)

Facts: In a Chinese story, the "banana yellow bones" of the mystic water spirit "Bro" Gao's

---

178 Ronald Hutton, *The Triumph of the Moon* (2001)

descendents rise up from the ashes of a wandering shaman's fire: "The shaman had said, 'Water is born from fire . . .' The fire burned blue turning to purple, purple to red, for exactly one day and one night. It was said that eventually eight sets of fragrant, banana yellow male bones emerged from the ashes. These were the sons of 'Bro' Gao."[179]

In Vodou, green bananas and bones are offerings to Legba, the supernatural Master of Passageways and opener of doors.[180]

In an early advertisement for bananas, "Josephine Baker, clad only in a girdle of bananas, sang a song with a refrain to the effect that she liked bananas because they had no bones."[181]

Banana Bones are a snack consisting of frozen banana dipped in chocolate or peanut butter and rolled with nuts.

In Literature: "'I say the magic words three times—Banana bones, banana bones, banana bones.' I held up the pencil horizontal at eye level and wiggled it up and down. 'Presto, it's rubber!'"
—Jon Scieszka, *2095* (1995)

Banath

(see also *banneth*)

Facts: *Banath* is the prankster deity of the Midkemia fantasy world popularlized by Raymond E. Feist.

Banneth

The magic word is Banneth.
—Peter F. Hamilton,
The Neutronium Alchemist: Conflict (1998)

Origins: Of Germanic origin, the word *banneth* means "to curse" or "to prohibit."

Facts: *Banneth* is the name of "the High Magus" in *The Confederation Handbook* by Peter F. Hamilton (2002).

Baraka

Mystique: There is speculation that the ancient Sufi saying "Baraka bashad," meaning "blessing be," is the source of the word *abracadabra*.[182] In any case, *baraka* is a "mysterious, wonder-working force which is looked upon as a blessing from God, a 'blessed virtue.'"[183] Put another way, "Baraka means blessedness and implies a mystical quality of divine protection."[184] Musician Brian Eno sees baraka as being "something between karma and fate. Certain people accrue baraka. They accrue the ability to attract interesting things to themselves, interesting and pleasant things. Now this seems to be manifestly true. That definitely happens, you know. You see people, you meet people to whom interesting things continuously happen. Why does this happen to them and not to others? Why is it happening to me? I think that some

179 Beatrice Spade, "The Birth of the Water God," *China's Avant-Garde Fiction*, edited by Jing Wang (1998)

180 Mal Leicester, *Classroom Issues* (2000)

181 Maguelonne Toussaint-Samat, *History of Food* (1992)

182 Doreen Valiente, *An ABC of Witchcraft Past and Present* (1973)

183 Edward Westermarck, *The Moorish Conception of Holiness* (1916)

184 Andy Griffin, "None Dare Call it Cantaloupe" (2003)

people are very good at being opportunistic in a good way, and in a large scale way."[185]

Meanings:

- Blessing, a blessing passed from one person to another
  —Nick Jenkins, "The Opinionated Traveler" (2002)

- Breath of life, breath of God

- Essence of life
  —National Peace Corps Association (1998)

- Fragrance of the divine

- Saintly

Origins: The word *baraka* traces back to Ancient Persia.

Barbathiaoth
(see also *ablanathanalba sisopetron*)

Origins: This magic name, part of a spell for salvation, is featured on "a silver tablet found in Beroea, in Macedonia."[186]

Facts: *Barbathiaoth*, described as a "word of power" and written in "the Old Script" with a boxwood twig, is part of an old woman's incantation in *Lord of the Isles* by David Drake (1997).

Variations and Incantations: Iao barbathiaoth ablanathanalba
—David Drake, *Lord of the Isles* (1997)

Barrada Nikto
(see also *clatto verata nicto*)

Origins: This phrase makes reference to "Klaatu, Barada, Nikto," used to command the robot Gort in the film *The Day the Earth Stood Still* (1951).

In Literature: "'Maybe we're forgetting something.' Daniel said, 'The magic word?' Mike smiled and shouted, 'Gort!' Daniel smiled. 'Barrada!' 'Nikto!' And when that didn't work, the fathers exchanged a last look, a last smile, and said the magic word together. Mike and Daniel whispered, 'Please!'"
—Patrick O'Leary, *The Impossible Bird* (2002)

Bazooka

Meanings:

- Short-range anti-tank rocket launcher

- Trombone-like kazoo

Origins: The word *bazooka* apparently originated in the 1930s from *bazoo*, a slang form of *kazoo*.

In Literature: "Bazookas, bazookas! That's the magic word, it's a regular fetish. Bazookas for everyone!"
—Jean Genet, *The Balcony*, translated by Bernard Frechtman (1958)

Beaurepaire

In Literature: "Riviere, lost in his own thoughts, attended to him as men of business do to a babbling brook; until suddenly from the

185 "An Evening With Brian Eno," *The Complete Music Magazine* (1982)
186 Christopher Faraone, *Magika Hiera* (1991)

mass of twaddle broke forth a magic word—
Beaurepaire . . ."
—Charles Reade, *White Lies* (1860)

Bee Loo Kila

In Literature: "Pratel shouted out three magic words. '*Bee Loo Kila.*' Suddenly a gaping hole appeared near the base of the hideous looking tree."
—Ted Lazaris, *Dragon Man and the Poseidon Encounter* (2004)

Beethoven, Chopin, Vivaldi, Bach

Facts: This magic phrase conjures the names of four great musical geniuses.

In Literature: Lisa Fiedler, *Know-It-All* (2002)

Begone

Remember the magic words,
"Begone! You have no power here!"
—Ellen Cannon Reed, *The Heart of Wicca* (2000)

Meanings: Go away. "Go away! Begone!"
—Brian Jacques, *Redwall* (2002)

Facts: "Persian poets say that Satan is sustained by his memory of the sound of God's voice when he said 'Begone!' That is his power."[187]

Begone is the classic word for banishing infernal spirits from the material plane,[188] typically said in a "huge and commanding" voice.[189]

Common Magician's Applications: Vanishing.

Variations and Incantations:

- Ali Zoom; Begone
  "Father Patrick twiddled his wrists like a second-rate magician: *Ali Zoom. Begone, Fatso.*"
  —Catherine Forde, *Fat Boy Swim* (2003)

- Begone, begone, begone
  —Charles Godfrey Leland, *Gypsy Sorcery and Fortune Telling* (1891)

- Begone, begone I say!
  —Kate McMullan, *97 Ways to Train a Dragon* (2003)

- Begone, now
  —Dave Juliano, *Armor of God* (2006)

- Forever begone
  —Mercer Warriner, *Full Moon Magic* (1998)

In Literature:

- "'Begone, fiend, or you shall know what magic really is!' the old wizard boomed."
  —Tony Abbott, *The Hawk Bandits of Tarkoom* (2001)

- "'By the beard of my Great-Uncle Humbug, begone!' the Good Magician said."
  —Piers Anthony, *Source of Magic* (1979)

- "'Begone!' he cried, hardly knowing if he was shouting or whispering."
  —Avi, *Midnight Magic* (1999)

---

187 Origin unknown

188 Bill Whitcomb, *The Magician's Companion* (1993)
189 Marc Zicree, *Magic Time* (2002)

- "'Begone!' The rustling, tapping, and flitter- ing stopped dead."
—Jonathan Stroud, *The Amulet of Samarkand* (2003)

Behold

And now *behold*—arise
[from your trance], my princess!
—Robert J. Tiess, *Yorick, Fellow of Infinite Jest*

Mystique: *Behold* is a command with a primal energy, indeed a supernatural power—the very caliber of word spoken by angels in the Bible. *Behold* means far more than simply "look." It calls upon spectators to "witness and be amazed." But it also does more. It calls upon spectators to be, if only for a moment, mystical "seers" endowed with profound spiritual insight and the power to perceive miracles. In other words, it invites everyone to participate in the magic, to suspend their disbelief and be convinced that "seeing is believing."

In 1883, the Hindu seer Sri Ramakrishna told the story of a king who once asked a yogi to impart Knowledge to him in one word. "The yogi said, 'All right; you will get Knowledge in one word.' After a while a magician came to the king. The king saw the magician moving two of his fingers rapidly and heard him exclaim, 'Behold, O King! Behold.' The king looked at him amazed when, after a few minutes, he saw the two fingers becoming one. The magician moved that one finger rapidly and said, 'Behold, O King! Behold.' The implication of the story is that Brahman [the world soul, the creative principle of the universe] and the Primal Energy at first appear to be two. But after attaining the knowledge of Brahman one does not see the two.

Then there is no differentiation; it is One, without a second—Advaita—non duality."[190]

Facts: Professional magician John Blood uses the magic word *behold* to help restore wonder in his audience and to re-establish the original role of magicians.[191] "From earliest times people have gathered around magicians for guidance, for learning, and for entertainment. The role of 'the magician' has been a valuable role in societies since the dawn of time. Sadly, the people of today regard magic as trivial entertainment. So many have lost touch with the magic of wonder. John Blood has as his key goal the restoration of wonder through learning and communication, hence [the name of his inspirational magic services], 'Behold! Learning.'"[192]

The word *beholden*—meaning "indebted" or "obligated"—derives from an old past participle of *behold*. When a magician speaks the word *behold*, perhaps there is a vestige of obligation in the following senses: gratitude, responsibility, fulfill-

----

190 *The Gospel of Sri Ramakrishna*, translated by Swami Nikhilananda

191 The ancient "druids" of Ireland, for example, were above all else poets: "While they occasionally carried magic wands and stones, in the far great majority of cases [their] only magic 'tool' was their voices. They were, emphatically, not 'pagan priests' and most of what we think of as priestly functions fell to the local king or tribal chief. They were sages, advisors, 'wizards'—their closest modern equivalents would be scholars sometimes called upon to be government advisors, although in many cases they were unaffiliated with the rulers and conducted what we nowadays would call 'private practice.'"—Seán Ó Tuathail, "The Excellence of Ancient Word: Druid Rhetorics from Ancient Irish Tales" (1993)

192 *BeholdLearning.com* (2005)

ment of a custom, and recognition of a binding promise. Considered in the context of *beholden*, the word *behold* bids the audience not only to look at the illusion at hand but to acknowledge the history and ingenuity behind it, and thereby honor all of the craft's forefathers.

Common Magician's Applications: Production. For example: "Fabrizio plunged his right hand into his pocket even as he held his left hand high over his head. 'Behold!' he cried, showing his left hand to be bare and open. All eyes went to this hand. Fabrizio made a fist. Next he shoved his right thumb into that fist and removed it, showing the right hand to be open and bare. Finally, he reached back into his left fist with fingers of his right hand and pulled out a long green ribbon. As gasps of astonishment came from the crowd, Fabrizio flipped the ribbon onto the master cook's lap. The cook stared with terror-filled eyes at the ribbon that lay upon his belly. 'Why . . . why . . . that's magic!' he cried. Leaping off his stool, he brushed away the ribbon as if it were a poisonous snake. 'That's what people call it,' Fabrizio replied coolly."[193]

Vanishing. For example: "'For my final act,' declared Matthew the Marvelous Magician, 'and my greatest miracle, I will make something appear from nothing!' With amazing grace and style he opened the wonderful looking box and showed it empty to the audience, and then re-closed it and asked for silence so he could summon something from nothing. The audience was silent as Matthew waved his arms around the box dramatically and hummed his silly tune, and then standing tall and proud he said, 'Behold, Something from Nothing!' and opened the box. . . . Out of the box flew what looked like an explosion of streamers and paper flowers . . . until the entire front of the stage was filled with beautiful and colorful flowers and streamers. . . . The audience jumped to their feet in wild cheers and he looked down through the streamers to see his mom crying and dad beaming."[194]

In Literature:

- "Luke then bowed his head. Then in a quick motion he rose up and said, 'BEHOLD!' And upon his word, a doorway to another world opened."
  —Ted Lazaris, *Dragon Man and the Poseidon Encounter* (2004)

- "'I am Mairelon the Magician!' he announced. 'Lend me your attention and I will show you wonders. The knowledge of the East and the West is mine, and the secrets of the mysterious cults of Africa and India! Behold!'"
  —Patricia C. Wrede, *Mairelon the Magician* (1991)

- "He put on a flowering robe, a turban, and a long, white cotton beard. He looked like a magician. 'Behold!' he cackled. 'Murko the Magnificent!'"
  —Jean Lewis, "Rainbow Brite Twink's Magic Carpet Ride" (2005)

Believe

There's that magic word BELIEVE.
—Bill Althaus, *The Examiner* (2004)

Mystique: All magic involves belief, since "seeing is believing," as the saying goes, and we "wouldn't have believed it if we hadn't seen it." There is a cultural given that without belief, no good things, no love, no Santa Claus, no God will exist for oneself.

193 Avi, *Midnight Magic* (1999)

194 Karl Bastian, "Matthew the Marvelous Magician's Miracle" (2002)

Facts: *Believe* is a favorite magic word for professional conjurer Dan Runfola, "Magician for All Occasions." A news feature about Runfola reported: "The magic word for the show was 'believe,' and children of all ages who attended Runfola's performance no doubt left in the firm belief that despite computer games and television, a crowd still reacts to a good magician."[195]

In Literature: "[T]he magic's in the word—believe."
—Treva McLean, *The Basic Humanity Handbook* (2003)

Benatir Cararkau
Dedos Etinarmi

Meanings: According to the 1652 grimoire *La Chouette Noire* ("Black Owl"), *Benatir* conjures the spirit of water, adding *Cararkau* conjures the spirit of the sea, *Dedos* conjures the spirit of earth, and *Etinarmi* conjures the spirit of air.

Origins: *Benatir Cararkau Dedos Etinarmi* are antiquated magic words to grant both invisibility and the power to penetrate any obstacle, even a brick wall. The phrase comes from an Egyptian book of magical talismans entitled *Treasure of the Old Man of the Pyramids*, "translated from the Language of the Magi" in the eighteenth century.[196]
Common Magician's Applications: Vanishing and penetration. When printed onto a silk in the form of an ancient talisman, *Benatir Cararkau*

Dedos Etinarmi can lend an ancient Egyptian mystique to any routine.

BENATIR CARARKAU
DEDOS ETINARMI

Figure 15. This invisibility and penetration talisman has an occult appearance but not an infernal purpose. It is based upon the research of Arthur Edward Waite in *The Book of Ceremonial Magic* (1913).

Bessen Berithen Berio

Origins: This phrase has been traced back to a creation myth of unknown origin and date, found on a magical papyrus from late antiquity, likely from Hellenized Egypt. "When [the Godhead] first laughed, light appeared and its splendor shone through the whole universe. The God of the cosmos and of the fire [was created]. Then: BESSEN BERITHEN BERIO, which are magic words."
—Marie-Louise Von Franz, *Creation Myths* (1972). "This is the one and only creation myth where God laughs," Von Franz notes.

---

195 Tom Boyle, "'Magician for all Occasions' Thrills Audience at Benson Memorial Library," *The Titusville Herald* (2005)

196 Arthur Edward Waite, *The Book of Ceremonial Magic* (1913)

Bet

Origins: Bet is derived from the old French *abeter* meaning "to urge on."

In Literature: "'What'll you bet?' said Jimmy. The Strollers began to sit up and take notice. The magic word 'bet,' when uttered in that room, had rarely failed to add a zest to life."
—P.G. Wodehouse, *The Intrusion of Jimmy* (1910)

Betelgeuse

Mystique: "Rigel, Betelgeuse, and Orion, too, spoke to her. There was no finer church, no finer choir, than the stars speaking in silence."[197] Star names are sometimes invoked "as the words of a prayer" as one abandons oneself to the vastness overhead and seeks to lose oneself below: *"Betelgeuse. Sirius. Orion. Antares. The sky is very large, and you are very small. . . . The Pleiades. Cassiopeia. Taurus. Heaven is wide, and you are very small.* Dead, but none the less powerful for being dead. . . . [He] turned his hands palm upward, in gesture of surrender. He reached beyond the stars, searching."[198] "And I search among the signs / For the flare, the pole-star, pulley toward the edge."[199]

Origins: *Betelgeuse* is a giant red star, *Alpha Orionis*, in the constellation of Orion. The star's name is a corruption of the Arabic *yad al jawza* ("hand of the central one" or "hand of the great one").

Facts: Chanting the name *Betelgeuse* conjures a trickster spirit in the Tim Burton film *Beetlejuice* (1988).

In H.P. Lovecraft's story "The Dweller in Darkness" (1944), Betelgeuse is home to the Elder Gods.

In Douglas Adams' *The Hitchhiker's Guide to the Galaxy* (1978), the character Ford Prefect comes from a planet "in the vicinity of Betelgeuse."

Variations and Incantations:

- Al Mankib
  This is an Arabic name for the star meaning "the shoulder," describing the star's position in the constellation.

- Bedalgeuze
  This is the Medieval Latin spelling of the star's name.

- Beetle juice
  "Sailors pronounce *Betelgeuse* 'Beetle juice' and so do I."
  —Basil Bunting, quoted in *The Oxford Anthology of English Literature: 1800 to the Present*, edited by Frank Kermode (1973)

- Beteiguex

- Betelgeux

- Betelgeuze

- Betelguex

In Literature:

- "A man is a cup able to hold his gill of the moon and magic, and only to yearn for Betelgeuse. It is his glory and his ruin that he is so quickly filled, and must forever know hunger."
  —Thomas Wolfe, *O Lost* (1929)

- From Alan Watts, "Incantation of the Stars" (1971), *Cloud-hidden, Whereabouts Unknown* (1974):

---

197 Mark Helprin, *Winter's Tale* (1983)
198 Diana Gabaldon, *Drums of Autumn* (1997)
199 Ruth Stone, "On the Mountain," *Book of Women Poets* (1992)

[T]he magician, his voice reverberating
without echo in the dark imaginary dome,
tells me the names of lights nearer home—
names whose strangeness to our tongue
measures the far immensity
of Aldebaran, bright horn of the Bull,
Arcturus, the Plowman's spear,
Betelgeuse and Rigel, the Hunter's jewels,
Vega, playing the Lyre, and Deneb, head of the swan.

- "He had a pull to the origin of things, the first day, the first man, the unknown sea, Betelgeuse, the buried continent. From passive places his imagination sprang a harpoon."
—Edward Said, "'All Interweavingly Working Together': Herman Melville's *Moby Dick*," *The American Mystery* (2000)

Beyond

Variations and Incantations:

- Above and beyond

- Great beyond

In Literature: "[H]is heart clenched with the beauty of that single magical word—Beyond."
—Stephen Bowkett, *Ice: A Frozen World* (2001)

Bibbidy-Bobbidi-Boo

A little bibbidy-bobbidy-boo goes a long way.
—Kristen Kidder,
"Average Joe: Hawaii," *PopMatters.com*

Mystique: These magic words are the stuff of enthrallment, of being "wrapped in a cloud of bliss, taking in the color and fantasy and bibbidy-bobbidy-boo of it all."[200]

Meanings:

- Believe it or not
"We found a card key in the ashtray of the rental vehicle. Anyway, it takes some footwork. But we run it down and—bibbity-bobbity-boo—it's a Comfort Inn . . ."
—John Case, *The Genesis Code* (1997)

- Magic word
"[O]ne 'bibbity bobbity boo' later, there she is dancing with the prince."
—Calvin Miller, *The Empowered Leader* (1995)
    "When the pre-schooler forgot to say please, Dana said, 'What's the magic word?' . . . 'Bibbidy bobbidy boo.'"
—*MommaSaid.net* (2005)

- Mumbo jumbo, gibberish
"*[G]obbledy-gook, helter-skelter*, or *bibbity-bobbity-boo* . . ."
—Bruce Hayes, *Metrical Stress Theory* (1995)

- "This way, that way, *there!*"
—*TheMagicCafe.com*

- Yada yada yada
"I beat you to death, pee on your body, we all go get drunk, bibbity, bobbity, boo."
—Warren Murphy, "Collaboration," *Murder Among Friends* (2000)

Origins: The phrase came down to us "from a Celtic spell meant to direct a thrown javelin or fired arrow unerringly to its intended target."[201]

Facts: These magic words were made famous by the song "Bibbidy-Bobbidi-Boo" by Jerry Liv-

---

200 Harry R. Moody, *The Five Stages of the Soul* (1997)
201 TheMagicCafe.com

ingston, Mack David, and Al Hoffman, from the Walt Disney film *Cinderella* (1950).[202]

Common Magician's Applications: Transformations.

Variations and Incantations:

- Alikazoola, mitchikaboola, bibbidy-bobidy-boo
  —Edward G. Rozycki, *"America 2000: An Education Strategy*: The Artifact of a Society Past (1999)

- Bibbedy-bobbedy-boo
  —Dorothea Jensen, *The Riddle of Pencroft Farm* (2001)

- Bibbidi-bobbidi-boo
  "And now for the magic words—Bibbidi-Bobbidi-Boo!" said the Fairy Godmother."
  —Walt Disney, *Cinderella* (1950)

- Bibbidy Bobbidy Boo
  —Harry R. Moody, *The Five Stages of the Soul* (1997)

- Bibbity bobbity
  "'Bibbity bobbity,' he said, rubbing his hands together."
  —Peter Abrahams, *The Fan* (1995)

- Bibbity bobbity boo-hoo
  "Electra looked vaguely disappointed, as if she might burst into a tearful 'bibbity bobbity boo-hoo.'"
  —Carole Nelson Douglas, *Cat in a Diamond Dazzle* (1996)

- Bibbity bobbity bumblebee
  —Jean R. Feldman, *Ready-to-Use Self Esteem Activities for Young Children* (1997)

- Bibbity-boo, undo his shoe
  —Jayne Castle, *Charmed* (1999)

- Bibidy-bobbidy-boo
  —Cheryl Charming, *Be a Star Magician!* (2002)

- Bibity-bobbity-boo
  —Adam Brooks Webber, *Modern Programming Languages* (2003)

- Bippety-boppety-boo
  —Richard Zacks, *An Underground Education* (1999)

- Bippidy-boppidy-boo
  —James M. Foard, *The Nebulous Hypothesis* (1996)

- Diggedy dobbidy cool
  —Imamu Amiri Baraka, *The Leroi Jones* (1960)

- Ibbity-boppitty-boo
  —Marcelle Langan DiFalco, *The Big Sister's Guide to the World of Work* (2005)

- Jiggedy bobbidy fool
  —Imamu Amiri Baraka, *The Leroi Jones* (1960)

- Pippity poppity pop!
  —Cheryl Charming, *Be a Star Magician!* (2002)

- Snippety-bobbity-boo!
  —*Action Adventure Excitement 9* (2003)

In Literature:

- "'What happened to *bibbity bobbity boo?* Cal asked Min. 'That was Disney, honey,' Min said. 'It wasn't a documentary.'"
  —Jennifer Crusie, *Bet Me* (2004)

- "*Bibbity bobbity boo*, I thought. *Alakazam.*"
  —Kim Harrison, *Every Which Way But Dead* (2005)

- "'Bibbidy, bobbidy, boo!' said Campbell. 'Now look, Daddy!' . . . He leaned over again. 'The ace of diamonds . . . the ace of hearts . . . the ace of . . . *clubs!* Whuh—Campbell!

202 Jon Burlingame, *Sound and Vision: 60 Years of Motion Picture Soundtracks* (2000)

How did the ace of *clubs* get there?' Delighted. 'It just—*did*!' 'Why—it's *magic*!'"
—Tom Wolfe, *The Bonfire of the Vanities* (1987)

- "Siggy saw the fairy godmother flying away ahead of them, north and east from San Clemente, trailing stars behind her as she flew. 'Bibbity bobbity boo,' she cried, and she was gone."
  —Orson Card, *Maps in a Mirror* (1990)

- "'Bibbidy Bobbidy boo.' Balaam transformed back into a man."
  —Oren the Otter, *The Lost Son of Nerr* (2004)

- "Force lines are invisible streams of energy that flow through the ground and the air. They're the source of power we tap into when we do our bibbity-bobbity-boo schtick."
  —Robert Asprin, *Myth-ing Persons* (2002)

- "'Bibbity-bobbity-boo,' said Sylvie. 'You're now a real boy.' 'You're thinking of *Pinocchio* but quoting *Cinderella*.'"
  —Orson Card, *Homebody* (1998)

- "'Beat it, willya! Shoo fly!' She waggled her hands at him. 'Bibbidy bobbidy boo! Take a hike, damnit!'"
  —Russ Anderson, "Hard Choices" (2001)

Bibbity Babbit

Common Magician's Applications: Pulling a rabbit out of a hat.

In Literature: "'Blasted bunnies!' he cursed. 'How was I to know that saying *Bibbity Babbit* summoned rabbits?'"
—Kate McMullan, *Class Trip to the Cave of Doom* (1998)

Bibbity-Boo

Meanings: "Something other worldly"
—James Harkness, quoted in *The Most Southern Place on Earth* by James C. Cobb (1992)

Variations and Incantations: Ibbity Bibbity Boo
—James Harkness, quoted in *The Most Southern Place on Earth* by James C. Cobb (1992)

In Literature: "[S]he opened her mouth and screamed words she hadn't used since a certain junior high pep rally—the words to the only spell she knew: 'Bibbity-boo, undo his shoe!'"
—Jayne Castle, *Charmed* (1999)

Bickery Stickery

In Literature: Deborah Hautzig, *Little Witch's Bad Dream* (2000)

Bim Bam Alakazam
(see also *alakazam*)

Facts: The words *bim bam* imitate the sound of bells[203] or booming explosions.

In Literature: "Bim! Bam! Alakazam! A man in a barrel went over a dam! He did it for money, the newspapers said: His pockets were empty *and so was his head!*"
—Ruth I. Dowell, *Move Over Mother Goose* (1987)

---

203 David Hurwitz, *The Mahler Symphonies* (2004)

Bingo

Bingo is the magic word.
—C. Forrest, *KlondikeMarketing.com* (2003)

Mystique: The very sound of *bingo* signals a win, the result of lucky numbers lining up in straight or diagonal rows. When fate magically comes our way, we exuberantly cry, "Bingo!"

Meanings:

- Eureka!
  "BINGO!—I had finally struck brain!"
  —Keith Ellis, *The Magic Lamp* (1996)
     "'Flibbing!' he exclaimed (which I decided must be like shouting 'Bingo!' or 'Eureka!' in our language)."
  —Bruce Coville, *Aliens Ate my Homework* (1993)

- Instantly
  "I'll hop behind that wheel and bingo!—I'm sober as a judge."
  —John Nichols, *The Magic Journey* (2000)

- Like magic
  "You can get a strange feeling that someone is on the way, or perhaps you suddenly feel compelled to do something, or go somewhere out of the ordinary—and bingo, there they are."
  —Susan Bowes, *Woman's Magic* (1999)

- This is it—Dotti Enderle, *The Burning Pendulum* (2005)

- Voilà
  "Now it's broken, now it's fixed. Now it's shells, now it's an egg. Bingo."
  —John R. Erickson, *Hank the Cowdog 24* (1995)

Facts: "Bingo" is the name of the hero in the parody novel *The Soddit* by A.R.R.R. Roberts (2003).

During a show at the Magic Castle, professional magician Tom Ogden called *bingo* "the magic word I learned in church."

Variations and Incantations:

- Bingo-zingo
  —Tim O'Brien, *In the Lake of the Woods* (1995)

- Lingo bingo
  "'Lingo bingo, Wordy itch, Hide yourself From Mother Witch!' POOF! The book disappeared."
  —Deborah Hautzig, *Little Witch Learns to Read* (2003)

In Literature:

- "You know it's been a good date if, at night's end, you find yourself thinking: 'Bingo!' Well, why not get the magic word out of the way earlier in the evening?"
  —Joshua Benton, "A Bottle of Pop, a Crispy Taco and Thou" (2002)

- "Jack fixed her with a trancelike gaze and chanted in the wizard's elderly irritable voice: 'Abracadabry, hocus-poo, Roger Skunk, how do you do, Roses, boses, pull an ear, Roger Skunk, you never fear: *Bingo!*'"
  —John Updike, "Should Wizard Hit Mommy?" *The Early Stories: 1953–1975* (2003)

Bip, Bomp, Bam Alakazam
(see also *alakazam*)

In Literature: This phrase is featured in Frankie Smith's song "Double Dutch Bus."

Blazimbo

Common Magician's Applications: Vanishing.

In Literature: "'You didn't say the magic word.' 'Huh?' In all her readings, Lucinda couldn't remember anything being said about a magic word. All words were supposed to be magic, if used properly. 'Blazimbo,' Xeno told her. 'If you want your magic to work, you've got to say Blazimbo.' Mabel snickered. 'You don't believe me?' Xeno asked. 'Watch.' Raising a perfectly manicured finger, he pointed it at Mabel. 'Blazimbo.' What happened next was, without question, the most amazing thing Lucinda had ever seen. One instant her best friend was standing by her side, the next she was gone. Vanished. Disappeared."
—Mike Baker, "Suffer a Witch," *100 Wicked Little Witch Stories* (2003)

Blessed Be
(see also *blessings*)

In Literature: "Forget hocus-pocus, abracadabra, and kaboom and begin transforming the world's 'Double, double toil and trouble' with your passionate 'Blessed be!'"
—Sarah Ban Breathnach, *Romancing the Ordinary* (2002)

Blessings

Mystique: Professional magician Kenton Knepper (The Mystic of Magic) says of the word *blessings*:

On stage and in personal life I often use this word, as I find it to be very powerful and magical. Many times I will sign my autograph with the word: *Blessings*. I do not define that word for others, as I have found that it has a power all its own. When I produce flowers or coins from the air, I remind the audience that it is important to count one's blessings. "For as you count your Blessings, so do you find yourself Blessed." One day I received an e-mail back from a person who was thrilled that they had "been Blessed." "I have never been Blessed before, let alone from the Mystic of Magic! What an honor. I feel different now, thinking of myself as Blessed." If you doubt the power of this word, when saying goodbye to a friend, say to them "Blessings!" Their reactions are worth observing. Use this word without a flip or degrading tone, naturally, and you will see that the word *Blessings* has Blessings of its own. All you have to do is use it to feel Blessed.[204]

Variations and Incantations: God bless you

"All you have to do is be the Light and assist anyone who comes to you. It's like saying three magic words: 'God bless you.' Then each person rises to the challenge of their own true self, their own Soul, their own God consciousness within."
—John-Roger, *Loving Each Day* (1989)

----

204 Personal correspondence (2005). The Mystic of Magic's website is *WonderWizards.com*.

Blickety Babka, Blackety Crow

In Literature: Deborah Hautzig, *Little Witch's Bad Dream* (2000)

Blitzyth Dorax Zooth

In Literature: "'Blitzyth, Dorax zooth!' he chanted. A bolt of energy exploded from the rod, crackling like a lightning bolt through the chapel."
—Douglas Niles, *Black Wizards* (2004)

Boneka
(see also *ranokoli*)

Meaning: The Great Spirit of Peace

In Literature: "[T]he chief invited a great council and organized the Society of the Magic Word. Every member promised that whenever the greeting 'Boneka' were given him, he would smile and bow and answer, 'Ranokoli.' The greeting meant 'Peace,' and the answer, 'I forgive.' Then, one by one, the law-giver called his councillors [sic] before him, and to each he said: 'The Great Spirit is in this greeting. I defy you to hear it and keep a sober face.' Then he said 'Boneka,' and the man would try to resist the influence of the spirit, but soon smiled in spite of himself, amid the laughter of the tribe, and said 'Ranokoli.' Thereafter, when a quarrel arose between two people, an outsider, approaching, would greet them with the magic word, and immediately they would bow and smile, and answer, 'I forgive.'"
—Irving Bacheller, *Silas Strong* (1906)

Boo

Common Magician's Applications: Transformation. For example, during a trick entitled "Fraidy Cat Rabbit," "The magician displays a black rabbit and places it into a large frame. The door to the frame is closed and the frame turned around, showing a brightly colored door on each side. The magic word 'Boo' is chanted, and when the door is opened, the black rabbit has turned white with fright."[205]

Boodoongapita

Origins: *Boodoongapita* originated in India.

In Literature: *Boodoongapita* is featured in a folk story about a fussy boy who learns from a traveling magician a magic word to make anything displeasing disappear.[206]

Booga Booga
(see also *ooga-booga*)

Facts: *Booga Booga* is a favorite magic phrase of professional magician Frank Tougas.[207]

The *Booga* hag is "a haunting spirit said to suck the soul out of you during the night," and may be scared away by indigo-colored doors.[208]

Variations and Incantations:

- Booga, wooga, cooga, booga, cooga, googa
  —Lois Griffith, *Action* (1997)

---

205 Bill Gormont, *EmpireMagic.com* (2004)
206 Gita Madhu, *TranslatorsCafe.com* (2004)
207 *TheMagicCafe.com* (2005)
208 Sue Monk Kidd, *The Mermaid Chair* (2005)

- Sanka dali; booga, booga
—Joe Nickell & James Randi, *The Mystery Chronicles: More Real-Life X-Files* (2004)

In Literature:

- "It was full of power it had stolen from me. It had the booga booga factor going for it."
—Jim Butcher, *Grave Peril* (2001)

- "Everything about the Djinn is one big, dark, booga-booga secret."
—Rachel Caine, *Windfall* (2005)

- "Sooner or later you gotta put on the gruesome mask and go booga-booga."
—Stephen King, *Danse Macabre* (1981)

Boogity Boogity Boo Yah

Facts: *Boogity Boogity BOO YAH!* is a favorite magic phrase of professional magician Professor Piper.[209]

Boohbah

Facts: This magic word, representing the power of imagination, is featured in the educational computer program "Boohbah" (2003) to stop action or make things happen.

Boom Boom Boom

Mystique: Like the explosions of fireworks, the magic words *boom boom boom* conjure a dazzling, threefold effect, each *boom* marking a transformation of energy.

Common Magician's Applications: Production. For example, "The magician covers the [mirror] glass with a silk, utters magic words, boom boom boom (secretly giving the glass a half-twist), and lifts off the silk to show the other compartment, the one filled with candy."[210]

Boomerang Toomerang Soomerang

Facts: This magic phrase is featured in the television series *Mister Rogers' Neighborhood*.

In Literature: "'Lady Elaine, please come back. We miss you!' 'Oh, sweet music to my ears,' said Lady Elaine, and then King Friday could hear her saying, 'Boomerang, toomerang, soomerang!' No sooner had she said the magic words and waved her magic boomerang than she and the Museum-Go-Round were right back in the Neighborhood of Make-Believe where they belonged."
—Fred Rogers, *Mister Rogers Talks With Parents* (1983)

Bouquet

Common Magician's Applications: Production of flowers.

In Literature: "'The tint is, perhaps, slightly pale. But the body is unquestionable. And as for the bouquet—' Ah, that magic Bouquet! How vividly that magic word recalled the scene! The little beggar boy turning his somersault in the road— the sweet little crippled maiden in my arm—the

209 *Ibid.*

210 Nathaniel Schiffman, *Abracadabra: Secret Methods Magicians and Others Use to Deceive Their Audience* (2005)

mysterious evanescent nursemaid—all rushed tumultuously into my mind, like the creatures of a dream: and through this mental haze there still boomed on, like the tolling of a bell, the solemn voice of the great connoisseur of WINE! Even his utterances had taken on themselves a strange and dream-like form."
—Lewis Carroll, *Sylvie and Bruno Concluded* (1889)

Brahman

Mystique: "Brahman was, at first, nothing else than the sacred word itself in the magic hymn and in the sacred myth; it was the magic word of power, the priests set in motion, which they attributed to the gods themselves and exalted above the gods, which they associated with the forces and the processes of nature, until it became identified—still in a mystic sense—with the ultimate principle of the world and nature itself."[211]

Meanings: "The word 'brahman' is the greatest word in the whole history of Indian Philosophy. On it hangs largely the development of Indian thought. The meanings assigned to it are numerous and bewildering. It has been explained and translated by such various terms as worship, devotion, fervor, prayer, hymn, charm, incantation, sanctity, holiness, priesthood, spiritual exaltation, sacred writ, Veda, Vedic formula, priestly order, holy work, priestly dignity, inspiration, force, spiritual power, ultimate reality, absolute. Thus it seems to mean almost anything."[212]

Breakfast

In Literature: "The magic word 'Breakfast' came simultaneously from them."
—H.G. Wells, *The Research Magnificent* (1915)

<Breath>

Mystique: "'While there's breath, there's life,' we say; and ever since Old Testament days it has seemed that the breath we inhale and exhale must in some way be the agent or carrier of life itself— a dollop of lifeless clay being transformed into a living being when the Divine Creator infuses the Breath of Life into its nostrils."[213] We can easily imagine that magicians have used puffs of breath to initiate magical effects since time immemorial. Modern-day magicians almost universally include a puff of breath to make magic happen, especially during silent performances. Such a breath acts as a silent magic word. The concept of breath as a creative force or divine spiritual energy is common to a great many religions and spiritual traditions. A puff of breath can be used to send energy "with a gentle power from within, rather like a kiss."[214]

Facts: "[T]hroughout the history of global magical practice, shamans employed their healing methods through the techniques of 'sucking' and 'blowing' air on and around patients. In the East, the control of one's personal flow of air is a central practice in the disciplines of yoga and tantric magic."[215]

211 Jean J. Waardenburg, *Classical Approaches to the Study of Religion* (1999)

212 Hervey DeWitt Griswold, *Brahman: A Study on the History of Indian Philosophy* (1900)

213 Stephen Toulmin and June Goodfield, *The Architecture of Matter* (1962)

214 Ann Moura/Aoumiel, *Green Magic: The Sacred Connection to Nature* (2003)

215 Timothy Roderick, *Wicca: A Year and a Day* (2005)

"Throughout the world, ancient tales talk of the Witches' Breath. More predominant in old Gaelic folklore, the breath of witches or wise-women was said to have magical properties. She could heal a wound with her breath. She could breathe life into a newly-born babe and take breath from the dying to ease their journey to the Summerlands."[216]

Common Magician's Applications: Breath is used as a magical trigger in a variety of tricks, including:

- Card effects
  "Addressing the spectator you say, 'Have you a magic breath? Well I will show you how to find out. If you have you can send your card to whatever position you please merely by breathing gently on the cards. Will you choose a number? Nine? Then just blow on the pack and think intently of that number as you blow.'"
  —Jean Hugard, *Encyclopedia of Card Tricks* (1937)

- Coin transformation
  "'A nickel is made from a rather soft metal,' remarks the performer. 'In fact, it is so soft that if I take it in my left hand and blow on it, it immediately becomes so malleable that I can, by slapping it onto my right hand, flatten it out like a pancake.'"
  —J.B. Bobo, *Modern Coin Magic* (1952)
     In his television special *Street Magic* (1997), professional magician David Blaine borrows a quarter from a spectator, takes a bite out of it, then blows on the coin to magically restore it visually.

- Linking and unlinking
  "Take the set of three [Chinese linking rings], folded together; hold the rings up in the left hand, blow on them, and let them fall one by one, linked."
  —Jean Hugard, *Hugard's Magic Manual* (1939)

- Unknotting
  "Place the hands on either side of the slip knot. Blow on the knot. At the same time, pull the hands apart, causing the knot to dissolve."
  —Karl Fulves, *Self-Working Rope Magic* (1990)

In Literature:

- "The power of magic is often believed to have resided in the breath or speech of the magician. . . . The basic idea in pronouncing spells and some other forms of magic is the power of the magician to produce results through his power of 'speech.'"
  —Morris Gross, "The Relation of Blessing and Cursing in the Psalms to the Evolution of Hebrew Religion" (1934), quoted in *Ritual Medical Lore of Sephardic Women* by Isaac Jack Levy (2002)

- "There is intrinsic magic in our breath. After all, it is the breath of life. Each one of us was formed by the breath. At birth, the breath of life must be forced from us to begin our normal breathing. A slap on the bottom usually starts us breathing. When we approach death, we cease breathing. Somebody can breathe life back into us, however, to return us to life."
  —Von Braschler, *Natural Pet Healing: Our Psychic, Spiritual Connection* (2003)

- "My wife has magic power, and if she blows her breath against your ships, she won't leave a person or animal, sheep or lamb or horse, alive within a distance of a hundred miles of any lake or sea."
  —"Céatach," as retold by Sean O'Sullivan in *Folktales of Ireland* (1966)

---

216 Janet Thompson, *Magical Hearth: Home for the Modern Pagan* (1995)

Brhaspati

Origins: "In the Vedic religion the gods are often represented as attaining their ends by magical means; in particular the god Brhaspati, 'the creator of all prayers,' is regarded as 'the heavenly embodiment of the priesthood, in so far as the priesthood is invested with the power, and charged with the task, of influencing the course of things by prayers and spells'; in short, he is 'the possessor of the magical power of the holy word.'"[217]

Bricklebrit

Origins: *Bricklebrit* is of German origin.

Facts: This magic word for the production of gold is featured in the Grimm's fairy tale "Gold-Donkey."

Brother

In Literature: "*Brother* . . . a magic word if I've ever seen one, abracadabra be damned."
—Eric Garcia, *Casual Rex* (2002)

Brumagem

In Literature: "What was the word—the magic word? Brumagem—that was it—Brumagem. An enchanting word! . . . A word to be repeated over to himself softly and secretly at night at the same time as Damn and Corsets."
—Agatha Christie, *Giant's Bread* (1930)

Brump Flump Clump

Facts: This is a magic phrase for materializing a bright yellow bulldozer in *Oral Storytelling and Teaching Mathematics* by Michael Schiro (2004).

Bunkum

All your magic is bunkum.
—Arthur Waley,
Monkey: A Folk-Tale of China (1942)

Meanings:

- Nonsense

- Outstanding, excellent
  —David K. Barnhart, *America in So Many Words* (1997)

Origins: Bunkum derives from the name Buncombe, a county in North Carolina which, in 1819, had a notoriously long-winded Representative.[218]

Variations and Incantations:

- bunco (meaning to swindle)

- bunk (nonsense)
  "History is bunk"
  —Henry Ford

217 James George Frazer, *The Golden Bough: A Study in Magic and Religion* (1890)

218 David K. Barnhart, *American in So Many Words* (1997)

In Literature:

- "Cara picks up her well-thumbed book of magic spells and flicks through the pages until she stops at a particular hex and smiles contentedly. 'Are you sure we should be doing this?' I don't believe in this load of old bunkum, but I wouldn't want Cara to conjure up something nasty with several heads and a spiteful nature in our living room."
—Carole Matthews, *Bare Necessity* (2003)

- "I remember it well! Its horn handle, so smooth and clear, glowing with the unmeaning, but magic word, '*Bunkum*;' and the blade significantly inviting you to the test, by the two monosyllables, '*Try me.*'"
—Charles W. Sanders, *Sanders' Union Fourth Reader* (1864)

But

Mystique: "[T]here's one word that is both splendid and terrible and I often ponder its mystery. The word is 'but.' A traffic cop of a word. A word of terror and beauty. For instance: 'I'd love to go out with you Saturday night, but . . .' 'You certainly have all the qualifications for the job, but . . .' Or: 'It was a lovely Christmas, but . . .' But—and there's the magic of the word—it can also be used in marvelous ways: 'I had planned to go away this weekend, but . . .' Or: 'We really didn't have an opening at the moment, but . . .' Or: 'The X rays do show a shadow there, but . . .' Or: 'I'm going to be busy until ten o'clock, but . . .' Thus it can be a word of hope."[219]

Professional magician Kenton Knepper (The Mystic of Magic) considers *but* "one of those power words people use against themselves and others with few being aware of this fact. The word 'but' tends to cancel out or erase what is said before it, and suggests that what follows it is the actual truth. I know at first you may not believe that, but such is the case as science has proved. If you ever were told, 'I love you but, you sure can be a pain' or 'I love you but . . .' followed by anything—chances are you focused on what was wrong with you. Rarely would you feel that you were loved. The words 'I love you' are canceled out because they are followed with the word 'but.' What you are likely to take to heart is what follows this: 'you are a pain' or 'you are so lazy.' In performance magic we use this to help people forget things we wish them not to remember, or to ensure they do not do something. 'You could look at the deck but what would it matter?' offers a seeming chance and then takes the option away stealthily. Next time you ask a friend for help and they refuse, see if they don't indeed try to have it both ways by saying something along the lines of: 'I'd love to help you BUT I have plans that day already.' Your friend may be willing to help usually, but the message this time is unmistakable and indirectly given: NO."[220]

In Literature: "Then the magic word appears, 'but.'"
—Tonya Denise Allen, *Words of Wisdom* (2001)

By Jingo
(see also *jingo*)

Meanings:

- Euphemism for the name of God; an oath
"'Why not?' he asked. 'Why not, by Jingo?'"
—T.H. White, *The Once and Future King* (1939)

- Surprise

------

219 Robert Cormier, *I Have Words to Spend: Reflections of a Small-Town Editor* (1994)

220 Personal correspondence (2005). The Mystic of Magic's website for magicians only is *Wonder Wizards.com*.

Common Magician's Applications: Production.

Variations and Incantations:

- By gee, by gosh, by jingo
  "[H]e whistled the ballad 'Oh, by gee, by gosh, by jingo' as though it were a hymn melancholy and noble."
  —Sinclair Lewis, *Babbitt* (1921)

- By jingo by gee by gosh by gum
  —e.e. cummings, "next to of course god america i" (1926)

- By the living jingo
  —Sir Arthur Conan Doyle, *The Return of Sherlock Holmes* (1903)

- High jingo!
  —Michael Connelly, *The Closers* (2005)

In Literature:

- "By jingo, that would be awful!"
  —James Joyce, *Ulysses* (1922)

- "I shall never forget it; by Jingo, it has served me for a most excellent good joke ever since."
  —Fanny Burney, *Evelina* (1778)

- "[B]y Jingo was not my Lolita a child!"
  —Vladimir Nabokov, *Lolita* (1955)

- "By jingo, I'm kerfoozled!"
  —Brian Jacques, *Lord Brocktree* (2001)

C

Cadabra
(see *abracadabra* and *kadabra*)

[He talked] such a curious, gentle, primeval cadabra that it drew her toward some violent unknown whirlpool and made her hum and shake.
—Barbara Trapido, *Temples of Delight* (1990)

Mystique: *Cadabra* is that flash when your mind is blown, like a hit of a powerful drug—"Sniff, cadabra," as novelist Rachel Timms puts it.[221] The word has an aura of necromancy to it, with its similarity to *cadaver.* It has all the impact of the longer word *abracadabra*, but without any dilly-dallying—it goes straight for the punch.

Meanings: Scholar William Isaacs explains that *cadabra* can be broken up into two root words: "*Ca* translates to 'as.' *Dabra* is the first person of the verb *daber*, 'to speak.'"[222] So *cadabra* means "as I speak," equivalent to "upon my command."

Facts: Jeff Bezos, the founder of the internet bookstore Amazon.com "originally planned to call the company Cadabra—a reference to the magic incantation. Fortunately for him, his friends convinced him that, while the name might have spellbinding connotations, it also sounded very similar to 'cadaver.'"[223]

Common Magician's Applications: Triggering. For example: "With your finger under his chin, gently push his chin up as you say '*Cadabra,*

---

221 *Whatever You Want* (2003)
222 *Dialogue: The Art Of Thinking Together* (1999)
223 Daniel Goleman, *Business: The Ultimate Resource* (2002)

now lift.' Be careful: you don't want to use a lot of pressure. Push just enough to move his head up, just before you say your magic words."[224]

Variations and Incantations:

- Cadavra
  The horror-comedy film *The Lost Skeleton of Cadavra* released in 2001.

- Kadabra

- Kedavra

In Literature:

- "When politicians prophesy that prices will float to their correct levels, they sound like magicians chanting prophecies that 'abra will rise, cadabra will fall.'"
  —Martin Feldstein, *New Ideas from Dead Economists* (1989)

- "The password to get into Abulafia had to be seven letters or fewer. Letters or numbers. How many groups of seven could be made from all the letters of the alphabet, including the possibility of repetition, since there was no reason the word couldn't be 'cadabra'? I knew the formula. The number was six billion and something."
  —Umberto Eco, *Foucault's Pendulum* (1988)

Cadabra-Abra
(see also *abra*, *cadabra*, and *abracadabra*)

Facts: This word is a transposed form of *abracadabra*.

Common Magician's Applications: Production. For example: "The magician says the magic words, 'Abracadabra,' lifts the glass and places it

(still face down) over the quarter. Suddenly, the quarter vanishes! Next the magician asks the audience to say the magic word . . . backwards ('CadabraAbra'). As this is said, he lifts the glass and places it where it was when the trick began. Once again the coin can be seen."[225]

Variations and Incantations: Ca-dab-rah-abra

"Scratch your head and say, 'I forgot to use the magic word. Let's see, I think it was CA-DAB-RAH-ABRA.'"
—Loris Bree, *Kids' Magic Secrets* (2003)

Canton, Hankow

Facts: *Canton* is an old English name for the Chinese city of Guangzhou. *Hankou* is a port town in Hubei province, China.

In Literature: "The President of the Club paused a moment to dwell on the magical words, and then repeated them, almost whispering. 'Canton and Hankow.'"
—William Saroyan, *Human Comedy* (1943)

Caterpillar

The magic word, caterpillar
—A.A. Milne, "Not that it Matters" (1920)

Mystique: The caterpillar dramatically transforms into a butterfly.
Facts: The Aztec word for the sacred cactus, *peyote,* means *caterpillar.*[226]

---

224 Loris Bree, *Kids' Magic Secrets* (2003)

225 Charles Kraus ("Charles the Magician") (2005)
226 Mary Crow Dog, *Lakota Woman* (1990)

Cei-u

Facts: *Cei-u* (pronounced "say you") is the magic word that gives comic book character Johnny Thunder (*Flash Comics*, 1940) the power to summon the Thunderbolt (his magical partner who appears as a puff of pink smoke).

Cha-Ka-Zoop-Ala-Zimba-Bam

Common Magician's Applications: Triggering, as recommended by magicians Ray Broekel and Laurence B. White Jr. in *Abra-ca-dazzle* (1982).

Chango

Mystique: *Chango* summons a great change. "Magical words are necessary for things to change. The chant and incantation must be said for the magic to happen. Potential is released through the initiation of vibration that can be felt with the whole body. . . . Vibration is both inside and out; everywhere. It is acausal. It is always there though sometimes too low to hear. The horns of the Tibetan lamas, the bells and fish knockers of Buddhists, the bells of cathedrals, and the call to pray from minarets; all of these disturb the cosmic silence announcing human being."[227]

Consider the incantation of change from *Merlin's Calling* (2002) by Mart Ettin:

> The magical words and melodious sounds that [we] create . . . are strung together into harmonies that resonate with the lively world all around us. . . .The mystery of our thoughts and words become incantations uttered in verse . . . In reverie, I sound out the changes that life brings and the changes that bring life. . . .
>
> *Change comes 'round through sudden twists of fate*
> *Change comes 'round with plans gone out of date*
> *Change comes 'round when lovers meet their mate*
> *Change comes 'round when love transforms to hate*
>
> *Change comes 'round with seasons here and gone*
> *Change comes 'round when dusk gives way to dawn*
> *Change comes 'round when salmon swim to spawn*
> *Change comes 'round when out of dark, light's born*
> . . .
> *Change comes 'round with the tracing of a maze*
> *Change comes 'round with the lifting of a haze*
> *Change comes 'round in a call for better days*
> *Change comes 'round in labyrinthian ways*

Ettin's verse makes for illuminating storytelling during magic routines showcasing changes.

Meanings: Change

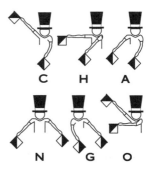

Figure 16. Silk flourishes can spell magic words. Here, *chango* is spelled through the semaphore flag signaling system. Semaphore adds mystique and meaning to even the simplest silk routines.

---

227 Eric Mark Kramer, *Modern/Postmodern: Off the Beaten Path of Antimodernism* (1997)

Facts: This magic word is typically spoken in conjunction with *presto*, to mean "change quickly."

In Santeria cosmology, *Chango* is the name of the ruler of thunder and lightning as well as virility.

In Chinese mythology, *Chang-O* is the name of an ancient sage who attained divinity during the T'ang dynasty.

Chango means "monkey" in Spanish.

Chazzerai

Origins: *Chazzerai* is of Yiddish origin, meaning "rubbish."

In Literature: "[W]ith a wave and the magical word chazzerai."
—Suzanne Finnamore, *Otherwise Engaged* (1999)

Cheereeboo Cheereebah Cheereebee

Origins: This magic phrase originated in Hungary.[228]

In Literature: Henning Nelms, *Magic and Showmanship: A Handbook for Conjurers* (1969)

Ching Ching Gada-Ching Gada-Gada-Ching

In Literature: "I picked up the dorje and chanted a bit—nonsense words, Asiatic sounding, insectile, similar to what I recalled of the Secoya language, came into my head and I called them out. 'Ching! Ching! Gada-ching! Gada-gada-ching!'"
—Daniel Pinchbeck, "Breaking Open the Head," excerpted in *Book of Lies* by Richard Metzger (2003)

Chittery-Chattery-Chongerty-Chee

In Literature: "Bastinda raised the wand with her left hand. Pointing it skyward she chanted, '*Chittery-chattery-chongerty-chee.*'"
—Sherwood Smith, *The Emerald Wand of Oz* (2005)

Chosi

Origins: *Chosi* is of African origin. Fatima Dike explains that when a mother would tell her child a bedtime story from African folklore, she first required the child to say the protective magic word *chosi*. "Especially if the story is told in the daytime. So you have got to say 'chosi,' the magic word. In the daytime, it's the word that stops all the evil fairies from giving you horns because you are telling stories in the daytime. In the evening, you say 'I am paying attention, please go on, I want to hear.'"[229]

---

228 Henning Nelms, *Magic and Showmanship: A Handbook for Conjurers* (1969)

229 Quoted in *South African Theatre: As/And Intervention*, edited by Marcia Blumberg and Dennis Walder (1999)

Christmas

Variations and Incantations: Pretty-bitty please with Christmas trees

"'What are the magic words'? Her children squealed with delight. 'Pretty-bitty please with Christmas trees!'"
—R.L. Stine, *More & More & More Tales to Give You Goosebumps* (1997)

In Literature:

- "Soon I shall be far away in Croydon; alas, unhappy fate which sends me from the few people with whom my heart would wish to stay. But Christmas!—that is the magic word I conjure with."
  —D.H. Lawrence (1908), *The Letters of D. H. Lawrence: Volume 1, September 1901–May 1913* (1979)

- "Charlene handcuffed Eddie, who got into the trunk. She locked the trunk and roped it shut. Then, swiftly, she brought out a screen and put it in front of the trunk. The crowd buzzed with excitement while Charlene walked back and forth across the stage, posing like a game-show hostess on TV. She checked her watch dramatically, then called to the audience. 'Say the magic words, y'all: "Merry Christmas!"' 'Merry Christmas!' the crowd shouted. . . . Amazin' pushed the screen back and held his arms over his head, the handcuffs dangling from one wrist. The trunk was still padlocked and roped shut."
  —Cherie Bennett, *Searching for David's Heart* (1998)

Chudley

In Literature: "Wave your hands around and say some magic words. ('Chudley!')"
—Bart King, *The Big Book of Boy Stuff* (2004)

Cigam Si Noisulli Dna Noisulli Si Efil

Facts: This is professional magician Tony Thompson's favorite magic phrase. He explains: "If you say that from right to left it's 'Magic is illusion, and illusion is life.'"[230]

Circulus Rotundus
(see also *rotundus reversus double plus*)

Origins: This magic phrase is Latin for "round circle."

Common Magician's Applications: Linking rings. For example, "[N]ow I'll use a magic spell. *Circulus Rotundus!* . . . Aha! The two loops are linked!"[231]

<Clapping Sound>

Facts: Professional magician Michael Matson suggests that claps from the audience can be effective triggers for magic effects. He encourages magicians to have their audiences clap as an alternative to speaking a magic word or waving a magic wand. He explains: "When I perform the

---

230 From a 1998 interview
231 Janice Eaton Kilby, *Book of Wizard Magic* (2003)

serpentine silk effect, wherein a handkerchief was tied into a knot and magically animates to untie itself, I have the audience clap in order to make the magic happen. I claim that their clapping wakes up the handkerchief and causes it to move by itself. I urge the audience to clap very loud and fast, saying that the louder and faster they clap the sooner the magic will happen! Of course, I milk the effect and have the handkerchief untie itself rather slowly compared to the audience's rate of clapping. While the audience is still clapping at the conclusion of the effect, I smile slyly and take a huge bow while shouting 'Thank You' as though all of the applause is just for me! This always gets a few laughs." Matson also likes to use hand claps as a trigger while performing the rising cards, the haunted matchbox, the rising wand, and other such feats of magic that animate the inanimate.[232]

---

232 Matson adds: "The animation of the inanimate is a very strong feat of magic. When you can apparently turn an inanimate object into something alive and responsive to the environment, it can appear as though the object is enchanted and the magic is happening without any obvious means of control on the part of the magician. Every time I think of this concept I am reminded of the story 'Beauty and the Beast,' wherein characters were transformed into objects such as clocks, candlesticks, tea pots, and cups. These household objects came to life and interacted with other characters, which brings a greatly appealing magical quality to the story. Keep this in mind the next time you witness or perform magic where objects seem to move by themselves or have life-like characteristics such as the serpentine silk, rising wand, rising cards, haunted matchbox, etc. Make your magic come alive!"—Michael Matson, personal correspondence (2005). Matson further discusses clapping triggers on his website *MichaelMatson.biz*.

Common Magician's Applications: Triggering. For example: "The performer, wearing a *borrowed* coat, is handcuffed (hands behind) by a member of the audience, who may use his own irons. He is then placed in a sack, the mouth of which is tied, *and sealed with private seal*, above his head by any person present. In this condition the performer is lifted bodily into a solid mahogany brass-bound trunk, which, having been subjected to a thorough examination, is now corded and double-locked, and keys retained by audience. To make things DOUBLE sure, this box, which actually contains the performer—there are no stage or scene traps employed—is now lifted into another similar solid mahogany brass-bound trunk, also thoroughly examined by the audience, corded, and cords sealed *anywhere desired by audience*, also double-locked, and keys retained by audience. The double trunk containing the performer is now lifted into a curtained enclosure, absolutely devoid of trickery, as is the stage under it. The performer's assistant, usually a lady, now says: 'I will enter the cabinet and clap my hands three times, and you will please notice the effect.' This the lady does, and, WITHIN ONE SECOND after the third clap, the curtains are drawn asunder, and—lo, and behold!—the PERFORMER HIMSELF emerges free, but in his shirt sleeves,

Figure 17. The hand clap represents primal power, as in this woodcut from 1697 emblem book. In clapping as in prayer, hands come together when opposites unite.

i.e., minus the borrowed coat. On the trunks' being opened, the lady is discovered tied and sealed in the sack *only three seconds ago* occupied by the performer. She is handcuffed (hands behind) with the same irons, and—miracle of miracles—she is wearing the same *borrowed* coat, and *all seals are intact.*"[233]

Clatto Verata Nicto

(see also *Barrada Nikto*)

Origins: This phrase makes reference to "Klaatu, Barada, Nikto," used to command the robot Gort in the film *The Day the Earth Stood Still* (1951).

Facts: These magic words are used to claim the *Book of the Dead* in the film *Army of Darkness* (1993).

Close Your Fingers and Cross Your Eyes

Facts: These words begin a spell to create a rabbit in the *Bewitched* television series. The spell continues: "Get Ready for a Big Surprise; The Rain Is Dry, the Night Is Sunny; Hold and Behold a Cottontail Bunny!" The spell to get rid of a rabbit is as follows: "Close your fingers and cross your eyes. Get ready for a new surprise. Bats in the belfry, pigs in a poke. Lose this bunny before I choke."

Club in a Sack

Mystique: *Club in a sack* recalls the fertility rites associated with early magic, the club symboliz-

ing the male reproductive organ, the sack symbolizing the womb, and the two joined in sacred union.

In Literature: "[The] youngest brother [in the Grimm fairy tale 'The Magic Table, the Golden Donkey, and the Club in the Sack'] becomes a wood-turner, but his reward, upon completing his apprenticeship, is neither food nor money; instead, it is a 'club in a sack.' Whenever the owner of this enchanted object utters these magic words, a club immediately jumps out of the bag and, prancing around, begins to beat mercilessly anyone who happens to be standing nearby."
—Valerie Paradiz, *Clever Maids: The Secret History of the Grimm Fairy Tales* (2005)

Coincidentia Oppositorum

Meanings: Fusion of opposites; reconciliation of contraries

The magical phrase *"coincidentia oppositorum"* can either be dismissed as nonsense or extolled as dialectical profundity. With reference to the absolute to which the idea is supposed to lead us, it remains ambiguous. At times it seems to mean: God is the coincidence of opposites. At other times the idea is only a springboard from which we are supposed to leap in order to touch the absolute—no one can tell how. But whoever makes the leap falls back to his starting point. . . . This ambiguity hints at a reality the truth of which comes to life only within ourselves through our thinking, yet which is not present merely because we think.
—Karl Jaspers, *Anselm and Nicholas of Cusa* (1974)

---

233 Ellis Stanyon, *Magic* (1903)

Origins: These magic words were discussed by the Christian philosopher Nicholas of Cusa (Nikolaus Krebs) (1401–1464).

Coldpot

HARRY: What's the magic word?
MIDGIE: Coldpot!
—Mary Chase, *Midgie Purvis* (1963)

Mystique: With the purity of a singing bowl, this mystic word resonates alchemy and conjures images of a witch's cauldron. Recalling the "cold pot" of metallurgy, this odd compound word fuses a rounded form ("pot") with a degree of intensity ("cold"), suggesting alchemical coagulation.[234] Indeed, *coldpot* is brimming with expectations, unlikelihoods, fulfillments of high commands, and even a dollop of danger.

Like black holes bending the very fabric of space, cold pots are famous for disrupting the flow of time. Lest you forget, "Nothing makes time pass more slowly than waiting for a cold pot to boil."[235] The quaint folk wisdom that a watched pot won't boil actually speaks to the "observer effect" in physics, in which the act of witnessing changes the beheld phenomenon. It's as if the cold pot is saying, "Don't look at me—I'm merely the vehicle for the change you desire. Focus on what's important, and take all the time you need."

A cold pot calls for a spark, as the Sufi mystics have said. For "fire is put under the cold pot, not the pot which is boiling over."[236] Ignition and expectation—both are at the heart of the magic word *coldpot*. Within the word itself is contained the possibility of highly-unlikely events coming to pass. Statistically speaking, "a cold pot of water could spontaneously come to a boil; it is simply not very likely. But unlikely events are quasi-certain to happen if we wait long enough."[237] The sparkling occurrence of highly-unlikely events is the very heart of magic.

Granted, *coldpot* resonates with risk, as one is "especially [to] avoid pouring hot water into a cold pot"[238] so as to avoid "rapid and uneven thermal expansion, which can easily crack the pot."[239] A cold pot would seem to demand the basic principle of homeopathy: "like with like" (cold water being best suited to a cold pot). The fact that "we can see water condense on the outside of a cold pot placed over a gas flame"[240] further illustrates the concept of "like with like." A cold pot also demands that a process (such as the heating of water) occur in its proper time (slowly warming by degrees). In terms of magic, the word *coldpot* testifies to an effect occurring in the fullness of time, according to resonant coincidences ("like with like").

The "fuzzy logic" of hybrid system science helps to illuminate how a cold pot clears one's mind of base instincts and allows high-level mental commands (what we might call the intentions of spellworking) to be carried out unhindered by reflexes (what we might liken to undermining distractions). Physicist Michael Branicky explains:

> Consider the act of picking up a pot on the stove. You plan to pick the pot off the burner and place it on a plate. On a lower level, your brain commands your muscles to perform the task. If all is

234 For example, "a cold pot full of something congealed" is described in *The Heirs* by G. Y. Dryansky (1978)

235 This old saying is recalled by Leon Uris in *A God in Ruins* (2000)

236 Jalal al-Din Rumi, *Tales from the Masnavi* (1961)

237 Herman Daly and Joshua Farley, *Ecological Economics* (2003)

238 Thomas J. Elpei, *Participating in Nature* (2002)

239 A. D. Livingston, *Duck and Goose Cookbook* (1997)

240 Knut Schmidt-Nielsen, *Animal Physiology: Adaptation and Environment* (1997)

right, you perform the task as planned. However, if the pot is too hot, your reflexes will override the "higher level planning" and command your hand to move quickly away from the danger of getting burned. A low level intelligence (your reflexes) refuses to carry out the "higher level" plans, saving you some pain. However, they only act when it is necessary to do so. Your hand does not jerk away from a cold pot.[241]

From neural nets to the web of magic, a cold pot speaks of the fulfillment of high commands, unencumbered by base instincts.

Consider these intriguing lines by the poet Tristan Corbiere which take us back to the witch's cauldron:

For us the cold pot the kettle calls black,
Our gall ladled out is our only surplus.
To be sure it's for that, not the honey-pot, I'm
covetous.[242]

Corbiere begins by turning a familiar saying inside out. Instead of "the pot calling the kettle black," he suggests that we are the cold pot that the kettle calls black. He places us inside the sacred space of the pot. The ladling out of gall alludes to entrails tossed into the pot (à la the classic recipe of the three "weird sisters" in Shakespeare's *Macbeth*). Transmuted by the alchemy of the pot, our gall (literally our bitterness) is purified and sweetly released. Here, described in three short lines, is the Magnum opus of the cold pot. Base matter transforms into golden honey.

Speaking of sisters around a cauldron in *Macbeth*, in the Santal language "cold pot" is the name for a tribe of girls.[243] The name refers to a

creation myth about how the children of the first human pair met. It's the perfect name for any community that dares to begin "stirring a cold pot and stok[ing] a long-dead fire that would get things going, the outcome of which was unknown, and couldn't even be guessed at."[244]

In Literature:

- "My mouth is parched for want of a cold pot."
—Anthony Burgess, *Nothing Like the Sun* (1964)

- "You've always got to start with a cold pot."
—Ronni Lundy, *Shuck Beans, Stack Cakes, and Honest Fried Chicken* (1994)

Colloportus

Origins: *Colloportus* combines two Latin words meaning "bind together" (*colligere*) and "door" (*portus*).

In Literature: *Colloportus* is used to magically seal a door in the *Harry Potter* novels by J.K. Rowling.

Command

Command is a strong magic.
—Joseph Conrad, *The Shadow Line* (1915)

When I speak, let magic begin.
What I command, be held within.
—Patricia Telesco, *Goddess in my Pocket* (1998)

Mystique: In *The French Revolution: A History* (1837), Thomas Carlyle describes how an authoritative word of command is literally a magic spell that can work wonders. "Discipline we called a

241 "On-line, Reflexive Constraint Satisfaction for Hybrid Systems: First Steps," in Oded Maler (Ed.), *Hybrid and Real-Time Systems* (1997)

242 "Paris By Day," *The Centenary Corbiere* (2003)

243 Paul Olaf Bodding, *A Santal Dictionary* (1936)

244 Ralph Hunter, *Winter's Stormy Rage* (2001)

kind of miracle: in fact, is it not miraculous how one man moves hundreds of thousands; each unit of whom it may be loves him not, and singly fears him not, yet has to obey him, to go hither or go thither, to march and halt, to give death, and even to receive it, as if a Fate had spoken; and the word of command becomes, almost in the literal sense, a magic-word? Which magic-word, again, if it be once forgotten; the spell of it once broken! The legions of assiduous ministering spirits rise on you now as menacing fiends; your free orderly arena becomes a tumult-place of the Nether Pit, and the hapless magician is rent limb from limb."

Meanings:

- An authoritative order that brooks no disobedience

- The Word of God

In Literature:

- "It's a good step from the Officers' Home to the Harbour Office; but with the magic word 'Command' in my head I found myself suddenly on the quay as if transported there in the twinkling of an eye, before a portal of dressed white stone above a flight of shallow white steps. . . . The broad inner staircase insinuated itself under my feet somehow. Command is a strong magic."
  —Joseph Conrad, *The Shadow Line* (1915)

- "Magic ball bounce high, I command you."
  —Jim Wiese, *Magic Science* (1998)

- "By the powers of ancient Goll, I command this carpet to fly!"
  —Tony Abbott, *Secrets of Droon 13* (2001)

- "By the Lords of Magic, I command you to stop."
  —Andrew Attias, *Bogg* (2002)

Compound Interest

Facts: This is a magic phrase recommended by professional magician Karl Fulves for tricks involving bankbooks. For example, when making a coin magically travel from a deposit slip to a bankbook, he suggests: "All I have to do is say the magic words 'Compound Interest,' you remark. As you say this, wave the pen over your pocket and over the bankbook. Remove the paper from your pocket and tear it to bits to show that the coin has vanished. Then tip the bankbook, allowing the coin to slide out into view."[245]

Confidence

Mystique: The magic word *confidence* suggests mutual trust, certainty of truth, self-assurance, and the sharing of secret matters.

Origins: The word *confidence* is derived from the Latin *confidere*, meaning "have full trust."

In Literature: "The magical words 'in confidence' seemed to be a kind of Open Sesame."
—Agatha Christie, *Dumb Witness* (1937)

Confundus

Origins: *Confundus* is from the Latin word meaning "to perplex" (*condfundo*).

In Literature: *Confundus* is a confusion spell in *Harry Potter and the Goblet of Fire* by J.K. Rowling (2000).

245 *Self-Working Paper Magic* (1985)

Constantinople

Mystique: Tell us about Constantinople! . . . Is it true the streets are paved with precious stones, and the fountains spew liquid gold?
—Donna Cross, *Pope Joan* (1996)

Place names, especially ones steeped in history (like the "wonders of the ancient world"), are potent with magic. Several books[246] discuss the primordial magic power inherent in naming things. Suffice it to say that names "have an occult associative and symbolic power. They are charms."[247] Now called Istanbul, Constantinople is the former Byzantine capital. "Byzantium is the 'magic place,'"[248] a picturesque, romantic city that has served as the "bridge between east and west" and "the crossroads of the universe."[249]

Origins: *Constantinople* took its name from the Roman Emperor Constantine, who moved the capital of the Roman empire to Byzantium in 324 CE.[250]

Facts: This is the magic word that crooked hypnotist "Voltan Polgar" uses to hypnotize Woody Allen's character in the film *The Curse of the Jade Scorpion* (2001).

Contact

Meanings: *Contact* is an electrical connection, an activation through physical touch.

In Literature: "And then, with less than seconds left, came the magic word: 'Contact!' Armstrong spoke first: 'Tranquility Base here, the Eagle has landed.'"
—John Jackman and Wendy Wren, *Nelson English: Student Book 5* (1996)

Crack Cronk Crooky

Facts: This is a magic phrase for materializing a parrot in *Oral Storytelling and Teaching Mathematics* by Michael Schiro (2004).

Crazzabelam

Facts: This is a magic word granting invisibility, as discussed in *Writing Prompts* by Justin McCory Martin (2001).

Creativity
(see also *abracadabra*)

Mystique: *Creativity* is at the heart of that grand magic word *abracadabra*: "I create as I speak." John William Gardner notes that *creativity* is a magic word that people use as an incantation to empower innovation, and that *creativity* (like *abracadabra* before it) has become vulgarized over time even though its deeper meaning retains the power to liberate. Gardner explains: "When we speak of the individual as a source of renewal, we call to mind the magic word *creativity*—a word of dizzying popularity at the moment. It is more than a word today; it is an incantation. People think of it as a kind of psychic wonder drug, powerful and presumably painless; and everyone wants a prescription. It is one of our national

246 See *Magic in Names and Other Things* (1920) and *The Language of Names* (1997).

247 Justin Kaplan, *The Language of Names* (1997)

248 Helen Vendler, quoted in *Hagia Sophia, 1850–1950* by Robert S. Nelson (2004)

249 Stephen Turnbull, *The Walls of Constantinople AD 324–1453* (2004)

250 *Ibid.*

vices to corrupt and vulgarize any word or idea that seems to have significance or relevance or freshness. And so we have done with the word *creativity*. But that should not lead us to neglect the idea behind the word. Granted that much of the current interest in the subject is shallow. Still it is more than a fad. It is part of a growing resistance to the tyranny of the formula, a new respect for individuality, a dawning recognition of the potentialities of the liberated mind."[251]

Creo Herbamus Satisfus

Facts: This magic phrase is a pseudo-Latin spell meaning "satiate the person in question."

In Literature: Balanced Alternative Technologies Multi-User Dimension, *Bat.org* (2004)

Cullen, Rayburn, Narz, Trebek

Facts: This is a spell that conjures zombies (actually names of game show hosts: Bill Cullen of *To Tell the Truth*, Gene Rayburn of *Match Game*, Jack Narz of *Concentration*, and Alex Trebek of *Jeopardy*), chanted by cartoon character Bart Simpson in the episode "Dial Z For Zombies" from *The Simpsons* television series.

Cushlamocree

Mystique: *Cushlamocree*—the word is sheer poetry. Semiotics experts teach us that over time magic words lose their original sacredness as their syllables evolve arbitrarily, gaining instead a purely poetic or aesthetic function. "Such a [poetic] dimension is implicitly found in every metamorphosis undergone by the magic sign in its passage from light to enlightening, from the world's external language to the world of internal language, from sacred to profane, from iconic to iconoclastic, from imagery to imaginary, from nature to culture and from the creation of the world to the world of creation."[252] As a result of how magic language naturally evolves, magicians involuntarily resort to poetic means, just as poets involuntarily resort to magic means.[253]

Facts: *Cushlamocree* is a magic word from the comic strip "Barnaby" (1942–1952) by Crockett Johnson.

D

Dabra Ca Abra

Facts: *Dabra ca abra* reverses the syllables of *abracadabra*.

Variations and Incantations: Hocus pocus, chicken bones choke us, dabra ca abra, boom! —*TheMagicCafe.com* (2001)

----

251 John W. Gardner, *Self-Renewal* (1995)

252 Traian D. Stanciulescu, "Signs of Magic: On the Archetypal Roots of Culture" (2004)

253 Lucian Blaga (1985), quoted in "Signs of Magic: On the Archetypal Roots of Culture" by Traian D. Stanciulescu (2004)

Danger

The singing, thundering, magical words made her seem doubly dangerous, doubly alluring.
—Aldous Huxley, *Brave New World* (1932)

Meanings:

- Fun
"Big danger usually means big fun."
—Todd O'Neill, "Doctor Danger Ratings," *DoctorDanger.com* (2002)

- No limit
"The world is mine cause I'm in it, and danger means no limit."
—C-Murder, "Constantly in Danger" (1998)

- Potential risk

- Uncertain effect

Origins: The word *danger* comes from the Old French *dangier*, which in turn comes from the Latin *dominus* ("lord," connoting power and authority).

Variations and Incantations: Dangerous
"'Dangerous.; That was like a magic word."
—Victor Emmanuel Chapman, *Victor Chapman's Letters from France* (1917)

In Literature: "Danger? Old fellow, you just said the magic word!"
—Tony Abbott, *The Hawk Bandits of Tarkoom* (2001)

Dee-dee-dee-dee-dee-dee Cadabra

(see also *cadabra*)

In Literature: From UW Faculty Alumni Staff and Students, "Closing Song," *FASS or Fiction* (1983):

Dee-dee-dee-dee-dee-dee, Cadabra.
Dee-dee-dee-dee-dee-dee, And abra.
Dee-dee-dee-dee-dee-dee, These are the magic words, ya!
Dee-dee-dee-dee-dee-dee, A Hocus!
Dee-dee-dee-dee-dee-dee, A Pocus!
Dee-dee-dee-dee-dee-dee, To send us back!

Dee Num Fiddle Giggle Gargle

In Literature: John Burningham, *Cloudland* (1999)

Desturi

Meanings: Respected custom(s)

Origins: *Desturi* is of Swahili origin.

In Literature: "*Desturi* means custom in Swahili and is a magic word to unfold the inexplicable. Customs are sacred, unquestionable, instantly accepted without reserve."
—Kuki Gallmann, *African Nights* (2000)

Devotion

Meanings:

- Prayers

- Loyalty

- Religious observance

Origins: *Devotion* is from the Latin *devotio*, meaning "zeal."

In Literature:

- From Frithjof Schuon, "Truth and Devotion," *Songs for a Spiritual Traveler* (2002):

  Devotion—a sound, a wondrous word,
  Fragrant with love and holy silence;
  A magic word, whose beauty is enough
  To convince us of the power of Truth.

- "They . . . had followed honor; and this was sanctified even more in their eyes by the magic word devotion."
  —Alphonse de Lamartine, *History of the Girondists* (1847)

Diffindo

Origins: *Diffindo* is from the Latin word meaning "to cleave."

In Literature: *Diffindo* is a spell to tear things apart in *Harry Potter and the Goblet of Fire* by J.K. Rowling (2000).

Diggedy Dobbidy Cool
(see also *bibbidy-bobbidy-boo*)

In Literature: Imamu Amiri Baraka, *The Leroi Jones* (1960)

Diggi Daggi, Shurry Murry, Horum Harum, Lirum Larum, Rowdy Mowdy, Giri Gari, Posito, Besti Basti, Saron Froh, Fatto Matto, Quid Pro Quo

Facts: This magical phrase occurs in Mozart's opera *Bastien und Bastienne* (based upon a 1752 operetta by Rousseau entitled *Le Devin du Village* [The Village Soothsayer]): "Bastienne is a shepherdess in love with Bastien, a shepherd [who is infatuated with a wealthy girl]. . . . [I]n comes the fortuneteller Colas. . . . [who] promises help through reading aloud from his book of magic. This is nothing but a lot of nonsense [words]."[254] The pair is finally reconciled, and in the final chorus they sing the magician's praises.[255]

Ding Bing Ping Swing Zunk

Facts: This is a magic phrase for materializing a puppy dog in *Oral Storytelling and Teaching Mathematics* by Michael Schiro (2004).

---

254 Henry W. Simon, *100 Great Operas and Their Stories: Act-By-Act Synopses* (1989)

255 Steve Boerner, "The Mozart Project" (1997)

Dionysus

He comes, the sudden Lord,
A rhythmic Spike of Light,
To cleave you with that spike:
Himself, His flowing Word.
Strike, O Poem. Strike!
—Stanley Kunitz,
"For the Word is Flesh" (1930)[256]

Facts: Dionysus is a god of ancient Greek and Roman mythology, patron of the theatre, wine and agriculture, law and civilization. He is associated with the secret rites of the mystery religions.

In Literature: "'Dionysus' had been Nietzsche's magic word to shake the world out of its slumber."
—Rudiger Safranski, *Nietzsche: A Philosophical Biography* (2002)

Dogura-Magura

Origins: This is a Japanese equivalent to *abracadabra*. *Dogura-Magura* "is a word in the Kyushu dialect for 'magic used by Christians' (Kyushu, especially the Nagasaki area, was one of the first places in Japan where European merchants and Jesuits made settlements.)"[257]

Facts: *Dogura-Magura* is the title of a 1935 work of avant-garde Gothic literature by Kyûsaku Yumeno.[258]

Variations and Incantations: Dogra Magra

Doip

Meanings: Spontaneity; joyfully defying nature

In Literature: "I'd come to fly-fish, and trout were taking flies everywhere. But as the air turned blue I was first distracted by a dinky trout, not ten feet behind me, that began jumping over and over, ludicrously high in the air. This little guy leapt so high so often that I began to laugh. I mean, all earthly creatures are supposedly opportunists—fish, humans, and transnational corporations alike. By nature we slurp the maximum number of bugs or profit flows via the minimal expenditure of energy, thus aggrandizing our bulk, be it bodily or financial. But this troutlet was defying its nature. There were flies all over the river, any of which it could have effortlessly sipped. It ignored them all to leap effortfully high into the blue, catch nothing, then fall back with a splash that made the same tidy sound every time: Doip! This trout child was jumping not as a career move but in random celebration (Doip!), jumping the way my four-year-old or a good comedy sometimes jumps (Doip!); jumping in spontaneous, reasonless defiance of the whole tragic idea that every effort on Earth must have a bottom line, profit margin, or edible bug at the

---

256 "The poem itself is a magic ritual. The 'He' [Dionysus] . . . is the sudden Lord, a rhythmic Spike of Light, Himself, his flowing Word, and the Poem. This flurry of identities is a mystery of simultaneous beings not attributes. He is the spike *and* the word which the spike causes to flow. The poem, like the god, embodies *and* enacts its mystery. Kunitz here, as elsewhere, insists on the magical properties of language in poetry." —Gregory Orr, *Stanley Kunitz* (1985)

257 Kyûsaku Yumeno, *Dogura-Magura* (1935), translated by Gishokitty.

258 John Clute and John Grant, *The Encyclopedia of Fantasy* (1999)

end of it (Doip!). Edified, I turned upstream—and spotted an exceedingly large trout troubling the sunset-colored surface, not 50 feet away. I readied my rod. . . . I'd learned a magic word I believed might keep lust from interfering with art. I began waving my wand. Hard-to-describe laws of motion were enacted. Energy gathered and dispersed. Line looped and flew. I noticed, first on the river, then in the sky, that the evening star had shown. Letting fly my one chance, I spoke the magic word into the blue: 'Doip!'"
—David James Duncan, "The War for Norman's River," *Sierra Magazine* (2000)

Dominocus
(see also *hocus pocus*)

Meanings:

- Lord's

- Master's

Origins: *Dominocus* is of Latin origin, "apparently a variant (or pun?) of *dominicus* (Lat.: 'lord's, master's')."[259]

Facts: "Dominocus the Magician" is the stage name of professional magician Alvin E. Mueller.
   Dominocus commonly appears after the magic words *hocus pocus*.
   In the Neverwinter role-playing game, Mojosephus Dominocus is a character with "a great magical aura" about him and whose past is "shrouded in mystery" (Shawn Schultz, *Never winterConnections.com* [2002]).

---

259 Steven Moore, *A Reader's Guide to William Gaddis's The Recognitions* (1982)

Variations and Incantations:

- Dominokus

- Diamondocus
   —*Uncle John's Electrifying Bathroom Reader For Kids Only!* (2003)

- Hocus, pocus, dominocus
   "'I thought of a spell,' Ann whispered. 'Try hocus, pocus, dominocus.'"
   —Jane Resh Thomas, *The Princess in the Pigpen* (1989)

In Literature: William Gaddis, *The Recognitions* (1952)

Don't Stop
(see also *go*)

Facts: This magical phrase conjures a law of physics known as *inertia*: an object in motion tends to remain in motion.

In Literature: "My friend held his breath, waiting for the two magic words of wisdom that would solve all his problems. The leader said, 'Don't stop.' And, of course, that's all it is. If you want to remain successful, *don't stop* doing what made you successful. It's difficult, it's unavoidable, and it's the simplest thing in the world."
—Gordon Bethune, *From Worst to First* (1998)

Doodee Doodee Doodee

Facts: These are the magic words of professional magician Wizzo (Marshall Brodien).

Variations and Incantations: Doodee doodee doodee doo
—William Shakespeare, *King Lear* (c. 1605)

Double Fuffle Guggle Truffle

Facts: This is a magic phrase for opening a locked door in *Oral Storytelling and Teaching Mathematics* by Michael Schiro (2004).

Double Trouble

Mystique: This magic phrase recalls the hags' cauldron spell from Shakespeare's *Macbeth*: "Double, double, toil and trouble; / Fire burn, and cauldron bubble."

Common Magician's Applications: Production, as in the "Double Your Money" trick described by Cheryl Charming in *Miss Charming's Book of Bar Amusements*: "[C]hant 'double trouble' three times . . . Rub your hands together. Open your hand, and Wow! One bill turned into two bills."

Dove

Mystique: The dove is the classic magician's companion and a symbol of love, communication, peace, purity, eternity, the spirit set free.

"Long before Christians adopted the dove as an emblem of spirit, ancient people considered this bird a symbol of the transition from one state of consciousness to another and the bringing of spirit down to earth. Sacred to the Great Mother, the dove represented peace, innocence, gentleness, and chastity. . . . Homer said that both Aphrodite and Hera could transform themselves into doves. The oldest oracle of Zeus was the Oracle at Dodona; there, a dove lived in a special oracular tree and was said to speak with a human voice."[260]

Facts: The DC Comics character named Dawn Granger (1988) uses the magic word *dove* to transform into a heroine called *Dove:*

Dawn can only turn into Dove when she is in danger. At such a time, all she has to do is speak the word "Dove," and she is transformed into a magical being that is made up almost completely of pure Order. As Dove, she is linked directly into the Primal Source of Order. This gives her the ability to see the underlying pattern in all situations, and to rapidly assimilate that information, sort it, and make sense out of it. Because of this, she seems to have lightning-fast reflexes, but that's not really the case. Actually, she figures out what her opponent will do before he does it, and reacts to it before his move begins. Thus, if you try to grab her, you will find yourself clinging to empty air, since she would have expected the blow to come before you made a move, and would be long gone before you started to go after her. She is also very good at using an opponent's force against him, so taking a swing at her, or shooting something at her, more often than not ends up coming right back at you. Finally, as Dove she has a perfect eidetic memory, forgets nothing, and notes all sorts of details the average person would miss. In her words (regular series, issue #1), she is the "ultimate strategist." To quote Barbara and Karl Kesel, Dove's creators, from issue #15 (regular series): "As the boulder flies toward Dove, she notes everything about

----

it—its size, mass, slow rotation. She correctly identifies all 3,427 of its weak points. She calculates more than 10,000 possible reactions, and settles on one. Her timing is flawless."[261]

Every time a magician speaks a magic word like *dove* and performs a lightning-fast feat of prestidigitation, one could say he taps into a "Primal Source of Order" as the character Dawn Granger does.

Dreams Begin

There is a song sleeping in all things
that dream on and on,
and the world begins to sing
if you only find the magic word.
—Joseph von Eichendorff,
"Schöne Fremde" (1834)[262]

Mystique: "The chief spoke in a low, pleasant tone. 'Dreams begin.' With two words of magic he completely captured the attention of my mind. Instantly all barriers between us melted away. The mere glance of an eye or slightest change of expression on the old man's face carried his full meaning."[263]

Drizzle Drazzle Droozzle Drome

Facts: These magic words are featured in the cartoon series *King Leonardo* (1960): "Drizzle Draz-zle Droozzle Drome, time for this one to come home!"

Dum Altrakh, Antra-Khii

Mystique: "The power of words . . . is not in their comprehensibility—it is often, as we find in [in the poetry of Edgar Allan] Poe, a function of their incomprehensibility, their indefinitiveness. . . . [I]ncomprehensible words . . . have a great power over people."[264]

In Literature: "[The silver arrows' hiding place] can be found by pronouncing the magic words 'Dum Altrakh, Antra-Khii!' while facing the wall."
—Petteri Sulonen, "The Curse of Al-Rumil" (1999)

E

Ea

By the magic of the Word of Ea . . .
The great prince Ea, lord of magic.
—Semitic incantation, quoted in *Semitic Magic*
by R. Campbell Thompson (1908)

Meanings:

- The act and structure of creation
  —Mary E. Zimmer, "Creating and Re-creating Worlds with Words: The Religion and Magic of Language in *The Lord of the Rings*" (2004)

261 Steven Viscido, "Dove!" (2005)

262 Translation from Theodor Wiesengrund Adorno, *Notes to Literature* (1991)

263 F. Bruce Lamb, *Kidnapped in the Amazon Jungle* (1994)

264 Rachel Polonsky, *English Literature and the Russian Aesthetic Renaissance* (1998)

- Babylonian deity of water, creation, wisdom, and magic (Enki in Sumerian mythology)
  "In ancient Babylon, [Ea was] the god of water who was also 'Lord of Wisdom'; the patron of magic, arts, and crafts, and the creator of people."
  —Nevill Drury, *The Watkins Dictionary of Magic* (2006)

- "It is"
  —Mary E. Zimmer, "Creating and Re-creating Worlds with Words: The Religion and Magic of Language in *The Lord of the Rings*" (2004)

- "Let it be"
  "[Ea] is used by Iluvatar, J. R. R. Tolkien's God-figure, to actually bring the world into existence."
  —*Wikipedia.com* (2006)

- Magic word with "the power to do what it says"
  —Mary E. Zimmer, "Creating and Re-creating Worlds with Words: The Religion and Magic of Language in *The Lord of the Rings*" (2004)

- Universe
  —J. R. R. Tolkien, *The Silmarillion* (1977)

Origins: *Ea* is of Semitic origin, meaning "living." "In Babylonia the great god Ea was reputed to be the inventor of magic, and his son Marduk, the chief deity of Babylon, inherited the art from his father."[265]

Facts: In Babylonian mythology, the Water of Life "can be obtained only by means of pronouncing a magic word known only to the god Ea."[266]

"In a magical incantation describing the primitive monster form of Ea it is said that his head is like a serpent's, the ears are those of a basilisk, his horns are twisted into curls, his body is a sun-fish full of stars, his feet are armed with claws, and the sole of his foot has no heel."[267]

Eagle Agle Oggle Ungle

Facts: This is a magic phrase for materializing an eagle in *Oral Storytelling and Teaching Mathematics* by Michael Schiro (2004).

Ecce Sum Simon Magus

Meanings: Behold, I am Simon the Magician

Facts: Simon Magus was a Gnostic teacher from Samaria and prominent miracle worker during the rein of Claudius Caesar. He is mentioned in the New Testament's Book of Acts. *Magus* means "worker of magic."

These magic words are used in "The Power of Simon Magus" Tarot card routine by professional magician Peter Marucci.[268]

Eenie, Meenie, Minie, Moe
(see also *Fee Fie Foe Fum*)

Mystique: The incantation *Eenie meenie minie moe* puts a matter at hand into the hands of fate. The words have a spiritual, poetic quality. Poet Rodger Kamenetz recalls passing Allen Ginsberg "in the audience during a teaching by the Dalai

265 James George Frazer, *The Golden Bough: A Study in Magic and Religion* (1890)

266 W.O.E. Oesterley, *Immortality and The Unseen World: A Study in Old Testament Religion* (1921)

267 Lewis Spence, *Myths and Legends of Babylonia and Assyria* (c. 1920)

268 *Oneline-Visions.com* (2005)

Lama in New York. While others were dutifully chanting Tibetan syllables, Ginsberg was intoning 'eenie meenie miney mo.'"[269] The phrase is closely associated with the action of counting. Historian Moustafa Gadalla notes that words accompanying an action are of tremendous significance: "The *magic word*, the incantation, actuates the power and endows the ritual acts with a magical religious effect."[270]

Meanings:

- Counting
—Alan Cohen, *A Deep Breath of Life* (1996)

- Guessing game
"Why would he turn salvation into an eenie-meenie-minie-mo guessing game?"
—Bruce Bawer, *Stealing Jesus* (1998)

- Luck of the draw
"Looks like eenie, meenie, minie, moe to me."
—Michael Connelly, *The Narrows* (2004)

- Multiple choice
"The 'eenie, meenie, miney, moe' ending in which the murderer could have been any one of the suspects . . ."
—Carolyn Wheat, *How to Write Killer Fiction* (2003)

Origins: The phrase is "based on a counting system that predates the Roman occupation of Britain, that may even be pre-Celtic. If so, it is a rare surviving link with the very distant past. It not only gives us a fragmentary image of how children were being amused at the time Stonehenge was built, but tells us something about how their elders counted and thought and ordered their speech."[271]

Variations and Incantations:

- Eenie-meenie-chili-beanie
—Lou Ann Walker, *A Loss For Words* (1987)
"'Eenie-meenie-chili-beanie,' as Bullwinkle Moose used to say, the spirits are about to speak."
—Stephen King, *Bag of Bones* (1998)

- Eenie-meenie-miney-mo
"[I]n the midst of my mental eenie-meenie-miney-mo . . ."
—Joanna Weaver, *Having a Mary Heart in a Martha World* (2000)

- Eenie-meenie-minie-mo
"'Eenie, meenie, minie, mo,' I muttered to myself, and headed for the center cell."
—Diana Gabaldon, *Outlander* (1991)

- Eenie-meenie-minie-mo, Fet-tuc-ci-ne Al-fre-do
—Janet Podleski, *Looneyspoons* (1997)

- Eenie meenie mynie mo
—Jon Scieszka, *Knights of the Kitchen Table* (1991)
—Jerry Spinelli, *Space Station Seventh Grade* (2000)

- Eenie meenie mynie moe
—Richard Rodriguez, *Brown* (2003)

- Eenie meenie op-sa-keenie, Ooo aaa oo be-lee-nie, Ah-chie kah-chee Li-ver-a-chee
—This incantation is part of a children's clapping game (T. Berry Brazelton, *Touchpoints 3 to 6* [2001]).

- Ena mena mona mite
—*Notes and Queries* (1854)

In Literature: "I went to the four levers. None of them were marked. There was only one way to figure out which was the right one. I had to call upon all my Traveler experience and special powers to figure it out. It's called . . . 'Eenie,

269 *The Jew in the Lotus* (1994)

270 *Egyptian Mystics: Seekers of the Way* (2003)

271 Bill Bryson, *Made in America* (1994)

meenie, miney . . . *mo!* I pulled on 'mo' and with a grinding screech, the floor began to move."
—D.J. MacHale, *The Lost City of Faar* (2003)

- -

ℰgg

NINA: What [is the] magic word?
RUSS: (whispering). Eggs.
—Arnold Bennett, *The Love Match* (2004)

Mystique:

> The bird fights its way out of the egg.
> The egg is the world.
> Who would be born must first destroy a world.
> The bird flies to God.
> That God's name is Abraxas.
> —Hermann Hesse, *Demian* (1925)

Ripe with symbolism, the egg has been a favorite prop of magicians throughout the ages, inherited from "magic's connection with fertility rites. Magic celebrates tumescence and erection, fecundity and growth, attraction and breeding, birth and resurrection: . . . eggs are produced one after another from an empty pouch that has been touched by a magic wand . . . Magic reiterates the mystery of regeneration. It serves to remind us of the miraculousness of the creation's continuity."[272]

But why would *egg* be used as a magic word? "[T]he very word *egg* means 'to incite to action,'" explains gynecologist Christiane Northrup, M.D. "The egg literally 'eggs on' new life. . . . Although we've been led to believe that [a mother's] egg merely sits there and waits to be 'acted upon' by the sperm, newer research has shown that the

Figure 18. The Cosmic Egg contains all of the numerals and alphabetical letters, showing how all that can be numbered or named is contained in one primal form.

egg is not a passive participant in reproduction. First of all, the egg actually sends out a signal that attracts sperm to it. And it selects the sperm that will enter it. Once fertilized, eggs become the original mothers. They see potential and facilitate it into becoming reality."[273] *Egg*, then, is a perfect magic word, both broadcasting a signal to create as well as facilitating a new reality.

Meanings:

- Circle of time (as in Druidic culture)
  —Gerald Massey, *The Natural Genesis* (1883)

- Consciousness (as in Aztec culture)
  —John Mini, *The Aztec Virgin* (2000)

- Fertility, "the renewal of life in the face of death"
  —George Robinson, *Essential Judaism* (2001)

- Human frailty
  —Chris Roberts, *Heavy Words Thrown Lightly* (2004)

- Soul
  —Chris Roberts, *Heavy Words Thrown Lightly* (2004)

272 Lee Siegel, *Net of Magic: Wonders and Deceptions in India* (1991)

273 Christiane Northrup, *Mother-Daughter Wisdom* (2005)

Facts: The mystical "philosopher's egg" was "one of the main goals of any alchemist, a substance that among other things was thought to effect the transmutation of ordinary metals into gold."[274]

Egypt

In Literature: "Egypt! What wondrous pictures are conjured up by that magic word! Scenes of white-robed priests moving in solemn procession through columned aisles to the sound of stately music; . . . of royal pageants wherein King and Queen, bedecked in silks and cloth of gold, embroidered with a mine of gems, pass through the crowded lines of their acclaiming subjects; scenes of light and life and colour, which cannot fail to rouse our admiration, even our awe: such are some of the pictures that rise before us at the sound of the mystic name."
—F. H. Brooksbank, *Legends of Ancient Egypt* (1914)

Elprup

Facts: This is the magic word that Donnie Osmond spoke on *The Donnie and Marie Show* (late 1970s) to transform into Captain Purple. The word is *purple* spelled backward.

Emptiness

Mystique: "'Emptiness' is the magic word that names the essence of the universe."[275]

Common Magician's Applications: Vanishing.

Engorgio

Origins: *Engorgio* is from the French word meaning "to swallow greedily."

In Literature: *Engorgio* is a spell causing things to swell in size in *Harry Potter and the Goblet of Fire* by J.K. Rowling (2000).

Ephphatha

Origins: *Ephphatha* is an Aramaic word used in incantations to cure deafness.

Facts: In the New Testament, Jesus uses the word *Ephphatha* to heal a deaf man.[276]

Meanings: Be opened

In Literature: "Those words are the very words of his magic curative power, as he actually spoke them: 'Ephphatha,' the magic word that healed deafness, and 'Talitha, kum!' the magic words that raised the dead."
—Norman Weeks, *The Test of Love* (1992)

E Pluribus Unum

Meanings: "From many, one"; unity out of diversity

274 Brian Clegg, *The First Scientist: A Life of Roger Bacon* (2004)

275 Stephan Beyer, *Cult of Tara: Magic and Ritual in Tibet* (1978)

276 Jaroslav Pelikan, *Jesus through the Centuries: His Place in the History of Culture* (1985)

Origins: *E Pluribus Unum* is a Latin phrase from a poem attributed to Virgil.

Facts: The evil magician in Doug Henning's musical *The Magic Show* (1981) uses the magic phrase *E Pluribus Unum* while producing wine bottles.

E Pluribus Unum is the name of a coin gimmick developed by magician Timothy Wenk.

E Pluribus Unum is included in the Great Seal of the United States, the words held in the eagle's beak.

Common Magician's Applications: Dollar bill restorations. For example, the magician explains, "There is a motto printed on every dollar bill. It's an old Latin phrase—a magic spell of sorts. It says, *E pluribus unum.* 'Out of many, one.' Out of many torn pieces . . . comes a single dollar bill!"

In Literature: *E Pluribus Unum* is a wizard's incantation in Harvard Lampoon's *Bored of the Rings* (1969).

Figure 19. *E pluribus unum* appears on a scroll held by the eagle on the Great Seal of the United States. Image courtesy of the U.S. Government Printing Office (2002).

Ɛp-pe, Ƥep-pe, Ꝁak-ke! Hil-lo, Hol-lo, Hel-lo! Ƶiƶ-ƶy, Ƶuƶ-ƶy, Ƶik!

In Literature: "In her cupboard, the Witch had a Golden Cap. This cap had a charm. Whoever owned it could call three times upon the Winged Monkeys, who would obey any order they were given. The Witch put on her Golden Cap and said the magic words: *Ep-pe, pep-pe, kak-ke! Hil-lo, hol-lo, hel-lo! Ziz-zy, zuz-zy, zik!* The sky drew dark, and a low rumble sounded through the air. There was the rushing of many wings, and the Winged Monkeys swooped down to do the Witch's bidding."

—L. Frank Baum, *The Wonderful Wizard of Oz*, as retold by Grace Mabie for Troll Illustrated Classics (1993)

Ɛpplekedepple
(see also *abracadabra*)

Facts: This variation of *abracadabra* was coined by professional magician Steve Charney.[277]

Ɛt Cetera Ad Ꞑauseam

Origins: *Et cetera ad nauseam* is a Latin phrase. *Et cetera* means "and the rest," and *ad nauseam* refers to something repeated tiresomely (literally "to sickness").

---

277 *Hocus Jokus: 50 Funny Magic Tricks Complete with Jokes* (2003)

In Literature: "I will enslave the world—by the magic of words. . . . Et cetera ad nauseam." —Henry Miller, quoted in *Researching Organizational Values and Beliefs* by J. Barton Cunningham (2001)

Eucalyptus Leaves

Facts: Professional magician Annie Erlandson uses the magic phrase *Eucalyptus leaves* in her performances with a koala bear puppet named Sydney.

Eureka

You wiggle your fingers and—eureka!
—Irv Furman, *Amazing Irv's Handbook of Everyday Magic* (2002)

Mystique: That sudden, impassioned sound of accomplishment, *eureka*, is "a word of magic . . . a dot of light on a night as black as pitch."[278] It marks the special moment when a spark of inspiration seems to come out of nowhere. "Eureka, or should I say *abracadabra*. I've found the magic."[279]

Meanings:

- Aha!
  "[L]ooking at the symbols in your dreams can suddenly give you a *Eureka!* moment." —Ariana, *House Magic* (2001)

- Bingo!
  —Bruce Coville, *Aliens Ate My Homework* (1993)

- Breakthrough
  —David Wolfe, *Puzzlers' Tribute* (2001)

- I found it!
  —Edward Eager, *Magic by the Lake* (1957)

- I've got it!
  —Sig Lonegren, *The Pendulum Kit* (1990)

- Realization, insight, illumination, epiphany
  —L. Michael Hall, *User's Manual for the Brain, Vol. II* (2003)
  —Richard Florida, *The Rise of the Creative Class* (2003)

- This is it!
  —Brian Jacques, *Redwall* (2002)

Origins: *Eureka* is a Greek word, famously associated with the great mathematician Archimedes.

Variations and Incantations:

- Bravo Viva Kudos Whoopee Eureka Hallelujah Abracadabra
  "Chant this string of magic words five times a day: 'Bravo Viva Kudos Whoopee Eureka Hallelujah Abracadabra.'" —Rob Brezsny, "Free Will Astrology" (2005)

- Eureka, abracadabra, yo-ho-ho
  "[S]cenes of imagination and wonder spring to life as if by magic. The studio shakes and rattles as eruptions of multicolored smoke billow forth amidst exclamations of eureka, abracadabra, yo-ho-ho, and then—poof! Another painting appears." —Don Maitz (2005)

In Literature:

- Terry Kay, *The Valley of Light* (2003)

- "[A] great light broke over his face. 'Eureka!' he cried. 'At last, at last! After all these years! . . . I found it! We've done it! We're successful, we're famous, we're heroes!'" —Edward Eager, *Magic by the Lake* (1957)

----

278 Terry Kay, *The Valley of Light* (2003)
279 Eddie Segrum, "Segrum Secret" (2004)

Evanesco

Origins: *Evanesco* is from the Latin word meaning "to vanish."

In Literature: *Evanesco* is a vanishing spell used in *Harry Potter and the Order of the Phoenix* by J.K. Rowling (2003).

Except

Mystique: "One and one will always equal two. Everything in creation follows a rigid set of physical laws—everything, except . . . *Except*. Ah, what a magical word. In those six simple letters lie all the possibilities of the imagination."[280]

Exercise

Mystique: "No means are known whereby the faculties of the mind can be developed but by exercising them. By the potent spell of the magic word *Exercise*, is evoked all human power. The proof of this proposition is found in multitudes of facts."[281]

F

Fadatta Fadatta Fadatta, Beepum Boopum Bah! Ratta Datta Boom Sh-h Ahfah Deedee Bobo

In Literature: Beverly Cleary, *Henry and the Clubhouse* (1990)

Fa La La and Do Re Mi

Facts: This magic phrase is composed of musical syllables. *Fa* is the fourth note of a muscial scale, *la* the sixth, and *do, re, mi* the first three.

In Literature: Lisa Fiedler, *Know-It-All* (2002)

Father
(see *abba*)

> She expected action because she
> had invoked the magic word: *father*.
> —Carolyn Russell, *Beyond the Lies* (2004)

Mystique: *Father* and its informal form *Dad* "are magical words, a symbol of honor, connectedness, ownership. These words have a very special meaning."[282]

In Literature: "A man hardly feels sure of his manhood till the magic word *father* is put in the

---

280 Jim Brown, *Black Valley* (2003)

281 James Pyle Wickersham, *Methods of Instruction* (1865)

282 Isolina Ricci, *Mom's House, Dad's House* (1980)

vocative case and applied to him direct, and the apotheosis of woman comes with maternity."
—William Hawley Smith, *The Evolution of "Dodd,": A Pedagogical Story* (1884)

Fazammm

In Literature: "Magic word. . . . Fazammm. Just like that. Ahahahahaha."
—Terry Pratchett, *The Truth* (2000)

Fee-Fie-Foe-Fum

There was magic in the words,
a weird magic that beat through
Matt's head and drummed in his blood.
—Christopher Stasheff,
Her Majesty's Wizard (1986)

Mystique: There is a musical quality to *fee-fie-foe-fum* that echoes oral ballads and rhymes associated with childhood, such as "Old MacDonald's" chorus of "e-i-e-i-o" (the final "e-i-o" matching the vowel sounds of "fee-fie-foe") and "Eenie Meenie Miney Mo" (the final words "Meenie Miney Mo" again matching the vowel sounds of "fee-fie-foe").[283] "The sonorous part of spells and incantations can be taken just as rows of syllables that the intellect refuses to understand. In fact, [it] is a sacred language, sometimes spoken only by the performer. Nevertheless, an enormous psychological power is attributed to these incomprehensible and magic words. . . . [T]heir musi-

cality can capture everyone."[284] As the visionary French Jesuit, paleontologist, and philosopher Pierre Teilhard de Chardin put it, "magical words are much more *felt* than understood."[285]

Meanings: Where? Why? How? Whom?
—*PlanetFusion.co.uk*

Origins: This phrase was made famous by the "Jack and the Beanstalk" fable. It is perhaps a Doric dialect (a blend of English, Gaelic, and Norse), in which the *wh* sound is pronounced *f*.[286]

Facts: In the 1947 cartoon *Mickey and the Beanstalk*, Willie the Giant "has the power to change his form with the utterance of a few magic words—'Fee Fi Fo Fum,' of course."[287]

Variations and Incantations:

- Abracadabra. Fee Fo Fi Bloody Fum
  "Abracadabra. Fee Fo Fi Bloody Fum. And just when everyone thinks you're going to produce the most ludicrously faked bit of cheese-cloth ectoplasm, or a phoney rap on the table, it comes. Clear as a bell. Quite unexpected. The voice of truth!"
  —John Mortimer, *Rumpole of the Bailey* (1978)

- Feee fiii fooo fum

- Fee Fee Fi Fo Fum
  —LaVern Baker, the title of a 7-inch single recording

----

283 Experimental psychologist David Rubin of Duke University studies why people remember such rhymes and cites the examples used here (Dennis Meredith, "Mining the Meaning of Memories," *Duke Magazine* [March 1998]).

284 Mirela Vlaica, "Forms of Magic in Traditional Mentality" (2003)
285 *The Future of Man* (1959)
286 *PlanetFusion.co.uk*
287 Daniel Briney, a review of "Walt Disney Treasures: Mickey Mouse in Living Color, Volume 2" (2004)

- Fee Fi Fo Fum
  —Mary Norton, *Are All the Giants Dead?* (1997)

- Fee-Fi-Foe-Fam
  —Edward Crosby Wells, *Jack and the Jade Beanstalk* (1983)

- Fee-Fi-Foe-Fam-And-Fum-Dee-Dum-Dee-Dum-Dee-Dum-Dee-Dum
  —Edward Crosby Wells, *Jack and the Jade Beanstalk* (1983)

- Fee Fie Fo Fum
  —Mary Westmacott, *Giant's Bread* (1930)

- Fee Fie Foe et Cetera
  —Gregory Maguire, "Fee, Fie, Foe, et Cetera," *The Green Man: Tales From the Mythic Forest* (2002)

- Fee Fie Foe Foobar
  —Richard Powers, *Plowing the Dark* (2001)

- Fee, Fie, Foe, Fumbug!
  —Carole Nelson Douglas, *Cat in a Midnight Choir* (2002)

- Fee Fie Foh Fum

- Fee Fi Foh Fum

- Fe-Fo-Fum
  —Guy Boothby, *Dr. Nikola Returns* (2001)

- Fe Fa Fi-fo-fum
  —Andrew Lang, *The Red Fairy Book* (1890)

- Fie fau fum
  —William Shakespeare, *King Lear* (c. 1605)

- Fi Fie Foe Fum

- Fi fy fo fum
  —*AsianAvenue.com*

- Finnk Fime Fudd
  —James Joyce, *Finnegan's Wake* (1939)

- Foo; Phum; Fee fie foe
  —Orson Scott Card, *Treasure Box* (1996)

- Fy fa fum
  "Fy, fa, fum, I smell the bloud of an Englishman."
  —Thomas Nash (1590)

- Phi Phie Pho Phum

- Yabba-dabba-doo-fiddledy-dee-tiddly-pom-fi-fi-fo-fum
  —Daniel C. Dennett, *Consciousness Explained* (1991)

In Literature: "He experienced a *fee fie fo fum* moment, smelling human blood—or more to the point, inhuman blood, something not quite earthly."
—Meg Wolitzer, *The Position* (2005)

Ferula

Origins: *Ferula* is from the English word *ferule*, meaning a rod or cane.

Common Magician's Applications: Production of a magic wand.

In Literature: *Ferula* is a spell that conjures a wooden rod in *Harry Potter and the Prisoner of Azkaban* by J.K. Rowling (1999).

Fetch Boy

Facts: This is a magic phrase recommended by professional magician Karl Fulves for tricks involving dog props, such as his "Houdini Hound" paper-bag puppet.[288]

---

288 *Self-Working Paper Magic* (1985)

Fiddleson Faddleson Spirits That Fly, Let Me Give It Another Try

Facts: These are magic words for trying something a second time in the *Bewitched* television series.

Fill Jomble, Fill Jumble, Fill Rumble-Come-Tumble

Facts: Philosopher Alan Watts recalled "the mysterious utterance of the old man of Spithead, who opened the window and said 'Fill jomble, fill jumble, Fill rumble-come-tumble.' . . . Once you have seen this you can return to the world of practical affairs with a new spirit. You have seen that the universe is at root a magical illusion and a fabulous game, and that there is no separate 'you' to get something out of it, as if life were a bank to be robbed. The only real 'you' is the one that comes and goes, manifests and withdraws itself eternally in and as every conscious being. For 'you' is the universe looking at itself from billions of points of view, points that come and go so that the vision is forever new."[289]

Flagrate

Flagrate with this oil of ink.
—Alfred Henry Lewis, *Richard Croker* (1901)

Origins: *Flagrate* is from the Latin word meaning "blaze" (*flagro*).

In Literature: *Flagrate* is a spell for conjuring fire from a wand in *Harry Potter and the Order of the Phoenix* by J.K. Rowling (2003).

Flahboodeeflee

Facts: This is a magic word coined by Marc Bissonnette (2004).

Flash Bam Alakazam
(see also *alakazam*)

In Literature: Will Friedwald, *Jazz Singing* (1990)

Flibbing

Facts: *Flibbing* is the equivalent to "Bingo!" or "Eureka!"[290]

In Literature: Bruce Coville, *Aliens Ate My Homework* (1993)

Flurr Ecke Ecke Ecke Ecke Ben Yan Bjorn

Facts: This magic phrase to transform anything into a toaster is from the television series "The Rottentrolls" (1998).

Focus

We must be in the center of the magic focus.
—Piers Anthony, *Geis of the Gargoyle* (1995)

289 *The Book: On the Taboo Against Knowing Who You Are* (1966)

290 Bruce Coville, *Aliens Ate My Homework* (1993)

Your focus invokes The Magician.
—Richard Gordon, *The Intuitive Tarot* (1994)

Mystique: The magic word *focus* is a cornerstone, a linchpin, bringing attention to the heart of the matter. *Focus* is a magic word of powerful concentration. It's the point of convergence.

Variations and Incantations:

- Focus focus
  This is a variation of *hocus pocus*.

- Focus. Focus. Dominocus.
  "'Focus. Focus. Dominocus,' Shahen chanted, twiddling her fingers in the air."
  —Laura Pace, "Musical Theater Program for Special Needs Students Falls on Hard Times," *Pittsburgh Post-Gazette* (2004)

- Hocus pocus focus
  "Gaze into the crystal ball and whisper, 'hocus pocus focus.'"
  —Vickie L. Milazzo, *Create Your Own Magic for CLNC Success* (2003)

Foken Falk
(see *mikkel myyra*)

Origins: These are folkloric magic words for transformation into a bird.

Football Touchdown, Toilet Plunger, Hocus Pocus, Woof

The magic in words is that the
story can make the picture.
—Christina Baldwin, *Storycatcher* (2005)

In Literature: "'And to reverse this amazing effect,' I boomed in my biggest stage voice, 'you simply reverse the spell.' I waved my linked hands around and chanted, 'Football touchdown, toilet plunger, hocus pocus, woof!' I slipped my fingers apart and raised the now free circles over my head. 'Ta da!' Talk about a 'Do or Die' trick. If the samurai liked it, we lived. If not—"
—Jon Scieszka, *Sam Samurai* (2001)

Fortune
(see also *gold*, *money* and *treasure*)

The magic word *fortune* always retains
some glamour in the ears of men.
—Alexandre Dumas,
The Man in the Iron Mask (1850)

Origins: *Fortune* is of Latin origin. "*Fortuna* is the Roman personification of good luck and success."[291] She is the "changeable goddess,"[292] "mistress of human events."[293] "She used Her special magic to create abundance wherever She smiled."[294]

Facts: In the Italian fairy tale "Fortunatus," the goddess Fortuna bestows a magic purse that yields ten pieces of gold whenever one reaches into it.[295]

291 K. Van Der Toom, *Dictionary of Deities and Demons in the Bible* (1999)
292 Matthew S. Santirocco, *Unity and Design in Horace's Odes* (1986)
293 Benedetto Fontana, *Hegemony and Power* (1993)
294 Nancy Blair, *The Book of Goddesses* (2002)
295 Michael Nerlich, *Ideology of Adventure* (1987)

Variations and Incantations: Fortuna
"By the power of Fortuna . . ."
—Deborah Gray, *How to Turn Your Ex-Boyfriend into a Toad* (1996)

In Literature: "[I]t was that magical word 'fortune' that had made the most profound impact on her."
—Barbara Taylor Bradford, *A Woman of Substance* (1979)

Frappa Wappa

Facts: This is a magic phrase that "makes any object you choose grow larger," as discussed in *Writing Prompts* by Justin McCory Martin (2001).

Friday

Mystique: "Friday has always been a magical word, the sign on the border between work and leisure, between hard work and serious fun."[296]

Fumble Gralley Goggle Ho Hee

In Literature: John Burningham, *Cloudland* (1999)

G

Galli Galli Galli
(see also *gilli-gilli-gilli*)

Meanings: "This circle shall never be broken"
—Stewart James, *Abbott's Encyclopedia of Rope Tricks for Magicians* (1945)

Origins: This magic phrase originated in Egypt.[297]

Facts: *Galli galli galli* is said many times very rapidly.

Variations and Incantations:

- Galli-Galli-Galli-Galli Houp
  "A conjurer dressed in tinsel drew from his sleeve endless many-coloured handkerchiefs, and from his mouth twenty small live chicks, crying all the time in the voice of the sea-bird: '*Galli-Galli-Galli-Galli Houp!*'"
  —Lawrence Durrell, *Balthazar* (1958)

- Galli Galli Galli Wum Wum Wum Pus Pus Pus
  —Josephine Demmond, *Derren the Different Dragon* (2004)

In Literature: Henning Nelms, *Magic and Showmanship: A Handbook for Conjurers* (1969)

---

296 Gordon Hughes and R.M. Fergusson, *Ordering Lives* (2000)

297 Henning Nelms, *Magic and Showmanship: A Handbook for Conjurers* (1969)

Gamble Grumble Groumble

Facts: This is a magic phrase (in conjunction with clapping three times) for activating a crystal ball in *Oral Storytelling and Teaching Mathematics* by Michael Schiro (2004).

Gargle Giggle Fiddle Num Dee

In Literature: John Burningham, *Cloudland* (1999)

Garwallah

Origins: "[The famous professional magician] Thurston . . . used to use 'Garwallah' as a magic phrase. At one point, a Turkish spectator laughed uncontrollably . . . and later, after having been brought backstage, explained that 'Garwallah' was Turkish for 'Hey, Taximan!'"[298]

Gazeeka Gazooka

Facts: This is professional magician-comedian Mike Carnevale's magic phrase.[299]

Ghht Mar Nak Grttzt
(see *qmʃbtʃ*)

In Literature: Balanced Alternative Technologies Multi-User Dimension, *Bat.org* (2004)

Giggle-Gaggle-Goo

In Literature: "The King placed the casket on a small table before him, and then, after a solemn look at the expectant faces, he said slowly: 'Giggle-gaggle-goo!' which was the magic word that opened the box. At once the lid flew back, and the King peered within and exclaimed: 'Ha!'"
—L. Frank Baum, *The Surprising Adventures of the Magical Monarch of Mo* (1903)

Gilli-Gilli-Gilli
(see also *galli galli galli*)

Origins: This magic phrase originated in India.

Facts: *Gilli-gilli-gilli* is sung in the Jewish Sabbath song "Minnimet."[300]

Common Magician's Applications: Restorations. For example: "[A] shawl, borrowed from an uneasy member of the crowd, is cut into shreds and then, after the wave of a magic wand, a puff of magic breath, and the muttering of magic words—'gilli-gilli-gilli' or 'yantru-mantru-jãlajãla-tantru'—it is whole again."[301]

----

298 *TheMagicCafe.com* (2004)
299 Judy Bannon, "Rope Tricks, Rabbits, It Must be Magic" (1999)

300 Temple Israel of Hollywood Outreach
301 Margaret A. Mills, *South Asian Folklore: An Encyclopedia* (2003)

In Literature:

- "Kabir stepped forward holding what appeared to be a rope, an old bicycle chain which Ibrahim Pasha had encased in a woven cotton tubing that was knotted at each end. He wiggled the device for all to see as his father, with English words, proudly announced the 'Old Indian Rope Trick!' Kabir set the rope on the ground and waved his hands over it as he said the magic words, '*Gilli-gilli-gilli!*' And then he lifted it again, turning it and carefully holding it so that the links of the concealed bicycle chain stretched straight out, parallel to the ground. The rope, to the delight of the small crowd, seemed to defy the most basic laws of nature, as if to prove that the intractable force that pulls all things to earth could, if one only knew the secret, be overcome. Anything is possible for the conjurer."
  —Lee Siegel, *Net of Magic* (1991)

- Stephanie Jones, *As Long as You Love Me* (2000)

Go
(see also *don't stop*)

Mystique: "That magic word 'Go'" is a gleeful yell, a "spirit-stirring sound" that encapsulates "joy at the prospect of getting under way."[302]

Common Magician's Applications: Vanishing. For example: "Five cards are selected by yourself or a member of the company, and thrown faces up on the table. You then announce that you are going to cause one of the cards to disappear, and ask a person to name the particular card. This is done and you collect the five cards in the left hand, squaring all together, and giving them a 'fillip' with the fingers of the right hand, say 'Go! Did you see the card disappear?' 'No!' 'Really—well I am not surprised but I will show you that it has done so.' Deal out the cards on the table, and sure enough there are only four. Pick up the cards again and treat them in the same way as before. Deal out again and the lost card re-appears—there are now five on the table."[303]

Variations and Incantations:

- Go away
  "Now you tell your two volunteers that on the count of three they are to pull the rope and the knot will disappear. One, two, three they pull the cord but when you slide the toilet roll away the cord is in a knot. Of course, you forgot to say the magic words 'Go Away.' You pass the cord through . . . and say the magic words, and this time there is no knot."
  —School Performance Tours, "Teachers' Resource Pack for Ventriloquist and Magician" (2005)

- Go go go
  "During the traditional sponge ball routine where the sponges vanish and transport from one magician's hand to the other, or from the magician's hand and into a spectator's hand, the volunteer simply says the magic words, 'Go, go go!' to make the magic happen. The climax of the ['Go Go Gone' sponge balls] effect is when the spectator opens his hand and discovers that his 'Go' sponges have now transformed into the word 'Gone!'"
  —Illusion Warehouse, *TrickSecrets.com* (2005)

302 Josiah Gregg, "On the Trail," *A Great Plains Reader* (2003)

303 Ellis Stanyon, *Magic* (1902)

God Bless You
(see *blessings*)

In Literature: John-Roger, *Loving Each Day* (1989)

God Is Great

In Literature: "Ibrahim Pasha combed his long, cinder-gray beard with his fingers and parted his darker moustache. He placed a bidi in his mouth, lit it, took a deep puff, and muttered the magic words: 'God is great.'"
—Lee Siegel, *Net of Magic: Wonders and Deceptions in India* (1991)

Gold
(see also *fortune*, *money* and *treasure*)

Gold. It was a magic word.
—Catherine E. Chambers and Allan Eitzen, *California Gold Rush* (1998)

Mystique: "Their great magician is Gold," wrote Richard Henry Savage. "In power, in pleasing witchery of potent influence; insidious flattery of pleasure; in remorseless persecution of the penniless, all wonders are its work. Ariel, Mephisto, Moloch, thou, Gold! King Gold! and thy brother, Silver!" (*The Little Lady of Lagunitas* [1892]).

In Literature:

- "'Gold!' And at that magic word all eyes were strained greedily forward."
  —Charles Kingsley, *Westward Ho!* (1855)

- "Wiglaf had said the magic word: gold."
  —Kate McMullan and Bill Basso, *Class Trip to the Cave of Doom* (2003)

- "The mountain gnomes of this mystic wilderness are already in terror lest some fortunate fool may utter the one magic word, 'Gold.' It will call greedy thousands from the uttermost parts of the earth to break the seals of ages, and burrow far below these mountain bases. Through stubborn granite wall, tough porphyry, ringing quartz, and bedded gnarled gneiss, men will grope for the feathery, fairy veins of the yellow metal."
  —Richard Henry Savage, *The Little Lady of Lagunitas* (1892)

- "Gold! gold! that is the magic word with which the world is ruled. I will have gold—I will rule the world."
  —Louise Muhlbach, *Berlin and Sans-Souci* (1858)

- "You said the magic word 'gold' again, Ghend. I could sit here all day and listen to you talk about it."
  —David Eddings, *The Redemption of Althalus* (2000)

- "That is when the exciting and magical word *gold* entered our conversation."
  —Donald Trump, *Churches, Jails, and Gold Mines* (2003)

- "The Protectorate was overrun by British officers, and their reports and itineraries never failed to contain, with a marvellous unanimity of iteration, the magic word—Gold."
  —Richard F. Burton, *To the Gold Coast for Gold, Vol. 1* (1883)

Figure 20. Seven alchemical symbols for gold.

- "To cover up the crime the culprits would hint that they had found the gold in the mysterious Indian country of the 'Black Hills.' And the magic word 'Gold!' would once again travel by the frontier grapevine from one settlement to another."
—Charles Windolph, *I Fought with Custer* (1987)

Gotcha

In Literature:

- *Gotcha* is "the magic word that only works for older brothers" on their young siblings, as when playing cops and robbers.
—William J. Webbe, "My Brother and Me," *Making Our Own Fun* (2004)

- "'Gotcha,' he says, displaying the mouse in his cupped hands."
—Audrey Niffenegger, *The Time Traveler's Wife* (2004)

Grabatto

Origins: *Grabatto* is a magic word for amulets, mentioned in the *Gremoire du Pape Honorius* (1800).

Grablada

In Literature: "The magic word I would like you to remember, the one that could save our lives as well as yours, is GRABLADA."
—Ted Lazaris, *Dragon Man and the Poseidon Encounter* (2004)

Great Googly-Moogly

Origins: The phrase *Great Googly-Moogly* is delivered in the song "Stranded in the Jungle" (1956) by The Jacks.[304]

Common Magician's Applications: Triggering. For example: "Lean forward, say your magic words (I still like 'Great Googly-Moogly') and gently but firmly press your finger against his forehead."
—Bart King, *The Big Book of Boy Stuff* (2004)

Variations and Incantations:

- Good googly-moogly
—Brad Warner, *Hardcore Zen* (2003)

- Great Googa Mooga Shooga Wooga
—Radio DJ Frantic Ernie (1952)

Great Powers

In Literature: "Over the whole scene . . . had loomed the commanding magic of the words 'the Great Powers'—even more imposing in their Teutonic rendering, 'Die Grossmächte.'"
—H.H. Munro, *The Complete Saki* (1976)

Great Scott

Meanings: *Great Scott* is an exclamation equivalent to *Eureka!*

Facts: To begin his show, professional magician The Great Scott (Scott Green) tells his spectators that the magic words are *Great Scott!* "Throughout

304 Vladimir Bogdanov, *All Music Guide to Soul* (2003)

the show, Scott has the audience yell the magic words to make his magic happen."[305]

H

Greece

Mystique: "To almost all, is Greece a magic word. Her romantic history—the legacies she has left us—our early recollections, identifying with her existence as a nation, all that is good and glorious;—no wonder these things should have shed a bright halo around her,—and have made each breast deeply sympathise with her in her unwonted struggle for freedom."[306]

Gweezy Yahmi

Facts: These exotic-sounding magic words actually condense the phrase "go easy on me."

These words are featured in a video entitled "Adventures in Customer Courtesy." "By touching their hands to their temples and saying the magic words 'gweezy yahmi,' . . . customer service heroes invoke Kirby the Leprechaun, a customer service magician."[307]

Habble Gum Gam Gibble

Facts: This is a magic phrase for materializing a squirmy worm in *Oral Storytelling and Teaching Mathematics* by Michael Schiro (2004).

Variations and Incantations:

- Bondo gum gam gibble
  —Michael Schiro, *Oral Storytelling and Teaching Mathematics* (2004)

Haddle Faddle Rooster's Cry, As the Sun Climbs in the Sky

Facts: These are magic words for renewal in the *Bewitched* television series.

Hakim Zambini

Facts: Zambini is the name of a circus psychic in the "Food for Thought" episode of the *Tales from the Crypt* television series.[308]

Zambini is the name of the magician hero in the Zip comic books[309] of the 1940s. "Zambini the Magician used his magic amulet to fight crime. Zambini had no powers apart from his miracle-working red amulet."[310]

305 *TheGreatScott.com* (2005)

306 A. Bushman, *A Love Story* (1841)

307 The Entrepreneurship Institute of Canada

308 *TVtome.com*

309 Cash Gorman, *MLJ Golden-Age Encyclopedia* (2004)

310 Jess Nevins, *Golden Age Directory* (2004)

Common Magician's Applications: These words are suggested for use with the "Zambini Coin Box" illusion, in which "A small brass box with a lid is shown, together with a solid brass disc, the size of a £1 coin. The disc is placed inside the box, and the lid placed on. The magic words 'Hakim Zambini' are spoken, and the lid removed to reveal that the brass disc has been converted into a genuine £1 coin."[311]

Happis Crappis

Facts: These are magic words used by professional magician Al Flosso.
In Literature: "Magician Al Flosso said, 'Happis Crappis,' which is tough to beat."
—Bart King, *The Big Book of Boy Stuff* (2004)

Happy Birthday

Facts: These are magic words professional magician Andrew Martin favors when he performs at children's birthday parties: "Instead of 'abracadabra,' the magic words are 'Happy Birthday!'"[312]

Harrahya

Mystique: The magic word *harrahya* could be likened to the shout of a martial artist delivering a karate chop, focusing power toward an amazing conclusion.

Origins: The word is exclaimed by a High Priestess at the end of an ancient chant.[313]

Ha-Ya-Ba-Ra-La

Origins: The magic word *ha-ya-ba-ra-la* is of Indian origin.

Facts: This word is the equivalent to *abracadabra*. It was popularized by children's writer Sukumar Roy (d. 1923).

In Literature: Sukumar Roy, *Ha-Ya-Ba-Ra-La* (1928)

Heba Haba

Facts: These are the trademark magic words of professional magician Heba Haba Al (Al Andrucci), who performed in the years following World War II and became known as "the grandfather of Chicago bar magic." Asked how he got his name, Heba Haba Al recalled, "One night I was doin' a trick and they said, 'Say the magic word.' And I said, 'Heba haba heba haba.' And they started callin' me Heba Haba."[314]

Hee Ho Goggle Gralley Fumble

In Literature: "Then the Queen said the magic words backward. She either said, 'Hee ho goggle

311 *MerlinsofWakefield.co.uk*
312 Quoted by Annie Cieslukowski, "Planning the Perfect Child's Party," *Toledo Blade* (2004)
313 Lady Sheba, *Lady Sheba's Grimoire* (1972)
314 Mike Houlihan, "Magic Moments With Funny Jim [Krzak]," *Chicago Sun-Times* (2004)

gralley fumble,' or 'Nee se bari waggle teetum,'
or was it 'Dee num fiddle giggle gargle?'"
—John Burningham, *Cloudland* (1999)

Heep

Facts: *Heep* is a word coined by Charles Dickens
for his novel *David Copperfield*. It refers to a grand
deception.

In Literature: "'HEEP!' With this last repetition
of the magic word that had kept him going at all,
and in which he surpassed all his previous efforts,
Mr. Micawber rushed out of the house; leaving
us in a state of excitement, hope, and wonder,
that reduced us to a condition little better than
his own."
—Charles Dickens, *David Copperfield* (1850)

Heka

Meanings:

- Isis, Goddess of Magic, Great Enchantress,
  One Whose Words Come to Pass Without
  Fail
  "As a God, Heka is said to be the first-made
  thing and it is because of Magic that all the
  Deities live. The ancient Egyptians conceived of magic as a living force, a primordial power, the energy of the universe. They
  believed it to be the essential energy that infuses and underlies all things, spiritual and
  physical. Magic connects everything and
  allows the levels of Being to interpenetrate
  and affect each other. Magic is required to
  ascend to the realm of the Deities, every
  ancient Egyptian's *post mortum* goal. By har-
  monizing with the thread of magic that is
  woven in all things, human beings can commune with the Deities, grow, have effect in

the world, and be spiritually renewed. As
Lady of Magic, Isis is the patroness, embodiment, and most-potent wielder of this
sacred, living energy. By Her magic, Isis not
only turns the stars in the heavens, but heals
us, protects us, and can lift us up in spiritual
communion with Her."
—M. Isidora Forrest, *New Worlds of Mind and
Spirit* (2001)

- Magic, act of
  —M. Isidora Forrest, *New Worlds of Mind and
  Spirit* (2001)

- Magic, force of; a magical power that ener-
  gizes the universe
  —Brian P. Copenhaver, *Hermetica* (1992)

- Magic word or formula
  —Rosemary Clark, *Sacred Tradition in Ancient
  Egypt* (2000)

- Magician
  —Nisut Hekatawy I, "Daily Devotions From
  Her Holiness Nisut Hekatawy I" (2003)

- To control powers
  —A. Rosalie David, *Handbook of Life in Ancient Egypt* (1998)

Origins: "Egyptologists translate the Egyptian
word *heka* . . . as 'magic.'"[315] Her Holiness Nisut
Hekatawy I suggests: "Heka is more accurately
translated from its root, *hek*, meaning to rule or
to be in authority, and from its determinative related to speech. Thus, some Egyptologists refer to
heka as 'authoritative utterance' or 'speaking with
meaning or intent.' Its hieroglyph is a compound
of two hieroglyphs: the lamp-wick meaning the
phonetic soft *h* sound, and the outstretched arms
meaning the *ka* sound. In an esoteric way, one
could read this combination of hieroglyphs using
the meaning of the word *ka*, the personality or

---

315 M. Isidora Forrest, *New Worlds of Mind and Spirit*
(2001)

unseen 'double' of a human being, and say that *heka* is 'the fire that comes from inside the *ka*,' or, in reference to the use of hand gestures along with special words in the system of *heka*, 'fire/light that comes from the hands.'"[316]

Variations and Incantations:

- Hekau
  "There's a story about the Egyptian sun god Ra and his granddaughter, Isis, goddess of the Nile. One day Ra was bitten by a snake and despite his divine powers he became deathly sick. He called for Isis, who was known across the land as 'the great sorceress who heals.' Isis mixed seeds, juniper berries and honey to make a balm, but before giving her treatment she demanded to know the secret word which was the source of all Ra's powers. This was a terrible price for the sun king to pay but, as Isis pointed out, he had no choice. The secret word given to Isis was *hekau*. Isis poulticed the wound and to make sure her cure worked, spoke the magic word. Ra recovered, and Isis basked in her new status. But there is more to the story. The serpent who bit Ra had been made by Isis herself. . . . Ra made a treaty with all serpents forbidding them to bite ever again, but snakes being what they are, they soon returned to their natural ways. So Ra gave his magic word to a north African tribe of snake charmers, the Psylli, and charged them with keeping serpents at bay."
  —Gail Bell, *The Poisoner* (2001)

- Hika
  —M. Isidora Forrest, *New Worlds of Mind and Spirit* (2001)

- Hike
  —M. Isidora Forrest, *New Worlds of Mind and Spirit* (2001)

Hekas Hekas Este Bebeloi

Meanings: "Far, far from this place be the profane." These words are intended to banish negative influences and unwanted entities.
—Chic Cicero, *The Essential Golden Dawn* (2003).

Origins: This phrase has been traced back to Ancient Greece and was "originally uttered at the Eleusinian Mysteries,"[317] annual sacred celebrations held in honor of Demeter and Persephone.

Helion Melion Tetragrammaton
(see also *Tetragrammaton*)

Origin: The word *Tetragrammaton* refers to the four Hebrew letters (Yod, He, Waw and He) spelling the unpronounceable divine name, sometimes transcribed as "Jehovah."

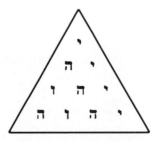

Figure 21. This Kabbalistic depiction of *Tetragrammaton* arranges the letters of the Great Name in the form of the sacred Pythagorean Tetractys (or "Mystic Tetrad," a triangular symbol of cosmic harmony).

316 "Daily Devotions From Her Holiness Nisut Hekatawy I" (2003)

317 Hermetic Order of the Golden Dawn, "Golden Dawn Glossary" (1997)

In Literature: "After the usual anointings, incantations, and foot stamping, he uttered the thunderous magical words 'Helion, Melion, Tetragrammaton.'"
—Iain McCalman, *The Last Alchemist* (2003)

Herbidacious

Facts: The magic word *Herbidacious* began every adventure in the BBC's animated series *The Herbs* (1968), concerning various animals living in the walled English country garden of Sir Basil and Lady Rosemary.

Hey Presto
(see also *presto*)

Variations and Incantations:

- Hey presto Abracadabra
  "Shoes. Come to me. Hey presto. Abracadabra. Shoes, I say!"
  —Diana Wynne Jones, *Witch Week* (1982)

- Hey! Presto! Fly!
  "An old saying has it that when Gargantua was born his first 'yell' was 'I want a drink.' Something similar must be said of [professional magician] Mons. J. Caroly, only the expression in his case must surely be, 'Hey! Presto!! Fly!'"
  —Ellis Stanyon, *Magic* (1902)

- Hey presto! Now you see it, now you don't
  "[W]hat if in full view of those eyes I had, like Bebb, committed it, pulled my own rabbit out of my own hat? Hey presto! Now you see it, now you don't, in reverse."
  —Frederick Beuchner, *Lion Country* (1971)

- Hey presto pass
  —Wilkie Collins, *The Woman in White* (1860)

"Mr. Parker has a new trick: The Vanishing Financier. Absolutely no deception. Hey, presto, pass! and where is he? Will some gentleman from the audience kindly step upon the platform and inspect the cabinet?"
—Dorothy L. Sayers, *Whose Body?* (1923)

In Literature:

- "Hey, presto, you asked me to examine your hat and all those wonderful things."
  —Sorana Salomeia, "Simsalabim" (2004)

- "But hey, presto, the mirror is breathed on and the young knighterrant recedes, shrivels, to a tiny speck within the mist."
  —James Joyce, *Ulysses* (1922)

- "Come here, my jolly little Mouse! Hey! presto! pass! I transform you, for the time being, into a respectable lady."
  —Wilkie Collins, *The Woman in White* (1860)

- "[L]ook back at the papers—hey, presto!—all the blanks are filled."
  —Jack Finney, *Time and Again* (1970)

- "His ultra-bright hey-presto look was insolent."
  —Saul Bellow, *The Dean's December* (1982)

- "'Hey presto,' he said. The door swung open."
  —Georgia Byng, *Molly Moon Stops the World* (2004)

Hfuhruhurr
(see also *qmfbtf*)

Facts: This mumbled word is used to summon an invisible swordsman in the film *¡Three Amigos!* (1986).

"Dr. Michael Hfuhruhurr" is a character in the film *The Man with Two Brains* (1983).

Higgledy Piggledy

Meanings:

- "Every which way"

- In random order

- Topsy turvey

Facts: This phrase is a favorite of professional magician Emazdad (Clive Hemsley). He says he prefers original-sounding phrases so that he doesn't appear to be using "someone else's magic."[318]

Variations and Incantations: Higgledy Piggledy Pop
—Maurice Sendak

In Literature:

- "By whatever higgledy-piggledy chance, space arose, time arose, laws of physics arose."
  —John Archibald Wheeler, *Geons, Black Holes, and Quantum Foam* (1998)

- From *An Appalachian Mother Goose* by James Still (1998):

  Higgledy, piggledy, my smart hen,
  She lays goose eggs for gentlemen;
  Gentlemen come from miles away,
  To see goose eggs my hen doth lay.

- -

High Jingo
(see also *jingo*)

Mystique: *High Jingo* exalts the name and conjures up the power of a wise magician named *Jingo*.

Meanings: "Higher up manipulation"
"'[H]igh jingo' [is] beat cop slang for cover-up and conspiracy by police brass."
—Rod Cockshutt, "Elmore Leonard and Michael Connelly Shine," *The News and Observer* (June 12, 2005)

Origins: *High Jingo* dates back to 1670.

Variations and Incantations:

- High Jinko
  This phrase originally meant "the Great One on High" (Ivan Terrance Sanderson, *Follow the Whale* [1956]).

- To my high jingo, to my low jingo
  —James Raymond Masterson, *Tall Tales of Arkansaw* (1942)

- Snip-snap-snorum-High Cockolorum-Jingo
  This is a variation of the card game *Snip-snap-snorum* (Cuthbert Bede, *Notes and Queries* [1862]).

In Literature: "'High jingo,' Bosch whispered to himself as he hung up."
—Michael Connelly, *The Closers* (2005)

- -

Hi Hae Haec
Horum Harum Horum

Origins: *Hi hae haec horum harum horum* are Latin pronouns with the sound of a mysterious incantation.

In Literature: "'We are traveling magicians,' replied Steve. 'You may have heard of us, for by our power this new river has begun to flow. Rhombustas is my name, and this is my familiar Balcazar.' 'I don't believe it,' said an incredulous one from behind. 'Very well, gentlemen; we can't help that. But if you give us some apples we'll prove

our right to the title.' 'Be hanged if we will give you any apples,' said the boy who held the basket, 'since it is already proved that magicians are impossible.' . . . 'In that case,' said Steve, 'we—we—' 'We will perform just the same,' interrupted I, for I feared Steve had forgotten that the time was at hand when the stream would be interrupted by Job, whether we willed it or not. 'We will stop the water of your new river at twelve o'clock this day, when the sun crosses the meridian,' said Rhombustas, 'as a punishment for your want of generosity.' 'Do it!' said the boys incredulously. 'Come here, Balcazar,' said Steve. We walked together to the edge of the stream; then we muttered, *Hi, hae, haec, horum, harum, horum,* and stood waving our wands. 'The river do run just the same,' said the strangers derisively. 'The spell takes time to work,' said Rhombustas, adding in an aside tone, 'I hope that fellow Job has not forgotten, or we shall be hooted out of this place.'"
—Thomas Hardy, "Our Exploits at West Hardy" (1892)

Hili Hili Mili Mili

Origins: *Hili hili mili mili* (also *hili hili kili kili*[319]) is a "meaningless"[320] mantra of Buddhist origin. Similar mantras include *hala hala* and *hulu hulu*.[321] These words invoke planetary forces.[322]

Facts: This phrase is "similar to the magic words, such as 'abracadabra,' found in other traditions."[323]

319 Pratapacandra Ghosha, *Durga Puja* (1871)

320 *The Roots of Ayurveda* (1998)

321 Tad Wise, *Blessings on the Wind* (2002)

322 Philippe Cornu, *Tibetan Astrology* (1997)

323 Robert A. Yelle, *Explaining Mantras: Magic, Rhetoric, and the Dream of a Natural Language* (2003)

Hinks Spinks, the Devil Winks

Origins: This is from a children's counting-out rhyme,[324] an echo of magical incantations and charms from ancient times. The word *spinks* recalls the Sphinx of mythology.

Hiram Abif

Origins: *Hiram Abif* is a name from a legend studied in Freemasonry, concerning "freedom of speech, conscience, and thought."[325] The legend became a central part of Masonic ritual in the year 1730.

Facts: These are the magic words of professional magician Howard Thurston (1869–1936): "During Thurston's stage show, he was known to say, 'pronounce the magic words *Hiram Abif* and the rooster and the duck will change places.'"[326]

<Hissing Sound>
(see also *popping sound*)

Variations and Incantations:

- Hist
  "As they landed, Rolf waited a clear view, then gave a short sharp 'Hist!' It was like a word of magic, for it turned the three moving deer to three stony-still statues."
  —Ernest Thompson Seton, *Rolf In The Woods* (1911)

324 *Notes and Queries* (1854)

325 Paul M. Bessel, "The Hiram Abif Legend" (1999)

326 "Masons and Magicians," *Mill-valley.freemasonry.biz*

In Literature:

- "The 'hissings and murmurings' . . . of magicians."
—Edward Peters, *The Magician, the Witch and the Law* (1978)

- "Jack Starhouse could make [cats] dance wild dances, leaping about upon their hind legs and casting themselves from side to side. This he did by strange sighs and whistlings and hissings."
—Susanna Clarke, *Jonathan Strange & Mr. Norrell* (2004)

- "He raised his hands slowly and extended them, cupping them around the precariously balanced globe without touching it. He bent his head and began to whisper. The words hissed and sizzled in the confined space of the wagon, rough and saw-edged."
—Patricia Wrede, *Mairelon the Magician* (1991)

Hocus

(see also *hocus pocus*)

This is Julius the Magnificent.
I seem to be suffering from partial amnesi
and can't remember what comes after *hocus*.
—Ron Goulart,
Elementary, My Dear Groucho (1999)

Meanings:

- Bewitch
"[T]he lurid Mangaian legend in which infernal deities hocus and destroy the souls of all . . ."
—Robert Louis Stevenson, *In the South Seas* (1896)

  "Could she hocus them again, by playing her charms and beguiling them with sweet words and fair promises?"
—George MacDonald Fraser, *Flashman and the Mountain of Light* (1990)

- Conjuring
"[I]f it's hocus, it's clever hocus indeed. . . . You must admit that it smacks rather of clairvoyance, or the cleverer sort of conjuring trick."
—Michael Kurland, *Death by Gaslight* (1982)

- Illness
"Many of us have fallen to hocus and some have already passed on."
—C.S. Haviland, *Faith & Fairies* (2005)

- Magician
"I say, old hocus, have you such a thing / About you,—feel your pockets, I command.— / I want this instant, an invisible ring."
—John Keats, "The Cap and Bells," *The Mask of Keats: The Endeavour of a Poet* (2000)

- Sham
"'They're going middle-class respectable, and it embarrasses the hell out of them when you get drunk and tell people about panhandling in New Orleans or that hocus wedding in Texas.' 'It wasn't hocus.'"
—Tim Sandlin, *Sex and Sunsets* (1987)

- Spike
"'The night afore the last day o' the last election here, the opposite party bribed the bar-maid at the Town Arms, to hocus the brandy and water of fourteen unpolled electors as was a stoppin' in the house.' 'What do you mean by "hocussing" brandy and water?' 'Puttin' laud'num in it,' replied Sam."
—Charles Dickins, *Pickwick Papers* (1837)

- Trick, deceive
"I thought maybe you was trying to hocus me again."
—Mark Twain, *The Adventures of Huckleberry Finn* (1883)

- Unintelligible
—Allan H. Meltzer, *Keynes's Monetary Theory* (1989)

- Unscientific
"I did not understand that valuable artifacts would be removed entirely from my own care to be subjected to some experimental hocus voodoo by an amateur."
—Elizabeth Ann Scarborough, *Channeling Cleopatra* (2002)

- Voodoo, superstition; nonsense, poppycock
"Hocus. I've seen what she does. Herb tea and a couple of joss sticks."
—Graham Joyce, *Dark Sister* (1999)

In Literature:

- Poet William Carlos Williams described Carl Sandburg as a writer "of excellent hocus."
—Paul L. Mariani, *William Carlos Williams: A New World Naked* (1981)

- "[I]f I hocus you, why you hocus me in return; so it isn't so very unfair, you know."
—Anthony Trollope, *Orley Farm* (1860)

- "Frankly, sir, the exercise strikes me as pure hocus!"
—Michael Kurland, *Death by Gaslight* (1982)

- From *The Rebel Scot* (1647) by John Cleveland, quoted in *The New Oxford Book of Seventeenth-Century Verse* (1991):

Before a Scot can be properly cursed,
I must like Hocus swallow daggers first.

Hocus Pocus
(see also *hokus pokus, sucop socoh*)

Hocus Pocus, gilded words and paper flowers
laid sprinkled around.
—Sorana Salomeia, "Simsalabim" (2004)

Mystique: These primal, rhyming syllables echo the transcendental incantations of Latin rites, reverberating through hallowed cloisters.

They invoke an ancient, unworldly power, especially when enunciated slowly and authoritatively. They conjure a mastery over the power to change one nature or form into another. The words actually constitute a formula: $A \Rightarrow B$, meaning that the substance of A (represented by the name *Hocus*) transmutes into the substance of B (now *Pocus*). The formula is a distillation of the intention: "May that which we call *Hocus* be changed into *Pocus*." This distillation, "Hocus Pocus," thereby epitomizes the act of transmutation itself. One can easily imagine a Medieval alchemist, huddled over his instruments, muttering such a formula to himself, as "Hocus Pocus" would be the equivalent to "Lead Gold" ("[May this base metal] Lead [transform into purest] Gold").

"Hocus Pocus" has been called the original entertainer's phrase. Alas, the profound impact of the phrase has diluted over the years, and modern audiences are likely to consider it nonsensical or to associate it with meaning "cheap trickery." However, its age-old power need not disappear forever. When spoken in a voice that disallows mockery, "hocus pocus" recalls the profound mystery that is at the heart of all worldly changes. "Now, a little hocus-pocus. It doesn't matter if you don't believe in hocus-pocus; the basis of this concept is real enough."[327]

Meanings:

To each his own hocus-pocus, that's what I say.
—Alan Wall, *The School of Night* (2001)

- Angelic name
"Behind each word—though in our wisdom we may be able to discern its humble origin—a celestial power was posited. Sometimes the apotheosis of the word achieved the height of extravagance . . . *Hocus Pocus*, for example, was a Prince on high—or two

---

327 Stuart Wilde, *Silent Power* (1998)

princes, to be exact. The literature of Jewish magic was predominantly an anthology of magical names."
—Joshua Trachtenberg, *Jewish Magic and Superstition* (1939)

- Art of conjuring
—Michael Chabon, *The Amazing Adventures of Kavalier & Clay* (2001)
    "[S]ome hocus-pocus of conjuring priests . . ."
—G.W.F. Hegel, *Phenomenology of Spirit* (1979)
    "A new and improved hocus pocus."
—*The Conjurer's Guide* (1808)
    "Hocus pocus in perfection."
—*The Conjurer's Museum* (1800)

- "Bring about change"

- Confusion
"There's no need to confuse poor Achilles (or the rest of us) with hocus-pocus about what 'almost' happened."
—Douglas R. Hofstadter, *Gödel, Escher, Bach: An Eternal Golden Braid, 20th Anniversary Edition* (1999)
    "Amid all the hocus-pocus, confusion reins. We have made a mystery out of something that is simply a practical, unamazing exercise in self-sufficiency."
—John Rosemond, *John Rosemond's New Parent Power* (2001)

- Deception, sham
—Jeffery Paine, *Adventures with the Buddha* (2004)
—Kim Daniels, *Clean House, Strong House* (2003)
    "They concern themselves only with deception and hocus-pocus, and spend their time in vain cleverness and dazzlement . . ."
—Israel Zinberg, *A History of Jewish Literature* (1975)

Figure 22. The hocus pocus formula of transmutation.

- Distraction
"Call attention to the seemingly impossible conditions under which you have subjected yourself. Caution each man to hold tightly onto your wrists, then go through the necessary hocus pocus as you pretend to make the coin pass."
—J.B. Bobo, *Modern Coin Magic* (1952)

- Dramatic air
"With many flourishes and the hocus-pocus of a magician he extracted the ring from his vest pocket and placed it on my mother's finger."
—Michael Gold, *Jews Without Money* (1930)

- Flashy act
"Give 'em the old hocus pocus."
—Fred Ebb, "Razzle Dazzle," *Chicago* (1975)

- Flight of fancy
—Lloyd Cope, *Astrologer's Forecasting Workbook* (1995)

- Gibberish
"[The vaudeville hypnotist] would chant some hocus-pocus gibberish while waving the handkerchief in front of a volunteer's face."
—Roberta Temes, *The Complete Idiot's Guide to Hypnosis* (2000)

- Guru, spiritual leader
"[M]y friend, philosopher, hocus-pocus and guide."
—Louis H Sullivan, *Kindergarten Chats and Other Writings* (1918)

- Hanky panky
"If there's been any hocus pocus, it seems probable that she's at the bottom of it."
—Agatha Christie, *Crooked House* (1948)

- Hex
"She proceeded to make a hocus-pocus sign with two fingers in the general vicinity of her friend's womb."
—Cheryl Sterling, *What Do You Say To A Naked Elf?* (2005)

- Incantation
—Hajo Holborn, *The Civilization of the Renaissance in Italy* (2002)
"Why didn't the priests say the hocus-pocus over them, and make them all good again?"
—Jerry Z. Muller, *Conservatism* (1997)

- Intuitive wisdom, as from one's "sixth sense"
—Vicki Iovine, *The Girlfriends' Guide to Pregnancy* (1995)

- Jargon, esoteric language
"The cops, district attorney, judge, and jury don't want a bunch of scientific hocus-pocus, they want straightforward information to help them decide what to do."
—Larry Ragle, *Crime Scene* (1995)

- Joke, folly
"But suppose the whole matter were really a hocus-pocus. Suppose that whatever meaning you may choose in your fancy to give to it, the real meaning of the whole was mockery. Suppose it was all folly."
—G.K. Chesterton, *The Napoleon of Notting Hill* (1904)

- Magic
"They play *hocus pocus* tricks enough there . . ."
—Royall Tyler, *The Contrast* (1787), anthologized in *Early American Drama* by Jeffrey H. Richards (1997)
"She is the magician, the one who possesses the hocus-pocus."
—Koren Zailckas, *Smashed* (2005)

- Magic word
"Now square the packet, mutter a hocus pocus or two and fan the cards face up."
—Theodore Annemann, *Annemann's Card Magic* (1977)
"Louis mumbled a little hocus-pocus in a foreign language."
—Rick DeMarinis, "Medicine Man" (1988), anthologized in *Borrowed Hearts* (1999)

- "Magical incantation in the language of the gods"
—Carlos Eire, *Waiting for Snow in Havana: Confessions of a Cuban Boy* (2003)
"[They] began to mutter their hocus-pocus."
—Henry Wadsworth Longfellow, "Christus: A Mystery" (1872)

- Magician
"Hocus-Pocus Junior" was the name of an early book on magic tricks published in 1763 (James Randi, *The Magic World of the Amazing Randi* [1989]).
"I went to see one Mr. Morrison, the *hocus pocus* man."
—Royall Tyler, *The Contrast* (1787), anthologized in *Early American Drama* by Jeffrey H. Richards (1997)

- Magic trick
"[S]ome hocus-pocus, some card-sharping trick . . ."
—Fyodor Dostoyevsky, *Notes from the Underground, Great Short Works of Fyodor Dostoyevsky* (1968)

- "Make something happen"

- Mental focus
"Hocus Pocus" is associated with the word focus partially by virtue of its rhyme. In the following quotation, even though "hocus pocus" is used pejoratively, the association to focus as a related magic word is self-evident: "'Focus, focus, focus,' [he muttered] over and over and over, a mantra. Briody thought he might as well be saying hocus-pocus, for all the good it was doing him."
—Thomas Kelly, *Empire Rising* (2005)

- Mirage or illusion
—Henry Miller, *Plexus* (1987)

- Mumbo-jumbo
"Blathering Zen hocus-pocus like a wise old man on the mountaintop."
—James W. Hall, *Forests of the Night* (2005)

- Mystery
—Brian M. Alman and Peter T. Lambrou, *Self-Hypnosis* (1991)
"[T]here were crystal orbs, scrying glasses, skulls from tombs, saints' knucklebones, spirit sticks that had been looted from Siberian shamans, bottles filled with blood of doubtful provenance, witch-doctor masks, [and so on] . . . Magicians love this kind of thing; they love the hocus-pocus mystery of it all (and half believe it, some of them) and they *adore* the awe-inspiring effect it has on outsiders. Quite apart from anything else, all these knickknacks distract attention from the real source of their power: us."
—Jonathan Stroud, *The Amulet of Samarkand* (2003)
"A genuine sleep scientist or mental health professional is not likely to calm patients' fears or solve their problems by describing recurrent nightmares as mysterious hocus pocus."
—Leslie Halpern, *Dreams on Film* (2003)

- Mysticism
"It sounded hocus-pocus-y to me, to call on higher powers to protect me from evil, but on some intuitive level I sensed it might be helpful, and I certainly needed all the help I could get."
—Candace B. Pert, *Molecules of Emotion* (1999)

- Paranormal, psychic phenomenon
—John Kenneth Muir, *Analytical Guide to Television's* One Step Beyond, *1959–1961* (2001)

- "Prince [angel] on high," as in Judaic magical rites during the Middle Ages
—Gustav Davidson, *Dictionary of Angels: Including the Fallen Angels* (1994)

- Ritual
"[W]e hear of a red heifer, slaughtered with elaborate hocus-pocus by 'Eleazer the priest.'"
—H.L. Mencken, *Treatise on the Gods* (1930)

- Shamanism
"[A]ll this hocus-pocus stuff—sorcery and shamanism—is blanketly proscribed."
—David Carson, *Magic of the Ordinary* (2003)

- Sleight-of-hand
"A little trick, a bit of hocus-pocus."
—Fyodor Dostoevsky, *The Brothers Karamazov* (1880)
"Cheap hocus-pocus, simple sleight of hand."
—Jostein Gaarder, *Sophie's World* (1996)

- Something that defies logic
"It's simple and logical—not hocus-pocus at all."
—*The Atkins Essentials* (2003)

- Stuff and nonsense
—Geraldine McCaughrean, *1001 Arabian Nights* (2000)

- Superstition, primitive belief system
—Michio Kaku, *Hyperspace* (1994)

"Poetta became convinced that the burning of specific candles could cure or fix any problem from bad breath to bunions on the feet. She even went so far as to share some of her knowledge with me, but I can't remember all that hocus-pocus mess."
—Debra Phillips, *The High Price of a Good Man* (2003)

"[H]e must know as well as I do that the ceremonies are mere hocus-pocus. There is nothing to be afraid of there."
—Robin George Collingwood, *The Principles of Art* (1938)

"The reign of hocus pocus is not yet over. What can be said is that we have rid ourselves of a great burden of superstition and misery."
—Daniel Usher, *Political Economy* (2003)

• Unknown quantities
"[What are dreams?] Incredible body hocus pocus. The truth is, we still don't know what they are or where they come from."
—*A Nightmare on Elm Street* (1984), quoted in *Dreams on Film* by Leslie Halpern (2003)

• Unscientific
"[H.P. Blavatsky's *Isis Unveiled*] covered everything from magic and psychic powers to ancient races, secret teachings, and Hindu philosophy. Its basic premise was that the occult is not hocus-pocus but a true science, based on profound knowledge of the secrets of nature, lost to modern humanity but known to the ancients and to a few highly evolved human beings."
—Gary Lachman, *A Dark Muse: A History of the Occult* (2005)

• Witchcraft
—Eugene H. Peterson, *The Message Remix* (2003)
—Ngaire E. Genge, *The Book of Shadows: The Unofficial Charmed Companion* (2000)

Origins: In a fifteenth-century German-Jewish manuscript, a magical formula of mystical names is spelled out. "One of the incantations in it . . . contains the names 'Akos Pakos,' the earliest literary occurrence of the terms which, with slight orthographic variations, have become the hallmark of pseudo-magic in a dozen European tongues—our Hocus Pocus. It is known in European literatures only since the beginning of the seventeenth century. The origin of the term is uncertain—it has been claimed as of both Jewish and Christian derivation—but whatever its origin there is no doubt that it has been preserved for us by German Jews."[328]

Some scholars trace the origin of *hocus pocus* to the Welsh phrase meaning "a goblin's hoax": *hovea pwca*[329] (the *w* in Welsh being a true "double u," pronounced *oo*). *Hocus pocus* may also have evolved from the name of a mythological sorcerer in Norse folklore, Ochus Bochus.[330] Medieval Italian performers appealed to a legendary Italian wizard, also known as Ochus Bochus, for help with their illusions. This wizard's name was misspelled by a German author as "Hogges and Bogges."[331]

A great many people mistakenly assume *hocus pocus* is a corrupted Latin phrase from the Roman Catholic Eucharist: *hoc est enim corpus meum* bishop of Canterbury in 1694,[332] and is generally considered to be a baseless "polemic against the Catholic notion . . . of transubstantiation."[333]

The Oxford English Dictionary has associated *hocus pocus* with a mock-Latin nonsense

328 Joshua Trachtenberg, *Jewish Magic and Superstition* (1939)
329 *Wikipedia.com*
330 David Louis, *2,201 Fascinating Facts* (1983)
331 Cathleen Ann Steg, "Focus on Hocus Pocus," *Scouting*, Sept. 2001
332 Michael Quinion, "Hocus Pocus," *WorldWideWords.com*
333 *LaputanLogic.com*

("this is my body"), in which a wafer is transformed into the body of Christ through the mystery of transubstantiation.[334] This controversial speculation is attributed to John Tillotson, Archphrase: *hax pax max Deus adimax*. However, Victor Hugo, in *The Hunchback of Notre Dame* (1831), claims that *hax pax max* isn't nonsense at all but rather "refers to medicine. [It is a] formula against the bite of mad dogs." Whatever its true origin, *hocus pocus* is certainly a contraction of *hocus-pocus, tontus talontus, vade celeriter, jubeo*, a phrase uttered by the court magician of King James (see the quotation from *A Candle in the Dark*, below).

Facts: "Hocus pocus was originally an entertainer's phrase. Unlike *abracadabra*, it never appeared on amulets or in spell books."[335]

The phrase became synonymous for *trick* or *deception* in the seventeenth century[336] and *juggler* in the eighteenth century.

The contraction *hocus* is the source of the word *hoax*, coined in the late eighteenth century.[337]

The contraction *hocus* combined with *bunkum* to create the word *hokum*.[338]

Some etymologists argue that the card game "poker" derives its name from the contraction *pocus*.[339]

Hocus Pocus Junior is the name of an early "how-to" magic book published in 1634.[340]

In 1584, Reginald Scot mentions *hocus pocus* as a magic word in his book *The Discoverie of Witchcraft*.[341]

The theme song to the *Candid Camera* television series (1948) featured the words hocus pocus: "With a hocus-pocus, you're in focus. It's your lucky day. Smile! You're on *Candid Camera*."

Common Magician's Applications: Changing. For example: "The magician urged the audience to shout out any magic words that they knew. Hocus Pocus became the audience's mantra. 'Help me do this trick by saying hocus-pocus on three,' the audience was urged. The trick failed. 'Hmmmm. Let's say it louder,' urged the magician. Shouts of 'Hocus Pocus' filled the air and the cane magically changed into two handkerchiefs."[342]

Restoration. For example: "The conjurer then says, 'I will now restore the string by saying a few magic words. However, while I do so, you must help me by pulling on both ends of the string. Are you ready? Pull. Hocus pocus, abracadabra, alakazam!' . . . When the conjurer removes his hand, the string is seen to be completely restored and will stand the closest examination."[343]

Variations and Incantations:

- Bogus-pocus
  —Jonathan Kellerman, *The Conspiracy Club* (2003)

- By hocus or by pocus
  —John H. Ritter, *The Boy Who Saved Baseball* (2003)

334 "The highest drama of the week was ushered in by uttering that secret, sacred phrase that, when it reverberated around the massive nooks and crannies of medieval cathedrals, sounded more like 'hocus-pocus' than 'hoc est corpus meum.'"—Leonard I. Sweet, *A Cup of Coffee at the Soul Cafe* (1998)

335 Allan Zola Kronzek, *The Sorcerer's Companion: A Guide to the Magical World of Harry Potter* (2001)

336 Michael Quinion, "Hocus Pocus," *WorldWide Words.com*

337 *Ibid.*

338 H.L. Mencken, *The American Language* (1919)

339 Phil Gordon, *Poker: The Real Deal* (2004)

340 *Ibid.*

341 John Granrose, *The Archetype of the Magician* (1996)

342 Lynne Ober, *Pelham-Windham News* (2003)

343 Henning Nelms, *Magic and Showmanship: A Handbook for Conjurers* (1969)

- Hocky, pocky, dominocky
—American Folklore Society, *The Journal of American Folklore* (1918)

- Hocum pocus
"[B]ringing in an endless parade of preachers with their eternal prayers and priests with their hocum pocus incantations . . ."
—Orson Scott Card, *Prentice Alvin* (1989)

- Hocum Pokum
"Hocum, Pokum, France and Spain / Nine times round the world and back again."
—From an early medieval folk play, quoted in *Nowhere in America* by Hal Rammel (1990)

- Hocus Crocus, Esquilocus
—James Joyce, *Finnegans Wake* (1939)

- Hocus Focus
Recommended for use with Chuck Leach's "Eclipse Wallet" illusion.

- Hocuspocus
"The Devil had always some new hocuspocus to make some little word pop out of their mouths."
—Jacob Grimm, *Teutonic Mythology Volume II* (1883)
          "The hocuspocus position . . ."
—R. Burling. "Cognition and Componential Analysis: God's Truth or Hocuspocus" (1964), quoted in *Routledge Dictionary of Language and Linguistics* by Hadumod Bussmann (1996)

- Hocuspocus minimocus. Abracadabra. Einszwei-drei!
"Magic incantations. Lem's step-grandmother mumbling as she circumcised a fresh loaf of rye bread or pulled a loose tooth from his mouth: 'Hocuspocus minimocus. Abracadabra. Eins-zwei-drei!'"
—Peter Spielberg, *Hearsay* (1992)

- Hocus pocus abracadabra alakazam
"I'd been coveting from afar this cool wooden hanging with three levels that say 'Hocus Pocus, Abracadabra, Alakazam'—because I heart the magic."
—G. Bond, "Shaken & Stirred" (2004)

- Hocus Pocus Alimagocus
Spoken by a magician named Waldo the Magnificent to bring a mannequin to life in the 1980s television series *Today's Special*.

- Hocus pocus alacazam
"[The Great Pepperoni] announces he will levitate him, says the magic words ('Hocus pocus alacazam. You eat salami, I'll take the ham.'), the other levitates horizontally under his blanket. A clown whips off the cover. He's been holding a pair of boots out horizontally from under a blanket."
—Stefan Brecht, *Bread and Puppet Theatre* (1988)

- Hocus pocus, chicken bones choke us, dabra ca abra, boom!
—*TheMagicCafe.com* (2001)

- Hocus-pocus diddily-ocus
—Rex Weyler, *Greenpeace: How a Group of Ecologists, Journalists, and Visionaries Changed the World* (2004)

- Hocus Pocus Dominocus
"Hocus pocus, dominocus, I whispered over and over to myself. I didn't want to forget them. They were the words that disappeared things and changed them into other things. This was useful information. I'd try them right away on baby brother. If they worked, I'd try them on my homeroom teacher, the one who gave me a 'U' in conduct for no reason at all on my last report card."
—Marcia Mascolini, "Hocus Pocus Dominocus," *Front Street Review*

"'Hocus-Pocus-Dominocus,' she is to be transformed into this ravishing beauty."
—Vince Corbett, *The Marvelous Maverick* (2004)

- Hocus Pocus Fishbones Chokus
—Ali Bongo, professional magician. This phrase was picked up in Virginia Henley's novels *The Dragon and the Jewel* (1991), *Seduced* (1994), and *The Border Hostage* (2002).

- Hocus-pocus flim-flam
"Nothing happened. Gogoud tried again, saying the magic words 'Hocus-pocus, flim-flam.'"
—Marek Kohn, "Sir Teo's Quest" (2000)

- Hocus-pocus Hexenschuss
Uttered by the witch in the opera Hänsel und Gretel: "She waves a juniper bough, utters the words '*Hocus-pocus Hexenschuss*'—and they are paralyzed."
—Henry W. Simon, *100 Great Operas and Their Stories: Act-By-Act Synopses* (1989)

- Hocus-pocus, Habeas corpus
—Karen Joy Fowler, *Sister Noon* (2002)

- Hocus-pocus, Hicksius-doxius
—Aphra Behn, *The Rover, the Feigned Courtesans, the Lucky Chance, the Emperor of the Moon* (2000)

- Hocus pocus lemon nokus
From a children's clapping game, transcribed by T. Berry Brazelton in *Touchpoints 3 to 6* (2002).

- Hocus Pocus, Madam'mnocus
—Mike Greene, "Hypnotizing Chickens: A Cautionary Tale," *Mystic River Review* (2002)

- Hocus pocus mumbo jumbo
—John Wooden, *Coach Wooden's Pyramid of Success* (2005)

"The 'hocus-pocus, mumbo-jumbo' mystification of traditional African beliefs found in many Western films . . ."
—Melissa Thackway, *Africa Shoots Back* (2003)

- Hocus Pocus, Now you see it, now you don't
—Peter R. Breggin, *Talking Back to Ritalin* (2001)

- Hocus pocus-pocus
—Roger Van Noord, *Assassination of a Michigan King* (1988)

- Hocus pocus pocus hocus
"Chant: 'Hocus Pocus, Pocus Hocus,' and wave your hands in the air."
—*ScoutXing.com* (2002)

- Hocus Pocus, toilet plunger, football touchdown, woof
"I moved my hands back and forth, around and around, chanting, 'Hocus pocus, toilet plunger, football touchdown, woof!' I crashed the two circles together, then held them up, now linked together. 'Ta da!'"
—Jon Scieszka, *Sam Samurai* (2001)

- Hocus pocus zippity-doo-dah
—Ntozake Shange, "Spell #7 Geechee Jibara Quick Magic Trance Manual for Technologically Stressed Third World People," *Honey, Hush!* (1998)

- Hocus pokus
—Annie Modesitt, *Confessions of a Knitting Heretic* (2004)

- Hocus-pokus Hanky-panky
—Steven C. Smith, *A Heart at Fire's Center: The Life and Music of Bernard Herrmann* (1991)

- Hogie-pogie
Lakota Chief Wallace Black Elk's phrase for a magician's illusions (*Black Elk: The Sacred Ways of a Lakota* [1991]).

- Hokuspokus
—Jürgen Köller (2003)

- Hoocus Poocus Dominocus
—Karin Michels (2005)

- Hopeless Focus
  —Professional magician Steve Charney, *Hocus Jokus: 50 Funny Magic Tricks Complete with Jokes* (2003)

- Hukus-Pukus
  —Professional magician Steve Charney, *Hocus Jokus: 50 Funny Magic Tricks Complete with Jokes* (2003)

- Horcty Porcty Dominorky
  This phrase appears in a choral warm-up chant of the Harvard Noteables. The chant is entitled "Aktamalygawhat?":

  Aktamaly Gazali Gazamti Yamti Yedi Yahoo
  Inkti Minkty Yedde Gazinkti Yamti Rei Yahoo
  Wing Wang Tricky Tracky
  Poo Foo Joozy Woozy
  Skizzle Wizzle Wang Dang
  Horcty Porcty Dominorky

- Itcha, kitcha, dominicha
  —American Folklore Society, *The Journal of American Folklore* (1918)

- Jiggery-pokery
  —Carl Jung, *Memories, Dreams, and Reflections* (1961)

- Locus-Pocus
  —Julia Oliver, *Music of Falling Water* (2001)

- Mumbo-Pocus
  —Frank Zappa, *The Real Frank Zappa Book* (1989)

- Oacha, poacha, domond oacha
  —American Folklore Society, *The Journal of American Folklore* (1918)

- Ocha, pocha, domo noche
  —American Folklore Society, *The Journal of American Folklore* (1918)

- Ocus-Pocus
  —Edward Eager, *The Time Garden* (1958)

- Orky Porky Dominorky
  This phrase occurs in the last line of the University of Redlands school cheer. The cheer, written by C. Merle Waterman, was originally called the "Psalm of Collegiate Thanksgiving." It is now called "Och Tamale":

  Och Tamale
  Gazolly Gazump
  Deyump Deyatty Yahoo
  Ink Damink
  Deyatty Gazink
  Deyump Deray Yahoo
  Wing Wang
  Tricky Trackey
  Poo Foo
  Joozy Woozy
  Skizzle Wazzle
  Wang Tang,
  Orky Porky Dominorky
  Redlands!
  Rah, Rah, Redlands!

- Otcha, potcha, dominotcha
  —American Folklore Society, *The Journal of American Folklore* (1918)

- Otchey, potchey, otchey, dotchey
  —American Folklore Society, *The Journal of American Folklore* (1918)

- Ozy, pozy, doma-nozy
  —American Folklore Society, *The Journal of American Folklore* (1918)

In Literature:

- "[O]bscured in a mist of hocus-pocus and imposture . . ."
  —J.J. Clarke, *The Tao of the West* (2000)

- "I will speak of a man . . . that went about in King James's time and long since . . . who called himself 'The King's Majesty's most excellent Hocus Pocus,' and was so called because at the playing of every trick he used

to say: 'Hocus-pocus, tontus talontus, vade celeriter, jubeo,' a dark composure of words, to blinde the eyes of the beholders, to make his Trick pass the more currently without discovery, because when the eye and the ear of the beholder are both earnestly busied, the Trick is not so easily discovered, nor the Imposture discerned."
—Thomas Ady, *A Candle in the Dark* (1655)

- "Kay took off Merlyn's hat and put it on Sir Ector, and Sir Ector said, 'Well, bless my soul, now I am a nigromancer. Hocus-Pocus."
—T.H. White, *The Once and Future King* (1939)

- From Moliere, *Tartuffe* (1669), translated by Richard Wilbur (1961):

Are you so dazed by this man's hocus-pocus
That all the world, save him, is out of focus?

- From Johann Wolfgang Von Goethe, *Faust* (1908), translated by Walter Kaufmann (1961):

You have the brazen impudence
To do your hocus-pocus here?

- "'Newton was an alchemist,' he says. 'His genius was as much hocus-pocus as anything else, his *Principia* and his *Opticks* and the laws of gravity were almost accidents, the voodoo man's sideline. His main interest was deciphering the secret codes of the universe, and he computed the year that Jason found the Golden Fleece.'"
—Janette T. Hospital, *The Last Magician* (1992)

- "From time to time jagged streaks of lightning illuminated the sky, hocus-pocus from the heavens. Lucy oohed and aahed, caught up in the wonder of it."
—Earl Emerson, *Poverty Bay* (1997)

- "A little hypnotic ability, a little hocus-pocus, and they can make people believe anything."
—Neil Gaiman, *American Gods* (2002)

- "What, do they consult Jugglers and Hocus-Pocusses? No certainly they consult Witches or Wizzards, and Diviners."
—Joseph Glanvill, *Saducismus Triumphatus: Or, Full and Plain Evidence Concerning Witches and Apparitions* (1688)

Figure 23. Doctor Johannes Faust and Mephistopheles from Christopher Marlowe, *Tragic Historie of D. Faust* (1631).

- "Hocus, pocus, dominocus . . . if someone was mean to me, I'd lie in bed at night imagining him (or her) with a big X on his face. The results worked very nicely. The next day the boy was invisible to me, completely insignificant—I no longer saw him."
—Jessica Treat, "Honda" (2000)

- "Hocus Pocus, a simple gesture and, like a wonder, red roses fell out of your hat in a cascade."
—Sorana Salomeia, "Simsalabim" (2004)

- "When in doubt, try hocus pocus."
—T.A. Barron, *The Merlin Effect* (1994)

Hokus Pokus

(see also *hocus pocus*)

A conjuror with a satchel of
'Hokus Pokus' slung round his neck.
—Leslie Stephen,
Dictionary of National Biography (1901)

Meanings:

- Deceit
"Hokus-pokus promises."
—John Moody, *The Truth About the Trusts* (1904)

- Jargon
"This hokus pokus was probably invented by lawyers."
—Clarence Morris, *The Justification of the Law* (1971)

- Magic
"Perhaps Frankie possessed a hokus-pokus touch."
—Gordon H. Fleming, *The Dizziest Season* (1984)

- Mirage; illusion
"[I]f I hadn't seen it with my own eyes, I should declare it be a Never, Never land—a hokus pokus that never did exist."
—John Jacob Niles, *One Man's War* (1929)

- Mumbo jumbo
"[J]ust the sort of thing one calls in English 'mumbo-jumbo' (or in German *Hokus-pokus*)."
—Karl Popper, *The Myth of the Framework* (1994)

- Nonsense syllables
—Nicola Pressburger, *Homage to the Eighth District* (1990)

- Secret
"The hokus pokus is to apply to the nut and stem of the whip and flat top of the insu-lator a coat of Plio-bond, a glue which will stick anything to anything."
—*Air Facts* (1938)

- Vulgar sorcery
—Helmut Hoffmann, *The Religions of Tibet* (1961)

Origins: *Hokus pokus* is the Germanic/Scandinavian spelling of *hocus pocus.*

While traveling through Arabia, Jonathan Raeban records a magician announcing "every new transformation" with the words "haukus boaukus." He writes, "I was as interested to discover where 'hokus pokus' came from as I was in the reappearance of the Ace of Spades or the missing banknote."[344]

Facts: The book *The Little Man* by Erich Kästner (1966) features a famous conjuror named Professor Hokus von Pokus.

In 1625, the playwright Ben Johnson reported a stage magician called Hokus Pokus.[345]

Variations and Incantations:

- Hokey Pokey
—Professional magician Steve Charney, *Hocus Jokus: 50 Funny Magic Tricks Complete with Jokes* (2003)

- Hokus, hokey, hokum
—Henry J. Taylor, *Men and Moments* (1966)

- Hokus Jokus
—Professional magician Steve Charney, *Hocus Jokus: 50 Funny Magic Tricks Complete with Jokes* (2003)

- Hokus mokus
"[I]t'll be hokus-mokus all the blessed time."
—Joan Aiken, *The Stolen Lake* (1981)

---

344 *Arabia Through the Looking Glass* (1979)
345 Allan Zola Kronzek, *The Sorcerer's Companion: A Guide to the Magical World of Harry Potter* (2001)

- Hokus Pocus
  —Thomas Hart Benton, quoted in *Benton, Pollock, and the Politics of Modernism* by Erika Doss (1991)

- Hokus-pokery
  —John Tyler Bonner, *First Signals* (2000)

- Hokus, Pokeus, Dominocus
  —Edward B. Grothus, "Nuclear-Free News" (2005)

- Hokus Pokus, Abra Kadabra
  "'Now I am going to show you the most magnificent skill of my entire life as a magician. I will raise the covers on the buildings before you by saying, Hokus Pokus, Abra Kadabra.' Then the covers turned into white eagles and flew away."
  —Ilyas Halil, *House of Cards* (2000)

- Hokus pokus alla gazam
  "The performer rolls the egg back and forth across the selected card. While doing this he utters the magic words, 'Hokus pokus alla gazam.' Then he states that the egg will name the card selected."
  —John Scarne, *Scarne on Card Tricks* (1950)

- Hokus Pokus Dominokus
  —Hal Reid, *Directions Magazine* (1998)

- Hokus Pokus Holderbusch
  This is a spell of disenchantment which Gretel hears the witch pronounce in the opera *Hänsel und Gretel* by Engelbert Humperdinck (1893)

- Hokus pokus jiminy smokus
  —Bessie Whitmore Stillman, *Training Children to Study* (1928)

- Hokus-pokus, popalorum, Stickstun, stickstun, cockalorum jig
  "A walking stick served him as a wand, and this he waved three times slowly and majestically, while he repeated in solemn tones this singular legend—'Hokus-pokus, popalo-

rum, Stickstun, stickstun, cockalorum jig.' Thereupon the curtain went back, and lo! Sunday appeared sitting upon a throne of state, robed in a long crimson mantle, which made him look like an emperor."
  —Bracebridge Hemyng, *Jack Harkaway and His Son's Escape from the Brigands of Greece* (1908)

- Hokuspokus filiokus
  —Jens Vigen (2003)
    This is the Norwegian equivalent of *hocus pocus*.
  —Charles E. Funk, *Horsefeathers: And Other Curious Words* (1958)

In Literature:

- "There was no attempt to hide deceit behind a curtain of impressive hokus-pokus."
  —Abraham Kuyper, *Women of the Old Testament* (1964)

- "The worst fear of all: fear of death with no priest around to perform his little 'hokus pokus and holy oil' skit over him on his death bed."
  —Robert H. Muller, *From Radical Left to Extreme Right* (1976)

- "[A]n 'artistic hokus-pokus,' as unreal as the character himself, but which on that very account helps the illusion and makes the hole plausible."
  —Robert Wooster Stallman, *The Houses that James Built* (1961)

- "I am not the only one here who can use hokus-pokus, as you call it. You may be surprised to learn that you, Jack, are blessed with more than average hokus-pokus power."
  —Willow Skye Robinson, *Prince of New Avalon* (2004)

- "Like a sorcerer chanting an incantation I mumbled, Hokus-pokus, hokus-pokus."
  —Louis Paul Lochner, *Always the Unexpected* (1956)

- "That was the old way, gossip, when Iniquity came in like Hokus-Pokus in a juggler's jerkin, with false skirts like the Knave of Clubs!"
—Alan Seymour Downer, *The British Drama* (1950)

- "So the Magician took the little round box from his belt and the little white pebble from the little round box and he rubbed the pebble once crossways and twice crossways and said 'Hokus, pokus!'"
—Johnny Gruelle, *Orphan Annie Storybook* (1989)

Hola Noa Massa

Origins: These words have been attributed to Albertus Magnus[346] (also known as Saint Albert the Great), the 13th-century German philosopher, theologian, and scientist.

Facts: *Hola Noa Massa* was found written in "an Elizabethan manuscript in the British Museum."[347]

This phrase is purportedly part of a chant to prolong orgasm.

In Literature: "'Hola Noa Massa!' spoke the strange booming voice. And back came a chorus intonation: 'Janna, janna! Hoa, hoa! Sabbat, sabbat! Molock, Lucifer, Asteroth!' Those, I fancied, were the names of pagan gods and devils. As the last syllable died away, something came into view beyond the window glass."
—Manly Wade Wellman, *Fearful Rock and Other Precarious Locales* (2001)

Holes in the Rain

Facts: This is a magic phrase for time travel in the novel *The Wooden Sea* (2001) by Jonathan Carroll: "Closing my eyes, I said, 'Holes in the rain.' The phrase that sent me back to my future."

Home
(see also *there's no place like home*)

Home, of course.
—Murilo Rubião,
The Ex-Magician and Other Stories (1979)

Mystique: "There is a magic in that little world, home; it is a mystic circle that surrounds comforts and virtues never known beyond its hallowed limits" (Robert Southey).

Origins: "The ancient root word *ham*, from which our word 'home' came, meant the triangle where two rivers meet which, with a short wall, can be defended. At first the word 'home' meant safety, then gradually comfort."[348]

Facts: The following lines are from "a magic spell for the Far Journey" by Yu Ch'ing: "[T]he deeper secret within the secret: The land that is nowhere, that is the true home."[349]

Variations and Incantations:

- Happy Home
"As a little girl, I would often chant and sing two words, which I had decided were magic words. These words were *happy home*, and how I came by them I don't know, but I

---

346 Gerina Dunwich, *Wicca Candle Magick* (1989)
347 Migene Gonzalez-Wippler, *The Complete Book of Spells, Ceremonies and Magic* (1988)
348 John Steinbeck, *America and Americans* (1966)
349 *Secret of the Golden Flower*, translated by Richard Wilhelm (1955)

believed if I said and sang them often enough, it would change things."
—Norma Fox Mazer, *When She Was Good* (2000)

In Literature:

- "The men of the regiment appreciated their homes more than any other thing (except perhaps the good cooking) that they had left behind. 'I never knew how much home was worth until deprived of it,' Houghton wrote and later added, 'We find that same reference paid the word "home" in every company of the regiment. There is something magical in the word.'"
  —Nancy Niblack Baxter, *Gallant Fourteenth* (1980)

- "At dawn he convened this assembly and could say no more than the magical word 'home' before his men were racing to their boats to do just that."
  —Lawrence A. Tritle, *From Melos to My Lai* (2000)

- "Old Marheyo whispers the magic words 'home' and 'mother' knowingly in Tommo's ear."
  —Laurie Robertson-Lorant, *Meville: A Biography* (1996)

- "[He] called to the coachman 'Home!' The magic word seemed to effect the horses, for they started at a brisk trot, and within a couple of minutes the carriage was out of sight."
  —Marie Corelli, *Thelma* (1887)

Hooey

Meaning: Nonsense
"[S]he investigates rituals and attends conventions, and takes part in all manners of bunkum

and hooey, or rather, magic and the supernatural."
—Rick Kleffel, "Christine Wicker is 'Not In Kansas Anymore'" (2006)

Facts: *Hooey* is the magic word used to activate the "Magic Hooey Stick" for testing psychic ability. Spectators may also be encouraged to recite the following mantra to warm up the stick: "Itzabeem locotada manzuneetee kolaseetseim."[350]

Ho'okalakupua

Facts: *Ho'okalakupua* is a Hawaiian word for "magic," referring to "use of the spiritual power [*mana*] that is resident within nature.... [A]ny use of *mana* to create wondrous change was an act of magic."[351]

Hoopla

There's a lot of hoopla that goes on to make the event much more interesting.
—W.C. Madden & John Peterson, *The College World Series* (2005)

Meanings:

- Attention-attracting commotion
  —Evan Morris, "The Word Detective" (2003)

- Boisterous celebration
  —Evan Morris, "The Word Detective" (2003)

---

350 John Banister-Marx, "The Incredible Magic Hooey Stick" (1998)

351 Scott Cunningham, *Hawaiian Magic and Spirituality* (2001)

Origins: Hoopla originated in the late 19th century as a "simple shout of excitement or surprise."[352]

Facts: Hoopla is the proper name of the carnival game in which one tosses small wooden hoops over square pegs.[353]

In Literature: "You appear on the stage with a napkin on one hand and a serviette grasped between the five fingers of the other. And waving it above your head you then with a series of intonations such as 'hoopla' or 'abracadabra' manage to make the first . . ."
—Clement Freud, "Welcome to Just a Minute!" (1977)

Hopla Yado Yado Bido Bido Pif Paf Plouf Tic Toc Rah Rah Rah Tralala
(see also *hoopla* and *pif paf poof*)

In Literature: Raymond Federman, *Take It or Leave It* (1976)

Hottentot Tatertot

In Literature: Bart King, *The Big Book of Boy Stuff* (2004)

Houdini Lives

Facts: This magic phrase refers to the great magician Harry Houdini.

In Literature: "It helps to know the magic word if you want to get into the Famous Houdini Museum in Scranton, Pennsylvania. I tried 'Abracadabra,' and it worked, but by the time I left, I was wiser. The real magic word, or words, to be more precise, are, and you have to yell them, 'Houdini Lives!'"
—*RoadtripAmerica.com* (2005)

Hour

In Literature: "'Hour' is a magical word: of all the units of time it is the most imponderable. Either it is interminable, or so fleeting. One finds it difficult to believe there are a full two dozen in a day."
—Thomas M. Disch, *Neighboring Lives* (1980)

Hovu-haga, Somasa

In Literature: "Next he squeezed the rock, mumbling spirit words, Hovu-haga, somasa, which were his private, spirit-magic words. 'Hovu-haga, haga, somasa,' he murmured."
—Virginia Hamilton, *The Magical Adventures of Pretty Pearl* (1986)

---

352 John Banister-Marx, "The Incredible Magic Hooey Stick" (1998)
353 *Ibid.*

How

Mystique: The word *how* is an "irresistible trigger" that catches the audience's attention.[354] *How* is the way a trick is done, and it causes the audience to wonder about the implied secret itself.

Huey Fooey Chop Suey Gefilte Fish

Facts: These were the magic words of professional magician Tom Kovnats.[355]

Hugger-Mugger
(see also *mumbo jumbo*)

Mystique: Though originally a nonsense phrase, *hugger mugger* has taken on its own mystique and often conjures a conspiratorial aura.[356] It's a confusing jumble[357] that perhaps betrays a "secret haste,"[358] and it often occurs amidst swirling fogs[359] or in "smoke-filled rooms."[360]

Meanings:

- Clandestinely

- Untidy

Origins: These words were coined by William Shakespeare and appear in his play *Hamlet*, meaning in context "without proper ceremony."[361]

In Literature:

- "I loved to go to her in the thick of the Adriatic winter when, in a hugger-mugger of fogs, the market seemed a tiny kingdom in the sky."
  —Marlena De Blasi, *A Thousand Days in Venice* (2002)

- "[T]he dark superstition and medieval hugger-mugger of the romantic [architectural] styles."
  —James Howard Kunstler, *Geography of Nowhere* (1993)

I

Iae-Yog-Thu-Sot

Facts: These are magic words featured in the computer game "Shadow of the Comet" (1994).

I Am

The magic is in the words *I am*.
—Melody Beattie, *The Lessons of Love* (1994)

Facts: *I Am* is a divine name in the Bible. For example, Yahweh identifies himself to Moses as "I am that I am" (Exodus 3:14). Jesus said, "Very truly, I tell you, before Abraham was, I am" (John 8:58).

---

354 Chuck Crawley, "The Magic Word *How* and Why You Must Use It" (2005)

355 Ontario Genealogical Society (2005)

356 "'All very hugger-mugger.' He was brimming with delight in the conspiracy."—Ellen Feldman, *Lucy: A Novel* (2003)

357 *Kaplan's Word Power* (2003)

358 Carla Lynn Stockton, *Shakespeare's Hamlet* (2000)

359 Marlena De Blasi, *A Thousand Days in Venice* (2002)

360 Eugene H. Peterson, *God's Message for Each Day* (2004)

361 Folger Shakespeare Library, *Hamlet* (1992)

Variations and Incantations: I Am Love
—Jim Britt, *Rings of Truth* (1999)

Ibbity Bibbity
(see also *ipitty bipitty* and *one-ery two-ery ickery ann*)

Origins: *Ibbity Bibbity Sibbity Sab* "was an old counting-out rhyme like 'Eenie, meenie, miney, mo' and . . . 'Onerie twoery ickery ann.'"[362]

Variations and Incantations:

- Ibbity, bibbity, canaga
  —Helen M. Bezansky, *Whimsy By Hoot* (2003)

- Ibbity bibbity canal-boat
  —John B. Sanford, *The People from Heaven* (1995)

- Ibbity bibbity casaba
  —Betty MacDonald, *Mrs. Piggle-Wiggle's Magic* (1985)

- Ibbity-bibbity-ka-nah-ba
  —John O'Hara, *Butterfield 8* (1935)

- Ibbity bibbity kinAYbo
  —Hortense Calisher, *Sunday Jews* (2002)

- Ibbity bibbity knabe
  —Elois Hubbard Linscott, *Folk Songs of Old New England* (1939)

- Ibbity bibbity sibbity sab
  —Hortense Calisher, *Sunday Jews* (2002)
  —John B. Sanford, *The People from Heaven* (1943)

- Ibbity, bibbity, zibbity, zab
  —American Folklore Society, *The Journal of American Folklore* (1918)

- Ibbity, bibbity, zibbity, zee
  —American Folklore Society, *The Journal of American Folklore* (1918)

Ibbity-Boppitty-Boo
(see *bibbidy-bobbidi-boo*)

In Literature: Marcelle Langan DiFalco, *The Big Sister's Guide to the World of Work* (2005)

Ibbidy Zibbidy
(see *ibbity bibbity*)

In Literature: *Uncle John's Electrifying Bathroom Reader For Kids Only!* (2003)

I Believe
(see *believe*)

In Literature: "[H]is life had been revolutionized by three simple phrases, each beginning with two magic words: *I believe*."
—Norman Vincent Peale, *Positive Imaging* (1982)

I Do

The magic words "I do."
—Geoffrey Block, *Enchanted Evenings* (1997)

In Literature: "'I do!' The magic words that make one out of two."
—Ira Gershwin, "Tomorrow is the Time," *The Complete Lyrics of Ira Gershwin* (1993)

---

362 Martin Gardner, *Famous Poems From Bygone Days* (1995)

If
(see also *what if*)

Much virtue in If.
—William Shakespeare, *As You Like It* (c. 1600)

Variations and Incantations: If only
  "Always remember those two magic words: if only."
  —Gil Friedman, *How to be Totally Unhappy in a Peaceful World* (1997)

In Literature:

- "[T]here is even a momentary reference to 'the little magic word *if.*'"
  —Jane Milling, *Modern Theories of Performance* (2001)

- "Everything that had happened in the last months rang of the magic word 'if.'"
  —Richard Helms, *The Valentine Profile* (2002)

Iggly Wiggly Woo

Facts: This is a magic phrase attributed to magician Mark Cheetham.[363]

Ili Mili Phuh Phuh

Origins: *Ili mili phuh phuh* is an apparently nonsensical mantra of Buddhist origin.

Facts: This phrase is "similar to the magic words, such as 'abracadabra,' found in other traditions."[364]

I Love To Read
(see also *love*)

Facts: Professional magician Marty Hahne tells an audience of children that the magic words are not *abracadabra* but *I love to read.* "Before each trick, he [has the children] wiggle their fingers and say the 'magic' words."[365]

I Love You
(see also *love*)

To find that excelsior feeling,
that effervescent feeling,
that legendary feeling that is magic . . .
that is what love does.
—Judy Zebra Knight & Ramtha,
That Elixir Called Love (2003)

Mystique: "There aren't any magical words, really. The words just hold the magic. They give it shape and form, they make it useful, describe the images within. I'll say this, though: Some words have a power that has nothing to do with supernatural forces. They resound in the heart and mind, they live long after the sounds of them have died away, they echo in the heart and the soul. They have power, and that power is very real. ["I love you."] Those three words are good ones."[366]

In Literature:

- "There are six magic words. The first three are, 'I love you.' And the second three are, 'God bless you.' They can cause miracles to happen."
  —John-Roger, *The Way Out Book* (1980)

363 Emazdad, *TheMagicCafe.com* (2003)
364 Robert A. Yelle, *Explaining Mantras: Magic, Rhetoric, and the Dream of a Natural Language* (2003)
365 Michelle Jones, "Magician Helps Kids Discover Power of Reading," *St. Petersburg Times* (2000)
366 Jim Butcher, *Grave Peril* (2001)

- "Without question, those three magic words 'I love you,' are the most sought-after message of all."
—Sandra Merrill Covey, *The 7 Habits of Highly Effective Families* (1997)

- "This magic word, this spell which opens all gates, doors and passages of the world sounds [like] 'I love you,' and your golden elixir is 'Love.'"
—Bozena T. Klejne, *The Rainbow Butterfly* (2003)

- "You don't remember the magic words, 'I love you'? And that if you say the magic words, then everything after that will be okay?"
—Alan Hollingsworth, *Flatbellies* (2001)

Illusion

In Literature:

- "I absently rubbed my lucky money clip between the fingers on my free hand as lightning cracked, a flock of white doves exploded into the night sky over the gothic church cathedral next door and somewhere Doug Henning spoke the magic words 'ill-LOO-jun.'"
—Daniel S. Fettinger, "The Magical Money Clip: A Love Story" (2005)

- "Tristan . . . rode with a sword graven with magical words of *Truth* and *Illusion*, cleaving one from the other, and wielded that weapon against the Shadow of shadows."
—C.J. Cherryh, *Fortress of Eagles* (1998)

Imadodo

Facts: This word sounds like the phrase "I'm a Dodo."

Common Magician's Applications: Transformations. For example: "'The magician explained that he knew some secret words that would change the water to any color,' you say as you pick up the large glass of water. 'He asked the audience what color they would like, and they said, "green." The magician said that the magic word for green was "Imadodo," and when he poured the water into the empty glass, it would turn green.'"[367]

Imagine

Mystique: "[T]here is always a door—imagination. 'Imagine' has the word *image* in it, and also a piece of the word *magic*. To imagine is how we create the door that leads from the impossible to the possible. The magic of it is just that we don't really know how or why it works."[368]

Variations and Incantations: Imagination

In Literature: "Whatever the situation, the key is applying the magic word—time out for drumroll—*imagination*."
—Gary McCord, *Golf For Dummies* (1999)

367 Laurence B. White Jr., *Shazam! Simple Science Magic* (1991)

368 Linda Tellington-Jones, *The Tellington TTouch* (1993)

Immo Haud Daemonorum, Umquam et Numquam, Urbi et Orbi, Quamquam Azazel Magnopere Thoth et Urim et Thummim In Nomine Tetragrammaton. Fiat, Fiat. Amen.

Meanings: The first two phrases of this spell mean "By no means condemn (damn), at any time whatsoever." The rest of the spell is incomprehensible.

Origins: This phrase is partially Latin and partially pseudo-Latin.

In Literature: "There are a very few extremely powerful amulets that . . . are very rare. I have never handled such an amulet, nor have I seen one, but it is said that one was owned by King Solomon, and that Simon Magus somehow contrived to steal one, so that for a time he seemed to be a very great magician indeed. These amulets of which I speak are so powerful that they do not appear to be magic at all. They do not respond to any of the standard tests. Yet, I am told that they will respond to this test: Place the amulet in your left hand, cross yourself three times, and say the following prayer: *Immo haud daemonorum, umquam et numquam, urbi et orbi, quamquam Azazel magnopere Thoth et Urim et Thummim in nomine Tetragrammaton. Fiat, fiat. Amen.* Then, if the amulet is truly one of those I have described above, it will produce a tingling senesation in the hand."
—John Bellairs, *The Figure in the Shadows* (1975)

Imperio

Origins: *Imperio* is from the Latin word meaning "command."

In Literature: *Imperio* is a spell for putting one under your command in *Harry Potter and the Goblet of Fire* by J.K. Rowling (2000).

Incendio

Origins: *Incendio* is from the Latin word meaning "to set fire to."

In Literature: *Incendio* is a spell for conjuring fire in *Harry Potter and the Goblet of Fire* by J.K. Rowling (2000).

Indocilis Pr ivata Loqui

Origins: *Indocilis Privata Loqui* is a Latin phrase meaning "not apt to disclose secrets."

Facts: This "regal" phrase is attributed to the first Caesar: "Never . . . was there within the same compass of words, a more emphatic expression of Caesar's essential and inseparable grandeur of thought, which could not be disguised or laid aside for an instant, than is found in the three casual words
—*Indocilis Privata Loqui* (Thomas De Quincey, *The Caesars* [1832–34]).

Indocilis Privata Loqui is the motto of Great Britain's Magic Circle society (founded 1905).

Inexplicable

In Literature: "Inexplicable—that's the magic word."
—Clayton Thomas (2003)

Inka Dinka Doo

Origins: This magic phrase sounds like "a completely other language."[369] It was popularized by a novelty theme song by Jimmy Durante in 1934.

Variations and Incantations:

- Inka dinka dink
  —Don DeLillo, *Libra* (1989)

- Inka Dinka Doom
  —Robert Dunn, *Sunspot Boulevard* (2000)

- Inka dinka rinka doo
  These are magic words spoken by Tabitha Stephens in the television series *Bewitched*.

Inshallah

Meanings:

- "God willing"

- "If Allah wills"

Origins: *Inshallah* is of Arabic origin.

In Literature: "*Inshallah* is Lilly's magic word. It is from the language that she knows ought not to be used by day except in an emergency. Because the words are like wishes from a genie—don't waste them. Lily has not even a rudimentary understanding of Arabic; it is, rather, dream-like. At night in bed, long after lights-out, she and Frances speak the strange language. Their bed language. Frances uses half-remembered phrases and tells fragments of old stories, weaving them with pieces of songs, filling in the many gaps with her own made-up words that approximate the sounds of Mulla's Old Country tongue. Lily converses fluently in the made-up language, unaware which words are authentic, which invented, which hybrid. The meaning resides in the music and the privacy of their magic carpet bed. Arabian Nights."
—Ann-Marie MacDonald, *Fall On Your Knees* (1996)

Intuition

In Literature: "[H]e introduced me to my first real magic word—and it wasn't *Abracadabra* or *Hocus Pocus! 'Intuition,'* Doc said, portentously. 'The most magical word of all. The source of all real magic.'"
—Craig Karges, *The Wizard's Legacy: A Tale of Real Magic* (2002)

Inuck-Ch-Uck

Facts: This is a magic word of transformation spoken by the character Apache Chief in the television series *The All-New Super Friends Hour* (1977).

Ipitty Bipitty
(see also *ibbity bibbity*)

Facts: These are magic words from the *Bewitched* television series. They began a spell for manifesting a Caesar salad: "Ippity bipitty salad green, oil, vinegar, chi-chi-bean, I call on Caesar's eternal soul, here and now to fill this bowl."

---

369 Don DeLillo, *Libra* (1989)

İpswobego

Common Magician's Applications: Professional magician John Mulholland suggests that one's patter "may be far-fetched but must sound reasonable. As an example, it is permissible to claim that the magic word 'Ipswobego' will cause an object to disappear but in the next trick, where something quite different occurs, it is well to devise another magic word. The audience will accept, while realizing it is silly, that a magic word caused something to happen. They will not accept, because it becomes too absurdly silly, that the same word will cause something else to happen."[370]

İs

Mystique: "The most profound statement that can be made about something is the statement that 'it is.' . . . The word *is* is the most magical word. It is a short, inconsequential little word and does not even sound special. Yet the word *is* is the greatest hymn to the 'thereness' of things. We are so thoroughly entangled in the web of the world that we are blind to the unfolding world being there before us."[371]

İsh-ka-loo-la-osh-ka-loo-la-bosh-ka-loo-la-lum

In Literature: "[W]hen they got back to where the poor bird was the green fairy did a magical trick. He took two pieces of wood, and three little stones, tossed them up in the air, and pronounced this word: 'Ish-ka-loo-la-osh-ka-loo-la-bosh-ka-loo-la-lum!' and in an instant that bird's leg was all well again, and it sang its song some more, just like this, only, of course, I can't sing it very well: 'Oh fie lum did-e-laddie ah! Oh tra la did-e-lay! Hum dum dum diddle-ideum, Tu rum lum skiddle-day!'"
—Howard Roger Garis, *Johnnie and Billie Bushytail* (1910)

İsm-El-Azam

Meanings:

- The absolute
- The great name of Allah
- The hidden greatest name

Origins: *Ism-El-Azam* is of Arabic origin.

Facts: This magic phrase, originating from Arab alchemists, "is believed to be extremely powerful in any type of invocation."[372]

Variations and Incantations:

- Al-Ism Al-Azam
- Ism al-Azam

İthni Asme Ata, İthni Manamee, Drutha Lotacata

Facts: This incantation, spoken while walking in a circle, is from Clive Barker's *Abarat* (2002).

370 *Mulholland's Book of Magic* (1963)
371 John O'Donohue, *Beauty* (2004)
372 Migene Gonzalez-Wippler, *The Complete Book of Spells, Ceremonies and Magic* (1988)

It Is All Right

The welcome sound of these
two magic words, All Right!
—D.H. Lawrence, *Aaron's Rod* (1921)

In Literature:

- "Magic occurs between parent and child. I recall awful nights as a fledging father with a crying infant, my first child. Night after night, she would scream and I would yell just as wildly in my mind. But magic occurred. Sometimes, I would pick her up, hold her close to me and say, 'It is all right. It is all right.' This is word magic. It was not all right from the everyday-life point of view. She was miserable and I was too. Besides, she could not understand what I said. Furthermore, I could not understand it either. But both of us were made content. 'It is all right.' That was a conviction about her, me, our relationship and our future. This is very basic magic."
—Robert E. Neale, *Magic and Meaning* (1995)

- "Mr. B. was also made to sleep in one minute, and rendered deaf to the loudest noises, till the magic words 'All right' awoke him."
—William Gregory, *Animal Magnetism or Mesmerism and its Phenomena* (1909)

It Is Time
(see *now* and *presto*)

In Literature: "'It is time.' Salvador would never forget as long as he lived the ring of these three magic words, 'It is time.'"
—Victor E. Villaseñor, *Rain of Gold* (1991)

It Sil Heve

Origins: This is a Dutch phrase meaning "it shall happen."[373]

Itty Itty Boom Boom

Common Magician's Applications: Production.

In Literature: "Now, for those in the audience, I want you to note that there is nothing in Char's hat. With a flick of the wrist and by saying the magic words—Itty, itty boom boom—I am able to pull a rabbit . . . from Char's hat."
—"The Great Leandro," *Writing.com* (2005)

Iwanna

Meanings: *Iwanna* is a childlike contraction of the words *I want a*, or *I want to.*
In Literature: "'Iwanna' is a chant, a magic incantation, which by simple repetition is believed to bring about a desired object or event. 'Horsie!' [two-year-old] Lawrie screams in ecstasy as the car passes a farm. His parents hold their breath. Then it comes. 'I wanna horsie. I wanna horsie. I wanna horsie.'"
—Selma H. Fraiberg, *The Magic Years* (1959)

---

373 Jane Ewart, *Holland* (2003)

Izzy Wizzy Let's Get Busy

Origins: The phrase *Izzy Wizzy Let's Get Busy* was "probably invented by Harry Corbett"[374] in the late 1940s.

Variations and Incantations:

- Izzy wizzy let's get busy. Tum diddly-um dum dum-dum.
  "Aldur held out his hand and a magical wand appeared. Waving the wand, he softly spoke the magic words 'Izzy wizzy let's get busy. Tum diddly-um dum dum-dum.' Then next thing Belgarath noticed was that Aldur had disappeared."
  —Stuart Langridge, *Kryogenix.org*

- Izzy-wizzy-wizzy
  —Gerald Kersh, *Night and the City* (1946)

J

Jigaldee Pigaldee Piggaldee Deeeee, Iggalee Pigaleee Alakazee

In Literature: This is an incantation for removing hiccups in the novel *The Key to the Land of Dogs* by Gareth M. Wilson (2004).

Jiggedy Bobbidy Fool
(see also *bibbidy-bobbidy-boo*)

In Literature: Imamu Amiri Baraka, *The Leroi Jones* (1960)

Jiggery Pokery
(see also *hocus pocus*)

Some magical illusion produced
by jiggery-pokery.
—Keith McCarthy,
The Silent Sleep of the Dying (2004)

Mystique: "Extraordinary visual wizardry"[375]— that's *jiggery pokery* in a nutshell.

Meanings:

- Action with astonishing results
  —Betty Kirkpatrick, *Cassell's Thesaurus* (2001)

- Conartistry, cheating
  "Then I see some more swindling and jiggery-pokery . . ."
  —Dorota Maslowska, *Snow White and Russian Red* (2005)
  "[W]hen politics becomes little more than dirty tricks and jiggery-pokery, and back-room deals . . ."
  —Thomas Singer, *The Vision Thing* (2000)

- Clever deception, outwitting
  —David Irving, *Nuremberg: The Last Battle* (1996)
  "[Y]ou're too clever for jiggery-pokery."
  —Nicholas Freeling, *Flanders Sky* (1992)

- Double-talk
  —Paul Sillitoe, *A Place Against Time* (1996)

---

374 Ian Peacock, "Word of Mouth" radio interview for BBC4

375 Toby Rose, quoted in *Lars Von Trier: Interviews* by Jan Lumholdt (2003)

- Fakery
—Marian Keyes, *The Other Side of the Story* (2004)

- Fictional
"Elspeth, what jiggery-pokery Canterbury tale have they hoaxed you with?"
—Patricia Veryan, *The Riddle of the Deplorable Dandy* (2002)

- Finesse
"[W]ith a little sly jiggery-pokery . . ."
—David Buser, *Beginning Active Server Pages 3.0* (2000)

- Good-natured foolery
—Brad Strickland, *The Specter from the Magician's Museum* (2001)

- Hanky-panky, fooling around
"They don't mind winking at a bit of jiggery-pokery when a fellow's single, but once he's married, he daren't let 'em find out about it, or they'll cut him."
—Mercedes Lackey, *The Gates of Sleep* (2002)

- Hocus pocus, trickery
"I could not forgive him for having dismissed Mephistopheles by a mere trick, a bit of jiggery-pokery."
—Carl Jung, *Memories, Dreams, and Reflections* (1961)
"[N]ot excepting Mumbo-Jumbo and Jiggery-Pokery . . ."
—Dorothy L. Sayers, *The Mind of the Maker* (1941)
"The universe is what it is and can't be changed by jiggery-pokery."
—Robert A. Heinlein, *Glory Road* (1963)
"The sword-swallower turned in a slow circle, swaying, to show there was no jiggery-pokery. No blade was sticking out of his back, he had taken the whole thing down."
—Madison Smartt Bell, *Anything Goes* (2002)

- Intrigue
—Thomas Pynchon, *Mason & Dixon* (1997)

- Magical spells, enchantment
—Michel de Montaigne, *An Apology for Raymond Sebond* (1987)
"Hitherto, except in exploration fantasies, the fantastic element was brought in by magic. Frankenstein, even, uses some jiggery-pokery magic to animate his artificial monster."
—Patrick Brantlinger, *A Companion to the Victorian Novel* (2002)

- Mischief, practical jokes, pranks
"Catching on to this spirit of devil-may-care jiggery-pokery, the government played their own little prank on the Delavels . . ."
—Harry Pearson, *The Far Corner* (1994)

- Mumbo jumbo
"[T]he scientific jiggery-pokery . . ."
—Thomas Pynchon, *Mason & Dixon* (1997)

- Mystic words
"By the use of the mystic words hanky-panky, jiggery-pokery, all-my-eye and what-goddam-fools-we-been . . ."
—John Dickson Carr, *The Curse of the Bronze Lamp* (1945)

- Nonsense
"The first stanza begins with a double-dactyl nonsense line like 'Jiggery-pokery.'"
—Jay M. Pasachoff, *The Teaching of Astronomy* (1990)

- Ritual
"[T]he whiskers of the male leopard for their jiggery-pokery . . ."
—Donald MacIntosh, *Travels in the White Man's Grave* (1998)

- Special effect
"[Lars von Trier's film *Europa* caused a huge stir at Cannes], not so much for its subject matter but for its extraordinary visual wizardry, involving the overlaying of colored and black-and-white images and various other sorts of jiggery-pokery."

—Toby Rose, quoted in *Lars Von Trier: Interviews* by Jan Lumholdt (2003)

- Stuff and nonsense
  —Anton Pavlovich Chekhov, *Ivanov* (1967)

- Unscientific, speculative
  "[S]cientists could not care less about such 'philosophical jiggery-pokery.'"
  —Jesper Hoffmeyer, *Signs of Meaning in the Universe* (1996)

Origins: *Jiggery-pokery* is a nonsense phrase of uncertain origin, dating to the late nineteenth century. There is speculation that it derives from an earlier phrase of Scots dialect, *joukery-pawkery* (the root words *jouk* meaning "to dodge" and *pawk* meaning "trick").[376]

Facts: *Jiggery-pokery* is one of the plagues and misfortunes that was contained inside Pandora's box of mythology. There were, among other things:

> *Carbuncles, Quagmires, and Jiggery-Pokery,*
> *Colic, Depravity, Lummoxes, Louts,*
> *Barbed Wire, Insomnia, Practical Jokery,*
> *Treachery, Lechery, Deluge, and Droughts.*"[377]

"[T]he Detection Club in Britain, shortly after its foundation in 1928, asked its members to swear an oath promising that their detectives would 'well and truly detect the crimes presented to them' without reliance on 'Divine Revelation, Feminine Intuition, Mumbo-Jumbo, Jiggery-Pokery, Coincidence or the Act of God.'"[378]

In Literature:

- "'Delightful phrase,' Lady Barre murmured with sensuous eyes. 'Jiggery-pokery.'"
  —Marc Lovell, *That Great Big Trenchcoat in the Sky* (1988)

- "But this talk of sorcery and such jiggery-pokery, you know, is the outside of enough."
  —Joan Aiken, *The Cuckoo Tree* (2000)

Jingle Bells

Facts: These magic words make reference to the traditional Christmas song by the same name.

In Literature: "When he got to his money magic trick you knew for sure he had never done a children's magic show before. When he asked the audience to chant the magic words Jingle Bells, Arnie took that as a cue instead and started playing 'Jingle Bells.' The money trick he was attempting to perform fell out of his hands and all the kids rushed the stage to grab the falling paper money while the rest of the crowd sang Jingle Bells as loud as they could. But the show must go on and the magician picked up another trick even though the crowd was singing so loud that you could not hear a word he was saying."
—Sandy Dykes, "The Great Santa Claus Escapade," *Inside Magic* (2002)

Jingo
(see also *by jingo*, *high jingo*)

Origins: This magician's catchphrase "dates from the late seventeenth century and is first recorded in the forms 'by jingo!' or 'high jingo!' as a bit of conjurer's patter when some item was re-

---

376 *Encarta Dictionary* (2005)
377 As retold by Jeanne Steig in *A Gift From Zeus* (2001)
378 Julian Symons, *Bloody Murder: From the Detective Story to the Crime Novel* (1972)

vealed as though by magic (the opposite of 'hey presto!', used when something was ordered to disappear). 'By jingo!' was also used around this

Figure 24. *Jingo* depicted in the form of a sigil, a graphic representation meant to capture the "essence" of the word and channel its magical energy like a circuit board.

time as another of the many euphemisms for 'by God' or 'by Jesus' and so became an interjection to show one's surprise or to give emphasis."[379]

There is speculation that *jingo* is derived from a Basque name for God (*Jainko*). "Jingo is the modified Kingo, the Mentula [fertility] type of deity.... 'By Jingo' is a common oath, but the more emphatic form is 'by the *living* Jingo'; that identifies the [Egyptian] Ankh with the living one.... This sense of life enters into our words jink and 'high-jinks.' Jink is to be gay and ebullient with life. 'High jinks' are the very festival of frolic life."[380]

Facts: *Jingo* (also *Jingu*) is the name of a legendary Empress who ruled Japan until 270 and

came to be considered a fertility goddess a century later.[381]

Jingo became the root of the word *jingoism*, referring to an aggressive patriotism, after appearing in a hit music-hall song of 1877. The song, written by "The Great MacDermott" during the Russo-Turkish war, featured the lyrics:

> *We don't want to fight*
> *But by jingo if we do,*
> *We've got the ships, we've got the men,*
> *We've got the money too.*[382]

Jitanjáfora

Meanings: *Jitanjáfora* is said to express everything because it means nothing.[383] It is a playful appeal to fantasy.[384]

Origins: This magic nonsense word for obtaining euphonic results was coined by Mexican writer Alfonso Reyes[385] in his book *La Experiencia Literaria* (1942). "Jitanjáfora is a term for the use of onomatopoeia in Spanish Afro-Caribbean poetry . . . to invoke an aesthetically Africanist sensibility into the poetic expression. . . . [J]itanjáfora does not literally mean. It means nonliterally: it evokes, not denotes; it must be thought about. To that end, it makes the other into a self.

379 Michael Quinon, *WorldWideWords.com* (2004)

380 Gerald Massey, *A Book of the Beginnings Vol. 1* (1881)

381 Bernard Faure, *The Power of Denial: Buddhism, Purity, and Gender* (2003)

382 Wilfred Funk, *Word Origins* (1950)

383 Augusto Monterroso, "Entre la Niebla y el Aire Impuro" (2005)

384 Hugo J. Verani, "The *Vanguardia* and its Implications," *The Cambridge History of Latin American Literature: Volume 2* (1996)

385 Leopoldo de Trazegnies Granda, *Diccionario Literario* (2005)

It reconstitutes what it re-envisions—the cultural roots of African spirit—leaving out the meaning of what it is imitating, admitting that it does not really know."[386]

Variations and Incantations: PrestoChango, Shazam! Jitanjáfora!
—Gustavo Pesoa, "Collateral Beauty" (2003)

Josta Ablati Agla Caila

Origins: This phrase is comprised of "four magical words God spoke with his mouth to his servant Moses," each the name of an angel, as discussed in the *Grimorium Verum* (a.k.a. "The True Clavicule of Solomon"), originally translated from the Hebrew in 1517.[387]

Junky Monkey, Stinkeroozer, This Old Apple Is a Loser

In Literature: Deborah Hautzig, *Little Witch Goes to School* (1998)

Jurisprudence

Origins: *Jurisprudence* is of Latin origin, meaning the theory or philosophy of law.

Facts: According to the 17th-century *Grimoire of Armadel*, the spirit Samael teaches "Magic, Necromancy, Jurisprudence, and all of the Occult Sciences."[388]

Law professor Ronald Dworkin suggests that jurisprudence relies upon "the faculty of making clear what was dark without making it dull." "[C]larity enhances rather than disspates the power of an idea. That is magic, and it is the magic that jurisprudence needs to work."[389]

In Literature: "'Jurisprudence!' exclaimed the thick voice of the public prosecutor, who was aroused from his stupor by this magic word; 'let us talk jurisprudence.'"
—Charles de Bernard, *Gerfaut: Immortals Crowned by the French Academy, Vol. 4* (1838)

K

Ka Nama Ka Lajerama

Facts: This magical Lemurian phrase appears in Marvel's *Conan*, *Kull*, *Red Sonja*, and *Sub-Mariner* comics as an ancient spell for testing suspected Serpent Men in disguise.

Kaboom

In a word: *kaboom*.
—Harlan Coben, *Fade Away* (1996)

Mystique: *Kaboom* is a bombshell. It's an entire pyrotechnics display in a single magic word. It's a

---

386 David Colón, "Other Latino Poetic Method" (2001)

387 Gustav Davidson, *Dictionary of Angels: Including the Fallen Angels* (1994)

388 S.L. MacGregor Mathers, *The Grimoire of Armadel* (1980)

389 *Philosophy of Law and Legal Theory* (2003)

sparkling firecracker,[390] and at the same time it's a heart racing with excitement: "My heart was pounding a steady kaboom-kaboom at a rate of about 120. Oh, this was going to be fun."[391]

Facts: Kaboom is the name of a card trick designed by Jon Allen involving a small bomb prop (*Misdirections.com*).

In Literature:

- Sarah Ban Breathnach, *Romancing the Ordinary* (2002)

- "[W]ave a magic wand, chant a few magic phrases, and presto, kaboom, abracadabra, the magic just happens."
  —Sirona Knight, *Dream Magic* (2000)

- "Try raising power again, but this time when you 'Kaboom' it, envision a circular web of golden sticky stars around, above, and below you."
  —Silver Ravenwood, *To Stir a Magick Cauldron* (2003)

Kadabra

(see also *abra*, *abracadabra*, and *cadabra*)

Facts: *Kadabra* is the name of the walled, glass-roofed capital city of the Okar nation of Mars in *Warlord of Mars* by Edgar Rice Burroughs (1913).

In the Pokemon card game, the character Abra evolves into Kadabra and finally into Alakazam, who has strong psychic powers.

Variations and Incantations:

- Cadabra

- Kadabra Sesameanie
  "To make a wish-granting genie appear, just say, with childlike candor: Kadabra, Sesameanie, I conjure me a genie."
  —Reneau H. Reneau, *Misanthropology: A Florilegium of Bahumbuggery* (2004)

- Kedavra

Kalamazoo

Origins: *Kalamazoo* is a Potawatoni and Algonquian Indian word.

Meanings:

- Boiling pot
  —Dick Branch, "Kalamazoo County Brief History" (2005)

- Boiling water

- Morning mist rising steam-like from the surface of water
  —Dick Branch, "Kalamazoo County Brief History" (2005)

- River crossing

- River that empties into Lake Michigan

- Swirling rapids
  —Dick Branch, "Kalamazoo County Brief History" (2005)

In Literature: "When my roommate and I were high [on LSD], we both became imbued with a sense of magical power. We stared at the candle flame, trying to change its color. Nothing happened. My roommate suggested that we utter a magic word. We tried 'Abracadabra.' The color did not change. We tried 'Open Sesame' to no avail. I shouted 'Kalamazoo!' Believe me,

----

390 "[B]oys outside didn't lose fingers setting off kabooms . . ."—Amy Klatzkin, *A Passage to the Heart* (1999)

391 Richard Marcinko, *Rogue Warrior* (1992)

we both saw the color of the flame change from orange to blue! It remained blue for five minutes. At that time, my roommate blew out the flame. We were quite shaken by the experience but wanted to try it again. We relit the candle. The flame was orange. We uttered the magic word. It turned blue. This was several days ago. Neither of us has dared to light the candle and utter the magic word. We knew the flame would change from orange to blue as soon as one of us said 'Kalamazoo!' And then where would we be?"
—Stanley Krippner, "Psychedelic Experience and the Language Process," *Journal of Psychedelic Drugs* (1970), quoted in *The Ecstatic Imagination: Psychedelic Experiences and the Psychoanalysis of Self-Actualization* by Daniel Merkur (1998)

Kambok Lovage Zweibach Zim, Koombek Levege Zweindol Zim

In Literature: Han Nolan, *Dancing on the Edge* (1999)

Kapusta

Facts: This is a "memory word," a "secret code word that only you know the real, true meaning of . . . a key word that would trigger [a] memory . . . jog loose a cherished moment."[392]

In Literature: "I started them off with a magical word of my own. 'Kapusta.' It was the name of the yellow-eyed, slate-grey cat who came to live with me after Greg died. I smiled when I said the word—I knew they wouldn't understand it and I let it linger as an example to them of just

how mystical and obscure their memory word could be."
—Theodore Menten, *After Goodbye* (1994)

Kazam
(see also *alakazam*)

KAZAM!, we will have magic.
—Grant Dixon,
Event Horizon: Hamilton Amateur Astronomers (1999)

Mystique: *Kazam* is the "onomatopoetic description of the Big Bang."[393]

Meanings:

- Instantly
  —Eryk Hanut, *The Road to Guadalupe: A Modern Pilgrimage to the Virgin of the Americas* (2001)

- Magic word
  —Terry Pratchett, *Sourcery* (2001)

- Vanish, disappear
  "Just kind of vanished—*kazam!*"
  —Frederick Barthelme, *Elroy Nights* (2003)
      "[W]e have just two bales to go when the shift whistle blows. Kazam! Everyone splits."
  —Mike O'Connor, *When the Tiger Weeps* (2004)

Origins: The root of *kazam* is echoed in many languages. In Greek, "cassuma" is a cunning trick. In Arabic, "kazam" can refer to a sword, an oath, and avarice. In Hindi, "kasam" is an oath.[394]

Facts: A machine for molding plywood into complex curves was invented in 1941 and called "Kazam!"[395] It took something flat and made it three-dimensional, like magic.

---

392 Theodore Menten, *After Goodbye* (1994)

393 Robert V. Gentry, *Creation's Tiny Mystery* (2004)
394 John Morris, *The New Nation Vol. 4* (1880)
395 Charlotte Fiell, *Design of the 20th Century* (2001)

Common Magician's Applications: Vanishing, triggering.

Variations and Incantations:

- Ka Zam
"When he tried the words 'Ka Zam' an eagle appeared!"
—Marlene Karkoska, "The Knight and the Wizard" (2005)

- Kazaam
Kazaam is "a made-up interjection" that "has meaning only within itself."
—Raymond J. Corsini, *Dictionary of Psychology* (2002)

- Kazam kazoo
"[A]ll of a sudden, the carrot he held in his hand turned—*kazam! kazoo!*—into a squawking, and no doubt very shocked, little parrot."
—Tim Kennemore, *Circle of Doom* (2001)

- Kazzam
—Thomas Blood, *Madame Secretary* (1997)
"Miss Sorrel picks up silver-topped ebony cane, bangs it three times on floor and kazzam! I'm a frog."
—Nicky Singer, *Feather Boy* (2001)

In Literature:

- "'I think I would prefer a bit of magical assistance.' 'I'm not very good at it,' said Rincewind. 'Never got the hang of it, see, it's more than just point a finger at it and saying *Kazam*—' There was a sound like a thick bolt of octarine lightning zapping into a heavy rock slab and smashing it into a thousand bits of spitting, white-hot shrapnel, and no wonder."
—Terry Pratchett, *Sourcery* (2001)

- "One day, out of nowhere, he was gone! Kazam!"
—Dorothea Benton Frank, *Isle of Palms* (2004)

- "When the moon and the stars arrived to execute their mother [goddess Coatlicue], *kazam!* The sun jumped out of her womb (don't ask me how) and cut his sister the moon in two pieces."
—Eryk Hanut, *The Road to Guadalupe: A Modern Pilgrimage to the Virgin of the Americas* (2001)

- "[K]azam, poof, it bounces back to him."
—Steve Martini, *The Arraignment* (2003)

- "With a 'Kazam!' Nina turns herself into a monkey."
—Scholastic ETV Consortium, "The Wild World: Nina's Strange Adventure" (2001)

- "'Do you have glasses?' 'KAZAM!' Michael pulled two paper cups out of his pockets."
—Joyce Faulkner, *Losing Patience* (2004)

- "She steps into blue jeans, throws on this big white billowy blouse, slips on some shoes, and leaves the room. *Kazam*, like that—I can't see where she's going, and her other rooms barely exist to me. She just leaves. I'm left."
—William Tester, *Head: Stories* (2000)

Ƙedaᴠra
(see also *cadabra* and *kadabra*)

Mystique: Even more than its cousin *cadabra*, the magic word *kedavra* is shrouded by an ominous, dark aura of necromancy. Through its very own feat of mentalism, the word conjures a *cadaver* in one's subconscious.

Origins: This word is of Aramaic origin.

Facts: The word *kedavra* is a part of a killing curse in J.K. Rowling's *Harry Potter* novels.

In Literature: "The only surviving Death Eaters are too decrepit these days to even say the word 'Kedavra,' let alone cast the spell."
—Caius Marcius, *Snape-Specific* (2004)

Kerblunkity-Blink

Origins: This phrase was coined by Thomas Theodore Turner (1851–1927).

Variations and Incantations: Kerblinkity-blunk

In Literature: "Who can forget the sonorous 'plop' with which he uttered that mystic word, 'Kerblunkity-blink!'"
—Hilary Willson, *Ampleforth Journal* (1940)

Kesk Ma'sik

Meanings: Changing from reality to non-reality.
—Micmac elder Michael W. Francis, quoted in *Visions of Sound* by Beverly Diamond and Franziska Von Rosen (1994)

Origins: *Kesk ma'sik* is of Micmac (Maritime Algonquian) origin.

Facts: Similarly, according to Micmac elder Michael W. Francis, *kesk matiket* means a magician, and *kesk mta'q* means "making a magic sound."[396]

Kha-khe, Khi-khi

Origins: This magic phrase is of Sioux origin.

Facts: According to Native American storyteller Zitkala-Sa (1876–1938), these magic words are to be said by a medicine man with the croaking voice of a buzzard.[397]

In Literature: "With every step he pronounced magic words, 'Kha-khe, Khi-Khi!' with a croaking voice."
—Zitkala Sa, "Buzzard Skin and the Sea Monsters," *Dreams and Thunder* (2001)

Khabs Am Pekht
(see also *konx om pax*)

Say the Mystic Words, Khabs Am Pekht.
—Israel Regardie, *The Golden Dawn* (1989)

Meanings:

- Attainment of the star
  —"Musings on Mystic Phrases," *Aletheia* (2000)

- May light be extended in abundance upon you
  —"Musings on Mystic Phrases," *Aletheia* (2000)

Origins: "Recent investigation, with the assistance of the British Museum, has revealed that the most probable Egyptian origin for this phrase is 'hbs m pht,' pronounced 'khebs m pekht.' The word *khebs* actually means *star* or *lamp* rather than *light*, and the word *pekht* is a noun from the verb *pekh*, meaning 'to reach or attain.' The museum thought that *extension* was a possible but unlikely translation. Thus, the most accurate translation of 'Khabs am Pekht' is rendered as 'the attainment of the star,' a phrase of particular and peculiar significance. The corruption *Konx om Pax* is, at least according to the museum, 'a complete mystery,

---

396 Beverly Diamond & Franziska Von Rosen, *Visions of Sound* (1994)

397 Zitkala Sa, "Buzzard Skin and the Sea Monsters," *Dreams and Thunder* (2001)

being neither Greek nor Coptic nor indeed a rendering of the hieroglyphics.' As the Fellowship of Isis documents note, 'initiates [of the Elusian Mysteries] were dismissed with two barbarous words, *Konx Ompax*, of which perhaps the Hierophants themselves did not comprehend the import' . . . they had been introduced by the first Egyptian mysteries. To us the words in question appear to be Syriac, and signify, 'be vigilant, be innocent.' Another offered version is 'light is strength.'"[398]

Ӄine-Ahora

Meanings:

* "Don't talk about it"
  "[Clint Eastwood] was asked about the possibility of [Oscar] nominations for his flick [*Mystic River*]. He responded, 'Kineahora! Kineahora!' The *[USA Weekend]* reporter retorted, 'Pardon?' Eastwood said, 'That's a Jewish expression meaning 'Don't talk about it. It's bad luck.'"
  —Nate Bloom, *Jewish News Weekly* (2004)

* "May you be spared the evil eye"

Origins: *Kine-ahora* is a Yiddish expression. It combines the German "no" with the Hebrew "evil eye."[399]

Facts: This is a magic phrase to ward off bad luck: "We knock on wood or utter the magical phrase kine-ahora . . ."[400]

----

398 Fehta Murghana, Liner Notes for "Konx: Wholly Ghost" (2002)

399 Helen Stavropoulos Sandoval, "Yiddish for Jews," *New Bridges Newsletter* (1999)

400 Althea J. Horner, *Working with the Core Relationship Problem in Psychotherapy* (1998)

Variations and Incantations:

* Kin Ahora

* Kineahora

* Kineahora poo-poo-poo
  —Jessica Coen, *Gawker.com* (2005)

In Literature:

* "Her mother would call it hexing yourself; Robin would say it was 'giving yourself a kine-ahora.'"
  —Paula Martinac, *Home Movies* (1993)

* "Rose spat into her hand. 'Kine-ahora, don't say such a thing, don't even think such a thing to yourself."
  —Marge Piercy, *Gone to Soldiers* (1987)

Ӄing

Origins: *King* is of Germanic origin and signifies a ruler or person of supreme importance.

In Literature: "[C]alled forth by the magic word 'king,' the Open Sesame word."
—Ruth Rendell, *Road Rage* (1997)

Ӄlondike

What alchemy—
for the Klondike was a magic place.
—Spike Walker, *Alaska: Tales of Adventure from the Last Frontier* (2002)

Mystique: The late 1800s "was an age of yearning, and the Klondike had taken on a mythic aura. It was more than a goldfield, more than a piece of geography: it was Beulahland, the panacea to all the fears and torments of the era, an answer for the lonely, an inspiration to the God-fearing, a bulkwark against the frailties of the flesh. For if the creek beds were said to be paved with gold, were not also the streets of the New Jerusalem?"[401] "There was a certain magic in the word Klondike that conjured up visions of unlimited profits."[402]

Origins: During the gold rush (starting in 1897), the Canadian government established in the Yukon territory a region whose name, Klondike, emerged as a "magic word" that thrilled the entire nation.[403]

In Literature:

- "It was the valley of the Klondike, magic word."
  —Rex Beach, *The Winds of Chance* (1918)

- "[E]very store window screamed the magic word *Klondike*."
  —Will Hobbs, *Jason's Gold* (1999)

- "[T]he magic word of Klondike was carried into camp."
  —Harry De Windt, *Through the Gold-Fields of Aliska to Bering Straits* (1898)

- "The name had always seemed part of a magical incantation, used to call the wonderful out of the actual. Now here I was face to face with the Klondike."
  —Thomas McGuire, *99 Days on the Yukon* (1977)

Klopstock

Mystique: As Elizabeth von Arnim suggests, though *Klopstock* is unmusical to the ear, the word

has the power to induce "tears of rapture" when spoken with intense joy.[404]

Origins: The German poet Friedrich Gottlieb Klopstock (1724–1803) inspired "joyous idealism."[405]

Facts: "Klopstock, in his *Messiah*, makes the Magi six in number, and gives the names as Hadad, Selima, Zimri, Mirja, Beled and Sunith."[406]

In Literature:

- "I drank my tea quietly, going on at the same time with my interrupted afternoon reading of [Goethe's] *Sorrows of Werther*, in which I had reached a part that has a special fascination for me every time I read it—that part where Werther first meets Lotte, and where, after a thunderstorm; they both go to the window, and she is so touched by the beauties of nature that she lays her hand on his and murmurs 'Klopstock,'—to the complete dismay of the reader, though not of Werther, for he, we find, was so carried away by the magic word that he flung himself on to her hand and kissed it with tears of rapture. I looked up from the book at the quiet pools and the black line of trees, above which stars were beginning to twinkle, my ears soothed by the splashing of the mill stream and the hooting somewhere near of a solitary owl, and I wondered whether, if the Man of Wrath were by my side, it would be a relief to my pleasurable feelings to murmur 'Klopstock,' and whether if I did he would immediately shed tears of joy over my hand. The name is an unfortunate one as far as music goes, and Goethe's putting it into his heroine's mouth

401 Pierre Berton, *The Klondike Quest* (1983)
402 Pierre Berton, *Prisoners of the North* (2004)
403 Susan Kollin, *Nature's State* (2001)
404 *The Solitary Summer* (1899)
405 Kuno Francke, *Social Forces in German Literature* (1896)
406 Ebenezer Cobham Brewer, *Character Sketches of Romance, Fiction and the Drama: Volume II* (1892)

just when she was most enraptured, seems to support the view I sometimes adopt in discoursing to the Man of Wrath that he had no sense of humour. But here I am talking about Goethe, our great genius and idol, in a way that no woman should."
—Elizabeth von Arnim, *The Solitary Summer* (1899)

- In 1748, Klopstock, "in the three opening cantos of his *Messias*, sounded that morning call of joyous idealism and exalted individualism which was to be the dominant note of the best in all modern German literature. No one has more vividly described the magic spell which the name of Klopstock exercised upon all aspiring minds of the middle of the eighteenth century than Goethe in *The Sorrows of Werther*."
—Kuno Francke, *Social Forces in German Literature* (1896)

Ƙlptzyxm

Origins: This magic word comes from the *Superman* comic books.

Facts: "The imp known as Mr. Mxyztplk [later changed to Mxyzptlk] first appeared in our dimension in Superman #30 (1st series, 1944) . . . For those who haven't seen the original story, you can find it in *The Greatest Superman Stories Ever Told* trade paperback. The bald little fellow in the purple suit and green bowtie creates all kind of havoc. . . . Mxy describes himself as a 'court-jester' from another dimension. The not very bright imp laughingly tells Superman that there is no way he can be tricked into saying the magic word 'Ƙlptzyxm' [his own name spelled back-

wards] that will return him to his own dimension. Oops. Saying the word, Mxy vanishes."[407]

Ƙommen

Meaning: *Kommen* is a German and Turkish imperative meaning "come."

In Literature: "[Ben Ali] Bay pushed up his long, full sleeves and held his white wand high in the air. There was a quick, rough command from the magician. 'Kommen!' And then a small, four-legged wooden pedestal table appeared standing beside the magician."
—Jim Steinmeyer, *The Glorious Deception: The Double Life of William Robinson, aka Chung Ling Soo, the "Marvelous Chinese Conjuror"* (2005)

Ƙonx Om Ᵽax
(see also *Khabs am Pekht*)

Meanings:

- Light in Extention
—Hermetic Order of the Golden Dawn, "Golden Dawn Glossary" (1997). This refers to the divine light extending itself into manifestation.

- Light rushing out in one ray
—"Musings on Mystic Phrases," *Aletheia* (2000)

Origins: Not without controversy, this phrase has been traced back to Ancient Greece and was "originally uttered at the Eleusinian

---

407 Sean Hogan, "Superman: Special Reports: Mr. Mxyztplk," *SupermanHomepage.com* (2004)

Mysteries,"[408] annual sacred celebrations held in honor of Demeter and Persephone.

Variations and Incantations:

- Khabs am Pekht
  This is an Egyptian version of the phrase.[409]

- Konx ompax

Ko-Sahn

Mystique: *Ko-sahn* is the type of name that evokes the "sacred power of storytelling at its best—the verbal repetition of names that are able to call into being an entire tradition. It involves a collective remembering or *anamnesis* that makes the listener immediately present to the past in all of its fullness."[410]

Origins: *Ko-sahn* is the name of Kiowa Indian origin. While seeking out his Kiowa heritage, author N. Scott Momady met a one-hundred-year-old seer named Ko-sahn in Oklahoma, and as he wrote *The Way to Rainy Mountain* (1969) he realized that Ko-sahn had a full existence within his imagination.

In Literature: "My eyes fell upon the name Ko-sahn. And all at once everything seemed suddenly to refer to that name. The name seemed to humanize the whole complexity of language. All at once, absolutely, I had the sense of the magic of words and of names. Ko-sahn, I said, and I said again KO-SAHN. Then it was that that ancient, one-eyed woman Ko-sahn stepped out of

the language and stood before me on the page. I was amazed."
—N. Scott Momaday, *The Way to Rainy Mountain* (1969)

Kraalax-Heeroz

In Literature: "The mirror was blank. 'Kraalax-Heeroz,' she chanted quickly. The image returned."
—Douglas Niles, *Black Wizards* (2004)

Kron-Zhig
(see *perciphedron*)

Kum Kunka Yali, Kum Buba Tambe

Origins: This magic phrase originated in African folklore.

Common Magician's Applications: Levitation

In Literature: "He raised his arms, holding them out to her. '*Kum [kunka] yali, kum buba tambe*,' and more magic words, said so quickly, they sounded like whispers and sighs. The young woman lifted one foot on the air. Then the other. She flew clumsily at first, with the child now held tightly in her arms. Then she felt the magic, the African mystery. Say she rose as free as a bird. As light as a feather."
—Virginia Hamilton, *The People Could Fly* (1985)

---

408 Hermetic Order of the Golden Dawn, "Golden Dawn Glossary" (1997)

409 *Ibid.*

410 Belden C. Lane, *Landscapes of the Sacred* (1988)

L

Laha Laha Hala Hala

Origins: *Laha laha hala hala* is an apparently nonsensical mantra of Buddhist origin.

Facts: This phrase is "similar to the magic words, such as 'abracadabra,' found in other traditions."[411]

Lance Burton

Facts: Professional magician Lance Burton has a child chant his name three times to magically empower a penny. He tells the child to put the coin under a pillow, promising that it will transform into a dollar bill by morning. He encourages the child to "tell Dad what the magician said."

Legilimens

In Literature: *Legilimens* is a mind-reading spell in *Harry Potter and the Order of the Phoenix* by J.K. Rowling (2003).

Let Me Show You Something a Little Different

Facts: These are professional magician John Cassidy's magic words: "But remember: you are under oath! You must NOT repeat this trick. Just smile, shrug your shoulders, and use your magic words: 'Did you like that? Well, let me show you something a little different then.'"[412]

Let's Rock

In Literature: Tim Dorsey, *Florida Road Kill* (2000)

Levitation

Meanings: To rise into the air by supernatural means

Origins: *Levitation* is derived from the Latin word *levis*, "light."

In Literature: "His thoughts were consumed by that magic word—levitation."
—Theodore Taylor, *The Boy Who Could Fly Without a Motor* (2002)

Levram Niatpac
(see also *shazam*)

Facts: These words are "Captain Marvel," the comic book hero, spelled backwards.

---

411 Robert A. Yelle, *Explaining Mantras: Magic, Rhetoric, and the Dream of a Natural Language* (2003)

412 *The Klutz Book of Magic* (1989)

In Literature: Paulette K. Johnson, *Wings of Our Own* (2001)

Li

Meanings:

- Ceremonies, rites
  —Pao Chao Hsieh, *Government of China 1644–1911* (1966)

- Propriety
  "[T]his magic word means . . . propriety."
  —Pao Chao Hsieh, *Government of China 1644–1911* (1966)

- Right principles
  —Pao Chao Hsieh, *Government of China 1644–1911* (1966)

Origins: *Li* is of Chinese origin.

Liberty

Mystique: "[F]ew words are more important and none is less capable of precise definition than the magic word *liberty*."[413]

Origins: *Liberty* comes from the Latin word *libertas,* meaning "free."

In Literature:

- "There is greater magic in the word *liberty* than in all other words combined!"
  —C. A. Windle, *Word Pictures* (1919)

- "[I]n order that liberty be a magic word some liberty must be inviolable, must belong to a part of us that is also inviolable."
  —Ramananda Chatterjee, *The Modern Review* (1907)

- "The magic word liberty had not lost its power to stir to its depths the heart of this officer, and consequently produced upon him the exact effect they desired, by awaking enthusiastic memories of his youth, and a joy to which he had long been a stranger."
  —Constant, *Recollections of the Private Life of Napoleon Bonaparte, Vol. 11* (1895)

Lirum Larum

(see also *diggi daggi, shurry murry, horum harum, lirum larum, rowdy mowdy, giri gari, posito, besti basti, saron froh, fatto matto, quid pro quo*)

Origins: *Lirum larum* is of Germanic origin.

In Literature: Mozart, *Bastien und Bastienne* (1768)

Lisan-al-gaib
Shai-hulud Muad'dib
Kwisatz Haderach

Facts: This magic incantation is featured in *The Intercontinental Union of Disgusting Characters* by Roger M. Wilcox (1986). All of the words reference the science fiction novel *Dune* by Frank Herbert. Wilcox explains: "*Lisan-al-Gaib, Muad'dib,* and *Kwisatz Haderach* are all phrases used to describe [the character] Paul Atriedes. *Shai-hulud* is the name the Fremen use to deify the sandworms."

----

413 Carl Lotus Becker, *Safeguarding Civil Liberty Today* (1949)

Lit Flitt Latt Flight

Facts: This is a magic phrase for materializing a small glowing moon in *Oral Storytelling and Teaching Mathematics* by Michael Schiro (2004).

Lo and Behold
(see *behold*)

Lo and behold, it worked like a charm!
—Julie Powell, *Julie and Julia* (2003)

Common Magician's Applications: Production. For example, "[L]o and behold, we have two—no three—pretty scarves."[414] Or, "Lo and behold, the quarter is there!"[415]

Locus-Pocus
(see also *hocus pocus*)

Mystique: *Locus* means "place," so *locus-pocus* conjures a place where magic happens.

Facts: *Locus-pocus* is a variation of the magic phrase *hocus pocus.*

In Literature:

• Julia Oliver, *Music of Falling Water* (2001)

• From *The Rant Zone* (2001) by Dennis Miller:

> *My locus*
> *My focus*
> *My wand of hocus-pocus.*

Lolomi

Origin: *Lolomi* is a Hopi term meaning "perfect goodness be upon you."[416]

Facts: *Lolomi* is the name of a brave hero in the folklore of the Moqui Pueblos of Arizona. Legend has it that Lolomi protected his people from the threat of giants.

In Literature: "[The Moquis] are shy and suspicious of strangers, but if addressed by the magic word *lolomi*, their reserve is instantly gone. It is the open sesame to their hearts and homes, and after that the house contains nothing too good to bestow upon the welcome guest."
—Joseph A. Munk, *Arizona Sketches* (1891)

Long Ago and Far Away
(see also *once upon a time*)

In Literature: Tami Hoag, *Guilty as Sin* (1996)

Look, Look

Facts: *Look, look* is a favorite magic phrase of professional magician David Blaine.

In Literature: "The sole patter line from [David Blaine's] first special might be summed up thusly: 'Look. Look. Look . . . watch . . . watch . . . here . . . look.' Instead of telling us what to see, what to think, he uses words the way Andy Summers of the Police used guitar lines—sparingly, letting us fill in the pauses, the silences, with our own minds. He stares people hard in the face

---

414 Fay Presto, *Magic for Kids* (1999)
415 Klutz Press, *Coin Magic* (1997)

416 Laura M. C. Kellogg, "Our Democracy and the American Indian" (1920), *American Philosophies: An Anthology* (2002)

after the magic has happened, unanswering in their queries. And then he walks away."
—Brian Wendell Morton, "Blaine: The Stage is You," *Genii* (1999)

£ove

Love, that magic word.
—Alina Reyes, *The Butcher* (1988)

Mystique: Magic words emanate from the heart. . . . This is the real secret of words of power.
—Phillip Cooper, *Esoteric Magic and the Cabala* (2002)

"'How do we become one with the universal?' [a woman asked Sai Baba]. As he did whenever anyone asked about methods of realization, Baba merely smiled meaningfully and said the magic word: 'Love.' That mysterious word, the sound no one dared to say they did not understand."[417]

Variations and Incantations: I love you
"[T]hose three magic words 'I love you' . . ."
—Sandra Merrill Covey, *The 7 Habits of Highly Effective Families* (1997)

In Literature:

- "[T]he quivering lip and the agitated countenance of the one, and the quick-heaving bosom and the gushing eye of the other, as, from the long mute grasp they turned hurriedly away, constituted the only language that told the sensations of their hearts. It had never spoken before; but it had spoken distinctly now, revealing to them, for the first time, their own and each other's secret, and apprising them

that the deep, unanalyzed, unacknowledged feeling, that had been sleeping and gathering strength in their attracted bosoms, had a name; and that its name was only to be found in the magic word, Love."
—Daniel P. Thompson, *Locke Amsden; or, The Schoolmaster* (1852)

- "[H]e did manage to say the magic word, 'love.'"
—Marilyn Anderson, *Never Kiss a Frog* (2003)

- "The magic of love! It softened, not for the first time, her heart towards all humanity."
—Norman Douglas, *South Wind* (1917)

- "And yet there it was: The Word: The Magic Word: Love."
—John Rechy, *City of Night* (1963)

- "The reader can now relish the Cardinal's action in underlining the magic word 'love.'"
—United States Catholic Historical Society, *Historical Records and Studies* (1916)

- "That magic word . . . Shall I tell you what love is, Maskull?"
—David Lindsay, *A Voyage to Arcturus* (1920)

- "The magical word which shall break the bars of the prisons where the chains of the slaves are heard is Love."
—Georg Ebers, *A Thorny Path, Volume 2* (1892)

£umos

Origins: *Lumos* is from the Latin word meaning "light" (*lumen*).

In Literature: *Lumos* is a spell for conjuring light from a wand in *Harry Potter and the Order of the Phoenix* by J.K. Rowling (2003).

----

417 Lee Siegel, *Net of Magic: Wonders and Deceptions in India* (1991)

M

Machts Nichts

Meanings:

- I'm easy
  "'Naw, *macht nichts*, let's walk.' Jack pronounces it 'mox nix,' meaning 'makes no difference' or, in air force parlance, 'I'm easy.'"
  —Ann-Marie MacDonald, *The Way the Crow Flies* (2003)

- Matters not

- Never mind

- Whatever

Origins: This is a German colloquial expression.

Variations and Incantations:

- Mox Nix

- Mocks Nicks

In Literature: "She took a drag and waved both the smoke and the image away, dismissing them with the words she used to take the curse off all vexations, '*Machts nichts.*' I repeated the magical words under my breath. *Mox nix.*"
—Sarah Bird, *The Yokota Officers Club* (2001)

Madagascar
(see also *Constantinople*)

In [Madagascar] magic is preserved in its full glory.
—Alexis Rochon,
A Voyage to Madagascar and the East Indies (1792)

Mystique: Called by its natives "the Island of the Moon,"[418] "Madagascar is an island filled with magic and many taboos, or *fadys* as they are called."[419]

Facts: Madagascar is a deforested African island, the fourth-largest island in the world.
Madagascar is the magic word that crooked hypnotist "Voltan Polgar" uses to hypnotize Helen Hunt's character in the film *The Curse of the Jade Scorpion* (2001).

Magic
(see also *magick*)

The only word was *magic*.
—Mort Rosenblum,
The Secret Life of the Seine (1994)

What is the magic word?
Magic, said the god. Magic itself.
— Modern Poetry Association, "Poetry" (1936)

Mystique:

Discovering Magic means recognizing the illusory nature of the material world.
—Phillip Cooper,
Esoteric Magic and the Cabala (2002)

----

418 D.J. Conway, *Moon Magick* (1995)
419 Gerald Durrell, *The Aye-Aye and I* (1992)

"*Magic*. The word evokes childhood memories of fireflies dancing in the dark, of fairies living in the garden; of dreams being so real they lapse over into waking time. We blew the fizz off dandelions in order to have wishes come true, or wished upon the first rising star. We breathed in magic and were not at all surprised by the wonders we encountered."[420]

The concept of magic "seems to stir up in everyone some hidden mental forces, some lingering hopes in the miraculous, some dormant beliefs in man's mysterious possibilities. Witness to this is the power which the words *magic, spell, charm, to bewitch,* and *to enchant,* possess in poetry, where the inner value of words, the emotional forces which they still release, survive longest and are revealed most clearly."[421]

Since well before our conceptions of conjuring tricks or witchcraft, nature has been weaving her magic and surprising humanity with her wonders. Physicist B.K. Ridley[422] dispels the common association of magic with superstition. He explains that we are moved by natural forces of magic in a variety of ways through our everyday lives:

> What is not scientific is not necessarily superstition. Forces that move people exist which lie outside the scientific domain by their very nature—everyday forces, neither supernatural nor occult, plain to everybody, part of the human experience. Even our everyday language employs the image of the mechanical effect of a force when we speak of being moved by a certain purely mental experience. Who does not respond to the power of form, of colour, of symbols, and is this not what used to be called talismanic magic? Who is not delighted and moved by the artful use of words, incantations, names as essences, oratory, poetry, and is this not word magic? Is not the effect of harmony and melody magic? And is there not an elemental magic in the intuition of the craftsman, even in the "feel" of the technician for his machine, though it be a product of the highest technology? To say nothing of common sense? Surely the answer to all these questions is yes. Then these are nothing but the well-known elements of natural magic stripped of their superstitious and supernatural patina. Magic, thus defined, is the complement of science. It acts, not on material objects, but on human sensibility. At its highest intellectual development, reached in the seventeenth century just when science was beginning, magical theory could describe a cosmos full of meaning to the human spirit, a latter day Theory of Everything.

Appealing to human sensibility, magicians demonstrate magical truths not only through their manipulations of the animate and inanimate but also through the power of their charisma and the ritualistic atmosphere of their performances. Ultimately, Ridley says, magic is about those things that are timelessly unique, and that makes magic an elixir of life. He explains:

> Magical truth and scientific truth are complementary in their respective limits, the former associated timelessly with the unique, the latter timelessly with the recurrent. The timelessness is all. At one time to be educated was to be well versed in both, but one approach does tend to drive out the other. The scientist

420 Galen Gillotte, *Sacred Stones of the Goddess: Using Earth Energies for Magical Living* (2003)

421 Bronislaw Malinowski, *Magic, Science and Religion and Other Essays* (1948)

422 *On Science* (2001)

as such can never be a magus (though as a human being he may be!). Poetry, music and the fine arts embody magical truths. That is where to find them, abstracted. And magic, I believe, is the right word to use. At one time the activities of science and magic were virtually indistinguishable. The magic I mean is the potent liquor left behind by the distillation of science, freed from superstition and as near an elixir of life as we are likely to get.

Meanings:

- Amusement
  —R.G. Collingwood, *The Principles of Art* (1938)

- Art of causing coincidence
  —Chris McIntosh, quoted in *Northern Mysteries & Magick: Runes, Gods, and Feminine Powers* by Freya Aswynn (1990)

- Art of changing consciousness at will
  "The true definition of Magic, little one . . . does not center around spells or incantations, or the mysterious waving of arms . . . no. [T]rue Magic is 'the art and science of changing states of mind at will.' And as we have learned by experience, action follows thought."
  —Douglas Monroe, *The 21 Lessons of Merlyn: A Study in Druid Magic and Lore* (1992)

- Art of illusion
  "According to the illustrious magician Harry Houdini, magic is achieved through illusion. A simple example is an illusion created using smoke and mirrors. The illusion is called magic simply because it *appears* to be unexplainable."
  —Wayne Dyer, *Real Magic: Creating Miracles in Everyday Life* (1992)

"When we hear the word *magic*, we usually associate it with the work of master illusionists who perform amazing feats on stage or television in front of bedazzled audiences."
—Henry Barnard Wesselman, *The Journey to the Sacred Garden* (2003)

"Going back into history . . . magic was once the highest of all the arts, its performers famous the world over. Back in the day, attending the performance of a magician inspired awe and wonder. . . . Today, the word *magic* retains its elevated status only when used as an adjective to describe something else. . . . If a performance is sheer magic, a work of art magical, a meal so memorable that the chef is called a magician, this is still high praise indeed."
—John Case, *The Murder Artist* (2004)

- Charlatanry
  —Tayannah Lee McQuillar, *Rootwork* (2003)

- Intention intersecting with attention
  "My favorite definition of the word *magic* is what happens when intention meets attention."
  —Michelle T. Johnson, *Working While Black* (2004)

- Knowledge of supernatural powers
  "Magic is the greatest wisdom and the knowledge of supernatural powers . . . acquired by obtaining more spirituality and making oneself capable to feel and to see the things of the spirit."
  —Paracelsus, quoted in *Temple of the Cosmos: The Ancient Egyptian Experience of the Sacred* by Jeremy Naydler (1996)

  "Magic . . . is the manipulation of spiritual powers to achieve an end."
  —Winfried Corduan, *Neighboring Faiths* (1998)

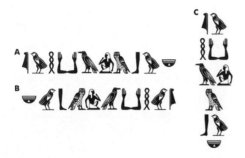

Figure 25. "Magic is everywhere" can be written three different ways in Egyptian hieroglyphics: left-to-right (A), right-to-left (B), and top-to-bottom (C). This figure is based upon an illustration in *Ancient Egyptian Magic* by Bob Brier (1980).

- Making possible the impossible
  "Magic is defined as making something possible that at first does not seem possible."
  —Sidney L. Friedman, *Your Mind Knows More Than You Do* (2000)

- Manifestation of desires
  "Magic involves reaching through the mirror into the sacred realms, connecting with the power that resides there, and then bringing it back into this physical world in order to manifest something—such as healing, for example. That's magic."
  —Henry Barnard Wesselman, *The Journey to the Sacred Garden* (2003)

- Miracle

- Mysticism

- Occult practices
  —E.M. Butler, *The Myth of the Magus* (1948)

- "Organisation of the imagination"
  —Paul Hine, *Condensed Chaos* (1995)

- Power

- Sleight of hand

- "Style and means of artistic expression by which the impression of the numinous comes into being"
  —Rudolf Otto, *The Idea of the Holy* (1923)

- Supreme wisdom
  —Chic Cicero, *The Essential Golden Dawn* (2003)

- Transformation, through a directed process
  "This is my definition of magic: Magic is transformation, brought about by will and skill in accordance with natural law."
  —Marion Weinstein, *Earth Magic* (2003)

- "Using the power of the mind to nudge probabilities."
  —Janina Renee, *Tarot Spells* (1990)

Origins: The word magic finds its roots in the Chaldean word *Maghdim* ("wisdom,")[423] as well as the word *magoi*, "a Median tribe or caste recognized in ancient Iran as specialists in ritual and religious knowledge."[424] Professional magician Tom Ogden elaborates: "Two thousand five hundred years ago, the Magi first visited Greece. The Magi (singular, Magus), a priesthood following the teachings of the Persian prophet Zoroaster, practiced astrology and other occult arts. The Greeks coined the term *magikos* to describe their mysteries. The Romans generalized the word's meaning with their Latin *magical* (meaning, essentially, the art of magic). The term referred to both the arcane practices, such as conjuring up spirits and foretelling the future, and the entertainer's performances of deception by nimble finger-work."[425]

---

423 Paul Christian, *The History and Practice of Magic* (1870), quoted in *The Essential Golden Dawn* by Chic Cicero (2003)

424 Georg Luck, *Arcana Mundi: Magic and the Occult in the Greek and Roman Worlds* (1985)

425 *The Complete Idiot's Guide to Magic Tricks* (1998)

Facts: "In Sanskrit [the] cosmic deception is called *maya*, which may be connected with the English word *magic*. . . . Personified, Maya is the cosmic magician, the creative power of the God-head: 'Charmer who will be believed,' says Emerson, 'by man who thirsts to be deceived.'"[426]

"The name [for the trace mineral] *manganese* comes from the Greek word for magic, because the ancient Athenians believed the element had magical properties."[427]

In the film *Bagdad Cafe* (1987), Jasmine (Marianne Sägebrech) uses the word *Magic* to trigger magical effects.

Professional magician Bill Wisch coined these two acronyms for the word *magic*: Males All Grownups into Children, and Mystification and Gratification in Combination.[428]

Common Magician's Applications: "Remove a penny from your pocket show it fair and square. Close your hand around the penny and before you can say the word 'Magic,' it disappears."[429]

Variations and Incantations:

- Abracadabra and let the magic begin!
  —*The Hindu* (2003)

- Let the magic begin!
  —Professional magician Duck Cameron, *DuckMagic.com* (2005)
  —Professional magician Colin Rose, *Colin RoseMimc.co.uk* (2005)
  —Professional magician Michael Bairefoot, *BairefootMagic.com*, (2003)

—Professional magician David Penn (2003) This is the name of Penn's touring cabaret show.

- Magick
  "Magick is the art and metaphysical science of manifesting personal desires through the collection and direction of energy. The letter 'K' has traditionally been added to the word magic to distinguish it from sleight-of-hand stage magic."
  —Raven Grimassi, *Encyclopedia of Wicca & Witchcraft* (2002)

In Literature:

- "I heard the magic word 'magic.'"
  —Lucius Apuleius, *The Golden Ass* (c. 200 CE), translated by E.J. Kenney (1999)

- "He knelt and spoke a single word—Magic."
  —J. Robert King, *Scourge* (2003)

Magick
(see also *magic*)

O, there's a Magick-musick . . .
—Henry Fielding, *The Tragedy of Tragedies* (1731)

Magick is what makes things happen.
—Edain McCoy, *Making Magick* (1997)

Mystique: "The 'k' in magick balances the energy of the word; the 'k' reaches for heaven while the 'g' roots down to earth."[430]

Meanings: "Some modern occultists spell their 'magick' with a k to differentiate it from the rabbit-out-of-the-hat kind of magic."[431] "Magick

426 Eknath Easwaran, *Dialogue With Death: A Journey Through Consciousness* (1981)

427 Robert C. Atkins, *Dr. Atkins' Vita-Nutrient Solution* (1998)

428 Personal correspondence (2005); *Wisch-Craft.com*

429 Tannen's Magic, *Tannens.com* (2004)

430 Jamie Wood, *The Wicca Herbal* (2003)

431 Dan Burton and David Grandy, *Magic, Mystery, and Science* (2003)

spelled with a 'k' denotes real magick—using your will to create form."[432]

"When your emotions evolve from anger to acceptance, that's magick. When you feel the connection between a ladybug and yourself, that's magick."[433]

Origins: Though popularly attributed to Aleister Crowley, the spelling of *magick* with a 'k' has been traced back to the alchemist John Dee, Queen Elizabeth's consultant. In *Archidoxes of Magic* (1656), Theophrastus Paracelsus uses three spellings: "Magick," "Magicke," and "Magic."

Facts: In 1653, a woman named Dorothy Magicke was imprisoned as an alleged witch in Middlesex.[434]

Variations and Incantations:

- Magic(k)

- Magicke
  In 1590, the poet Edmund Spenser wrote of Merlin's "Magicke slights" ("The Ruines of Time").

In Literature:

- "Magick is the most vital force in our lives. It gives us personal mastery over our destiny so we are no longer victims of fate. To study magick is to study life, and to understand the concept of controlled coincidence."
  —Lady Sabrina, *The Witch's Master Grimoire* (2001)

- Veteran theatre director Peter Brooks recalls: "Walking along Charing Cross Road one day, peering into the windows of the bookshops,

my eye had been caught by a fat volume on display. On its cover in large letters was printed the magic word *Magick*. At first I was ashamed at my interest and several times would enter the shop and pretend to rummage on other shelves before furtively turning its pages. Suddenly, a footnote caught my attention: 'A pupil who reaches the grade of Magister Primus can produce wealth and beautiful women. He can also call up armed men at will.' This was irresistible, and although the book was far too expensive for me, I bought it and at once set out to trace the author, whose very name, Aleister Crowley, was notorious enough to produce a thrill of excitement and fear. A letter to the publisher produced a phone number, which led to an appointment at an address in Piccadilly, where gentlemen-about-town lived in expensive service flats. The great magician was elderly, green-tweeded, and courteous. He had been known in the twenties as 'The Wickedest Man in the World,' but I think he was down on his luck. He seemed touched by my interest, and we met a few times, strolling along Piccadilly together where to my great embarrassment he would stand in the middle of the traffic at noon to raise his elaborately carved walking stick and chant an invocation to the sun. Once he took me into the Piccadilly Hotel for lunch, and again in the crowded and startled dining room, he roared out a conjuration across the soup. Later he allowed me to hide him in my bedroom in Oxford so that I could make a sensation by producing him at the height of a college party, and on the same occasion he outraged a waiter at the Randolph Hotel who asked him for his room number by bellowing, 'The number of the Great Beast, of course—666!' When I did my first production in London, *Doctor Faustus*, he agreed to be magical adviser and came to a rehearsal, having first made me promise that no one should know who he was, as he just wanted to watch unseen from the back of the stalls. But when

---

432 Silver Raven Wolf, *Silver's Spells for Prosperity* (1999)

433 Jamie Wood, *The Enchanted Diary* (2005)

434 James Sharpe, *Instruments of Darkness: Witchcraft in Early Modern England* (1997)

Faustus began his incantation, it was too much for him and he was on his feet, roaring impressively, 'No! No, no! You need a bowl of bull's blood. That'll bring real spirits, I promise you!' Then he added with a broad wink, 'Even at a matinee.' He had demystified himself, and we laughed together."
—*Threads of Time* (1998)

- "'Tell us how you did your trick,' Sam said. 'Now. A bargain's a bargain.' Merilynn glanced around. 'Magick. Magick with a k.' Sam looked annoyed. 'Magick with a k. That's just New Age Wicca hokum.' 'You're wrong.' Merilynn looked triumphant. 'Look it up, Sam. Magic is sleight of hand, tricks of a stage magician. Illusions. Magick is the real thing. I can do a little of that.'"
—Tamara Thorne, *Merilynn* (2003)

Make It So

In Literature: "I became Captain Picard on *Star Trek*, uttering the most magical of words: Make it so."
—Trish MacGregor, *The Everything Love Spells Mini Book* (2002)

Mambo Jambo
(see also *mumbo jumbo*)

Meanings: Greeting similar to "What's happening?"
—Stephen F. Soitos, *The Blues Detective* (1996)

Origins: *Mambo jambo* is a Swahili phrase.[435]

---

435 Stephen F. Soitos, *The Blues Detective* (1996)

Marathon

Origins: *Marathon* is the name of a Greek town, made famous by the legend of the hero Pheidippides.

In Literature: "Marathon became a magic word at Athens. The Athenian people in succeeding ages always looked back upon this day [when the Persians departed] as the most glorious in their annals, and never tired of hearing its praises sounded by their orators and poets."
—William Smith, *A Smaller History of Greece* (1892)

Matba

Meanings:

- "Bring forth," "let it be forthcoming"
—S. Liddell MacGregor Mathers, *The Sacred Magic of Abramelin the Mage, Book III* (translated 1898)

- Coin
—Raphael Patai, *Jewish Alchemists* (1994)

Origins: *Matba* is a magic word for obtaining small coins. The word is found in eighteenth-century Kabbalistic treatises.

Facts: As a talisman to be carried in one's money purse, *matba* was to be written on a square of paper.

Common Magician's Applications: Coin production. To add mystique to a coin routine, a sleight-of-hand magician can use such a marked square of paper as a production prop, perhaps in conjunction with an anecdote about the alchemists of old and their quest for spiritual riches (symbolized by gold).

Figure 26. The *matba* formula for coin production.

Matches, Matches

Common Magician's Applications: Production. For example, the magic words *matches, matches* are recommended when producing headless matches in *Scarne's Magic Tricks* by John Scarne (1951).

Mazak Hala
(see also *alakazam*)

Origins: This magic phrase is a backward-spelling of *alah-kazam*.

Facts: *Mazak Hala* is a "wicked incantation" spoken by an old soothsayer with a long white beard and holding a twisted staff in *4 Hundred and 20 Assassins of Emir Abdullah-Harazins* by Joseph DeMarco (2004).

Mea Maxima Culpa

Meanings:

- I am guilty

- My most grievous fault

Origins: *Mea maxima culpa* is a Latin phrase.

Facts: The evil magician in Doug Henning's musical *The Magic Show* (1981) uses the magic phrase *mea maxima culpa* during his act.

Variations and Incantations: Mea culpa, mea culpa, mea maxima culpa

---

Mekka-lekka-hi, Mekka-hiney-ho

Facts: This magic phrase was popularized by the children's television series *Pee-Wee's Playhouse* (1986): "One of Pee-wee's visiting pals to pop into the Playhouse was in the form of a genie—a disembodied, turban-topped talking head named Jambi. Always a jokester, Jambi swiveled his head and worked his magic much to Pee-wee's rapture; he granted wishes if Pee-wee chanted along with him ('mecca-lecka-hi, mecca-hiney-ho')."[436]

Variations and Incantations:

- Meka-leka-hi, Meka-hiney-ho

- Mecca Lecca Hi, Mecca Hiney Ho

- Mekka Lekka Hi, Mekka Lekka Hiney Ho —Naomi Judd, *Naomi's Breakthrough Guide* (2004)

---

436 Stephen Cox, *Dreaming of Jeannie* (2000)

- Mekka lekka hai, mekka haini ho; Mekka lekka hai, mekka chani ho
  —*Cockahoop Times* (2003)

- Mekka Lekka Hi, Mekka Heiny Ho; Mekka Lekka Hi, Mekka Chonni Ho

- Mekka Lekka Hi, Mekka Heiny Ho; Mekka Lekka Hi, Mekka Chonney Ho

- Mekka lekka hi, mekka hiney ho; Mekka lekka hi, mekka chiney ho
  —"Ask Ken!" (1997)

In Literature:

- "It might as well have been Abracadabra, hocus pocus, or meka-leka-hi, meka-hiney-ho. It was a magical incantation in the language of the gods."
  —Carlos Eire, *Waiting for Snow in Havana: Confessions of a Cuban Boy* (2003)

- "A massive frozen glass door stood in my way, which I opened with ease, by repeating the chant 'Mecca lecka hai, mecca heiney ho,' and using the handle."
  —*TikiRoom.com* (2004)

- "We'd let those kids know that they're loved and valuable, and deserving of healing. 'Mekka Lekka Hi, Mekka Lekka Hiney Ho. Fear be gone when we say 'go.'"
  —Naomi Judd, *Naomi's Breakthrough Guide* (2004)

Melos

Meanings:

- Christ
  —Phillip Tovey, *Inculturation of Christian Worship* (2004)

- Solomon
  —Phillip Tovey, *Inculturation of Christian Worship* (2004)

- The fearful sword of fire
  —Phillip Tovey, *Inculturation of Christian Worship* (2004)

Origins: The word *Melos* appears in the magical amulets and eucharistic liturgies of Abyssinian Christianity. "The magic is based on the idea of words of power. The greatest magicians were given these words, which by repetition are able to accomplish the desired effect. Moses and Solomon were great magicians, but greatest of all was Christ who gave some of his powers to his mother. . . . It would seem that [Melos] is a magic word for Solomon, a variation on that name spelt backwards. Melos is connected with a sword of fire in other Ethiopian magic texts, and is regarded as meaning in the secret language Christ."[437]

Mesopotamia

Facts: Also known as "the blessed word" (ca. 1870), *Mesopotamia* is "a magic word" owing "much of its charm and potency to its sonority."[438]

Mesopotamia refers to the ancient cradle of civilization between the Tigres and Euphrates rivers, site of the Sumerian, Babylonian, and Assyrian cultures.

437 Phillip Tovey, *Inculturation of Christian Worship* (2004)
438 Eric Partridge, *A Dictionary of Clichés* (1978)

Miggle Maggle Muggle Mi

In Literature: "Orko waved his arms and the orbiting objects began to spin faster and faster. 'Annnnd now for the magic words! Miggle, Maggle, Muggle, Mi!'"
—Stephen R. Sobotka Jr., "Gargoyles: Power & Honor" (1998)

Mijoter

Meanings: "The magic word . . . *mijoter* . . . describes that condition of near suspension in which there is, nonetheless, a whispering movement, a tiny bubble rising here and there to break a . . . still surface—and it means, at the same time, a slow ripening."
—Richard Olney, *Simple French Food* (1974)
Origins: *Mijoter* is of French origin. It means "to simmer."

In Literature: "*Mijoter* was the word she used, waving her hands like a conductor quieting an unruly orchestra."
—Elisabeth Luard, *Sacred Food* (2001)

Mikkel Myyra

Origins: This is a magic phrase from Finnish folklore, for transformation into an ant.

Common Magician's Applications: Transformation.

In Literature: "[T]he shoemaker spoke the magic words 'Mikkel myyra,' and became an ant. At once the princess repeated, 'Mikkel myyra,' and she too became an ant. Together they hurried out through the crack in the door. When they were outside the shoemaker said, 'Foken falk,' and became a bird. The princess repeated, 'Foken falk,' and set out flying with him."
—Richard Dorson, "The Shoemaker and the Princess," *Bloodstoppers and Bearwalkers* (1972)

Mirror Mirror

The magic is in you, and the mirrors reflect it.
—Uma Reed, *Developing Your Intuition with Magic Mirrors* (1998)

Mystique: *Mirror.* There is a "shivery thrill"[439] to the word. "Mirrors have been used as special, magical devices for thousands of years. . . . It is not surprising that the magical words 'Mirror, mirror on the wall' play such an important part in the story of Snow White."[440] As in Lewis Carroll's famous novel *Through the Looking Glass*, mirrors entice us with the idea that they might show "alternative worlds or realities."[441] Small wonder that mirrors have played such an important, historical part in the art of conjuring.

Figure 27. The Chinese symbol of "the mirror," one of the "Eight Precious Things."

---

439 Ian Irvine, *Dark is the Moon* (1999)
440 Richard Webster, *Soul Mates* (2001)
441 Stephen R. Donaldson, *Mirror of Her Dreams* (1986)

In Literature:

- "Mirror, mirror, mirror. The words reflected back and forth endlessly in his mind."
  —Ian Irvine, *A Shadow on the Glass* (1998)

- "This is a magic mirror. I know. You've probably heard of a magic mirror before. There was a magic mirror in *Snow White and the Seven Dwarfs*. Let me see if I can remember the magic words to say to the magic mirror. Mirror, mirror on the wall, who's the fairest of them all? That's right. Well, this isn't the same mirror, it's better. Here are the magic words to say to this mirror: Mirror, mirror in my hand, show me evil in the land."
  —Lisa Bany-Winters, "The Snow Queen," *On Stage* (1997)

Misin Nipso Puppy Yakie

Common Magician's Applications: Production.

In Literature: "'*Misin Nipso Puppy Yakie!*' she said. All sorts of things appeared. A sock. A glove. A pair of eye glasses. But no little dog."
—Susan Meddaugh, *Lulu's Hat* (2002)

Mississippi

There is magic in running water.
Who does not know it and feel it?
—Ernest Thompson Seton,
Wild Animals I Have Known (1898)

"On to the Tigris! On to the Euphrates!
The Mississippi! The Hanging Gardens of
Babylon!" His magic words drove them on,
frightened and giggling.
—Joyce Carol Oates, *Them* (1969)

Mystique: "If there is magic on the planet," said naturalist and philosopher Loren Eisley, "it is contained in the water." *Mississippi* is a fluid word rich with magical connotations. It's a word that meanders, gathering strength as it channels the mighty energy of converging rivers.

"A river seems a magic thing. A magic, moving, living part of the very earth itself—for it is from the soil, both from its depth and from its surface, that a river has its beginning."[442] Sir George Sitwell praised "the magic of water, an element which owing to its changefulness of form and mood and color and to the vast range of its effects is ever the principal source of landscape beauty, and has like music a mysterious influence over the mind."[443] Weaving their perennial spell, "Rivers run through our history and folklore, and link us as a people,"[444] says veteran journalist Charles Kuralt.

"As the word *Abraham* means the father of a great multitude of men," wrote Herman Melville, "so the word *Mississippi* means the father of a great multitude of waters. His tribes stream in from east and west, exceedingly fruitful the lands they enrich."[445]

Meanings:

At what point in its course does the Mississippi
become what the Mississippi means?
—T.S. Eliot

- Big river
  —Walter A. McDougall, *Freedom Just Around the Corner* (2004)

---

442 Laura Gilpin, *The Rio Grande* (1949)

443 *On the Making of Gardens* (1909)

444 "The Magic of Rivers" (date unknown)

445 "The River," a fragment appearing in the Norton Critical Edition (1971) of *The Confidence Man* (1875)

- Father of waters
"The river was dubbed 'the father of waters' by early French explorers in the 1700s, apparently [having] misinterpreted the Algonquin name for it meaning 'big river.'"
—Jerry R. Rogers (Ed.), *Water Resources and Environmental History* (2004)

- Gathering of waters

- River in the United States, one of the longest waterways in the world

- State in the southern region of the United States
"As one woman declared at a meeting of the Afro-American Genealogical and Historical Society of Chicago: 'When you say Mississippi, it's a magic word for black Chicagoans. It means memories, good and bad.'"[446]

Origins: *Mississippi* is generally believed to have originated from the Ojibwe (Chippewa) Indian words "mici zibi" meaning "great river" or "gathering in of all the waters" and the Algonquin word "Messipi."[447] "A great many scholars of our Indian languages have tried their hand at the word Mississippi; but the most of them are wrong," said Peter Vieau in 1889. "I used to be told that it is a Menomonee word, *mashchechepee* (the great river)."[448]

Facts: The word *Mississippi* is commonly used as a "countdown spacer" to accurately count down seconds: "One—Mississippi, two—Mississippi, three—Mississippi" and so on.

"Mississippi . . . is beloved by every young child for the very way it trips off the tongue as they spell all those repeated letters."[449]

In Literature: "Squinting through the smoke-laden air, I watch in disbelief as the [billiard] balls, now far more than sixteen in number, begin to scrabble around and arrange themselves at my feet. To me, the floor appears as a muddy flat. I recoil and gasp as the balls slowly shift into forms, shapes, characters—letters of the alphabet! First an *M*, then an *I*, then an *S*, until the word *Mississippi* holds statically, coagulated in a paste-like muddy gruel. Then, in a dizzying, anagrammatic, kaleidoscopic swirl, the balls reconfigure to form the word—*Murderer!*"
—Mark Stanleigh Morris, *Billy Goat Hill* (2004)

Mitchakaboola

Facts: This magic word typically introduces *bibidy bobbidy boo.*

Variations and Incantations:

- Midgidiboola
—Mike Albo, *The Underminer* (2005)

- Mitchakaboola Abbadazoola
—Francesca De Grandis, *Be a Goddess* (1998)

Mobilicorpus

Origins: *Mobilicorpus* is from the Latin words meaning "moveable" (*mobilis*) and "body" (*corpus*).

446 Michael Kammen, *Mystic Chords of Memory* (1991)

447 *Mississippi.gov* (2005)

448 transcribed by Reuben Thwaites, "Narrative of Peter Vieau," *Wisconsin Historical Collections* (1900)

449 Susan Ohanian, *Day by Day Activity Book* (1997)

In Literature: *Mobilicorpus* is a levitation spell in *Harry Potter and the Prisoner of Azkaban* by J.K. Rowling (1999).

Molly Molly Hung

Facts: This is the Cantonese equivalent to *abracadabra.*

In Literature: "On July 17, 2004 over 500 spectators were treated to a special show in Hong Kong and shouted out the magic word, 'Molly, Molly Hung.' What, haven't you used this magic word before in your show? It means 'Abracadabra' in Cantonese."
—Amadeo Swiss, "Fantasma Open up Magic Venue in Hong Kong" (2004)

Money
(see also *fortune, gold* and *treasure*)

Mystique: "Money—money—what a magic is in the word. It is the talisman . . . which more than all gives a man to himself, gives him leisure & independence, the means of cultivating his mind, of improving his nature."[450]

Meaning: Unit of magical energy
"Few understand that the dollar is a unit of magical energy, and the dollar bill itself a magical talisman. Although many words have been written by conspiracy theorists analyzing the Masonic symbols on the one dollar bill, no one has yet been able to sufficiently explain why these symbols are there, or what they really mean."
—Tracy R. Twyman, *Solomon's Treasure: The Magic and Mystery of American Money* (2005)

Facts: Professional magician Jeff McBride calls money "the greatest illusion ever created."[451]

In Literature:

- "I used the magic word. Money."
  —Joseph A. Haymes, *Desperate Summer* (2000)

- "Antoinette had used Nick's magic word—money."
  —Kieran Crowley, *Burned Alive* (1999)

- "'Money?' Pett, the student, became Pett, the financier, at the magic word."
  —P.G. Wodehouse, *Piccadilly Jim* (1918)

Monosodiumglutamate

Facts: *Monosodium Glutamate (MSG)* is the name of a flavor enhancer.

In Literature: "'There now, they enter the cage. Now the glorious Angelina will lock the ferocious porcuswine to the floor with heavy locks and chains. They are now in place. . . . Now, the magic word, *Monosodiumglutamate!*' The canopy dropped down, rose an instant later and they were gone. The audience roared with appreciation when they saw that the cage was empty."
—Harry Harrison, *The Stainless Steel Rat Joins the Circus* (2000)

---

450 Sidney Fisher, quoted in *Them Dark Days* by William Dusinberre (1996)

451 *The Magic of Jeff McBride* DVD (2003)

Motas Uaeta Daries Dardares Astaries Dissunapiter

Origins: This pseudo-Latin phrase was found in a book on Roman agriculture by Cato. It was meant to be chanted in cases of a fracture. "[I]t has no meaning for the uninitiated, whereas the powers to which it is addressed are supposed to understand it very well."[452]

Common Magician's Applications: Restoration.

Mumbo
(see *mumbo jumbo*)

In Literature: "Superstition! From our ancestors, savages, afraid of the dark, of themselves: mumbo words and magic lights to scare away ghosts."
—Tillie Olsen, *Tell Me a Riddle* (1956)

Mumbo Jumbo

It might be mumbo jumbo, but mystery and mumbo jumbo are a big part of ritual . . .
And if it works, why question it.
—Twyla Tharp, *The Creative Habit* (2003)

Mystique: Mythologist Joseph Campbell suggested that the "magic of art and the art of magic" both derive from a special kind of momentary experience of "reality-beyond-meaning," an experience that can't be put into words:

Hence the power of the meaningless syllables, the mumbo jumbo of magic, and the meaningless verbalizations of metaphysics, lyric poetry, and art interpretation. They function evocatively, not referentially; like the beat of a shaman's drum, not like a formula of Einstein. One moment later, and we have classified the experience and may be having utterable thoughts and describable feelings about it—thoughts and feelings that are in the public domain, and they will be either sentimental or profound, according to our education. But according to our life, we have had, for an instant, a sense of existence: a moment of unevaluated, unimpeded, lyric life— antecedent to both thought and feeling; such as can never be communicated by means of empirically verifiable propositions, but only suggested by art.[453]

According to Campbell, a magician's "mumbo jumbo" captures the unutterable, indescribable meaning of profound, unclassifiable experiences.

Meanings:

- Black magic
  "Cordelia, believing she had restored his soul with some black magic mumbo-jumbo, set him free."
  —Diana G. Gallagher, *The Casefiles: Volume 2* (2004)

  "[L]umped in with the worst practitioners of the so-called black magic or mumbo jumbo . . ."
  —Deirdre Bair, *Jung: A Biography* (2003)

----

452 Tore Janson, *A Natural History of Latin* (2004)

453 *Flight of the Wild Gander* (1951)

- Gibberish, incomprehensible language
"[T]he path to freedom gets overgrown by brambles of meaningless mumbo jumbo."
—Mihaly Csikszentmihalyi, *Flow* (1990)

"[I]t smacked of impenetrable mumbo jumbo, designed to hoodwink the public."
—Ron Chernow, *Alexander Hamilton* (2004)

"He thoroughly despised the *kahins*, whose oracles were usually unintelligible mumbo jumbo, and was always very careful to distinguish the Koran from conventional Arabic poetry."
—Karen Armstrong, *A History of God* (1993)

"[E]soteric and unintelligible mumbo-jumbo . . ."
—R.J. Chambers and G.W. Dean, *Chambers on Accounting* (2000)

- Jargon
"[T]ransforming the mumbo jumbo of medieval alchemy into hard science . . ."
—Rick Steves, *Florence and Tuscany 2005* (2004)

- Language intended to confuse
"[A] minor conjuror, a dabbler in fakery and mumbo jumbo . . ."
—Jonathan Stroud, *The Amulet of Samarkand* (2003)

- Magic spell
"My husband is sure that you worked some sort of mumbo-jumbo on me."
—Maxwell Maltz, *Psycho Cybernetics* (1989)

"All that mumbo-jumbo and magic nonsense."
—Brian Jacques, *Redwall* (1998)

- Magician
—Stephen F. Soitos, *The Blues Detective: A Study of African American Detective Fiction* (1996)

- Mystical incantation
—Lynne McTaggart, *The Field* (2003)

"[I]t seemed as though Dick were muttering jubilant mumbo-jumbo."
—Truman Capote, *In Cold Blood* (1965)

- Object with supernatural powers
"[A] Mumbo-Jumbo which has to be invoked . . ."
—Kay Redfield Jamison, *Touched With Fire* (1993)

- Obscure ritual
"'What on earth is she doing in there?' 'Her usual mumbo-jumbo, I suppose,' said Williams. 'Twigs, leaves, feathers, exotic powders, chicken bones.'"
—John Berendt, *Midnight in the Garden of Good and Evil* (1994)

- Rubbish
Interjection said with "'enlightened' scorn."
—Henry Lincoln, *Key to the Sacred Pattern* (1998)

- Supernatural
"Aren't we crossing into mumbo-jumbo territory here?"
—Harville Hendrix, *Keeping the Love You Find* (1993)

"Why do I always get sucked into this supernatural mumbo jumbo?"
—Sherrilyn Kenyon, *Night Pleasures* (2002)

- Superstition
—Eugene H. Peterson, *Christ Plays in Ten Thousand Places* (2005)

"[T]his is just verbal magic, mumbo jumbo, superstition in a modern form."
—Duke Maskell, *The New Idea of a University* (2002)

- What's up? What's happening?
—Stephen Soitos, *Blues Detective* (1996)

Origins: *Mumbo jumbo* is likely of Mandingo origin, derived from the name of the deity "Mama Dyambo" (literally meaning "ancestor with a pompon" or tuft on his hat).[454] There is a story of the "Mambo Jambo" talisman of eastern Senegal, reported in 1795 by Scottish explorer Mungo Park:

> Thought to be an idol in the shape of a grotesque snake—similar to the 'Rainbow Snake' which is worshipped by tribes further down the West African coast—the talisman was used by the Woolli River people to regulate village disputes by making sacrifices to the image. [Explorer Mungo] Park's journals record that he found a mask of the Mambo Jambo spirit somewhere near Tambacounda, towards the confluence of the rivers Gambia and Kouloufou. His story of the rituals associated with the fetish so confused his listeners back in Britain that the phrase *mumbo jumbo*, meaning hocus pocus or superstitious rigmarole, was introduced to the English lexicon.[455]

Some sixty years earlier, another explorer recounted: "At Night, I was visited by a Mumbo Jumbo, an Idol, which is among the Mundingoes a kind of cunning Mystery . . . This is a Thing invented by the Men to keep their Wives in awe."[456] Later, in 1799, Mungo Park concurred: "This is a strange bugbear . . . much employed by the Pagan natives in keeping their women in subjection"[457] through bewildering talk and meaningless ceremonies. However, since the eighteenth century, there have been no reports of any such deity in any West African tribe.[458]

The *Morris Dictionary of Word and Phrase Origins* suggests that *Mumbo Jumbo* is a "magician who makes the troubled spirits of ancestors go away. [The phrase] referred to the belief of some Mandingo peoples in the western Sudan that a high priest called the 'Mumbo Jumbo' had the power to protect his village from evil spirits."[459]

Variations and Incantations:

- Hugger-mugger
  —WordNet, Princeton University

- Mambo jambo
  —Dean Buchmeyer and Peter Gardner, *A Touch of Voodoo* (2000)

- Mambo jumbo
  —Muhd F. Khamsin, "Witches Cookbook," Young Writer's Club (1999)

- Mumbo-Pocus
  "[T]his transcends mere *Mumbo-Jumbo*, sending us reeling into the realm of Mumbo-Pocus."
  —Frank Zappa, *The Real Frank Zappa Book* (1989)

- Mumbo mumbo mumbo jakka dakka hippitippi
  —Balanced Alternative Technologies Multi-User Dimension, *Bat.org* (2004)

- Mumpo jumpo
  "[T]he professor of the mystic art to-day wears a white or embroidered waistcoat, pays rates and taxes, has a wife and family; and, instead of mystic adjurations of 'hocus pocus,' and 'abracadabra,' and 'mumpo

454 Robert Hendrickson, *Encyclopedia of Word and Phrase Origins* (1997)

455 *Insight Guide: Gambia and Senegal* (1999)

456 F. Moore, *Travels in Africa* (1738), quoted in *Take OurWord.com* (1999)

457 *Ibid.*

458 *Ibid.*

459 William and Mary Morris (1977)

jumpo,' issues invitations to his friends to come and see him at a theatre, an assembly room, or a public hall."
—Ellis Stanyon, *Magic* (1900)

In Literature:

- "The ultimate effect of the non-Euclidian geometries becomes nothing more than a magician's mumbo jumbo in which belief is sustained purely by faith!"
  —Robert M. Pirsig, *Zen and the Art of Motorcycle Maintenance* (1974)

- ". . . an intangible, impalpable, mysterious mumbo-jumbo virtue in it."
  —William Hope, "Pollution of Rivers," *Transactions of the National Association for the Promotion of Social Science* (1873)

Mutabor

Origins: *Mutabor* is a magic word from Arabian folklore.

In Literature: "The caliph and his grand vizier buy various things and finally notice a container full of dark powder to which is attached a piece of paper with strange letters on it. The learned Selim is able to decipher this writing, which explains in Latin that anyone who sniffs this powder and then says the Latin word *mutabor* will be transformed into the animal he chooses and will be able to understand the speech of animals. There is no danger in doing this since in order to resume human form the sniffer has only to bow three times to the east and then repeat the magic word *mutabor*. However, one must be very careful not to laugh during the process of sniffing and

transformation, for otherwise the magic world will instantly be forgotten."
—Harald Weinrich, *Lethe: The Art and Critique of Forgetting* (1997)

Mutatis Mutandis

Meanings: "The necessary changes having been made"

Origins: *Mutatis mutandis* is a Latin phrase.

In Literature: "Even in the absence of a reference to Lacan, we can recognize a hallmark Lacanian rhetorical gesture: *mutatis mutandis*, the magic words which allow different things to be *versions of* each other without the exact relation being spelled out."
—Edward R. O'Neill, "The Last Analysis of Slavoj Zizek" (2001)

Mystery

Mystery has a great appeal to human minds,
even when it's known to be fantasy.
—Lloyd H. Whitling,
The Complete Universe of Memes (2002)

Mystique: "The word *mystery* has a certain inherent hiddenness and a built-in quality of puzzlement."[460] However, it "does not mean a puzzle or a conundrum to be figured out. On the contrary: though a mystery may give rise to many interpretations, it can't be exhausted by any of them. Rather it serves as a window to a

----

460 Jeffrey L. Curry, *The Mysteries of the Kingdom* (2004)

higher reality; it speaks of, and elicits, a deeper truth within the mind."[461]

Origins: "The word *mystery* (*mysterion* in Greek) derives from the Greek verb myein, 'to close,' referring to the closing of the lips or the eyes. This 'closed' character of the mysteries may be interpreted in two ways. First of all, an initiate, or *mystes* (plural, *mystai*) into the *mysterion* was required to keep his or her lips closed and not divulge the secret that was revealed at the private ceremony. Vows of silence were meant to ensure that the initiate would keep the holy secret from being revealed to outsiders. . . . A second way to interpret the 'closed' nature of the mysteries relates to the closing and the opening of the eyes. Closed eyes brought darkness to the prospective initiate both literally and metaphorically, and the opening of the eyes was an act of enlightenment."[462]

In Literature: "[In a] wholly inexplicable way, Pierre felt himself surrounded by ten thousand sprites and gnomes, and his whole soul was swayed and tossed by supernatural tides; and again he heard the wondrous, rebounding, chanted words: 'Mystery! Mystery!'"
—Herman Melville, *Pierre, Or the Ambiguities* (1852)

N

Nee Se Bari Waggle Teetum

In Literature: John Burningham, *Cloudland* (1999)

Never

Well, I never! Who would have thought such a common word could work magic?
—Peggy Christian, *The Bookstore Mouse* (2002)

Mystique: Professional magician Kenton Knepper (The Mystic of Magic) notes, "I feel that every word is magical, for by defining, we create. By labeling anything, we limit it. When we limit something, it becomes a seeming reality. All that is in physical form is a compression, and words do compress a wide range of possibilities of experience into a single thing. Each word has a compression of its own limitation of experience. Limitation is not a bad thing. We must have limitation for anything to exist in any purposeful way. On the other hand, those of us who work in illusion (as well as a hopefully larger perspective) understand very well the deception that occurs by such limitation and labeling. 'I never want to touch the deck of cards at all' is something an audience later recalls as truth. But a good card sharp says such a thing as he hands the deck to a person to shuffle. The word 'never' creates the false impression that the card sharp never, ever touches the cards. In physical fact, he himself handled the cards as he gave them over for a shuffle. In the process

461 Richard Smoley, *Hidden Wisdom* (1999)
462 Marvin W. Meyer, *The Ancient Mysteries* (1987)

he has marked the cards or abused them in his favorite manner for his later benefit."[463]

Next Time

The next time.
Did there exist three more magical words?
—Kathleen O'Reilly, *Touched By Fire* (2002)

Mystique: *Next time* is a charm-like promise often accompanied by "better luck." It conjures a future in which anything can happen. "Using 'next' as a magic word will remind you to get on with the magic of believing," suggests Wayne Dyer, "rather than the anguish of doubt" (*Real Magic* [1992]).

In Literature: "The two most magical words in the English language . . . are *next time*. We have a chance to be different."
—David Baum, *The Randori Principles* (2002)

Ngh-Hlu-Khu-Wig

Facts: These magic words, to be intoned in a stern voice, are featured in the computer game "Shadow of the Comet" (1994).

Nikkety Nakkety Noo

In Literature: "Scraps waved the wand at Glinda and chanted, '*Nikkety nakkety noo, Smarts come back to you!*'"
—Sherwood Smith, *The Emerald Wand of Oz* (2005)

Nikstlitselpmur

(see also *rumplestiltskin*)

Facts: This is the name "Rumplestiltskin" spelled backwards, used as a magic word in the computer game "King's Quest 1."

No

She used one simple word. A very simple, one syllable, magic word that far too many people seem to have forgotten the usefulness of. . . . "No."
—Tiberius Alantheus,
"One Simple Word" (2004)

Mystique: "To be 'magic,' words do not have to have a mysterious sound, an esoteric meaning, or a special history."[464] "A little word. A simple sound. 'No.' Again. 'No . . . No. No no.' Get used to forming the sound. Tip of the tongue on the roof of the mouth, then a circle of the lips: 'NO!' Such a powerful word. A magical word. A word that gets you what you want."[465]

In Literature:

- "[S]tart religiously using the magic word 'no' in all your conversations with her."
  —Ron Louis and David Copeland, *How to Succeed With Women* (1998)

- "She began to plead with one spoken word: 'NO!' As if it were a magic word, presto! Danny came to himself."
  —Danny Rolling and Sondra London, *The Making of a Serial Killer* (1996)

- "[H]e was nearly overcome by the *Yezer Ha-Ra* [an 'evil inclination' that occurs in Jewish rabbinical writings], but resisted it with

---

463 Personal correspondence (2005). The Mystic of Magic's website for magicians only is *Wonder Wizards.com*.

464 John Granrose, *The Archetype of the Magician* (1996)
465 Jim Oliver, *Closing Distance* (1992)

his might and managed to shout, 'No!' Just as the magic word was uttered, the woman vanished along with the cottage."
—Carol K. Mack, *A Field Guide to Demons, Fairies, Fallen Angels and Other Subversive Spirits* (1999)

- "When we're kids, the magic words are 'please' and 'thank you.' When we get older, the magic word is 'no.'"
—Martin L. Rossman, *The Art of Getting Well* (2002)

Noctar Raiban

Origins: *Noctar Raiban* are antiquated magic words for mind reading from an Egyptian book of magical talismans entitled *Treasure of the Old Man of the Pyramids*, "translated from the Language of the Magi" in the eighteenth century.[466]

Figure 28. This mind-reading talisman has an occult appearance but not a diabolical purpose. It is based upon the research of Arthur Edward Waite in *The Book of Ceremonial Magic* (1913).

Facts: These magic words were believed to compel even "the most discreet man . . . to unveil his utterly secret thoughts."[467]

Common Magician's Applications: Mentalism. When printed in the form of an ancient talisman, *Noctar Raiban* can serve as a mystique-laden prop during a mentalism routine.

No-Kan-Du

Facts: This phrase is a play on the words "No Can Do."

No-Kan-Du is the name of a magician played by the animated character Krazy Kat, in the cartoon "The Crystal Gazebo" (1932).[468]

Nomee-Akwee-Petree

In Literature: "Eric closed his eyes and summoned up some magic words. 'Nomee-akwee-petree!' A blast of blue sparks burst from his fingertips."
—Tony Abbott, *Search for the Dragon Ship* (2003)

Nov Schmoz Ka Pop

Meanings: *Nov schmoz ka pop* is a nonsense phrase.

Origins: *Nov schmoz ka pop* was the catchphrase of "Little Hitchhiker," a popular Sunday comic

466 Arthur Edward Waite, *The Book of Ceremonial Magic* (1913)

467 *Ibid.*

468 Leonard Maltin, *Of Mice and Magic: A History of American Animated Cartoons* (1980)

strip character in Gene Ahearn's "The Squirrel Cage."[469]

"*Nov Schmoz Ka Pop?* That was the question raised by the omnipresent stranger in L'il Abner. No one knew what he meant; apparently he was speaking a dying language."[470]

Facts: These are the magic words of professional magician Steve Charney[471]

Variations and Incantations:

- Nov schmoz kapop

- Nov schmozz kepop

- Nov shmoz kapop

- Nov shmoz ka pop

Now

The magic word is NOW!
—Elisa Medhus, *Hearing is Believing* (2004)

Facts: *Now* is a magic word popularized by professional magician Doug Henning.

In Literature:

- "*Now* is the magic word of success."
  —David Schwartz, *The Magic of Thinking Big* (1987)

- "The advertiser plays on those magic Mom's words, like the word NOW. 'You have got to [go to] bed Johnny . . . NOW.' As a six year old child, you recall the power of Mom's command, and the physical consequences if you disobeyed."
  —Geoffrey Knight, "Covert Hypnosis" (2002)

- From Frank Zane, "The Present," *Mind, Body, Spirit* (1997):

  Where is this NOW
  when now you see it
  now you don't?

- "'What's the magic word?' I asked. 'Now!' she replied."
  —Dan Clark, *Puppies for Sale and Other Inspirational Tales* (1997)

- "You stupid, dumb bunny rabbit, you get out of there [the magic hat], NOW!"
  —Leslie Tryon, "The Magic Words Flashcards" (2005)

- "The magic hasn't even begun to take place. Not until . . . now!"
  —Tom Ogden, *The Complete Idiot's Guide to Magic Tricks* (1998)

- "I said the magic word, 'Now!'"
  —Darrell Max Craig, *Japan's Ultimate Martial Art* (1995)

- "An agent on the briefing podium almost forgot to say his magic word into his handset, and only just remembered in time: 'Now!'"
  —Brian Lumley, *Bloodwars* (1995)

---

469 Robert A. Buethe, *Cartoonacy.net* (2003)

470 Milt Rosenberg, "Milt's File" (2003)

471 *Hocus Jokus: 50 Funny Magic Tricks Complete with Jokes* (2003)

Now You See It, Now You Don't

(see also *now*)

The now-you-see-it
now-you-don't hands of a magician . . .
—Thomas L. Friedman,
From Beirut to Jerusalem (1990)

Mystique:

Life is an illusion. There one second, gone the
next. Now you see it, now you don't.
—Timothy Leary, *The Politics of Ecstasy* (1980)

"That old magician's cry 'Now you see it, now
you don't'"[472] is an exclamation of wonder at the
ephemeral marvels of life, marvels that many
people refer to as *maya* (a Sanskrit term). "Maya
means not so much illusion, but trickery, in the
sense of play. Now you see me now you don't.
Maya is the shapeshifter. You can never grasp it
. . . It is so beyond our ordinary understanding
that we can only exclaim, 'It just can't be true!
It's some marvelous error!'"[473] *Now you see it, now
you don't* describes two "magical states"[474] of reality and invokes the great cycle of creation and
destruction. Quantum physicists observe this cycle, describing things popping into existence out
of thin air and then blinking back out into the
great void.[475] Physicist Evan Harris Walker notes
that "It is important to understand that this now-
you-see-it-now-you-don't quirk of atomic reality

is not a magic trick but a part of the way nature
is."[476] Spiritual philosopher Alan Watts explains:

> [T]here are times when the world is,
> and times when it isn't, for if the world
> went on and on without rest for ever
> and ever, it would get horribly tired of
> itself. It comes and it goes. Now you see
> it; now you don't. So because it doesn't
> get tired of itself, it always comes back
> again after it disappears. It's like your
> breath: it goes in and out, in and out,
> and if you try to hold it in all the time
> you feel terrible. It's also like the game
> of hide-and-seek, because it's always fun
> to find new ways of hiding, and to seek
> for someone who doesn't always hide in
> the same place.[477]

Whereas physicists developed the Big Bang theory of creation, "Hundreds of years ago, theo-
logians developed a similar hypothesis called
creation ex nihilio. This is the doctrine that the
world sprang into being out of pure nothingness.
One moment there was void and emptiness, and
an instant later, quick as a divine heartbeat, a
whole universe pulsed into view. Now you see it,
now you don't: That's Life."[478]

Naturalist Richard Fortey discusses why a
magician's "now you see it—now you don't" is
so profoundly moving to his spectators. "In our
visually-dominated world sight is almost synonymous with understanding. We acknowledge light
dawning by saying: 'I see!' The metaphor of vision suffuses our attempts to convey comprehension: we bring issues into focus, we clarify our
views, we sight our objectives, we *look into* things.

---

472 Eugene H. Kaplan, *A Field Guide to Coral Reefs* (1999)

473 Roger Housden, *Ten Poems to Change Your Life* (2001)

474 *Michelin Must Sees: Las Vegas* (2004)

475 "Electrons, it seems, blink in and out of existence,
all the while. Now you see them, now you don't."
—Harry Wilson, *Freedom From God: Restoring the
Sense of Wonder* (2001)

---

476 *The Physics of Consciousness* (2000)

477 *The Book: On the Taboo Against Knowing Who You Are*
(1966)

478 Barbara Rohde, "For All the Gifts of Life," *All the
Gifts of Life* (2002)

We accept the evidence of our own eyes. The conjurer turns the veracity of sight head over heels: now you see it—now you don't. We find his tricks disturbing because we are so wedded to the truth of sight."[479] Perhaps a magic trick is sometimes disturbing, but more often than not the "'now you see it now you don't' [is] entangling, enticing, enthralling, [and yet] elusive," for it indirectly presents a "divine revelation" to human eyes: "indirectly—direct vision would be blinding—through the veil of language."[480]

Meanings:

- Apparition, "intangible nonentity"
  —Yael Navaro-Yashin, *Faces of the State* (2002)

- Changeability
  "[Ovid's *Metamorphoses*] is another of those fleeing-nymph stories, combined with the now-you-see-it-now-you-don't nature of Arcadian rivers. The river god Alpheus chases Arethusa, who *becomes* a river to *escape* a river."
  —Larry Habegger, *Travelers' Tales: Greece* (2000)

- Conjuring trick; sleight of hand
  —Deborah Debonshire, *Counting My Chickens* (2001)
  —Todd Boyd, *Young Black Rich and Famous* (2003)
  —Elizabeth Martinez, *De Colores Means All of Us* (1998)
  "[A] now-you-see-it-now-you-don't trick guaranteed to amuse and bewilder . . ."
  —Jerome Malitz, *Rocky Mountain National Park Dayhiker's Guide* (1993)
  "This 'now you see it, now you don't' conjuring trick, called 'regeneration' in the physics trade, is not magic at all, but a dra-

matic demonstration of quantum mechanics at work."
—Gordon Fraser, *Antimatter: The Ultimate Mirror* (2000)
  "It's the sleight of hand routine done with other parts of the body, now you think you see it, now you don't."
—Derek Smethurst, *Soccer Technique for Winning* (2000)
  "Autobiography is the magician's best trick: now you see him, now you don't."
—Debra B. Sostak, *Philip Roth—Countertexts, Counterlives* (2004)
  "The now-you-see-it-now-you-don't-sleight-of-hand rules . . ."
—John Edgar Wideman, *Brothers and Keepers* (2005)

- Demonstration of stagecraft
  —E.J. Clery, *The Rise of Supernatural Fiction, 1762–1800* (1999)

- Disappearing act
  "[P]ulling some sort of disappearing trick. Now you see it, now you don't."
  —Daniel M. Hausman, *Economic Analysis and Moral Philosophy* (1996)
  "[O]ne can only speak of the film as a conjurer's 'now you see it, now you don't' disappearance act."
  —Thomas Elsaesser, *Weimar Cinema and After: Germany's Historical Imaginary* (2000)
  "The Pleistocene extinction is a vanishing trick that falls under the heading, 'Now you see them, now you don't,' for at the time human beings were numerous all over the earth."
  —Charles Panati, *The Browser's Book of Endings: The End of Practically Everything and Everybody* (1989)

- Ebb and flow
  —Matthew Fox, *The Way of Conflict* (2004)

---

479 *Trilobite* (2001)

480 Nicholas Garnham, *Emancipation, the Media, and Modernity* (2000)

- Elusive, slippery
—Jerome D. Levin, *Theories of the Self* (1992)
—Ruth Robbins, *Pater to Forster, 1873–1924* (2003)

- Evanescent
—Edward Bliss Jr., *Writing News for Broadcast* (1994)

- Fleeting image
—Charles Hayes, *Tripping* (2000)

- Flick, flicker
"[A] flickering, *trompe-l'oeil* quality: Now you see it, now you don't."
—Lance Morror, *Evil: An Investigation* (2003)
  "There's something about the crimson flash of a snake's forked tongue or the now-you-see-it-now-you-don't flicker of a lizard's nictitating membrane, the clear film that acts as a third eyelid, that gives most people the willies—and thrills a select few."
—Osha Gray Davidson, *Fire in the Turtle House* (2001)
  "Then the electricity supply began to flicker—now you see it now you don't."
—John Lawton, *A Little White Death* (1999)
  "[W]ith the flick of a switch—now you see it, now you don't."
—Chris Lefteri, *Glass* (2004)
  "[H]is touches have a rather flickering appearance; now you see them, now you don't."
—Jacqueline A. Rankin, *Body Language of the Abused Child* (1999)

- Fluctuating pattern
—Elaine Shimberg, *Living With Tourette Syndrome* (1995)

- Game of appearance and reality
—Ian Stronach, *Educational Research Undone* (1995)

- Ghostlike
—David Punter, *The Gothic* (2004)

- Hide-and-seek game
—Rose Mary Dougherty, *The Lived Experience of Group Spiritual Direction* (2003)
—Biruté M.F. Galdikas, *Reflections of Eden* (1995)
—Mary N. Waters, *Private Rooms* (2000)
  "[T]he Hindu dramatic idea of the cosmos as an endless hide-and-seek game: now you see it, now you don't . . ."
—Alan Watts, *Philosophies of Asia* (1995)

- Illusion
—Solly Angel, *The Tale of the Scale* (2003)
  "Some will view this paradox as a 'smoke and mirrors' illusion—now you see it, now you don't. But this is the essence of paradox: it is and it is not; it is neither this nor that."
—Ernie Bringas, *Created Equal* (2003)
  "Christo and Jean Claude would probably wish the workings of constructing and dismantling the veil could be concealed like a magician's illusion. Now you see it, now you don't."
—C.J. Lim, *Realms of Impossibility* (2002)

- Incantation
"[H]e would kiss every five-pound note that went through his hands with the incantation, 'Now you see me, now you don't.'"
—Michael King, *Wrestling with the Angel: A Life of Janet Frame* (2000)

- Instantly
—Amber K., *Heart of Tarot* (2003)

- Magic, magical transformation
—Gail Herman, *The Icicle Forest* (2000)
—Jean M. Stehman, *Handbook of Dementia Care* (1996)
  "Magic. Now you see it, now you don't. Now it's broken, now it's fixed. Now it's shells, now it's an egg. Bingo."
—John R. Erickson, *Hank the Cowdog 24* (1995)

- Magic words
  —R.E. Oliver, *What is Transparency?* (2004)
  "'Now you see it, now you don't.' 'Huh?' 'It's what magicians say.' 'Oh, yeah. I do magic, too!'"
  —Rod Downey, *The Moralist* (2004)
  "This description seems almost like a magician's words—now you see it, now you don't. Quantum energy is now a wave, now a particle, and we don't know where it is or when it is."
  —Cletus Wessels, *The Holy Web* (2000)
  "Like a magician (now you see it, now you don't) the doctor restored Hector's allowance."
  —Jacques Barzun, *Berlioz and His Century: An Introduction to the Age of Romanticism* (1956)

- Magician
  "[F]ormer resident magician Max Kinsella, Mr. Now-you-see-him, Now-you-don't, was possibly involved in a murder, or three."
  —Carole Nelson Douglas, *Cat in a Neon Nightmare* (2003)
  "The belief about the use of sleeves originated back in the early days of theatrical performances when prestidigitators customarily wore huge robes with large sleeves. In those days the now-you-see-it-now-you-don't artists could conceal several rabbits and a bowl of goldfish up around their elbows."
  —Vincent H. Gaddis, "The Art of Honest Deception," *Strange Magazine* (2005)

- Mirage
  —Victoria Newhouse, *Towards a New Museum* (1998)
  —Chandra Talpade Mohanty, *Feminist Genealogies* (1996)

- Misdirection
  —Philip Gerard, *Secret Soldiers* (2002)

- Mystifying logic
  —Terry Eagleton, *The Ideology of the Aesthetic* (1990)
  —Neil Hertz, "Medusa's Head: Male Hysteria Under Political Pressure" (1983)

- Now; the present moment
  —W.S. Merwin, *Zen Wave: Basho's Haiku and Zen* (1978)
  "Where is this NOW / when now you see it / now you don't?"
  —Frank Zane, "The Present," *Mind, Body, Spirit* (1997)

- On-again-off-again
  —David Wiltse, *Heartland* (2002)

- One-step forward, two-steps back
  —Theodore M. Vestal, *Ethiopia: A Post-Cold War African State* (1999)

- Paradigm shift; Gestalt switch
  "[I]t is impossible to embrace a new paradigm until the old one has been relinquished. The perceptual shift is rather like the Gestalt switch—the 'now you see it now you don't' principle—which operates in the perception of visual illusions, and must occur all at once. Hence all important advances are sudden insights, or new ways of seeing."
  —Helen Graham, *Complementary Therapies in Context: The Psychology of Healing* (1999)

- Paradox
  —Joel S. Migdal, *Boundaries and Belonging* (2004)

- Passing quickly
  "[It was] described on official stationery from headquarters which Sullivan passed (now-you-see-it, now-you-don't) quickly before her eyes."
  —Maureen Howard, *Natural History* (1999)

"Her pale green eyes and now-you-see-it-now-you-don't smile hinted at an easily amused nature."
—Elizabeth Bevarly, *Her Man Friday* (1999)

- Peekaboo
  —Patricia Spyer, *Border Fetishisms* (1998)
  —Lynn Turgeon, *Bastard Keynesianism: The Evolution of Economic Thinking and Policy-Making Since World War II* (1997)

- Seasonal operation
  —Tim Hollis, *Florida's Miracle Strip* (2004)

- Shifting ambiguity
  —Jonathan Franzen, *The Twenty-Seventh City* (2001)

- Short glimpses
  —Malcom Bradbury, *To the Hermitage* (2001)

- Simulacrum
  —Ian Stronach, *Educational Research Undone* (1995)

- Skullduggery, scam
  —Michael H. Hyman, *The Power of Global Capital* (2003)

- Sometimes
  —John McWhorter, *Doing Our Own Thing* (2003)

- Syndrome "where increased visibility leads to a paradoxical disappearance"
  This syndrome occurs in minority groups struggling to be recognized even as they wish to remain unidentifiable (Brian Roberts, "Whatever Happened to Gay Theatre?" *New Theatre Quarterly 62: Volume 16, Part 2* [2000]).

- Teasing
  "These young women were tricksters of desire—now-you-see-it, now-you-don't flirtation and flair."
  —Cynthia Gralla, *The Floating World* (2004)

- Transitory thrills
  —Ken Emerson, *Doo-Dah: Stephen Foster and the Rise of American Popular Culture* (1998)

- Uncertainty
  —Sue Nelson, *How to Clone the Perfect Blonde* (2004)

- Unpredictability
  —Martin Kantor, *Distancing* (2003)
  —Anthony Easthope, *Privileging Difference* (2002)

- Wishy-washy
  —Arnold Aronson, *American Set Design* (1985)

Origins: Magicians started using the phrase *now you see it, now you don't* in the 1930s, at the same time people started saying the catchphrases "The greatest thing since sliced bread" and "That's all, folks!"[481]

Facts: The magic trigger in *now you see it, now you don't* is actually in the silence between the two phrases. The magic happens in the split second before *now you don't*.

This phrase is often described as "conjuring in reverse."[482] "Now you see it, now you don't—the rabbit seems to vanish back into the hat."[483]

Common Magician's Applications: "The Instant Vanish,"[484] in which something disappears "before one's very eyes."[485] For example: "'Now you see it, now you don't.' Charlotte made a sweeping motion, and just like that, the

---

481 Rick Jones, "20th Century Catchphrases" (2003)

482 Priscilla Vail, *Liberate Your Child's Learning Patterns* (2002)

483 David B. Cohen, *Out of the Blue: Depression and Human Nature* (1994)

484 Giovanni Livera, *Amazing Dad* (2001)

485 Marc Davenport, *Visitors from Time* (1994)

old coin was gone."[486] *Now you see it, now you don't* is especially associated with the ancient game of shells[487] or cups and balls.[488]

Variations and Incantations:

- Abracadabra, Now you see it, now you don't
  —Jodi Picoult, *Keeping the Faith* (1999)

- First you see it, then you don't
  —*Phrases.org.uk* (2003)

- Helter Skelter now you see it, now you don't
  —Jack Sarfatti, quoted in *The Dancing Wu Li Masters* by Gary Zukav (1979)

- Here one moment, gone the next
  —Paul Levinson, *The Soft Edge: A Natural History and Future of the Information Revolution* (1997)

- Hey presto! Now you see it, now you don't
  —Frederick Beuchner, *Lion Country* (1971)

- Hocus Pocus, Now you see it, now you don't
  —Peter R. Breggin, *Talking Back to Ritalin* (2001)

- Now you see 'em, now you don't
  —Scott Flansburg, *Math Magic for Your Kids* (1998)

- Now-you-see-me now-you-don't
  —Carl Sandburg, "Timesweep," *Honey and Salt* (1963)

- Now you think you see it, now you don't
  —Derek Smethurst, *Soccer Technique for Winning* (2000)

- Vê, não vê
  —Candace Slater, *Entangled Edens: Visions of the Amazon* (2002)

In Literature:

- Pedro Juan Gutierrez, *Dirty Havana Trilogy: A Novel in Stories* (2002)

- "[N]ow you see it, now you don't, the trick of a supreme magician who could—with cunning legerdermain under a silk handkerchief—transform a few seconds of tranquility into an eternity of chaos."
  —Judith Viorst, *Necessary Losses* (1986)

- "I was always suspicious of people, especially boys. Their smiles and words were like little balls in the hands of a magician: now you see them, now you don't."
  —V.C. Andrews, *Cinnamon* (2001)

- "[P]erhaps he is only the latest example of 'Now you see it, now you don't'—as stage magicians used to say during the Great Depression when the rabbit disappeared into the tall silk hat."
  —Donald E. Morse, *The Novels of Kurt Vonnegut* (2003)

- "She is similar to the famed leprechaun of Irish lore, a 'now you see it, now you don't' little creature."
  —Sue Ellen Cooper, *The Red Hat Society* (2004)

- "I reshuffled the cards and tried to concentrate on the trick. 'Just a deck of cards. Nothing up my sleeve. Now you see 'em. Now you don't.'"
  —Jon Scieszka, *Knights of the Kitchen Table* (1991)

---

486 Annie Bryant, *Out of Bounds* (2005)

487 Winthrop D. Jordan, *White Over Black* (1995). Consider also: "Pea under the shell—Now you see it now you don't." (William S. Burroughs, *Nova Express* [1964]). Additionally: "[P]roducing the effect of an elaborate shell game. Now you see it and now you don't." (Peter Wiggins, *Donne, Castiglione and the Poetry of Courtliness* [2000])

488 Clive Barker, *The Damnation Game* (1985)

- From Quincy Troupe, "Following the North Star Boogaloo," *Transcircularities* (2002):

Dropping a deuce or a trey quick
as a pickpocket off the slide by
sleight of hand trick, eased on by like mojo
*   with his yoyo*
pitter patter, now you see me, now you don't.

- "He wore a navy turtleneck and a 'now you see it, now you don't' expression."
—Carole Nelson Douglas, *Catnap* (1993)

- From Carl Sandburg, "Timesweep," *Honey and Salt* (1963):

The weasel gave me his lingo
of now-you-see-me now-you-don't.

- "Viper squeezed the talisman and became invisible again. Now you see me. Now you don't! she thought."
—Jacqueline Carrol, *Enter the Viper* (2001)

- "Only suddenly, the fish was gone. Now you see it, now you don't. No weight in the net. Vanished into thin air."
—Lewis Freedman, *Fishing For a Laugh* (1998)

- "There is nothing particularly magical about patterns except for their 'now you see it, now you don't' aspect. *The real magic is to make these invisible phantoms visible.* And, to accomplish this, you will need to reactivate your childhood interest in uncovering secrets."
—Farrell Silverberg, *Make the Leap* (2005)

O Tarot Nizael Estarnas Tantarez

Origins: *O Tarot Nizael Estarnas Tantarez* is an antiquated magical phrase for "reading the thoughts of all persons." These words come from an Egyptian book of magical talismans entitled *Treasure of the Old Man of the Pyramids*, "translated from the Language of the Magi" in the eighteenth century.[489]

Facts: In the original manuscript, the would-be mindreader is instructed to place a talisman with the magic words on his head and chant the phrase.[490]

Common Magician's Applications: Mentalism. When a magician holds to his forehead a prop in the form of a papyrus talisman and intones the mysterious words *O Tarot Nizael Estarnas Tantarez*, he can imbue his mentalism routine with an ancient Egyptian mystique.

Ocus Pocus
(see also *hocus pocus*)

Origins: *Ocus pocis* was used by the Ancient Romans to mean "quickly, at few words, the conjuror's word of command, as præsto."[491]

489 Arthur Edward Waite, *The Book of Ceremonial Magic* (1913)
490 *Ibid.*
491 Walter Savage Landor, *Imaginary Conversations of Literary Men and Statesmen* (1826)

O Tarot Minail
Estarnas Tanfarty

Figure 29. Emblazoned with hieroglyphic symbols, this mind-reading talisman has an occult appearance but not an infernal purpose. It is based upon the research of Arthur Edward Waite in *The Book of Ceremonial Magic* (1913).

Facts: This is a variation of the magic phrase *hocus pocus.*

In Literature:

- "'Ocus pocus!' it was saying. 'Come ghoulie, come ghaestie, come long-leggedy beastie!'"
  —Edward Eager, *The Time Garden* (1958)

- ". . . a lot of smoke to conceal the ocus pocus, the magic of the substitution."
  —Iakov Levi, "John the Baptist; Father and Lover" (2004)

Odin

Odin! Odin! Odin!
Come here when you are needed.
—Yves Kodratoff,
Nordic Magic Healing 1:1 (2003)

Mystique: "In the time before man, Odin was, and Odin was wise, but he wanted even more wisdom. He wanted the wisdom of the mystical knowledge and power that he knew he lacked. In order to achieve this, he must offer sacrifice, so he hung himself from the eternal world tree for nine days. At the end of the nine days, wounded in the side by a spear, without food, without water, and at the cost of one of his eyes, he fell from the tree screaming. And as he fell, the magic of the runes was suddenly revealed to him. And Odin gave this knowledge to men."[492]

Meanings:

- All-father

- Father of the Runes

- God of Wisdom

- Heaven
  —Herbert Spencer, *Works* (1892)

- The High One
  —William Vollmann, *The Ice-Shirt* (1993)

- Master Magician
  —James Hastings, *Encyclopedia of Religion* (1912)

- One, alone

- Pangs of death
  —Ajith Fernando, *Acts* (1998)

- Source of movement
  "The word Odin, according to the mythologist Jacob Grimm, in ancient times literally meant the 'source of movement.' Thus, Odin becomes the creator god, the source of all movement in the world."
  —Dean Williams, *Real Leadership* (2005)

- Supreme God
  —M. Mallet, *Northern Antiquities* (1847)

- The Wader
  "The word Odin means The Wader in the sense of a person wading through water. By

492 James Richard Larson, *The Eye of Odin* (2003)

extension it signifies the permeator, or the power that moves through all things."
—Manly P. Hall, *Horizon* (1946)

- Wind, the life-giving breath of heaven
  —Duncan Long, *Classical Mythology Super Review* (2002)

- Wisdom
  —George F. Fort, *Early History and Antiquities of Freemasonry* (1884)

Origins: In Scandinavian mythology, Odin is the name of a deified monarch who invented letters. Odin is "the counterpart to the Greek Hermes, likewise is the god of magic, poetry, divination and inspiration, who undertakes shamanic practices."[493]

Variations and Incantations:

- Votan

- Wednesday

- Woden

- Wotan

- Wuotan

In Literature:

- "In desperation, Samuel grasped the ring pin tightly in his hands, closed his eyes and shouted, 'Odin, Odin, Odin.' Nothing happened. Again, with his voice nearly choked with fear, Samuel gasped the magic words."
  —John Anacker, *Raven's Ring Pin* (2004)

- "You are blessed in the name of Odin."
  —Ed Fitch, *The Rites of Odin* (1990)

Ofano, Oblamo, Ospergo

Origins: *Ofano Oblamo Ospergo* was found written in "an Elizabethan manuscript in the British Museum."[494]

Facts: These words are purportedly part of a chant to prolong orgasm and were cited in evidence against alleged witches and warlocks in a sixteenth century tribunal.

In Literature: "How about *ofano, oblamo, ospergo*?"
—Peggy Christian, *The Bookstore Mouse* (2002)

Oh Mighty Isis

Facts: In the television series *Isis* (1977), the heroine is a high school teacher who discovered an ancient Egyptian amulet during an archaeological dig. By intoning the magic phrase "Oh mighty Isis!" she transforms into a superhero with the strengths and abilities of her Egyptian goddess patroness.

Om
(see also *aum, omega*)

The deep OM, the mystic word of might.
—George William Russell, "Magic" (1913)

Mystique: "[B]oth rhythm and melody find their synthesis and their solution . . . in the one profound and all-embracing vibration of the sacred sound OM. . . . OM is the quintessence, the seed-syllable (*bija-mantra*) of the universe,

493 Nigel Pennick, *Magical Alphabets* (1992)

494 Migene Gonzalez-Wippler, *The Complete Book of Spells, Ceremonies and Magic* (1988)

the magic word par excellence . . . the universal force of the all-embracing consciousness."[495]

"The extravagance of supposing that all human ideas, sensations, desires can be eventually compressed into one word, the utterance of which shall suffice to annihilate man, or at least to blend him forever with the Unknowable, may certainly be ridiculed . . . but there is poetry in the fancy, as well as a pseudo-philosophy immemorially old. For thousands of years,—perhaps for thousands of ages,—men have been seeking after this ideal of expression, just as they have pursued the delusions of alchemy, believed in the lies of astrology, hunted for the jewel in the toad's head, and the dragon-stone, and the self-luminous carbuncle. Various faiths aided the search; the Brahmins claimed to know the mystic Word, whose utterance elevated men to heaven;—the Buddhists held that the syllable OM gave power to enter Nirvana to those who knew its deeper signification;—in the Kabbala we read of the Name by the combinations of whose letters men have been created from dust;—in the Talmud we are told of the Ineffable Appellation of forty-two letters, revealed only to those beloved of the Lord;—nor is it necessary to cite the magical attributes which Islamic fancy lends to the name of Allah, engraved upon emeralds, or upon seals, or written upon . . . million[s of] charms . . ."[496]

Origins: *Om* is a Hindu mantra, signifying the totality of the universe. "Yogi practitioners maintain that reciting . . . mantra can grant chanters all kinds of magical abilities. As a result, mantra formulas are found throughout the Far East, in the religions of Hinduism, Tibetan Lamaism, and Buddhism."[497]

Figure 30. The mystic symbol *om* consists of three curves, one semicircle, and one dot. This diagram encapsulates Nitin Kumar's explication in "Om: An Inquiry Into Its Aesthetics, Mysticism, and Philosophy," *ExoticIndia.com* (2001).

Variations and Incantations:

- Aum

- Om mani padme hum

In Literature:

- "Pilgrim recited again the magic word *Om* to summon the local spirit."
  —Anthony C. Yu, *The Journey to the West, Volume 4* (1983)

- "According to popular legend the Oriental ascetic who concentrates his gaze on the centre of his body and his thoughts on the syllable 'Om' arrives at a peculiar mental condition. So the magic word on which she had so long meditated, had its hypnotic effect on Elodie."
  —William J. Locke, *The Mountebank* (1926)

495 Anagarika Govinda, *Foundations of Tibetan Mysticism* (1969)

496 Lafcadio Hearn, "Decadence as an Art," quoted in *Reading Emptiness* by Jefferson Humphries (1999)

497 Haha Lung, *Black Science* (2001)

Omega
(see *alpha and omega* and *om*)

Facts: The magic word *Omega* means literally "great Om."[498]

Omega is the last letter of the Greek alphabet.

Om Mani Padme Hum
(see also *om*)

Mystique: *Om mani padme hum* "has many layers of mystical meaning. It refers to the primal unity within a larger whole of what we today tend to think of as polarities: light and darkness, creation and destruction, fire and water, and woman and man."[499] "The most favoured and potent of all mantra—*om mani padme hum*—in essence represents the breakthrough (*om*) of seeing the absolute (*mani*, jewel) in the relative (*padme*, lotus) beyond time, space and individuality (*hum*). This mantra of liberation is written on rocks, flags, and prayerwheels and is regarded as the epitome of Buddhist teachings."[500]

Origins: "The ancient Sanskrit meaning of many mantras has been lost, yet they remain in use just for the magic that is attached to the sound."[501] *Om mani padme hum* is a "universal compassion" mantra from the Hindu and Buddhist traditions. Some consider the syllables to echo "the vibration that created the universe."[502]

Meanings:

- All hail the jewel within the lotus flower
  This means that "one has perceived and honors the divine child within the universal matrix."
  —Jean Houston, *The Passion of Isis and Osiris* (1995)

- "All is well with the universe, the force of good and love is everywhere and competent to help all beings out of every difficulty"
  —Robert Thurman, *The Tibetan Book of the Dead* (1994)

- "Amen the Thunderbolt in the Dark Void"
  —Jack Kerouac, *The Dharma Bums* (1958)

- "I surrender to the pearl within the lotus"
  —Lisa Marie Coffey, *What's Your Dosha, Baby?* (2004)

- "May the jewel of the lotus descent into your heart [of compassion]"
  —William Gammill, *The Gathering: Meetings in Higher Space* (2001)

- "The jewel of consciousness is in the heart's lotus"
  —Thom Ashley-Farrand, *Healing Mantras* (1999)

- "You and I are one"
  —Geo Takoma, *The Complete Idiot's Guide to Power Yoga* (1999)

Variations and Incantations:

- Om mani padme cow
  —Stephen Levine, *A Gradual Awakening* (1989)

- Om mani padme hung

- Om mani padme om
  —L. Ron Hubbard, *Battlefield Earth* (1982)

---

498 Barbara G. Walker, *Woman's Encyclopedia of Myths and Secrets* (1983)

499 Riane Eisler, *Sacred Pleasure* (1995)

500 R.K. Joshi, "The Religious World of Letterforms" (1996)

501 Michel Peissel, *Tibet: The Secret Continent* (2003)

502 Diane Stein, *Psychic Healing with Spirit Guides and Angels* (1996)

Figure 31. "According to Tibetan philosophy, the written seed character (letter) is as potent as a spoken one" (R.K. Joshi, "The Religious World of Letterforms" [1996]). This Tibetan Buddhist charm is inspired by a 19th century woodblock. It depicts sacred mantras and formulae binding a shackled figure. The mystic words *om mani padme hum* are featured at the bottom.

- Om Mani Pedmé Hung
  "Let everything dissolve into that purring stream, that songlike repetitive sound of Great Compassion's mantra. Om Mani Pedmé Hung."
  —Lama Surya Das, *Awakening the Buddha Within* (1997)

- Om mani peme hum

In Literature: "On the Mountain [of the Five Elements], inscribed in gold, are the magic words: OM MANI PADME HUM."
—Peter Schat, "Monkey Subdues the White Bone Demon," *The Tone Clock* (1984)

Om Yee Pesh
(see also *om*)

Mystique: The magic phrase *om yee pesh* is meant to sound like a sacred Hindu mantra.

In Literature: "Would the magic words be . . . Om-yee-Pesh?"
—Tony Abbott, *The Magic Escapes* (2002)

Once Upon a Time

Those beautiful, magical words that
transported me far, far away . . .
—Bettyclare Moffatt, *An Authentic Woman* (1999)

Mystique: "*Once upon a time*—what a magical phrase."[503] These are "the magic words that open the floodgates of a child's imagination."[504] And child-like imagination is ageless. "As all good magic begins with the magical phrase 'Abra-Cadabra!' or 'Hocus Pocus!' so all good story-magic begins with the magical phrase 'Once upon a time.'"[505] "The audience has come to the theatre to *believe*, to respond to the magical words, 'Once upon a time.'"[506] That's because magical words can give us "symbolic wings" with which to move from one world to the next with the speed of light.[507] The storyteller, as Marilyn Twintreess writes, "bring[s] words to magic and then magic comes to life."[508] "The spell of a story . . . the power of words . . . Now, let the magic begin!"[509]

Author Jane Yolen points out that for adults, "the world of fantasy books returns to

503 Margaret Lucke, *Schaum's Quick Guide to Writing Great Short Stories* (1999)

504 Dale Carnegie, *The Quick and Easy Way to Effective Speaking* (1990)

505 Mychael Wordsmythe, *Tales Told Vyctorious* (1997)

506 Frank Hauser, *Notes on Directing* (2003)

507 Eva Judy Jansen, *The Book of Hindu Imagery: Gods, Manifestations and Their Meaning* (1993)

508 *Stones Alive* (1999)

509 Barbara Mariconda, *The Most Wonderful Writing Lessons Ever* (1999)

us the great words of power which, in order to be tamed, have been excised from our adult vocabularies. These words are the pornography of innocence, words which adults no longer dare to use with other adults, and so we laugh at them and consign them to the nursery, fear masking as cynicism. These are the words that were forged in the earth, air, fire and water of human existence. And the words are: Good — Evil — Courage — Honor — Truth — Hate — Love."[510]

Facts: "The magical words 'once upon a time' in English set in motion a machine of considerable momentum which can hardly be turned off without the equally magical 'they lived happily ever after' or some near equivalent."[511]

In Literature:

- "[W]ords can not only take you to other worlds, they can create worlds of their own. You don't need *abracadabra*; *once upon a time* will do."
  —Alison Gopnik, *The Scientist in the Crib: What Early Learning Tells Us About the Mind* (2000)

- "[T]he fairy tale begins, 'Once upon a time . . .' and we know from these words that we are about to enter a world whose reality is strangely different from our rational, everyday reality. In the fairy tale, the insignificant frog may be a prince, people might sleep for hundreds of years, wishes can magically be granted, animals can talk and wear aprons, hats and other pieces of clothing, and things

generally are not always just what they seem to be. I suspect that children enter the world of the fairy tale primarily for the nonrational wonder and enchantment of it. I did."
—Eugene Burger, *Magic and Meaning* (1995)

- "An easy way to start your story is with the magical words 'Once upon a time,' and then let your myth unfold."
  —Patricia Montgomery, *Mythmaking* (1994)

- "'My shadow may be having coffee across the road from the library, but I am really here, like a worm in the library's heart,' [Mr. Mephistiana] shouted. 'I'll feast on words and wonders. I'll eat every single song, every single story.' 'How will we stop him?' cried Sam. 'We need a magic word or a good spell.' 'We need the books,' whispered Daisy. Her whisper ran around the mysterious forest like a secret wind. Something heard her whisper. Something moved in the trees around them. From out of the leaves came flocks of white parrots . . . thousands of them . . . millions of them. 'Say the magic spell!' they screamed. 'Call on the book-birds.' 'What spell?' asked Daisy. A parrot flew around her. 'Read me!' it cried, turning a flip in the air. There were black words on the white feathers across its back and over its wings. As it flew away, that parrot turned into an open book. Its wings became flickering pages. . . . 'Let's say it aloud.' . . . Then, together, Sam and Daisy shouted the magic words. 'ONCE UPON A TIME . . .' The whole forest sang a huge chorus around them. 'ONCE UPON A TIME . . .' White parrots came flying towards them. No! They were books, flapping their wonderful pages. From between those pages . . . from the leaves of the forest trees . . . words fluttered like black moths. The air was filled with little black wings as well as great white ones. Mr. Mephistiana's face twisted with

---

510 Quoted in *Magic and Meaning* by Eugene Burger (1995)

511 Robert Scholes, "Decoding Papa: 'A Very Short Story' as Work and Text," *New Critical Approaches to the Short Stories of Ernest Hemingway* (1990)

horror as words flew into his eyes and ears. He flailed his arms trying to beat away the books set free by the spell. . . . [T]he books flapped and Mr. Mephistiana flopped and faded. White pages beat him to nothing."
—Margaret Mahy, "The Word Eater" (1998)

- "[W]hen they would tell their own children the tale by candlelight in the warmth of their homes, on the streets where lamps burned under stars that still stirred the power to dream, they would always begin the tale with the same magic words: 'Once upon a time . . .'"
—Robert McCammon, *Swan Song* (1987)

One-ery Two-ery Ickery Ann

Origins: This children's counting-out rhyme has been traced directly back to "a gypsy magic spell in the Romany language." Children's rhymes are "a survival of incantations" and charms of priests and sorcerers from ancient times, vestiges of "divination by lot."[512]

Variations and Incantations:

- One-ry two-ery dickery Davy
—*Notes and Queries* (1854)

- One-ry two-ery ickery am
—*Notes and Queries* (1854)

- One-ry, two-ery, tickery, seven, Hallibo, crackibo, ten and eleven, Spin, span, muski-dan, Twiddle-um, twaddle-um, twenty-one
—Diana Hendry, *Harvey Angell Beats Time* (2000)

Onni Swakey Mollie Pons

Facts: Professional magician Steve Charney uses this magical phrase.

Oocha Coocha Bing Bang Bam, Alakazy Alakazam

Facts: This is an incantation for making a serpent hiccup in the novel *The Key to the Land of Dogs* by Gareth M. Wilson (2004).

Bing bang bam is an expression of a quick sequence of events, sometimes followed by a *boom* to signify the culmination.

Ooga-Booga
(see also *booga booga*)

Mystique: When intoned without mockery, the primitive syllables of *ooga-booga* conjure the "primal oohs and ahs from cave men and women . . . in those early human settlements,"[513] or perhaps the mysterious, exotic powers of tribal elders.

Meanings:

- God; higher power
"Great Ooga-Booga, can't you hear me talkin' to ya?"
—The Temptations, quoted in *Miles to Go* by Chris Murphy (2002)

"[P]eople felt when they died their 'spirit' went to the great ooga-booga in the sky . . ."
—*SciForums.com* (2003)

512 Charles Godfrey Leland, *Gypsy Sorcery and Fortune Telling* (1891)

513 Helen Godgson and Patti Britton, *The Complete Idiot's Guide to Sensual Massage* (2003)

- Jungle native chant
—James Howard Kunstler, *Geography Of No-where* (1994)

- Mumbo-jumbo
"The stuff where you play the records backwards and it's got some sort of ooga-booga about the Devil on it."
—Joe R. Lansdale, *The Drive-In* (1988)

- Nonsense
—Orson Scott Card, *The Memory of Earth* (1992)

- Occult; "otherworldly phenomena"
—Bernie Brillstein, *Where Did I Go Right?* (1999)

- Password
"After two rings, a voice spoke from the tiny handset. 'Ooga-booga?' 'Boola-boola,' Tollhouse responded. 'Hubba-hubba!' came the gratified reply."
—Harry Beard, *The Dick Cheney Code: A Parody* (2004)

- Primitivism
—Rick Steves, *Rick Steves' London 2004* (2003)

- Ritual
—Alexandra Robbins, *Secrets of the Tomb* (2003)

- Spirituality
"[There is] a spiritual component—what I sometimes laughingly refer to as ooga-booga moments."
—Ronna Lichtenberg, *Pitch Like a Girl* (2005)

- Spooky
"In desperation, soaps have started adding a lot of ooga-booga ghost storylines with voodoo, witchcraft, and, in the case of one, a Chucky-style creepy doll that comes to life."
—Celia Rivenbark, *We're Just Like You, Only Prettier* (2004)

- Voodoo
—Salman Rushdie, *The Satanic Verses* (1988)
"There were zombies in the building. Not ooga-booga magic-type zombies, but near enough."
—Richard Fawkes, *Nature of the Beast* (2004)

- Witchdoctor, head honcho
"Seems the Lord High Ooga-Booga wants to see you face-to-face 'fore he seals the deal."
—Tom Clancy, *Hidden Agendas* (1999)
"[H]e was like a guru, or a witch doctor, or some kind of far-out ooga-booga man . . ."
—Frank E. Peretti, *This Present Darkness* (1986)

Facts: "In the movie *Freaks* [1932], by Tod Browning, the freaks dance around a woman they've horribly mutilated, chanting, 'One of us, one of us, ooga-booga, one of us.'"[514]

Variations and Incantations:

- Ooga-booga looga-booga
"He wanted to run for his room the way he used to do when he was little, jabbering nonsense words—'Ooga-booga looga-booga' had been a favorite—while he pulled on his clothes and rubbed himself to get warm."
—Orson Scott Card, *The Memory of Earth* (1992)

- Ugah bugah hoogaloo ugh ugh
—C. Richard King & Charles Springwood, *Beyond the Cheers: Race as Spectacle in College Sport* (2001)

In Literature: "Were my nostrils flaring, my eyes pulsing red? I was about to shout 'Ooga-booga' and give the guy a heart attack when Scoby clambered from the rear of the truck . . ."
—Paul Beatty, *The White Boy Shuffle* (1996)

514 John Vernon, *A Book of Reasons* (1999)

Oola Moola

Facts: These magic words are featured in *A Genie's Big Book of Sickness Symptoms*, a fictional spell book discussed in *Little Genie: Double Trouble* (2004) by Miranda Jones: "She pointed at Ali and began to mutter some magic words. '*Oola, moola, poolo, pill, please make Ali look really ill.*'"

Oolong Caloophid Baeower Gazots

Facts: This magic incantation is featured in *The Intercontinental Union of Disgusting Characters* by Roger M. Wilcox (1986). The words *Oolong Caloophid* reference the humorous science fiction novel *The Hitchhiker's Guide to the Galaxy* by Douglas Adams. Wilcox explains: "Oolong Caloophid is . . . the author of that trilogy of philosophical blockbusters, 'Where God Went Wrong,' 'Some More of God's Greatest Mistakes,' and 'Who Is This God Person Anyway?'"

Ooo-Cha

In Literature: "'You may have teeth as big as daggers and claws as sharp as razors,' said Emily, 'but you certainly don't have any manners, so you can have this instead.' And she thunked the tiger over the head with her good witch wand and said the magic word, 'Ooo-cha!' Instantly the tiger vanished, and in her place stood a beautiful tiger lily. Emily plucked the tiger lily and off she skipped, whistling and singing, and smelling her lovely flower."
—Coleen Sydor, *Ooo-cha!* (1999)

Ooo Eee Ooo-Ah-Ah Ting Tang Walla-Walla Bing-Bang

Facts: This phrase is a love spell chanted in the song "Witch Doctor" by David Seville (1958). "It is a song of unrequited love cured by the magic incantations of the witch doctor."[515] Diana Winn Levine suggests that *ting tang* are the magic words and *walla walla bing bang* mean the magic is over.[516]

Oozita
(see also *atizoo*)

In Literature: In the BBC Puppet Theatre production *Tunnel Trouble* (1976) by Gordon Murray, *Oozita* is believed to be an *Open Sesame*-type magic word:

> WEATHERSPOON: *I've been thinking! If you were a magician, and you had built yourself a secret tunnel, how would you arrange for the entrances to open and close?*
> RUFUS: *Ah . . . ooh-ah . . .*
> WEATHERSPOON: *Well, I'll tell you! You'd have a magic word, like 'Open Sesame,' in The Arabian Nights.*
> RUFUS: *Ooh yes, Weatherspoon!*
> WEATHERSPOON: *Well look, Sire! The old stone, opposite Ampumpo's main entrance. Carved on the corner, a word, do you see!? Could it be the magic word? Carved by Ampumpo so he couldn't forget it?*
> NARRATOR: *Weatherspoon pushed aside a clump of weeds and a brick, and pointed out the letters. . . .*
> WEATHERSPOON: (slowly spelling) *O, O, 'Zed,' I, T, A.*

---

515 Bob McCann, "The Declension Song" (2003)
516 "Funny 50s and Silly 60s Activity Worksheet" (2005)

RUFUS: Go on, Weatherspoon! Say it!
WEATHERSPOON: Oozita!
NARRATOR: They all looked around. Nothing happened!

Open Sesame

Open Sesame! . . . as enticing as ever.
—Victoria Morna, *Younger by the Day* (2004)

Open sesame.
Anyone who knew that word must have
a head full of many fascinating things.
—Harriet Rubin, *Soloing* (1999)

Mystique: Magic words are classically associated with opening doors.[517] They are the keys for unlocking barriers, dissolving obstacles, revealing something *beyond*. They are the coveted guarded secrets[518] that grant admittance into inner chambers[519] and secret circles. *Open sesame:* these "two simple words change the landscape,"[520] invite us to "discover hidden treasures,"[521] and affirm "an entire range of extraordinary things . . . indescribable only because they have not been described."[522] With *open sesame*, "the impossible

and the unobtainable miraculously materialize before your very eyes."[523]

There is no more classic, no more straightforward magical key than *open sesame*. It exemplifies how precisely the *right* words are required for working magic. "When Ali Baba wanted to enter the cave of the forty thieves, he had to have the right password. He could yell out, 'Open, brown rice' or 'Open, shredded wheat' forever, but nothing was going to happen until he said, 'Open, sesame.'"[524] *Open sesame* is a badge of knowledge, of wisdom, of initiation, and of authority.[525]

Essayist Susan Cooper suggests that magic words like *open sesame* guide us to finding our way into the unconscious mind, the place where imagination resides, and we use them "because we know that's the only way to get into a place where magic is made. 'Open sesame!' I am shouting, silently, desperately to the door of my imagination."[526] Even before they begin working their magic, the words *open sesame* are, by definition, always called for at a magical time and place. In other words, before one speaks "open sesame," one is already standing between two worlds, at a magical threshold (or liminal zone—see *Abraxas*), ready to call upon a veil to be parted

----

517 As in *The Count of Monte Cristo* by Alexandre Dumas (1845): "We examined the grotto all over, but we never could find the slightest trace of any opening; they say that the door is not opened by a key, but a magical word."

518 David Britland, *Phantoms of the Card Table* (2004)

519 Reginald Hill, *Death's Jest-Book* (2004)

520 Jodi Picoult, *My Sister's Keeper* (2004)

521 Scott Cunningham, *Cunningham's Encyclopedia of Magical Herbs* (1985)

522 Marina Tsvetayeva, *Letters: Summer 1926* (1985)

523 Katie Hickman, *Dreams of the Peaceful Dragon* (1987)

524 Eknath Easwaran, *Meditation* (1978). Similarly: "Change the structure of the sentence; substitute one synonym for another, and the whole effect is destroyed. The spell loses its power; and he who should then hope to conjure with it would find himself as much mistaken as Cassim in the Arabian tale, when he stood crying 'Open Wheat,' 'Open Barley,' to the door which obeyed no sound but 'Open Sesame'" (Thomas Babington Macaulay, *Critical and Historical Essays* [1865], quoted in *Nets of Awareness: Urdu Poetry and Its Critics* by Frances W. Pritchett [1994]).

525 Freya Stark, *The Valleys of the Assassins* (2001)

526 *Dreams and Wishes* (1996)

and for a spectacle to unfold.[527] There's already electricity in the air, sizzling with the promise of a miraculous, legendary payoff. (Best of all, the acquisition will be effortless.) Novelist Henry James described such a magical instant: "that pitch of the wondrous was in everything, particularly in such an instant 'Open Sesame,' and . . . the vividness, the almost blinding whiteness of the light . . . struck her as the most beautiful she had ever seen in her life."[528] How true it is that "Magic words ma[k]e us see things in a different light."[529]

Steeped as they are in history and romantic tales of adventure,[530] the words *open sesame* are potent with mystery and intrigue, and they always transport the spirit back to that primal, womb-like cavern of wonders, that secret passage to other worlds.[531] As a pass phrase the words may well qualify as a "worst-kept secret," but their power has not diminished. Unlike phrases such as "hocus pocus" or "mumbo jumbo" that the general public so often uses derisively or mockingly, the literature attests that "open sesame" demands respect. It is simply *the* thing one says when faced with an obstacle.

---

527 For, as poet Jules LaForgue has said, "the Infinite is at our doors! at our windows! Open, and see those Far-Off Nights and all Time with them!" (*Selected Poems* [1890], translated by Graham Dunstan Martin [1998]).

528 *What Maisie Knew* (1897)

529 Howard Kaminsky and Alexandra Penney, *Magic Words* (2002)

530 As Nietzsche suggested, history and romance are hopelessly entwined, "once upon a time" being an "open sesame" to the past (Keith Jenkins, *The Postmodern History Reader* [1997]).

531 A similar concept is discussed by Gilles Neret in *Erotica 20th Century* (2001).

Meanings:

- Admission, ticket
  —Jennifer L. Scheidt, *On Miller's Death of a Salesman* (2000)

  "Since when has money been an open sesame to the Turf Club?"
  —James Clavell, *Noble House* (1986)

- Avenue
  "The child's smallness and inadequacy is the 'open sesame' to a future and to the unfolding of potentiality."
  —Thomas Moore, *Care of the Soul* (1992)

  "The single-track railway across the desert was the 'open sesame' to almost everything in Transcaspia, including the capture of the Merve oasis."
  —Peter Hopkirk, *Like Hidden Fire* (1994)

- Breaking and entering
  "Wonder signaled he was ready to perform his 'open sesame' act [to break down the door]."
  —Richard Marcinko, *Designation Gold* (1997)

- Certificate
  "Money was the coin of the urban realm from which we came,—the open sesame to the satisfaction of needs and wants."
  —Scott Nearing, *The Good Life* (1989)

- Clue, key evidence
  "You may have found our open-sesame, Holmes!"
  —Matthew Pearl, *The Dante Club* (2003)

- Controller
  "The cavern, apparently, required a human presence to operate it, a living *open*, *sesame* to switch on power and lights and to open doors."
  —Ian Douglas, *Luna Marine* (1990)

- Cue
  "[S]ome cue, an open sesame . . ."
  —Jose Saramago, *Blindness* (1999)

- Currency

"Now and then, from behind us, a couple of people or so would present themselves to haggle at the glass door. Once or twice it had opened to them. Since we were still at the back of the queue and looked like staying there I asked Lena what 'Open Sesame' they might have used. 'They pay in dollars,' she said."
—Philip Glazebrook, *Journey to Khiva* (1992)

"[S]eal (and otter) skins, once an open sesame to the teas and silks of China . . ."
—Roy Nickerson, *Sea Otters* (1998)

"[T]heir hands were thrust deep into pockets from which came the cheerful and open-sesame clinking of gold."
—Clarence E. Mulford, *Hopalong Cassidy* (1992)

- Doorway, portal

"With his elated attitude and keen observation, each rock became a doorway, an 'open sesame' to a new world of adventure."
—Pila Chiles, *The Secrets and Mysteries of Hawaii* (1995)

- Entrée

"His slightest wish seemed always to be translated instantly into the most impressive kind of reality. Trains were held; yachts materialized; the best suites in the finest hotels were flung open; airplanes stood waiting. . . . He was the open sesame to a new and glittering world that excited me as nothing in my life had ever done before."
—Eleanor Herman, *Sex with Kings* (2004)

- Floodgate

"My words were like an open sesame, because it immediately spewed forth eons of stored grievances against me."
—Tanis Helliwell, *Summer with the Leprechauns* (1997)

- Gatekeeper

"'[Y]ou're my open sesame.' Temple's tootsies curled again, sans shoes but with pleasure, as if they were the turned-up toes on an Arabian Nights slipper. 'It's amazing,' Matt went on, 'how many doors you've opened for me. To the past, and to the future.'"
—Carole Nelson Douglas, *Cat in a Crimson Haze* (1995)

- Guarantee

"A university degree used to be an open sesame to a professional position."
—Ken Robinson, *Out of Our Minds* (2001)

- Holy inscriptions

"They were, literally, precious, glowing open sesames. The ceiling of the throne room was sixty feet high, the walls covered with graffiti—poems, mottoes, sayings, *sura* from the Koran—all in graceful gold Arabic."
—Mary Lee Settle, *Spanish Recognitions* (2004)

- Ignition

"It might be the Open Sesame of the whole war."
—Douglas Porch, *The Path to Victory* (2004)

- Incantation, mantra

"[M]ore incantation or open-sesame mantra than a name . . ."
—John Edgar Wideman, *Hoop Roots* (2001)

"It would be their mantra, their creed, their open-sesame incantation that would slide back the door to the sacred treasure chamber."
—David Weddle, *Among the Mansions of Eden* (2003)

- Inspiration

—Michael Chekhov, *To the Actor* (1953)

"Morris's workshop was an Open Sesame to Clive's imagination."
—Graham Joyce, *The Tooth Fairy* (1998)

- Instantly
"The guarantee of compensation . . . opened the icehouse door quicker than 'open sesame.'"
—Richard Edward Crabbe, *The Empire of Shadows* (2003)

- Invitation
"Isabelle's fresh mellow voice was the open sesame to meeting many new friends and experiences."
—Bess Streeter Aldrich, *A Lantern in Her Hand* (1997)

"The breakup of this marriage only served to substantiate Ruzicka's belief that emotional involvement with a woman was an open-sesame to getting hurt."
—Ann Rule, *A Fever in the Heart* (1996)

- Irresistible command
"My words worked like open sesame to him, and he turned and raced out of the room."
—Rex Pickett, *Sideways* (2004)

"[A]s if by an open sesame as unarguably obeyed as it is planned to the last detail, public awareness is saturated with media analysis."
—Edward W. Said, *Culture and Imperialism* (1993)

- Key
"[I]t may take an electronic or mechanical Open Sesame to get in."
—Philip Jose Farmer, *The Dark Design* (1998)

"'Open sesame' opens doors, a wish becomes a tangible possibility."
—Arthur Kroker, *Life in the Wires* (2004)

"[A]n intruder in the writer's study, rifling through his drawers, hoping to find souvenirs of character in his old journals since they provide an 'open sesame' to his work."
—Brenda Wineapple, *Hawthorne: A Life* (2003)

"Who holds the wondrous crystal key, / The silent Open Sesame."
—Oliver Wendell Holmes, "The Flaneur" (1882)

- Key to the City
"It was a virtual 'open sesame' to Hollywood. Doors would finally swing wide for her."
—Ann Rule, *Heart Full of Lies* (2004)

- Letter of introduction
"Freya had obtained an impressive array of introductions from important people. . . . Armed with her open sesames, as she called them, Freya believed she could count on a month and a half . . . with virtually no expenses . . ."
—Jane Geniesse, *Passionate Nomad* (1999)

"This letter was an 'Open Sesame': its quite insignificant contents were luckily sealed up, but the name on the envelope had already served to get me through the entanglements of the Nihavend police; its mere production gave the impression that I travelled with the authority of governments behind me and when I handed it to anyone, I tried to cultivate a manner to correspond."
—Freya Stark, *The Valleys of the Assassins* (2001)

"Again Martins had marked his card with the open-sesame phrase: 'A friend of Harry Lime's.'"
—Graham Greene, *The Third Man* (1950)

- Love, an open heart
"[L]ove is the 'Open Sesame' of life."
—Sue Patton Thoele, *The Courage to Be Yourself* (2001)

- Magic charm
"[A]n open sesame that will allow us to identify the object of this pilgrimage no matter what form it may assume."
—Umberto Eco, *Travels in Hyperreality* (1986)

"I was going to get inside of reality and extract its essence, write down on paper

the magic metrical words that, read aloud, would do their open sesame."
—Richard Powers, *Plowing the Dark* (2000)

- Magic trick, gimmick
  —Ron Willingham, *Integrity Selling* (1989)

- Magic skill
  "For her they were magic skills, the open sesame to a remote but entirely desirable world."
  —Ann Corneliesen, *Women of the Shadows* (1976)

- Magic word
  —Peter C. Rollins, *Hollywood as Historian* (1997)
  "Rather than knocking on the door, he stood outside of it shouting, 'Open sesame!' And when I opened it, he laughed, 'Magic words! Working every time!'"
  —Lee Siegel, *Net of Magic* (1991)
  "It's the magic word all right, the golden key, the open sesame."
  —Keri Hulme, *The Bone People* (1986)
  "[H]oping to acquire an abracadabra or open sesame . . ."
  —Helen Valentine, *Better Than Beauty* (2002)
  "Colin and Susan roamed all over Stormy Point, and beyond, but there were so many rocks and boulders, any of which could have hidden the gates, that they soon tired of shouting 'Abracadabra!' and 'Open sesame!'"
  —Alan Garner, *The Weirdstone of Brisingamen* (1960)
  "A wave of a magic wand or a command of 'open sesame' would have been more appropriate, she thought, smiling inwardly at her strange fancies."
  —Marianne Willman, *The Mermaid's Song* (1997)

- "Mere sound"
  —Peter Kreeft, *Making Choices* (1990)

- Open up
  —Catherine Anderson, *Annie's Song* (1996)
  "The veil falls away, and our eyes are opened. It is only necessary to say 'Open sesame.'"
  —Paul Veyne, *Did the Greeks Believe in Their Myths?* (1988)

- Opening
  "'In the days when animals could talk,' an even more perfect Open Sesame than 'Once upon a time.'"
  —Michel Leiris, *Scratches* (1948), translated by Lydia Davis (1991)

- Passport
  "Jesus is the 'Open Sesame' to heaven."
  —Dwight Moody, quoted in *American Jesus* by Stephen Prothero (2003)
  "[T]he passport to their freedom, the open sesame to their enjoyment."
  —Erika Rappaport, *Shopping for Pleasure* (2001)

- Password, code word, secret word, watchword
  "I want to open her memory, but I don't have the password. I want to cry out, 'Open, sesame!' so that the door to this treasure cave will open, but it is permanently locked."
  —Madeleine L'Engle, *The Summer of the Great-Grandmother* (1974)
  "The problem is the password—the open sesame. Without that, there's nothing we can do. The door won't open for the wolf, no matter how hard he tries to disguise his voice. He can knock and say, 'Hi, it's me, your friend Rabbit,' but if he hasn't got the password, he gets turned away at the door."
  —Haruki Murakami, *The Wind-Up Bird Chronicle* (1998)

"I keep the gate locked and don't answer unless I hear the right open sesame."
—Moshin Hamid, *Moth Smoke* (2000)

"[T]he password, the 'Open sesame' unlocking the door of a past which one had ceased to take into account because, having seen more than enough of it, literally one no longer possessed it."
—Marcel Proust, *In Search of Lost Time, Volume 5*, translated by C.K. Scott Moncrieff and Terence Kilmartin, revised by D.J. Enright (1993)

"In fables, access is always controlled by 'secret words' like 'Open Sesame.'"
—James Dale Davidson, *The Great Reckoning* (2004)

- Propitiate
  —Theodore Ayrault Dodge, *Hannibal* (2004)

- Red carpet
  "This truth has been my passport and has been the open sesame to freedom and joy in all countries."
  —Joel S. Goldsmith, *Practicing the Presence* (1958)

  "When he . . . wanted to be first in line, all he had to do was start in the direction he chose, and his approach itself proved to be an 'open sesame.'"
  —Edwin H. Friedman, *Friedman's Fables* (1990)

- Safe conduct
  "[A] magical safe conduct, an 'Open, Sesame!'"
  —Ignacio Ellacuría and Jon Sobrino, *Mysterium Liberationis* (1993)

- Secret
  "It has found the secret of knowledge; the open sesame to all truth."
  —Arthur W. Lindsley, *Classical Apologetics* (1984)

"[D]iscovering the 'open sesame' to real living . . ."
—Edgar Cayce, *My Life as a Seer* (1997)

"'To weigh and consider'—that is the *open sesame* of right reading."
—Frank Haddock, *Power of Will* (1907)

"What is the open sesame to a thriving practice?"
—Vickie L. Milazzo, *Create Your Own Magic for CLNC Success* (2003)

- Secret passage
  "Perhaps, in some remote unborn century, a more fortunate explorer may hit upon the 'Open Sesame,' and flood the world with gems. But, myself, I doubt it. Somehow, I seem to feel that the millions of pounds' worth of gems that lie in the three stone coffers will never shine round the neck of an earthly beauty. They and Foulata's bones will keep cold company till the end of all things."
  —H. Rider Haggard, *King Solomon's Mines* (1885)

- Shortcut
  "I . . . knew the shortcut, the open sesame."
  —Philippe Sollers, *Event* (1987)

  "Here is the open-sesame way of representing the problem."
  —Jake Copeland, *Artificial Intelligence* (1993)

- Skeleton key
  "There is . . . a certain kind of 'open sesame' which seems less a charm than a skeleton key."
  —Vladimir Nabokov, *The Real Life of Sebastian Knight* (1941)

  "This increase in wealth and the prospect of its acceleration had become a kind of master-key, the ideological open-sesame of society."
  —Roy Porter, *English Society in the 18th Century* (1982)

"Back in high school and college, they had pored over books, believing that knowledge alone was the open sesame to financial and professional rewards."
—Dale Carnegie, *How to Win Friends and Influence People* (1936)

- Solution
"[A] magic 'open sesame' to all our problems . . ."
—A. Trevor Hodge, *Roman Aqueducts and Water Supply* (2002)

- Starting point
"[C]ertain ideas burst upon the intellectual landscape with a tremendous force. They resolve so many fundamental problems at once that they seem also to promise that they will resolve all fundamental problems, clarify all obscure issues. Everyone snaps them up as the open sesame of some new positive science, the conceptual center-point around which a comprehensive system of analysis can be built."
—Clifford Geertz, *Interpretation of Cultures* (1973)
"[The heart of a white cock] was the open sesame to many experiments."
—Idries Shah, *Oriental Magic* (1956)

- Stimuli, especially "the correct stimuli"
—Leslie Glass, *Stealing Time* (2000)

- Trigger
—Melvin Burgess, *Doing It* (2004)

- Voilà
"Aziz squeezes once, then releases her. 'Open sesame,' he says, 'the spell is broken.'"
—Diana Abu-Jaber, *Crescent* (2003)
"It was like a story out of a library book: he said the magic words and—Open, Sesame!—something amazing happened."
—Pete Hamill, *Snow in August* (1997)

- Wide open
"A door left even slightly ajar is 'open sesame' to a cunning ferret."
—Gary Bucsis and Barbara Somerville, *The Ferret Handbook* (2001)
"[T]he world split wide open, open sesame, for motorcycle entry only."
—Laurie Gough, *Kite Strings of the Southern Cross* (1999)

- Window
"The harem images offer an 'open sesame' to an alluring and tantalizingly forbidden world, seen as infinitely desirable to the instinctual primitive presumably inhabiting all men."
—Ella Shohat, *Unthinking Eurocentrism* (1994)

- Womb, vagina
—Gilles Neret, *Erotica 20th Century* (2001)

Origins: Popularized through Arabic mythology,[532] *open sesame* is widely thought to have been "inspired by the fact that the pods of the sesame plant burst open when the enclosed seeds reach maturity."[533] The name of the seed is over 4,000 years old and is "one of the few to have entered modern languages from the ancient Egyptian *(sesemt)*."[534]

However, vocal commands such as "open sesame" seem to hark back to ancient sonic technologies. Some researchers are convinced, for example, that sound vibrations were manipulated to levitate heavy stones during the building of the Great Pyramid. Umberto Eco suggests: "It is known that the Chaldean priests operated sacred machines by sounds alone, and the priests of Karnak and Thebes could open the doors of a temple with only their voice—and what else

---

532 J.J. Dewey, *The Lost Key of the Buddha* (2003)
533 François Fortin, *The Visual Food Encyclopedia* (1996)
534 Najmieh Batmanglijm, *Silk Road Cooking* (2002)

could be the origin, if you think about it, of the legend of Open Sesame?"[535]

See *sesame* for a discussion on how the word is related to the Egyptian *seshemu*, "sexual intercourse." From time immemorial, artists have shaped the female's sex "into an 'open sesame,' a doorway to another world . . . what [Rodin] called 'the eternal tunnel.' The sublime passage between these thighs leads us, via the pleasures of love, from woman to Genesis, from the carnal to the sacred."[536]

Facts: The magic phrase *open sesame* gained renown, of course, from *The Arabian Nights*. However, an authentic translation of the magic phrase is "Simsim."[537]

"Open sesame" has been called the "original password"[538] and the "international password."[539]

"Open Sesame" is a magician's stage name in the novel *The Fabulist* by Stephen Glass (2003).

If the words occur in a dream, they denote "a 'key' one has been looking for; a solution or means to accomplish something."[540]

"These words ['open sesame'] were, in effect, mantras. It's no fairy tale, it's a fact, when you know the 'magic' words, you can find the hidden treasure!"[541]

Common Magician's Applications: Escapes.

---

535 *Foucault's Pendulum* (1988)

536 Gilles Neret, *Erotica 20th Century* (2001)

537 Donald A. Norman, *The Design of Everyday Things* (1988)

538 Stephen L. Nelson, *Quicken 2000 for Windows for Dummies* (1999)

539 William H. Chafe, *Never Stop Running* (1998)

540 Mary Summer Rain, *Mary Summer Rain's Guide to Dream Symbols* (1996)

541 Shakto Parwha Kaur Kaisa, *Kundalini Yoga* (1996)

Variations and Incantations:

• Arise sesame
—Lauren Henderson, *Strawberry Tattoo* (1999)

• Open, open, open sesame
—Ann McCaffrey, *Acorna's Rebels* (2003)
—Meena Alexander, *Manhattan Music* (1997)

• Open Says Me
—Jeanne Rose, *The World of Aromatherapy* (1996)

    "*Open!* he thought at the door, feeling absurdly like an Arabian princeling in some ancient story. *Open sesame! Open says me!*"
—Stephen King, *Song of Susannah* (2004)

• Open Sez Me!
—Piers Anthony, *Swell Foop* (2002)

• Open Sesame, open sunflower
—Lexa Rosean, *Powerspells* (2001)

• Open sesame seeds
—P.D.Q. Bach, "The Seasonings," *Definitive Biography of P.D.Q. Bach* (1976)

• Open Sesame Voilà!
—Charles Busch, *Red Scare on Sunset* (1991)

• Open shazaam
—Milena McGraw, *After Dinkirk* (1998)

• Presto, Open Sesame!
—Audrey Niffenegger, *The Time Traveler's Wife* (2003)

• Voilà, Open Sesame!
—Thomas Beller, *Open City #15* (2003)
—Andrew Humphreys, *Time Out Shanghai* (2004)

In Literature:

• "She levered open the passenger door. It swung out like some Ali Baba mountainside to my unspoken 'Open, Sesame.' I had to jump back so it wouldn't knock me flat."
—Paul De Filippo, *Neutrino Drag* (2004)

- "She was reading 'Ali Baba and the Forty Thieves,' and every time she read 'Open sesame,' Matt sang out the magic words with her."
—Siri Hustvedt, *What I Loved* (2003)

- "He walked straight up to the rock, opened his mouth, and just before he spoke light dawned, and everybody else knew what two words he would say. The two words were, 'Open, Sesame!' Immediately the expected happened. A door in the rock opened. Beyond it yawned a vast cavern. 'It's the cave Ali Baba found. It's the cave of the Forty Thieves. It's *that* buried treasure!'"
—Edward Eager, *Magic by the Lake* (1957)

- "'How are you going to open it?' she asked. . . . 'Like this,' said Kazul. *'By night and flame and shining rock, Open thou thy hidden lock. Alberolingarn!'* As the sound of Kazul's voice died away, the iron gate swung silently open. 'That's a very unusual opening spell,' Cimorene commented, impressed. 'It wasn't always that complicated,' Kazul said. She sounded almost apologetic. 'I believe the first version was very simple, just 'Open sesame,' but word got around and we had to change it.'"
—Patricia C. Wrede, *Dealing With Dragons* (1990)

- "'There is the key to opening the gates,' Scott revealed. 'You speak into it.' 'What are you gonna do? Turn around and shout *Open Sesame?*' Scott shrugged without a hint of irony. 'The myth had to come from somewhere.' Then he spun on his heel to face the doors, pulled the device up to his mouth and in clear ancient Sumerian pronounced: *'Doors, open!'* There was a clank, loud and laborious. The sound of lock mechanisms disengaging, of hinges and counterweights swinging into action as slowly the main gates to the City of Atlantis swung open."
—Stel Paylou, *Decipher* (2001)

- "If you had to say 'Open Sesame' [to the owl statue] to get through the door, then that's what she would do. The bookcase slid open."
—Ann Pratchett, *The Magician's Assistant* (1997)

- "This opening up of the floodgates of his memory was not on account of any alchemy of mine, or charm I put upon him with my presence, or open sesame that I pronounced, but was perhaps vouchsafed because he sensed in me an audience whose interest was genuine, and because he found a melancholy pleasure in the telling."
—Grey Owl, *Tales of an Empty Cabin* (1936)

- "Rhyme wheeled up to the door, noticed the hands-free intercom. He said a boisterous 'Open, sesame' and the door swung wide. 'We get that a lot,' drawled the pert secretary when they'd entered."
—Jeffrey Deaver, *The Empty Chair* (2000)

- "On the video monitor, they saw Ted Fielding slap the polished sphere with his hand and shout, 'Open! Open Sesame! Open up, you son of a bitch!' The sphere did not respond."
—Michael Crichton, *Sphere* (1987)

- "'The next question is how we get inside.' 'Try saying "open sesame" and hope for the best.' Zavala stood back and bellowed the famous command from *Ali Baba and the Forty Thieves.* When nothing happened he tried again in Spanish, also to no avail. 'You know any more magic words?' he asked Austin. 'You just exhausted my entire repertoire,' Kurt said with a shrug."
—Clive Cussler, *Blue Gold* (2000)

- "[I]t was as if someone had said 'Open sesame.' All resistance seemed to fall away."
—James Huston, *Fallout* (2002)

- From Federico Garcia Lorca, "Venus," *The Collected Poems* (1988):

  Open sesame
  by day.
  Shut sesame
  at night.

- "[H]e mumbled, 'Open, sesame.' 'Louder, Fibich. Like you really mean it,' Rizka said. 'See that crack in the wall? Imagine it's going to open up in front of you.' With some added urging, Fibich took a great breath and, in a voice so strong that he startled himself, called out the magical password a few times until Rizka nodded approval."
  —Lloyd Alexander, *Gypsy Rizka* (1999)

- "From beneath the net-draped iron bed she pulled a stainless-steel briefcase. She touched index fingers to circles on either side of the latch, whispered 'Open sesame,' and the latch sprang open."
  —Kathleen Ann Goonan, *Crescent City Rhapsody* (2000)

- "'Open Sesame!' yelled Henry, just in case it might work."
  —Beverly Cleary, *Henry and the Clubhouse* (1962)

- "There, beneath the lip of the wood, she felt a metal shape, not unlike a trigger. She fingered it for a second, then closed her eyes, as if she expected the device to explode when she pushed it, but knowing she had no choice. 'Open sesame,' she whispered. The latch mechanism made a small thunking sound, and the door slid free."
  —John Katzenbach, *State of Mind* (1997)

- "Finally, Dhirendra found the word of power, the open-sesame, that restored animation to morose Sammy Hazaré. He leapt up on to a table, posed like a little garden statue and spoke the occult syllables. 'RDX,' he announced."
  —Salman Rushdie, *The Moor's Last Sigh* (1995)

- "Consumed multitudes are jostling and shaving inside me; and guided only by the memory of a large white bedsheet with a roughly circular hole some seven inches in diameter cut into the centre, clutching at the dream of that holey, mutilated square of linen, which is my talisman, my open-sesame."
  —Salman Rushdie, "The Perforated Sheet," *Mirrorwork: 50 Years of Indian Writing* (1997)

- "'Open see-same!' shouted the little girl [Patricia Highsmith], proud she knew this magical phrase. [Her stepfather] Stanley corrected her pronunciation to 'Sess-a-mi!' but when Patsy repeated the word, her spirit was crushed. . . . [Highsmith recollected:] 'I knew he was right, and I hated him because he was right like grown-up people always were, and because he had forever destroyed my enchanting, my 'Open See-same,' and because now the new word would have no meaning to me, had destroyed my picture, had become strange, unfriendly and unknown.'"
  —Andrew Wilson, *Beautiful Shadow: A Life of Patricia Highsmith* (2003)

- "When George was alone at a meal, formally served him in the dining room in his high chair, and he did not like something he was given to eat, he repeated the lordly gesture and the lordly phrase [his father's '*Enlevez-le*'] and was delighted to see that, like 'Open Sesame' in reverse, he could thus have the unhappy cabbage, or whatever it was, removed from sight."
  —May Sarton, *I Knew a Phoenix* (1954)

- "The magic influence of 'open sesame' could not have been more effective upon bolts and bars."
—Ben Macintyre, *The Man Who Would Be King* (2004)

- "'There's no door handle,' he called as I walked down the hallway of posters. 'Just say the magic words.' 'Abracadabra,' I said standing in front of the door. 'No,' called Ott. 'That's for getting in. The other words.' 'Open Sesame,' I said. The door swung open suddenly, missing me by a few inches."
—Stuart M. Kaminsky, *Now You See It* (2004)

- From Louis Zukofsky, *Complete Short Poetry* (1991):

  Open Sesame, Ali Baba, I, thy firefly, little errant star, call here,
  By thy magic I embrace thee.

- "[E]ven when my grandfather sat in his salmon upholstered lounge chair and trapped me between his crossed ankles, refusing to release me until I said the magic words, *Open sesame,* I never felt the desperate need to escape."
—Hope Edelman, *Mother of My Mother* (1999)

- -

Open Space

Facts: "'What are the magic words?' asks the magician. 'Open Space!' yell dozens of school kids watching one of Paul Becker's Great Environmental Magic Shows."[542]

Opopomoz

Origins: This is an Italian magic word from the animated film *Opopomoz* (2003), taught to a little boy by three mischievous devils.

- -

Oprah

Just say the magic word: Oprah
—Vince Vittore, *America's Network* (Jan. 1, 1995)

Meanings:

- Dust

- Fawn

- "She who turns her back"
—Adrian Room, *Cassell's Dictionary of First Names* (2002)

Origins: This is the given name of the successful talk-show host and media mogul Oprah Winfrey. The word is of Hebrew origin.

In Literature: "I had thought it would be difficult springing me from familiar duties for a sudden trip to Chicago, but everything is made easy by my use of a magical word. Saying 'Oprah,' I learn, is better than chanting 'abra-cadabra,' or even 'open sesame.' Uttering the name clears me of all responsibilities. To say 'going to Oprah' is like announcing a sacred pilgrimage. 'Oprah,' I say. 'Oprah, Oprah.' Maybe this new magic will overcome the old jinx."
—Ken Kuhlken and Alan Russell, *No Cats, No Chocolate* (2004)

---

542 "New Jersey's Great Northwest Skylands," *New JerseySkylands.WorldWeb.com* (2005)

Orchideous

Facts: *Orchideous* is derived from *orchid*, a type of flower.

In Literature: *Orchideous* is a spell to make a bouquet of flowers appear from a wand in *Harry Potter and the Goblet of Fire* by J.K. Rowling (2000).

Oso Yi Mi Ka

Meanings:

- "I am surrounded or sustained by circles of protective shamans"
  —Biodun Jeyifo, *Wole Soyinka* (2004)

- "I am surrounded by sorcerers"
  —Biodun Jeyifo, *Wole Soyinka* (2004)

Origins: This phrase is of Nigerian origin.

Ostagazuzulum

Facts: This magic word is from the BBC television series *Wizbit*, hosted by Paul Daniels. The title character is a giant magician's hat.

Variations and Incantations: Ostapazoozalem

Otserp Cigam Ees Em Ees Em

In Literature: "The magic words are these words, written and pronounced backwards: 'presto-magic-see-me-see-me.'"
—Bill Sheehan, *Marigold in Fourth* (2004)

Otto

Origins: *Otto* is a palindromic magic word for amulets, mentioned in the *Gremoire du Pape Honorius* (1800).

Ou're-yay Uts-nay

Mystique: Pig Latin initiates many children into the idea of secret words and the power of imbuing even common words with special meaning.

Origins: This phrase is "Pig Latin" for "you're nuts."

In Literature: Tamar Myers, *Assault and Pepper* (2005)

Owa Tagu Siam

Facts: These are magic words used by professional magician Amazing Gregory (Greg Stringer).

Spoken quickly, these words sound like "Oh what a goose I am."

Common Magician's Applications: Lighthearted humor. For example: "[B]y and large, the family of eight seated before the after-dinner carnage of take-out containers and half-empty tea glasses is appreciative, giggling, enthralled by each deft new sleight-of-hand. Except, that is, for Miranda, a freckle-faced strawberry-blonde at the end of the table scrutinizing the steakhouse's resident mage with a 10-year-old skeptic's discerning eye. Undaunted, the mustachioed magician holds a deck of cards before his diminutive critic and asks her to recite the magic words: 'Owa Tagu Siam (Oh what a goose I am).' Miranda plays along, looking more the jaded sophisticate than the sheepish victim, even after she realizes she's been had. Then Stringer caps the trick by waving his free hand with an exaggerated flourish and pulling the card she had chosen just a minute earlier out of her pony tail. 'Tough crowd,' Stringer says with a good-natured chuckle as he waves to Miranda's parents and siblings. An active professional magician for seven years, he knows that cynics are one of the hazards of the trade. 'Some people just don't want to be fooled.'"[543]

Variations and Incantations: O watta goo siam
—*MonkeyMadhouse.com* (2005)

P

Papa-Ooma-Mow Mow

Mystique: This incantation begins with the primal word *papa*, "a magic word that babies know."[544]

Origins: This chant is featured in the song "Surfin' Bird" by The Trashmen (1964).

Facts: The similar magic phrase "Paa paa paa oom papa mow mow" is featured in the Nintendo video game "StarTropics II: Zoda's Revenge" (1994).

Papparapa

Meanings:

- Nonsense

- Suddenly

- Incomprehensible
  It is called "papparapa" in Japan, meaning "I can't understand at all."
  —Hiroshima Daigaku (1975)

Origins: This is a Japanese version of *presto*.

Facts: *Papparapa* is a magic spell for teleportation in the *Dragon Ball* manga and role playing games.

Variations and Incantations: Pappapparaparapappappara
This Italian word captures the musical flourish of circus jugglers (*Intersound2000.com* [2005]).

Paradise

In Literature:

- "The magic word is 'paradise.' The next time you hear me say it, you will go into a very serene, meditative state. You will be completely at peace, and all will be well."
  —T.K. Rouse, *The Paradox of Paradise* (2001)

- "Today we are standing at a major crossroads. One fork of the road has a signpost inscribed with the magic word '*Paradise*'; the other fork also has a signpost bearing the word '*Doomsday*.'"
  —John O'Neill, quoted in *Chain Reaction* by Brian Balogh (1991)

----

543 Mike Gibson, "Being a Working Magician Ain't Easy—But Local Conjurers Make a Living with Tricks Up Their Sleeves," *Weekly Wire* (1997)

544 Gerry L. Spence, *Of Murder and Madness* (1983)

Pararin Ririkaru Parapora Magikaru

Facts: This is the magic phrase for transformations in the animated television series *Magical Emi (Mahou no Star Magical Emi)* (1985). The series is about a little girl who comes from a long line of stage magicians.

Pathfinder

In Literature: "There are magical words, magical apart from their meanings, physically magical, with a magic inherent in the sound itself, words that before they deliver a message already have a meaning, words that are signs and meanings unto themselves, that do not require comprehension, but only hearing, words of the animals, the child's dream language. It is possible that each person has in his own life his own magic words. In my life, the magic word was and remains—the Pathfinder."
—Marina Tsvetaeva, "Pushkin and Pugachev," *Marina Tsvetaeva—A Captive Spirit: Selected Prose* (1980)

Pax, Sax, Sarax

Origins: *Pax Sax Sarax* was found written in "an Elizabethan manuscript in the British Museum."[545]

Facts: This phrase is purportedly part of a chant to prolong orgasm. "The chanted words have no meaning. Their virtue lies in the fact that they sound impressive."[546]

In Literature:

- Peggy Christian, *The Bookstore Mouse* (2002)

- "He sneaks up behind her and places his hands over her eyes. Guess who. I can't. I'm your hypnotist, he says. He releases her eyes. Look into my eyes. She turns and looks into his eyes. Repeat after me. I will always hold a raw potato in my mouth while peeling onions. Julie repeats the words though they mean nothing to her. Barry continues: I am a rabbit who will eventually lay an egg. He listens carefully as she repeats it. I will fall in love with a handsome young Jewish man and live happily ever after. Rather than repeating Barry's word Julie—as though another's voice is speaking through her—says: Pax sax sarax afra afca nostra."
—Clarence Major, *Emergency Exit* (1979)

Pazoink

In Literature: World of Warcraft Europe, *WOW-Europe.com* (2005)

Peach, a Plum, a Half a Stick of Chewing Gum

Mystique: Children's rhymes resonate with nostalgia. With the phrase *a peach, a plum, a half a stick of chewing gum*, the innocence of children's voices invokes magical power.

----

545 Migene Gonzalez-Wippler, *The Complete Book of Spells, Ceremonies and Magic* (1988)

546 Richard Cavendish, *The Black Arts* (1967)

Origins: This incantation is part of a children's clapping game.

Variations and Incantations: A peach, a plum, have a stick of chewing gum
—Stephanie Calmenson and Joanna Cole, *Miss Mary Mack* (1990)

In Literature: "Say the magic word, a peach, a plum, a half a stick of chewing gum."
—T. Berry Brazelton, *Touchpoints 3 to 6* (2001)

Pee-Times-Co-Que-Time-Contra-Variant-Tensor

Facts: This magic phrase is based upon a mathematical equation.

In Literature: "[N]obody—not even the great Einstein—can, by covering a yardstick with a piece of cloth, waving a wand, and using some such magic phrase as: 'pee-times-co-que-time-contra-variant-tensor,' turn it into a brand new glittering alarm clock!"
—George Gamow, *One Two Three…Infinity* (1961)

Perciphedron

In Literature: In the poem "Why!" (1981) by Konstantin Pavlov, *Perciphedron* is a magic word written in white letters on the belly of a magical fish named "Kron-zhig," who lies on the bottom of the ocean and emerges from the deep every century to shriek her own name. Also on her belly is the magic word *Aburadan*, written in black letters. White birds peck at the black letters, and black birds peck at the white letters,

And Kron-zhig,
calmed, starts for the bottom.
But what is the meaning of the text? . . .

The meaning of the text is in the subtext.

I don't understand anything! Neither the text nor the subtext . . .

The birds eat only the text,
and afterwards spit out the subtext—
a stone,
they cannot digest and assimilate . . .
In another hundred years
everything will become clear.

But why only in a hundred years!
Why, why, why . . .

Because!
Because you're immortal!

Who will explain it to us in a hundred years!

Someone else.
If you don't kill him
with accusatory questions
while he is still in his mother's womb.[547]

Peterpiperpickedapeck ofpickledpeppers

Origins: Tongue-twisters such as "Peter Piper picked a peck of pickled peppers" originated as spells for divination and good luck that devolved into children's counting games, the object being "to repeat a difficult formula rapidly without an error."[548]

Facts: *Peterpiperpickedapeckofpickledpeppers* is a favorite magic word of magician Cliff G. He ex-

----

547 *Capriccio for Goya: Selected Poems 1955–1995* (2003)
548 Charles Godfrey Leland, *Etruscan Magic and Occult Remedies* (1897)

plains: "While it is not traditional, I always like to feed a volunteer the magic words 'Peterpiperpickedapeckofpickledpeppers.' I can say that very fast, and it gets a good audience reaction. Plus it is familiar enough to most people that the volunteer can probably say it (slower than I) but not look stupid."[549]

Variations and Incantations:

- Peter Piper picked a peck of pretty pickled peppers
  —Rodney Saulsberry, *You Can Bank on Your Voice* (2004)

- Peter Piper picked a peck of prickly pears
  —Emma Paddock Telford, *Good Housekeeping* (1894)

Petrificus Totalus

Origins: *Petrificus* is from the Latin word meaning "stone" (*petra*). *Totalus* is from the Latin word meaning "entire" (*tota*).

In Literature:

- *Petrificus Totalus* is a petrifying spell in *Harry Potter and the Philosopher's Stone* by J.K. Rowling (1997). It causes a person to freeze like a statue.

Phblthplbht
(see *qmjbtf*)

Facts: This is a magic word for conjuring an iron will.

In Literature: Balanced Alternative Technologies Multi-User Dimension, *Bat.org* (2004)

Pickwick

There, sure enough, in gilt letters of a goodly size, was the magic name of PICKWICK!
—Charles Dickens,
The Pickwick Papers (1836–1837)

In Literature: "[T]hough the words were inaudible, Sam saw by the motion of the two pairs of lips that they had uttered the magic word 'Pickwick.'"
—Charles Dickens, *The Pickwick Papers* (1836–37)

Piddlepaddlepodlepum

In Literature: "[S]he pronounced the magical word, 'Piddlepaddlepodlepum!' (only you mustn't say it, you know) and then she waved her magic wand three times. Then a wonderful thing happened. Grandpa's bushy tail, that had turned white because he was so old, got a nice silver-gray in an instant, and the pain in his back went right away. Then he straightened up, and he cried: 'Well, well, I certainly do feel better! I feel ever so much younger again. I guess I'm wrong about fairies being bosh. I'm ever so much obliged to you, my dear little lady. I surely do feel fine! Thank you so much!'"
—Howard Roger Garis, *Johnnie and Billie Bushytail* (1910)

Pif Paf Poof
(see also *poof*)

He's disappeared, Pif Paf Poof! Magic.
—*TodChat.com* (2003)

Meanings:

- Bing-bang-boom
  —Gerard Genette, *Mimologics* (1995)

- Magic
"Must be magic then. Abracadabra! Pif-Paf-Poof."
—*MoviePoopShoot.com* (2004)

- Magic word
Pif paf poof is the catchphrase of professional magician Geoffrey Durham's character "The Great Soprendo."
"[S]ome omnipotent being said 'pif-paf-poof' and all of creation sprung to life . . ."
—"Earth and Beyond Portal," *EBPortal.com* (2003)

- Password
"I hope Yoda does not tell Obi-Wan some secret password like pif-paf-poof!"
—*GalacticSenate.com* (2004)

Facts: *Pif Paf Poof* is a phrase from a universal language. For example, in *The Good Soldier Svejk and His Fortunes in the World War* by Jaroslav Hasek (1973): "The Hungarian . . . tried to explain something to him with the help of gestures. He pointed to his shot arm and said in international language: 'Pif, paf, poof!'"

Pif paf poof appears in the comic opera *The Grand Duchess of Gerolstein* by Jacques Offenbach (1967).

Pif-Paf is a Polish interjection meaning "Bang! Bang!"

Pif Paf is the name of a card game from Brazil.

In British folklore, *Pif* and *Paf* are names of "the country where cats are made," homeplace to the Breton fairies.[550]

Pif-paf is a British interjection meaning "Pow!" For example, "Pif-paf! a blow on the ear sent sparks flying before my eyes, and rolled my hat to the ground."[551]

Variations and Incantations:

- Pif paf piaf patapan
—Charles Nodier, quoted in *Poétique de la Coupure Chez Charles Nodier* by Hélène Lowe-Dupas (1976)

- Pif, paf, plouf
—Raymond Federman, *Take It or Leave It* (1976)

- Pif paf pof
—David Ascher, *Learning Python* (2003)

- Pif paf poof and voilà
—Matt Pilky, Angling Lines Forum, *RMC Angling.co.uk* (2004)

- Pif paf poof nanoolia
—*RiskyChris.com* (2005)

- Pif, paf, poof, tarapapa poom
—Jacques Offenbach, *The Grand Duchess of Gerolstein* (1867)

- Pif-paf-pouf
—Gerard Genette, *Mimologics* (1995)

- Piff, paff, poof
"I opened the door to the tank and asked her to step inside. 'Once inside please face the front, and place your hands through the holes on either side. And ladies, would you please hold hands with our sweet volunteer, so that the audience can plainly see that she remains in the box at all times.' I moved to the side so that the camcorder could see she was now restrained inside the box. 'Now I'm going to shut the door, like so . . . could you please wiggle your hands to show that you're alright . . . excellent . . . and now I'm going to say the magic words—Piff, Paff, Poof—and Susie, our young volunteer has now disappeared!'"
—Big Dave, "The Tuesday Club Episode Three: It's a Kind of Magic" (2003)

---

550 Lewis Spence, *Legends and Romances of Brittany* (1917)

551 *Blackwood's Edinburgh Magazine* (1898)

Piff Pang Poof Pop

Facts: These are magic words "that work wonders" in conjunction with a fairy godmother wand, according to Elizabeth Ingrid Hauser's *Princess Crafts* (2005).

Pink Platypus

Facts: These are professional clown-magician Sugar Plum's magic words for making an elephant disappear.

Pinky-Schminky, Alakazoo

Facts: These are magic words used by professional magician Steve Charney.[552]

Pinocchio

Mystique: The word *Pinocchio* invokes the character in literature and film who transformed from a puppet into a real boy through the power of wishes and belief in the possibility of magic.

In Literature: Sherrilyn Kenyon, *Tie Me Up, Tie Me Down* (2005)

Pippity Poppity Pop
(see also *bibbidy-bobbidy-boo*)

The magic is in the words.
—Gunter Gebauer, *Mimesis* (1996)

Variations and Incantations:

- Pipiti Popiti Pù
  —*Digilander.libero.it/ludozone* (2004)
- Pippity Pappity Peppity Poppity Puppity
  —Allen & Unwin, *Making Radio* (2000)
- Pippity Poppity Pip
- Pippity Poppity Poo

In Literature: Cheryl Charming, *Be a Star Magician!* (2002)

Please
(see also *thank you*)

That magic word 'please'
ought to be spoken more often.
—Lydia Ramsey, "'Please' Takes Abruptness
and Demand Out of Requests,"
Savannah Morning News (2002)

Mystique: "'Say the magic word.' Who among us can't remember that command? We heard it as children; we repeat it as adults. The word 'Please,' is, in truth, a magic word. It was magic to us as children because it transformed inaction into action. Our request was issued, and nothing happened. Then, either through demand or memory, we said the magic word and the arrested world came alive. As adults we hear the appeals of youngsters, and we reply, 'Say the magic word.' We sometimes surprise ourselves with the strength of our position and fully realize that we are quite prepared to deny the request if it is not accompanied by, 'Please.'"[553]

Of course, not everyone finds the word *please* to carry enough mystique to be used as a magic word during a performance of legerdemain. A Web diarist who goes by the name Philomedy

----

552 *Hocus Jokus: 50 Funny Magic Tricks Complete with Jokes* (2003)

553 John A. Taylor, *Notes on an Unhurried Journey* (1991)

has this to say on the matter: "In my experience, a magician has never said 'please' and made the woman reappear. Ali Baba didn't say 'Open Please.' There is nothing magic about it. If I ask 'What's the colorful word?' you would not say 'table.'"[554]

Facts: An enchanted doorknocker shaped like a gargoyle in Terry Pratchett's novel *Mort* (1987) requires his own version of "open sesame" (the word *please*) to allow someone to pass.

Variations and Incantations:

- Please please please please disappear
  —John Cassidy, *The Klutz Book of Magic* (1989)

- Please? Pretty please? Sim Salabim? Hocus Pocus? Open Sesame? Amen?
  —*Uqm.stack.nl/forum* (2003)

- Pleathe
  "'*Pleathe!*' she lisped, her face so radiantly sure t magic appeal of that word, that he could not disappoint her. 'The little witch!' he exclaimed. 'She could wheedle the fish out of the sea if she'd say please to 'em that way. But how that honey-sweet tone and the yells she was letting loose awhile back could come out of that same little rose of a mouth, passes my understanding.'"
  —Annie Fellows Johnston, *Georgina of the Rainbows* (1916)

- Pliss
  "'Yes, yes, hurry, come!' His eyes moved from the impassive face of Emerson to the equally inexpressive countenance of Emerson's son, and in desperation he tried the magic word again. 'Pliss? Pliss!'"
  —Elizabeth Peters, *Guardian of the Horizon* (2004)

In Literature:

- "'Perhaps there's a magic word or something.' 'I don't know any magic words,' said Tristran. He held the chain up. It glittered red and purple in the light of the setting sun. 'Please?' he said. There was a ripple in the fabric of the chain, and he slid his hand out of it."
  —Neil Gaiman, *Stardust* (2003)

- "I took a step toward him. 'Please.' I suppose the magic word worked, because he reached for the brass knobs of the high double doors and swung them wide."
  —Neal Shusterman, *The Dark Side of Nowhere* (1997)

- "The chicken started trotting. There was no way I was going to try the classic 'abracadabra' or 'hocus pocus' magic words to stop a charging chicken. And don't even remind me of that 'please' and 'thank you' mistake I made earlier in my career."
  —Jon Scieszka, *Summer Reading Is Killing Me* (1998)

- "'Magic word? What's the magic word?' The knocker perceptibly sneered. 'Haff you been taught nothing, miss?' . . . 'I have been *educated*,' she informed it with icy precision, 'by some of the finest scholars in the land.' The doorknocker did not appear to be impressed. 'Iff they didn't teach you the magic word,' it said calmly, 'they couldn't haff fbeen all that fine.' . . . '*Please* help me,' she said. 'Please!' 'See?' said the doorknocker triumphantly. 'Sooner or later *everyone* remembers the magic word!'"
  —Terry Pratchett, *Mort* (1987)

- "One friend I've never met in the material world is Eri, a librarian from North Carolina who has a wicked sense of humor: a sign on the floor of Eri's dwelling in Cyberion City says 'Caution, black hole.' If you make the mistake of looking in the black hole, you fall into the basement, where you discover that the look command only gets you the message 'The basement is dark.' Then you try a bunch of commands, and you get the message 'Say the magic word.' And if you say 'shazam' or 'abracadabra,' you get the message 'Say the magic word your mommy taught you.' When you say 'Please,' Eri's black hole lets you back into her living room."

—Howard Rheingold, *The Virtual Community: Homesteading on the Electronic Frontier* (1993)

- "Judy was fond of telling a story of long long ago when Pat had been four years old and was being trained to say 'please.' One day she could not remember it. 'What is the word that makes things happen, Judy?' she had asked. Oh, for such a magic word now . . . some word which would make everything right for Jingle."

—Lucy Maud Montgomery, *Pat of Silver Bush* (1933)

Plugh

Plugh is a command.
—Nick Montfort, *Twisty Little Passages* (2003)

Facts: This magic word is featured in early "interactive fiction" computer games such as "Advent" and "Colossal Cave."

Plugh is sometimes associated with the sounds of spitting[555] or snorting.[556]

In Literature: "On a whim, he suddenly shouted 'Plugh!' Predictably, nothing hap-

pened. He shrugged and opened the door."
—Robert G. Ferrell, *Tangent* (2004)

Pocuscadabra

(see also *abracadabra*, *cadabra*, and *hocus pocus*)

Facts: This magic word is from the Bugs Bunny cartoon "Transylvania 6-5000" (1963). Bugs the Magician uses the word to turn the menacing vampire Count Bloodcount into a "bumbling bat."[557]

Pon Chiki Non Non

Origins: "Pon Chiki Non Non" originated in India.

Facts: *PonChiki* is a Russian word for "doughnut."

Common Magician's Applications: Vanishing.
Variations and Incantations: Pon chiki pon chiki chiki pon pon pom
—*Anim-arte.com* (2004)

In Literature: "He threw the fish taveez into the air, and murmured the magic words: 'Pon Chiki Non Non!' The taveez vanished in mid-air."
—Surajit Basu, "Suraj and the Fever Fiend" (2005)

555 Michael Brown, *Nurses* (1992)
556 Anita Coons, *What About Me* (2003)
557 Steven Jay Schneider, *Horror Film and Psychoanalysis* (2004)

ꝑooſ

Poof, a puff of magic smoke.
—Ed Dee, *14 Peck Slip* (1995)

Poof, like *presto-chango.*
—Randy Wayne White, *Twelve Mile Limit* (2002)

They can make things appear
and disappear with poofs and smoke.
—N.E. Bode, *The Anybodies* (2004)

Mystique: "And then, poof! Like magic . . ."[558]
Poof is its own dazzling puff of smoke, suddenly there one moment and, just as quickly, gone the next. Invariably *poof* is a puff of smoke conjured by a magician. "He sprinkles his fingers through the air. 'Poof.'"[559] Yet as insubstantial as a puff of smoke may be, there's an undeniable concreteness to *poof* as a magic word. This concreteness reveals itself in how people use *poof* in a sentence: the most common phrase to follow *poof* is "just like that!" Just like how? Just like a magician makes something disappear—expertly, instantaneously, convincingly, totally, "for all the world" gone. Another concrete phrase that commonly follows *poof* is "the next thing you know." Before that elephant had time to take a single pounding step, *poof—the next thing you know* Doug Henning had made it vanish into thin air. "The next thing you know" implies "the first thing you know"—that being the magician's feat, which you witnessed with your very eyes. The spectator has solid knowledge of the magician's abilities. As the illusion's dazzling haze dissipates, the next thing you know is speechless awe expressed through thunderous applause.

Meanings:

- Appear out of nowhere
"Love is the magician of the Universe. It creates everything out of nothing. One moment, it isn't there, and the next—POOF—it appears in all its splendor, and you greet it with amazement."
—Barbara de Angelis, *Real Moments* (1994)

   "I want to make very clear to you that my gardens did not just *poof!!* appear suddenly overnight."
—Ellen Dugan, *Garden Witchery* (2003)

   "You are the one walking like a ghost—poof—here you are."
—Jessica Shattuck, *The Hazards of Good Breeding* (2003)

   "Within the concept of self-creation is the idea that once there was nothing—pure nonbeing . . . and then, 'poof,' there was something, like the rabbit out of the magician's hat. Only what happens is more stupendous than the feats of prestidigitation. In this magic show the rabbit comes from nothing by himself. There is no magician to bring him forth, no hat out of which to pull him, and no concealed rabbit or even partially becoming rabbit who emerges."
—Arthur W. Lindsley, *Classical Apologetics* (1984)

- Burst of light
"With a little poof of light . . ."
—Kathleen Ann Goonan, *Light Music* (2003)

   "Without even a *poof* or a clap of thunder—just appeared."
—Michael Kurland, *The Rite Stuff* (2004)

- Cleavage
"'I don't need wool stuffing to give me—' Mary broke off, too embarrassed to say the words. She waved her hands at her chest. '—Poof.' . . . Obviously, he didn't mind that she didn't have 'poof.'"
—Cathy Maxwell, *The Wedding Wager* (2001)

---

558 P.C. Cast, *Goddess of Light* (2005)
559 Diana Abu-Jaber, *Crescent* (2003). Similarly: "'Poof,' I said, and waggled my fingers as if I were casting a spell" (Paul Watkins, *The Forger* [2000]).

- Illusion
"How deep is the extent of the burial of mankind in his ignorance on this poof called earth."
—Jack Kerouac, *Some of the Dharma* (1956)

- Instantly, suddenly
"One day I'm the elf next door and then *poof* I'm a river."
—Harvard Lampoon, *Bored of the Rings* (1969)
"Poof! . . . all at once as if a magician had snapped his fingers."
—Kim Stanley Robinson, *Pacific Edge* (1995)
"While things didn't go 'poof' and change in an instant . . ."
—Hank Bordowitz, *Bad Moon Rising* (1998)
"What I feel is poof, it's gone, or poof, it's back."
—Gertrude Blanck, *Ego Psychology II* (1979)

- Like magic
"'Poof.' 'Yeah. Like magic.'"
—Mike Stewart, *Dog Island* (2002)
"Imagine a building supply warehouse that is never out of stock on any item, for the simple reason that the owner is a magician. If he runs out of rain gutters, he simply takes some scraps of lumber or a handful of nails and—*poof!*—turns them into the precise rain gutter that you require."
—Stephen Cherniske, *The Metabolic Plan* (2003)
"A thing is just a thing until you have the story that goes with it. Without the story, there's nothing to hold on to, nothing to relate this mysterious new thing to who you are—you know, to make it a part of your own history. So if you're like me, you make something up and the funny thing is, lots of times, once you tell the story, it comes true. Not poof, hocus-pocus, magic it comes true, but sure, why not, and after it gets repeated often enough, you and everybody else end up believing it."
—Charles de Lint, *Moonlight and Vines* (1999)

"A blink of an eye and, poof! Like magic."
—Jonathan R. Cash, *The Age of the Antichrist* (2000)
"Imagine for a moment a magician on a stage. At the crucial moment of the trick, a puff of smoke appears, and poof—the rabbit appears, the assistant is cut in two, or the box begins to levitate."
—LearningExpress, *GMAT Exam Success in Only 4 Steps* (2003)
"As you look closely at the still life on the table then step back slowly, poof! it becomes solid form. Magic? Yes, the painter is the magician."
—Donald Stanley Vogel, *Memories and Images* (2000)

- Magic trick
"Poof! Like a magic trick on a stage."
—John Katzenbach, *The Madman's Tale* (2004)
"With a poof, like an evil magician's trick, the door was filled with a luminous glow."
—Julie Johnston, *Adam and Eve and Pinch-Me* (1995)
"Like she had just appeared—or was disappearing, which was it?—into or out of smoke, poof, magic, like some trick."
—Carolyn Coman, *What Jamie Saw* (1995)
"Dalton flicked his hand like a magician going poof."
—Ralph Wetterhahn, *Shadowmakers* (2002)
"A poof of magic, like the magician you'd hired for my sixth birthday with his tricks of transformation."
—Constance Warloe, *From Daughters & Sons to Fathers: What I've Never Said* (2001)

- Magic word
"What are you . . . some type of magician or something? You waiting on some 'magic-poof' or something?"
—Akil, *From Niggas to Gods, Vol. II* (1996)

"[J]ust as a magician says 'Poof!' when something vanishes . . ."
—Joanna M. Lund, *The Arthritis Healthy Exchanges Cookbook* (1998)

"Poof. That's a spell word, magicians go 'poof.'"
—Tom Donaghy, *Northeast Local* (1996)

"Sometimes they appear out of nowhere and vanish, as if a magician said, 'Poof.'"
—Terry Lynn Taylor, *Answers from the Angels* (1993)

"'Poof,' he said, waving his magic wand."
—Henry Winkler, *Day of the Iguana* (2003)

"Poof, I'll make you disappear."
—Harlan Coben, *Gone for Good* (2003)

"'POOF!' The magician reached into a chalice by his side and dashed a pellet into a pewter dish; a smoky cloud smudged the air."
—Daniel McBain, *Art Roebuck Comes to Born with a Tooth* (1993)

- Offensive slang for an effeminate man
"Holding them out, she turned a circle while the diamond clasp exploded with light. 'Where do they come from? Do you just picture them in your mind and . . . poof?' 'Poof?' He decided she hadn't meant that as an insult."
—Nora Roberts, *A Little Magic* (1998)

- Presto-chango
—Randy Wayne White, *Twelve Mile Limit* (2002)

- Puff of smoke, powder, or dust
—Brady Udall, *The Miracle Life of Edgar Mint* (2002)

"[H]e'd tried to disappear. Displace himself outside his body. Poof. Puff of smoke."
—Jewell Parker Rhodes, *Magic City* (1997)

"[P]oof, like smoke . . ."
—Edward Hays, *The Passionate Troubadour* (2004)

"She laughs triumphantly, then disappears in a poof of smoke."
—Hillary DePiano, *The Love of Three Oranges* (2003)

"A Wizard waved her wand, and said some words, / and then, presto . . . poof of smoke . . . the ugly frog discovered that he was really . . . / A handsome Prince."
—L. Michael Hall, *Communication Magic* (2001)

"[H]e enjoyed the walk through the darkening streets, the cold air turning to smoke as it left his nostrils. Poof the Magic Dragon, he thought ironically."
—Val McDermid, *Killing the Shadows* (2000)

"[A] poof of dust . . ."
—Michael Spooner, *Daniel's Walk* (2004)

"The bag lands not far away from Ruby but explodes with a satisfying thud and wonderful poof, a big white cloud like a gloved magician might produce."
—Sara Pritchard, *Crackpots* (2003)

- Transformation
"Someone waves a magic wand and poof—everything that was ugly is magically new and remarkably gorgeous."
—Mary E. Hunt, *Cheapskate Monthly Money Makeover* (1995)

"No abracadabra and *poof*."
—Jim Munroe, *Flyboy Action Figure Comes with Gasmask* (1995)

- Unexplainable occurrence
"*It's a mystery.* That catchall phrase was used by her parents as liberally as salt for all unexplainable occurrences, the equivalent of *poof* to prestidigitators."
—Nina Solomon, *Single Wife* (2003)

- Vanish into thin air
"Poof! Into thin air they went."
—John Griesemer, *Signal & Noise* (2004)

"I wanted to tell you, but you disappeared, poof, like a magician's dove."
—Jenny McPhee, *No Ordinary Matter* (2004)

"[I]f you want to make a set of car keys go *poof!* pull one key from the ring and vanish it instead."
—Joel Bauer, *How to Persuade People Who Don't Want to be Persuaded* (2004)

"Poof! Gone like magic! Now ya see it, my friends, now ya don't."
—Stephen King, *The Drawing of the Three* (1990)

"Poof! You are vanished, invisible."
—Stephen Hunter, *Havana* (2003)

"[P]oof off to oblivion . . ."
—Reneau H. Reneau, *Misanthropology: A Florilegium of Bahumbuggery* (2003)

"'You need only say the word, and *poof!*' Like a sorcerer, she opened her fist in the air, flinging magic. 'We'll be gone.'"
—Lauren Belfer, *City of Light* (1999)

"Yet it was gone. Vanished, poof!"
—Patricia Monaghan, *The Red-Haired Girl from the Bog: The Landscape of Celtic Myth and Spirit* (2003)

Common Magician's Applications: Flame effects. Vanishing. For example, "A coin sits on a table. You pick it up, toss it high into the air, where it vanishes at the peak of its arc. 'Poof! Where'd it go?'"[560]

Variations and Incantations:

- Ay, fo! Poof
"Ay, fo! Poof, bad thoughts be gone."
—John Leguizamo, *Extreme Exposure: An Anthology of Solo Performance Texts from the Twentieth Century* (2000)

- Ka-poof
—Pam Smallcomb, *Trimoni Twins and the Changing Coin* (2004)

- Pif, paf, poof
Pif paf poof is the catchphrase of professional magician Geoffrey Durham's character "The Great Soprendo."

- Pif, paf, poof, tarapapa poom
—Jacques Offenbach, *The Grand Duchess of Gerolstein* (1867)

- Poof, begone!
"A disappearing act: 'Poof, begone!'"
—Avery Hart, *Knights & Castles* (1998)

- Poof! Whammo!
—Peter Straub, *In the Night Room* (2004)

- Poof! Woof! Soof! Soof! Woof! Poof!
"When I count to three, vanish. Poof! Woof! Soof! Soof! Woof! Poof!"
—I. Rivers, *Black Magic Woman* (2004)

In Literature:

- "Will she go poof in a puff of smoke?"
—Roald Dahl, "George's Marvellous Medicine," *The Roald Dahl Treasury* (1961)

- "'Just gone. Disappeared. Poof.' He paused. 'He's a magician. Poof. Get it?'"
—Lyn Hamilton, *The Moche Warrior* (1999)

- "Even now, I remember watching the strange apparition suddenly turn to stone. I walked over to where it stood among the rubble and dust of the fallen building, and saw that it had that hideous grin upon its lips. A thought occurred to me to say the magic word: 'Poof!' The Shadow Man turned to dust, vanishing before my eyes . . . but, before the last particle fell away I heard in the distance the deep and abiding laughter of the Wizard of Lei Chen singing on the wind."
—Craig Harris, "The Wizard of Lei Chen" (2004)

- "'Sometimes I can work magic better than Licleng. Watch me. Poof!' She raised her hands in a theatrical manner."
—Patricia Briggs, *Dragon Bones* (2002)

- "The drumroll continues, the clown staggers back and forth a bit, but James never wobbles, and then, the clown sticks his arms up straight in the air, the drumroll flourishes, and then—And then, James is gone. Just gone. Poof! The audience is stunned for a moment, silent, and then they get on their feet and begin to yell and cheer."
—Anne Ursu, *Spilling Clarence* (2002)

- "[A] bit of waving, a bit of mumbling, and POOF!—whatever one's heart desires. But each conjuration, each illusory spectacle, requires agonizing hours of study and concentration."
—Paul A. Thomsen, *Realms of Magic* (1995)

- "In my book, you're a goddamn wizard. A magician. *Poof*—the elephant vanishes from the stage. *Poof*—the magician's gone, cape and wand and everything."
—Robert Ludlum, *The Ambler Warning* (2005)

- "Just as no actor would attempt to walk on a stage, instantly begin crying, and expect to move the audience to tears, no real magician thinks that a performance consists of flapping and Inverness cape and—poof!—causing a lady to disappear."
—Jim Steinmeyer, *Hiding the Elephant: How Magicians Invented the Impossible and Learned to Disappear* (2004)

Popcorn

Mystique: Popcorn is transformative, going from small to large and from hard to soft in an instant, pulling its own rabbit and hat trick by surprising us with something white and fluffy from out of nowhere. Popcorn's transformation from kernels of seed symbolizes the magical potential for change when energy is applied. Since popcorn is the quintessential snack at the movies, people automatically associate it with entertaining, magical spectacles.

Common Magician's Applications: Restoration. For example: "Say the magic word, 'popcorn,' and pull the ends of the rope. The knot will pop off . . . revealing that two ropes have become one."[561]

<Popping Sound>

Mystique: "[H]issing, popping, clicking, groaning, and other seemingly inarticulate noises are characteristic forms of magical speech. The German historian of religion Rudolf Otto called such noises 'original numinous sounds.' Roman writers called them *voces magicae* (magical sounds). Neither human speech nor bestial grunt, the *voces magicae* provided a way of praying that could lay claim to the supernatural to a degree that ordinary language cannot. Making bizarre noises disengages the intellect, eliciting an altered state of awareness, more potent than, though perhaps not different in kind from, the hypnotic effect of ordinary chanting or singing. . . . A magical treatise . . . [entitled] the 'Eighth Book of Moses' [part of the Greek Magical Papyri] offers a partial interpretation of the hissing and popping noises. Popping is the sound made by the sacred crocodile when it rises from the Nile to take a breath; this is how the crocodile (who is a form of the god Horus) salutes the high god. Hissing is the sound made by the sacred snake that devours its own tail, emblem of the endless cycle of regeneration. Popping, moreover, is the

------

561 Karl Fulves, *Self-Working Rope Magic* (1990)

first element of the high god's secret name, and hissing the second; and popping and hissing, together with breathing, speaking, and laughing, are among the sounds the high god made when he called the world into being. If we fail to comprehend these sounds, it is because they are of a higher order than human speech, not a lower one. They echo divine speech; they are recovered fragments of the language of paradise. One of the magical papyri relates that the mere sound of them delights the gods."[562]

Porridge and Chips

Facts: This magic phrase is used by professional magician Clown Kevin.

Possible

In Literature: "A magic word, 'possible.'"
—Scott Smith, *Breaking 100, 90, 80* (2004)

Presto

Xav had the power to speak most things into existence with the magic word of presto.
—Anonymous (2003)

Mystique:

The name itself was almost magic on his tongue, like *presto* or *shazam.*
—Peter Abrahams,
Their Wildest Dreams (2003)

Presto is a flash—the very essence of spontaneity, the profound magic of the "instant" when something shifts. *Presto* says "magic is in the air. Do not try to figure it out; you cannot. It is the power of the unknown at work, and something special is about to happen."[563] The word itself begs to be spoken quickly, as if without thinking. Truly spontaneous speech is when the thought and the word are identical, like unselfconscious singing in the bathtub.[564] We capture that energy when we jump outside ourselves with "courage and humor and openness and perspective and carelessness, in the sense of burning your mental bridges behind you, outreaching yourself."[565] When a magician says *presto* in such a spontaneous way, the air is electric and his spectators are transfixed, astounded. *Presto* is the moment that will be etched in their memories, because it is the moment they opened up to the possibility of the impossible. Upon speaking the word *presto*, even the magician's mouth is open in amazement.

Presto is the moment when legends are born. Brandon Bays recalls such a moment while seeing ballet dancer Rudolf Nureyev in *Romeo and Juliet* at the Metropolitan Opera House. "[T]here was a moment when it seemed as if time stood still. It was as if Nureyev reached into the depths of his soul—into genius itself. He leaped into the air, and his legs spread into a full split; then, for a moment, it was as if he lifted even higher—as if he was practically floating in the air."[566] *Presto* moments happen often in the world of sports, as when a bat sends a ball soaring. That "whack" is the *presto* that brings everything to a standstill, "and in that gap of absolute silence the soul flashes forth—an immensity revealing itself . . . a presence of vastness . . . a greatness

---

562 Philip Zaleski, *Prayer: A History* (2005)

563 Jamie Sams, *Medicine Cards* (1988)

564 Allen Ginsberg, "Meditation and Poets," quoted in John Welwood, *Ordinary Magic* (1992)

565 *Ibid.*

566 Brandon Bays, *The Journey* (1999)

that can't be explained . . . and then *whack!*—ball hit, hair standing on end. Something great had revealed itself in that tiny instant. One heart, one breath, hair on end. We'd dropped into the 'Gap' for an instant and this vast truth had, in a flash, revealed itself."[567] What is that vast truth? Bay suggests that it's the same as Nureyev's inner genius: our own greatness flashes forth, we see ourselves in the mirror, we remember our own magic, and ripples of joy spread through the audience. The magic of those *presto* moments is what sweeps people up for a standing ovation. No wonder *presto* is such a popular magic word. It's the magic wand blooming into a bouquet. It's the miracle of levitation. It's every special effect that's especially effective. It's smoke and mirrors in a nutshell.

Meanings:

- At once, instantly
"Suddenly—presto!—it was over."
—Irvin D Yalom, *Love's Executioner* (2000)

- Like magic

- Magic words
"If anybody has given you to believe that you're coming to me for some kind of magic formula and—hey presto!—everything's back to normal again, then they've seriously misled you."
—Peter Robinson, *The Final Cut* (1990)

- Nimble
"'Prestidigitation. Sleight-of-hand tricks,' said the Wizard. 'It comes from *presto* meaning nimble and *digit* meaning finger.'"
—Jane Yolen, *The Wizard of Washington Square* (2005)

Origins: *Presto* is derived from the Italian word for *quickly*.

Facts: The Great Presto is a stage magician in the comic book *Uncle Sam Quarterly #2*.

Common Magician's Applications: Transformations, vanishing.

Variations and Incantations:

- Hey Presto
"'Hey, presto!' said the Magic Shopman, and then would come the clear, small 'Hey, presto!' of the boy."
—H.G. Wells, "The Magic Shop"

- Presto Chango
"I can change anything / with just one magic word."
—Arden Davidson, "Presto Chango!" (1998)
	"The fact that the energy of a response is not proportional to the magnitude of the result has contributed to the belief in verbal magic (the magician's 'Presto chango' converts a handkerchief into a rabbit)."
—B.F. Skinner, *About Behaviorism* (1974)
	"[O]ften used when performing a transformation . . ."
—Tom Ogden, *The Complete Idiot's Guide to Magic Tricks* (1998)

- Presto chango alakazam
—Jon Scieszka, *2095* (1995)

- Presto Chango! Ala Peanut Butter Sandwiches! Alakazaam!
—David E. Bell (2001)

- Prest-o Change-o

- Presto Alacazam
"Presto! Alacazam! By sleight of hand, the rules have been circumvented."
—D. Kirk Davidson, *The Moral Dimension of Marketing* (2002)

---

567 *Ibid.*

- Presto-digitation
—Ace Starry, *The Magic Life: A Novel Philosophy* (2003)

- Presto magic
"She just wanted me to pass her that morning like presto magic or something, but I was not planning on being a magician."
—Omar Tyree, *For the Love of Money* (2000)

- Presto vedo
"It were as if the Juggler had uttered the magic words, *presto vedo*, for when the bugle announced the hour for striking tents, all was done in a trice."
—Civil War news from *The Clinton Public*, "From the 107th Regiment, Camp Joe Kelly, Glasgow, KY, March 17th, 1863"

In Literature:

- "He looked as if he had rolled out of a Zen scroll, as if he said 'presto' a lot, knew the meaning of lightning and the origin of dreams."
—Tom Robbins, *Even Cowgirls Get the Blues* (1976)

- "By five-thirty the show has pulled out. Nothing is left but an unreal blue and a few banked clouds low in the north. Some sort of carnival magician has been here, some fast-talking worker of wonders who has the act backwards. 'Something in this hand,' he said, 'something in this hand, something up my sleeve, something behind my back . . .' and abracadabra, he snaps his fingers, and it's all gone. Only the blank, blank-faced magician remains, in his unruffled coat, bare handed, acknowledging a smattering of baffled applause. When you look again the whole show has pulled up stakes and moved on down the road. It never stops. New shows roll in from over the mountains and the magician reappears unannounced from a fold in the curtain you never dreamed was an opening. Scarves of clouds, rabbits in plain view, disappear into the black hat forever. Presto chango. The audience, if there is an audience at all, is dizzy from head-turning, dazed."
—Annie Dillard, *Pilgrim at Tinker Creek* (1974)

- "[W]hen they looked through [the spectacles] the little rabbit children saw that every thing was dark, and gloomy, and dreary, and even the sun seemed to be behind a cloud. Oh, it was as cold and unpleasant as it is just before a snowstorm. 'No wonder you were cross!' cried the fairy. 'But I will soon fix matters! Presto-chango! Ring around the rosey, sweet tobacco posey!' she cried, and then she rubbed first one pink finger on one glass, and then another pink finger on the other glass of the spectacles. And a most wonderful thing happened, she smiled as she held the glasses up in front of Sammie and Susie, and as true as I'm telling you, if everything wasn't as bright and shining as a new tin dishpan. Oh, everything looked lovely! The flowers were gay, and the sun shone, and even the green grass was sort of pink, while the sky was rose-colored."
—Howard R. Garis, *Sammie and Susie Littletail* (1910)

- "Munching a mouthful of fish, he tries to remember that thing about magic. What did he think? It seemed clever at the time. He is a bit befuddled but if he tries hard . . . He doesn't want to lose his audience now. 'Magic, it's like this, see.' He picks up the package of pigments and fumbles open the string. 'Here's these lumps of colors . . . my master—hey presto!—he turns them into trees, into beautiful ladies . . .' Inside, there is an onion. He has opened the wrong parcel. He chuckles. 'Hey presto, it's an onion!'"
—Deborah Moggach, *Tulip Fever* (1999)

Protection

The magic word "protection"
Will banish all dejection
—L. Frank Baum, "When McKinley
Gets the Chair, Boys" (1896)

Origins: *Protection* is of Latin origin, meaning "covered in front."

In Literature: "'I am not speaking against protection,' he said, and at the magic word 'protection' a dead silence again fell over the vast crowd. 'I say to you, 'Protect!' Protect, all of you, merchants, tradesmen, the great body of the commerce of this country; protect whatever you all decide together needs protection. But by the greatness and the power you have, by the Heaven that gave us this land of ours to till and to enjoy, protect also yourselves and your liberties."
—F. Marion Crawford, *An American Politician* (1884)

- -

Psukh

Origins: *Psukh* (also *psukhe*) is a Greek word and the origin of *psyche*.

Meanings:

- Breath of life

- Butterfly

- Psychic
  "I have a magic word, however: it's *psukh*, which is Greek for psychic."
  —Cecilia Tishy, *Now You See Her* (2005)

- Soul
  "The *psukh* is the Greek word for the soul. However in its original context, *psukh* means

much more than just soul. A person's psukh is the core of who they are—their deepest secrets, insights, feelings, hurts, wants, and dreams."
—Jon Foley, "More Than a Broken Heart," *AnythingAtAll.net* (2005)

- -

Pull

In Literature: "'[Y]ou are standing at a doorway through which you are about to pass, into a world where you must make your own way, must accomplish things that will establish the basis for your future lives. I'm going to help you in this by telling you a magic word. This word, if you use it properly, will allow you to go anywhere, do anything, accomplish whatever you want. . . . I know that by now you are all wondering what this magic word is,' he said. 'I will show it to you now. If you will all just turn around and look toward the back of the room, you will find that my magic word is inscribed in large letters on the rear doors of this auditorium.' The students did as the admiral suggested and turned around. Then they broke into gales of laughter. At the rear auditorium, written in very large letters on each door, was the word 'Pull.'"
—John Cramer, *Einstein's Bridge* (1997)

- -

Pum Pum Pum

Origins: This magic phrase originated in a folktale from India.

In Literature: Celia Barker Lottridge, *Ten Small Tales* (1993)

Puritto

Facts: This is the magic word to conjure a bubble-producing magic wand in the animated television series *Magical Emi (Mahou no Star Magical Emi)* (1985). The series is about a little girl who comes from a long line of stage magicians.

Purple Puppy Paws

In Literature: Heather L. Price and Deborah A. Connolly, "Event Frequency and Children's Suggestibility: A Study of Cued Recall Responses," *Applied Congnitive Psychology* (2004)

Putffuffa

In Literature: Lois Harvey, "A Sugar Heaven" (2005)

Pyrzqxgl

Origins: This word originates in L. Frank Baum's *The Magic of Oz* (1919).

Facts: In the *Oz* books, it is said that to transform people and objects, this word must be pronounced correctly. The Munchkin named Bini Aru, who discovered the word, hid away the pronunciation directions after Princess Ozma decreed that only Glinda could practice magic in the land.

Common Magician's Applications: Transformations.

In Literature: "He had discovered a new and secret method of transformations that was unknown to any other Sorcerer. Glinda the Good did not know it, nor did the little Wizard of Oz, nor Dr. Pipt nor old Mombi, nor anyone else who dealt in magic arts. It was Bini Aru's own secret. By its means, it was the simplest thing in the world to transform anyone into beast, bird or fish, or anything else, and back again, once you know how to pronounce the mystical word: 'Pyrzqxgl.' Bini Aru had used this secret many times, but not to cause evil or suffering to others. When he had wandered far from home and was hungry, he would say: 'I want to become a cow—Pyrzqxgl!' In an instant he would be a cow, and then he would eat grass and satisfy his hunger. All beasts and birds can talk in the Land of Oz, so when the cow was no longer hungry, it would say: 'I want to be Bini Aru again: Pyrzqxgl!' and the magic word, properly pronounced, would instantly restore him to his proper form. Now, of course, I would not dare to write down this magic word so plainly if I thought my readers would pronounce it properly and so be able to transform themselves and others, but it is a fact that no one in all the world except Bini Aru, had ever (up to the time this story begins) been able to pronounce 'Pyrzqxgl!' the right way, so I think it is safe to give it to you. It might be well, however, in reading this story aloud, to be careful not to pronounce Pyrzqxgl the proper way, and thus avoid all danger of the secret being able to work mischief."
—L. Frank Baum, *The Magic of Oz* (1919)

Qazam
(see also *kazam*)

Meanings:

- Breast
  —Alexander Lubotsky and Robert Beekes,
  Indo-European Etymological Dictionary (2004)

- Dwarf; unusually small figure of fantasy or
  folklore
  —Catherine Cobham, "The Poetics of
  Space in Two Stories by Hanan al-Shaykh"
  (2002)

Origins: *Qazam* is of Lakonian (Northern Cau-
casian) origin.[568]

Facts: *Qazam* is an alternate spelling of *kazam*.

Qmʃbtʃ

Mystique: Inaudibly mumbled and whispered
over the centuries, many magic words inevitably
become corrupted and lose their original meanings. Yet that doesn't necessarily mean that they
lose their power. "Indeed, sometimes understanding the words gets in the way," says Patricia Monaghan. "For example, the use of Latin
for Catholic chants continued for more than a
thousand years after the language fell from use,
and many people living today can still attest to
the mind-altering and hypnotic effect of hearing magnificent Gregorian chants without the
mind being bothered by meaning."[569] We have
seen throughout this dictionary that a mystery
offers its own special kind of potency, and magic
words have come to be considered efficacious to
the degree that they *are* strange and incomprehensible: "Rashi, in the eleventh century, proved
his familiarity with this phenomenon when he
wrote: 'The sorcerer whispers his charms, and
doesn't understand what they are or what they
mean, but . . . the desired effect is produced only
by such incantations.'"[570] *Qmʃbtʃ*, like the similarly incomprehensible *Hfuhruhurr*, is a testament
to the potency of mumbled syllables that carry a
powerful mystery.

Origins: This magic word is featured in the
computer role-playing game "Gorasul: The Legacy of the Dragon" (2001).

Quandog Quandoggli

Origins: This magic phrase was coined by
A.R.R.R. Roberts for his humorous novel *The
Soddit* (2003), a send-up of *The Hobbit*.

Variations and Incantations: Qua-aa-andoggli
"'Qua-aa-andoggli,' said Gandef, putting the
word through a strange musical contortion,
starting warbling and high and dropping to a
baritone for the final syllable."
—A.R.R.R. Roberts, *The Soddit* (2003)

---

568 Alexander Lubotsky and Robert Beekes, *Indo-
European Etymological Dictionary* (2004)

569 *Goddess Path* (2004)

570 Joshua Trachtenberg, *Jewish Magic and Superstition*
(1939)

Quid Pro Quo

(see also *diggi daggi, shurry murry, horum harum, lirum larum, rowdy mowdy, giri gari, posito, besti basti, saron froh, fatto matto, quid pro quo*)

Quid pro pro. . . . those three magic words.
—Bob Norman, "Corruption and Nothingness" (2003)

Meanings:

- Equality in exchange
- This for that

Origins: *Quid pro quo* is a Latin phrase.

In Literature: Mozart, *Bastien und Bastienne* (1768)

- -

Qwertyuiop Asdfghjkl Zxcvbnm

QWERTYUIOP. Probably, I thought, a spell.
—Ken MacLeod, *The Sky Road* (1999)

Meanings: Euphemism
"Shut the QWERTYUIOP up!" "Get the ASDF-GHJKL: out of here!"
—Brendan B. Read, *Home Workplace* (2004)

Origins: These magic words, "from which all others are made,"[571] come from the standard typewriter keyboard's three rows of letters.

Facts: The first e-mail message ever sent, composed by Ray Tomlinson in 1971, was "QWERTYUIOP."[572]

Qwertyuiop is the name of a yellow Martian in *The Snake and the Fox* by Mary Haight (1999).

In Literature:

- "Years ago, he showed her the keyboard's three magic words: QWERTYUIOP, ASDFGHJKL, ZXCVBNM from which all others are made. *Those three words are all you need, kiddo.*"
  —Andrew Lewis Conn, *P: A Novel* (2003)

- "'Qwertyuiop,' Finn whispered, surveying the landscape's rising dark cubist pyres."
  —Andrew Lewis Conn, *P: A Novel* (2003)

R

- -

Rabbit Cadabra

(see also *abracadabra*)

"Rabbits!" At that word,
that magic word, she revived.
—Virginia Woolf, "Lappin and Lapinova,"
A Haunted House and Other Short Stories (1938)

Facts: This phrase brings the classic magician's white bunny into the famous magic word *abracadabra*. The hare is a traditional Trickster archetype in folklore.

Rabbit-Cadabra is a picture book for children, featuring a vampire rabbit and characters from the *Bunnicula* series of books by James Howe (1993).

---

571 Andrew Lewis Conn, *P: A Novel* (2003)

572 Leonard Stern, *Guiness World Records Mad Libs* (2004)

In Literature: "Jack . . . waved his hand over the magic jellybeans. 'Presto! Chango!' he said. Nothing happened. He tried again. 'Rabbit Cadabra!' Still nothing happened."
—Joan Holub, *Jack and the Jellybeanstalk* (2002)

Ranokoli

Meaning: The Great Spirit of Forgiveness

In Literature: "[T]he chief invited a great council and organized the Society of the Magic Word. Every member promised that whenever the greeting 'Boneka' were given him, he would smile and bow and answer, 'Ranokoli.' The greeting meant 'Peace,' and the answer, 'I forgive.' Then, one by one, the law-giver called his councillors [sic] before him, and to each he said: 'The Great Spirit is in this greeting. I defy you to hear it and keep a sober face.' Then he said 'Boneka,' and the man would try to resist the influence of the spirit, but soon smiled in spite of himself, amid the laughter of the tribe, and said 'Ranokoli.' Thereafter, when a quarrel arose between two people, an outsider, approaching, would greet them with the magic word, and immediately they would bow and smile, and answer, 'I forgive.'"
—Irving Bacheller, *Silas Strong* (1906)

Rantorp

Origins: *Rantorp* is a name of Scandinavian origin.

Facts: The magic word *rantorp* changes people into chairs in the play *General Gorgeous* by Michael McClure (1982).

Rata-Pata-Scata-Fata

Meanings: Nonsense, gobbledygook
—Phillis Gershator, *Rata-Pata-Scata-Fata: A Caribbean Story* (2005)

Origins: Of Caribbean origin, *Rata-pata-scata-fata* is "an old-time Virgin Islands way of talking nonsense—Caribbean gobbledygook. It might be imitation Spanish, since the Islands are close to Puerto Rico, or perhaps it comes from one of the many West African languages that influenced local English Creole. At one time, there were sixteen African languages spoken in St. Thomas alone!"[573]

Facts: *Rata pata* means "leg of a rat" in Spanish.

In Literature: "What if I close my eyes and say a magic word, like *rata-pata-scata-fata*, three times?"
—Phillis Gershator, *Rata-Pata-Scata-Fata: A Caribbean Story* (2005)

Rat-Atar

Facts: This magic word (a palindrome) is suggested by professional magician John Mulholland.

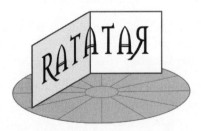

Figure 32. A palindromic magic word like *rat-atar* reads the same backwards.

----

573 Phillis Gershator, *Rata-Pata-Scata-Fata: A Caribbean Story* (2005)

Common Magician's Applications: "Here is a loop of string—or rather, two pieces of string tied together here, and here, with knots. Of course, what we want is one neat and knotless string and that is where magic comes in. In order to join the two pieces of string together, it is necessary to have nice, fresh, clean cut ends and these scissors will do that. A snip and one knot is out of the way. Put those fresh ends together, say the magic word 'rat-atar,' blow on the knot, and we have one fine, straight, knotless piece of string."[574]

Recipe

Origins: *Recipe* is from a Latin word meaning "receive."

Meanings:

- Set of instructions
- Something likely to lead to a particular outcome

In Literature: "They inscribe upon a sheet of paper, under the magic word 'Recipe,' the names of certain medicines, whereupon the Apothecary's assistant takes his mortar and pounds out of the wretched patient whatever health may still be left in him." —Archibald Cockren, *Alchemy Rediscovered and Restored* (1941)

Reduce, Reuse, Recycle

Facts: These are professional magician Steve Trash's magic words.

Reducio

Origins: From the Middle English *redusen*, *Reducio* means "diminish."

In Literature: *Reducio* is a spell for returning an enlarged object to its normal size in *Harry Potter and the Goblet of Fire* by J.K. Rowling (2000).

Relashio

Origins: *Relashio* is from an Italian word meaning "to release" (*rilascio*).

In Literature: *Relashio* is a spell for conjuring heat or sparks from a wand in *Harry Potter and the Goblet of Fire* by J.K. Rowling (2000).

Release

In Literature: "Now, say a magic word, such as 'release,' and watch the cards fall to the table." —Colin Francome and Simon Frost, *Magic* (2002)

Resurgam

Origins: *Resurgam* is a Latin word meaning "I shall rise again."

In Literature: "From the Potomac to the Rio Grande, from the grass-covered prairies of the West to the Atlantic shores, over every desolate hill and valley, on every wasted homestead, upon every ruined hearthstone, is written as with an

---

574 John Mulholland, *Mulholland's Book of Magic* (1963)

angel's pen, in letters of fire, the magic word RESURGAM!"
—Sallie Brock Putnam, *Richmond During the War* (1867)

Rethgual

Facts: "Remember that 'Laughter' spelled backwards is 'rethgual.' It means absolutely nothing, but it just might cheer you up."[575]

In Literature: "Now I shall release you by saying the magic word, 'Rethgual,' backwards. And that word is 'Laughter!' And, zap, the minute he said 'Laughter,' the magic word spelled backwards, the spell was broken and the golden goose and the farmer and the fisherman and the old lady went on their way."
—Stan Paregien, "The Magic Word" (1993)

Rhubarb

Mystique: In *Easy to Remember* (2000), William Zinsser counts *rhubarb* among his list of "magical words" with powerful connotations.

Facts: *Rhubarb* is the name of a magician's rabbit in *Prophet Annie* by Ellen Recknor (2000).

Ridas Talimol

Origins: *Ridas Talimol* are antiquated magic words for "commanding the elements." This phrase comes from an Egyptian book of magical talismans entitled *Treasure of the Old Man of the Pyramids*, "translated from the Language of the Magi" in the eighteenth century.[576]

Common Magician's Applications: Fire or water effects. When a magician uses magic words like *Ridas Talimol* (and/or the *Ridas Talimol* talisman) while summoning fire or controlling water, he brings an air of mystery to the illusion.

Figure 33. Depicting two sphinx-like creatures holding a font, this enigmatic "command the elements" talisman has an occult appearance but not an infernal purpose. It is based upon the research of Arthur Edward Waite in *The Book of Ceremonial Magic* (1913).

Riddikulus

Origins: *Riddikulus* is from a Latin word meaning "laughable" (*ridiculum*).

In Literature: *Riddikulus* is a spell for inciting laughter in *Harry Potter and the Prisoner of Azkaban* by J.K. Rowling (1999).

---

575 George Gilbert, "Originally Speaking" (2004)

576 Arthur Edward Waite, *The Book of Ceremonial Magic* (1913)

Ringcadabra

(see *cadabra* and *abracadabra*)

Common Magician's Applications: Linking. For example: "Ask your volunteer to pull on the ends of the laces and you say the magic word, 'Ringcadabra.' Let go of the knot in your right hand. Continue to hold the pencil in your left hand. The rings will seem to go right through the laces."[577]

Rinky-Dinky-Doo

In Literature: "[W]hen I was a youngster we used to go fishing and we would give out of bait every once in a while. Without bait, we used to say some magic words like 'rinky-dinky-doo, look out little fish, I am going to catch you,' and then we would spit on the hook."
—Reuben L. Johnson, quoted in United States Congress, Senate, Agriculture and Forestry Committee, *Feed Grain Act of 1963*

Rla-Gha-Has-Tep

Fearlessly say Rla-Gha-Has-Tep.
—"Shadow of the Comet Walthrough,"
The Spoiler.com (2008)

Facts: These are magic words featured in the computer game "Shadow of the Comet" (1994).

Rooglio-Fooglio-Vungerty-Vee

In Literature: "[Bastinda] transferred the wand to her right hand, and slowly pointed it toward the floor, chanting, '*Rooglio-fooglio-vungerty-vee.*'"
—Sherwood Smith, *The Emerald Wand of Oz* (2005)

Rotundus Reversus Double Plus

(see also *circulus rotundus*)

Origins: This magic phrase includes the Latin words *rotundus*, "round," and *reversus*, "to turn back."

Common Magician's Applications: Linking rings, as described in Janice Eaton Kilby's *Book of Wizard Magic* (2003).

Rumplesnitz

In Literature: "It can't be too short or it wouldn't be potent. . . . Here's a splendid word—'Rumplesnitz.' Do you think you can learn that?"
—Heywood Broun, *The Fifty-First Dragon* (1985)

Rumpelstiltskin

Magic words—abracadabra, Rumpelstiltskin.
—Richard Eyre,
Teaching Your Children Values (1993)

Origins: *Rumpelstiltskin* originated in a German folktale about a magical little man who has gold

577 Loris Bree, *Kids' Magic Secrets* (2003)

thread spun from straw. The secret of his true name is the source of his power.[578]

Facts: There is an "ancient tradition known as word magic: in folk tales (for example 'Rumpelstiltskin'), in scripture (the naming of the animals in Genesis), and generally, in the 'discovery' and naming of lands and even in the baptism of children; to give a name to (or to learn the name of) an artery, a nerve, a lymphatic duct is to have a sense of familiarity, perhaps even ownership or control."[579]

Variations and Incantations: Rumplestiltskin

In Literature:

- "There has to be a magic word, Rumpelstiltskin, something!"
  —Patricia, "Fare thee Well," *emxc.org*

- "'Should have said the magic word,' the girl said as she passed. ... Benedict engaged his mouth before thinking. 'Yeah. Rumplestiltskin.' Her forehead creased in a mock frown. 'Gorgonzola.' And with that she was gone, through the door and out into the street. Benedict stood and watched her disappear, ecstatic, heartbroken and relieved all at the same time. *Rumplestiltskin? What were you thinking? Jeez. Way to impress. Yeah, but it did the trick, dint it?*"
  —Matthew Collins, *Death by Lingerie* (2003)

- "It's a little like Rumpelstiltskin: if we wait for someone else to come along and wave a magic wand, naming us an artist, ('Ah- hah! You there! You are an artist!'), we may wait a terribly long time."
  —Julia Cameron, *The Vein of Gold* (1996)

- "It's the secret belief most of us carry forward from childhood, that we might have in us somewhere the capacity, like Rumpelstiltskin, to rupture and transmogrify out of a sheer tantrum of desire."
  —Barbara Kingsolver, *High Tide in Tucson* (1995)

Rune

The "flame-word rune" is the Word of the higher Inspiration, Intuition, Revelation which is the highest attainment of Thought.
—Sri Aurobindo, *Letters on Yoga, Vol. III* (1988)

Mystique: It is doubtful that any word captures the spirit of "esoteric knowledge"[580] more than *rune*. *Rune* is a primitive relic, a talisman with something of the sacred about it.[581] "The very word *rune* conjures up magical associations in the word hoard of Old English and Germanic languages."[582] "As a magical word, *rune* must be understood from self-created viewpoints, and as such its true 'meaning' cannot be communicated through profane, natural speech. As a magical word it is 'whispered in our ear' by the Odhinn [the god of poetry] within."[583]

578 S. I. Hayakawa, *Language in Thought and Action: Fifth Edition* (1991)

579 Albert Howard Carter, *First Cut* (1997)

580 Paul Rhys Mountfort, *Nordic Runes: Understanding, Casting, and Interpreting the Ancient Viking Oracle* (2003)

581 Mark Osteen, in his critical introduction to Don DeLillo's *White Noise* (1998)

582 Paul Rhys Mountfort, *Nordic Runes: Understanding, Casting, and Interpreting the Ancient Viking Oracle* (2003)

583 Edred Thorsson, *Runelore* (1987)

Meanings:

- Consultation
—Paul Rhys Mountfort, *Nordic Runes: Understanding, Casting, and Interpreting the Ancient Viking Oracle* (2003)

- Holy secret
—Willow Arlena, *Tarot of Transformation* (2003)

- Incantation
—Paul Rhys Mountfort, *Nordic Runes: Understanding, Casting, and Interpreting the Ancient Viking Oracle* (2003)

- Magical binding
—Edred Thorsson, *Runelore* (1987)

- Mystery
—Jean Marie Stine, *Empowering Your Life with Runes* (2004)

- Secret script
—Robin Lumsden, *The Allgemeine-SS* (1993)

- Whisper
—Nigel Pennick, *Magical Alphabets* (1992)

Origins: Of uncertain etymology, the word *rune* is found only in Germanic and Celtic languages.[584]

Facts: "The word *rune* denotes a poem or a piece of a poem. . . . Incidentally, it might be the root for the word *tune*."[585]

The word *rune* refers to an ancient writing system. "[T]wo Swedish runestones call their alphabet 'of divine origin.'"[586]

In Literature: "Saaski could feel her eyes stretching wider and wider. The word *rune* was echoing and re-echoing in her mind, filling all its spaces."
—Eloise McGraw, *The Moorchild* (1996)

Rushety Gushety Lickety-Split

In Literature: Deborah Hautzig, *Little Witch's Bad Dream* (2000)

Ruth

Origins: *Ruth* comes from the Hebrew *Rut* and means "compassion," "friend," or "mercy."

Facts: Ruth is the name of a Moabite woman from Jewish and Christian scripture.

In Literature: "'Ruth.' He had not thought a simple sound could be so beautiful. It delighted his ear, and he grew intoxicated with the repetition of it. 'Ruth.' It was a talisman, a magic word to conjure with. Each time he murmured it, her face shimmered before him, suffusing the foul wall with a golden radiance. This radiance did not stop at the wall. It extended on into infinity, and through its golden depths his soul went questing after hers. The best that was in him was out in splendid flood. The very thought of her ennobled and purified him, made him better, and made him want to be better."
—Jack London, *Martin Eden* (1909)

---

584 *Ibid.*

585 A.J. Drew, *A Wiccan Bible* (2003)

586 Heather O'Donoghue, *Old Norse-Icelandic Literature* (2004)

S

Sabbac

Facts: *Sabbac* is a magic word from the comic book *Outsiders* (2004) that transforms a villain into demon-form. Like *Shazam*, *Sabbac* is an acronym. It stands for the names of various demonic lords: Satan, Any, Belial, Beelzebub, Asmodeus, and Craeteis, endowing the speaker with the powers of each of these creatures.

Sabbac is the *Star Wars* equivalent to poker. In a game of sabbac, Han Solo wins the Millenium Falcon from Lando Calrissian.

Sabbac is an angelic name summoned in "The Conjuration of Thursday" for the purpose of obtaining love, merriment, pacification of strife, appeasement of enemies, healing of disease, and recovery of losses.[587]

Sadyk

Meanings:

- Friend
  —Nicholas Clapp, *Sheba* (2001)

- Truthful

Origins: *Sadyk* is an Arabic word.

Facts: *Sadyk* (also spelled *Sadak*) was the Phoenician god of justice,[588] father of the mysterious fertility demons known as the Cabiri and Dioscuri.

In Tibetan Buddhism, the *sadak* are deities dwelling on the Earth.[589]

In the film *The Blue Wand*, a thirteen-year-old boy named James asks his Grandfather about a tree branch displayed on the mantelpiece. "His Grandfather explains that it is a magic wand he bought in a market in Cairo when he was a young sailor on one of his many trips to the Middle East during the war. To make the wand work he must say the Arabic word of SADYK, which means friend." When James tries saying the magic word, "The wand starts humming and glows with a strange blue light. . . . A blue laser-like light shoots towards the wall and a little blue spot starts growing until the whole wall is a window to another world, with its edges glowing blue. Through the window James can see the trees of a forest through a fine mist. James grabs the wand and . . . crosses through the window to the forest on the other side. Here he is greeted by an Old man and some villagers, all dressed in old-fashioned Arabian clothes. They hail James as the young prince who has come to free them from the evil wizard who rules the Crystal City."[590]

Variations and Incantations:

- Sadak
- Sadik

Safety First

Facts: *Safety first* are the magic words professional magician Johnny Magic uses during his touring magic show that counsels children about peer pressure, gun and fire safety, and drug abuse.[591]

---

587 Lewis de Claremont, *The Ancient's Book of Magic* (1940)

588 George Raywood Devitt, *Home Lover's Library* (1906)

589 Reginald A. Ray, *Indestructible Truth* (2000)

590 Lino Omoboni, *BlueWand.co.uk* (2005)

591 Rhonda Rosner, "Amazing Magic Messages," *The Daily Record* (2001)

Salabim

(see *sim sala bim*)

Facts: *Salabim* is the name of a site in ancient Palestine, "on the road between Scythopolis and Neapolis," as noted by Saint Jerome.[592]

Samboobia

Facts: This is professional magician "Dandy Dan" Dyer's phrase for making magic happen.

Saritap Pernisox Ottarim

Origins: *Saritap Pernisox Ottarim* are antiquated magic words for opening locks. The phrase comes from an Egyptian book of magical talismans entitled *Treasure of the Old Man of the Pyramids*, "translated from the Language of the Magi" in the eighteenth century.[593]

Figure 34. Emblazoned with astrological symbolism, this lock-picking talisman has an occult appearance but not an infernal purpose. It is based upon the research of Arthur Edward Waite in *The Book of Ceremonial Magic* (1913).

Facts: These magic words were believed to grant the speaker the ability to "open all locks at a touch, whatever precautions have been taken to secure them,"[594] including the doors of prisons and fortified castles.[595]

Common Magician's Applications: Escapes. When used as a prop in the form of an ancient talisman, *Saritap Pernisox Ottarim* can lend an ancient Egyptian mystique to any escape routine.

Sator Arepo Tenet Opera Rotas

Meanings:

- The creator holds the working of the spheres [cycles of life] in his hands
  —Suzanne Alejandre, "The Sator Square" (2005)

- The farmer, Arepo, keeps the world rolling
  —Wolfram Research (1999)

- The sower, Arepo, holds the wheels with care
  —*Wikipedia.com* (2005)

Origins: This palindromic ancient charm (possibly untranslatable) dates back to the first century and was discovered as graffiti in the buried city of Pompeii. (Incidentally, *Pompeii* itself is a "centuries-old magic word."[596]) The charm's possible origin in Alexandria, Egypt (between 30 BCE and 50 CE) "best explains its wide popularity in the extant Coptic amulets, papyri,

---

592 Susan Weingarten, *The Saint's Saints* (2005)

593 Arthur Edward Waite, *The Book of Ceremonial Magic* (1913)

594 *Ibid.*

595 *The Black Pullet: Science of Magical Talismans*, an eighteenth-century treatise on necromancy and conjuration.

596 Walter Benjamin, *Reflections* (1978)

and ostraca, coming from Egypt, Nubia and Ethiopia."[597]

Facts: Written as a "magic square," the sentence reads the same left to right, bottom to top, top to bottom, and backwards.

**SATOR
AREPO
TENET
OPERA
ROTAS**

Figure 35. The famous Pompeiian magic square.

Saulem

Meanings: Asked for; desired.

Origins: *Saulem* is the Latin form of the Hebrew name *Saul*, as in the Old Testament. *Saulem* appears as a charm in the Medieval tale "The Moonbeam" (a.k.a. "The Foolish Thief") written by Pedro Alfonso sometime after 1106.[598] The author claimed to have translated his work from the Arabic. His story is "[p]art of the vast tradition of 'wisdom literature' going back to ancient Egypt, Mesopotamia, and India, [consisting] of ethical instruction, imparted in the form of philosophical disquisitions, maxims, and illustrative stories."[599]

In Literature: "[F]irst I climb up to a roof, then I seize a moonbeam and immediately repeat seven times the magic word *Saulem*. Thanks to

this extraordinarily marvelous word I'm able to descend to the garden on a moonbeam, I enter, and carry away everything of value that I find in the house. I return at once to the moonbeam and, uttering the word *Saulem* seven times, I go up with everything and take it away with me."
—Pedro Alfonso, "The Foolish Thief," *First Spanish Reader*, edited by Angel Flores (1964)

Scrumpledoggins

Common Magician's Applications: Production. For example, Master illusionist Uncle Dave "makes you shout the magic word, 'Scrumpledoggins,' to get the quarter" he produces from behind your ear.[600]

Secret

In Literature:

- "[Y]ou will . . . have the privilege of responding to a magic word: Secret!"
  —Lloyd H. Whitling, *The Complete Universe of Memes* (2002)

- "She had said the magic word . . . Secret!"
  —Wallace Neal Briggs, *Riverside Remembered* (1992)

Sedle Sedelie See

Facts: *Sedle Sedelie See, What Are Thee?* is a phrase used in conjunction with clapping three times for activating a magic slate in *Oral Storytelling and Teaching Mathematics* by Michael Schiro (2004).

---

597 Miroslav Marcovich, *Studies in Graeco-Roman Religions and Gnosticism* (1988)

598 Stanley Appelbaum, *Medieval Tales and Stories* (2000)

599 *Ibid.*

600 Justin Racz, *50 Relatives Worse Than Yours* (2005)

Seem-Salamay Foofoo

In Literature: "You want a miracle or what? You want Seem-Salamay Foofoo and Abracadabra? Then go to a magician."
—Rohinton Mistry, *Such a Long Journey* (1992)

- -

Selah

Mystique: "Is there anything more thrilling and awe-inspiring than the calm before the crashing of the storm, or the strange quiet that seems to fall upon nature before some supernatural phenomenon or disastrous upheaval? And is there anything that can touch our hearts like the *power of stillness?*"[601] *Selah* is that magical moment before a miracle occurs. It's that breathless instant of anticipation, of suspended disbelief. *Selah* is the pause in music, the stillness in the dance, the calligraphic circled space—emptiness enhanced. "Selah is a very old word. A mysterious and magical word. . . . But it is the best kind of word—because it can . . . mean whatever the speaker *wishes* it to mean."[602]

Meanings:

- Amen
  —James Stuart Bell, *The Complete Idiot's Guide to the Bible* (2003)

- Blessing
  —John McKinna, *Shark Lake* (2001)

- Crescendo
  —Zondervan, *New American Standard Bible* (2002)

- Freedom
  —Virginia Hamilton, *The House of Dies Drear* (1996)

- Pause
  "Is there any note in all the music of the world as mighty as the grand pause? Is there any word in the Psalms more eloquent than the word 'Selah,' meaning pause?"
  —L.B. Cowman, *Streams in the Desert* (1997)

- Quiet
  —Louie Giglio, *Facedown* (2004)

- "So be it"
  —John McKinna, *Shark Lake* (2001)

- "Strike up the band"
  —James Stuart Bell, *The Complete Idiot's Guide to the Bible* (2003)

- "Think calmly"
  —Joyce Meyer, *In Pursuit of Peace* (2004)

- True
  —John McKinna, *Shark Lake* (2001)

Origins: The "imperfectly understood" word *selah* is ubiquitous in the book of *Psalms.*[603] It appears over seventy times throughout the *Psalms,* "most likely referring to an instrumental interlude between verses or sections of vocal music."[604]

Selah is a Chinook word meaning "still water."[605]

Facts: The word *selah* appears on Kabalistic talismans as part of a special prayer "similar in nature but not identical to types of invocations."[606]

---

601 L.B. Cowman, *Streams in the Desert* (1997)
602 John McKinna, *Shark Lake* (2001)

603 Michael Coogan, *The New Oxford Annotated NRSV Bible with the Apocrypha* (2001)
604 Rory Noland, *The Heart of the Artist* (1999)
605 Scott Rutherford, *Insight Guide: Seattle* (2003)
606 Donald Michael Kraig, *Modern Magick* (1997)

Serpens Aut Draco Qui Caudam Devoravit

Meanings: Ouroboros of wisdom that protects and encircles everything

Origins: *Serpens aut draco qui caudam devoravit* is a Latin phrase meaning "snakes or dragons who swallow their tails."

In Literature: "*Serpens aut draco qui caudam devoravit*. They guard the treasures: the tree of knowledge in the Garden of Eden, the apples of the Hesperides, the golden fleece ... They're the serpents or dragons that the ancient Egyptians painted in a circle, with their tail in their mouth to indicate that they came from a single thing and were self-sufficient. Sleepless guardians, proud and wise. Hermetic dragons that kill the unworthy and allow themselves to be seduced only by one who has fought according to the rules. Guardians of the lost word: the magic formula that opens eyes and makes one the equal of God."
—Arturo Perez-Reverte, *The Club Dumas* (1996)

Figure 36. Ouroboros is an ancient Gnostic symbol.

Sesame

(see also *open sesame* and *simsim*)

You in your vest of Sesames and Ali-Babas.
—Jacob Glatstein (Yankev Glatshteyn),
"We the Wordproletariat" (1937),
Jewish American Literature (2001)

Mystique: "[I]t is a seed, a spiritual food, a magic word which opens a long-hidden, underground treasure-house."[607]

Origins: *Sesame* is "related to Egyptian *seshemu*, 'sexual intercourse.' The hieroglyphic sign of *seshemu* was a penis inserted into an arched yoni-symbol. Every ancient culture used some form of sexual symbolism for the idea of man-entering-paradise."[608]

Variations and Incantations: Open sesame "Sesame. Shall we say, 'Open Sesame!?'"
—Audry Couto McClelland, *Preconception Plain & Simple* (2004)

In Literature:

- "This magical word ... is the *sesame* of life, for it unveils for all to see fabulous treasures, captivating perspectives, extraordinary worlds—and what is even more, pleasures, joys, in short happiness!"
  —Susan K. Besse, *Restructuring Patriarchy* (1996)

- "[T]he diploma that opens the Sesame of success and wealth."
  —Katharine Washburn, *Dumbing Down* (1997)

---

607 George Painter, *Marcel Proust: A Biography* (1865), quoted in *Frank Lloyd Wright: A Biography* by Meryle Secrest (1992)

608 Barbara G. Walker, *Woman's Encyclopedia of Myths and Secrets* (1983)

Shabukalakazam

(see *allakazam*)

In Literature: "'Say the magic word . . .'
'Shabukalakazam?'"
—Sa'ar Chasm, "Five-Minute 'Body Parts'"
(2003)

Shallakazam

(see *allakazam*)

Variations and Incantations: Shalakazam
—Marek Kohn, "Sir Teo's Quest" (2000)

In Literature: "'Anybody know any incantations?' Leo shrugged. 'Abracadabra? Shallakazam?'"
—Charles Harrington Elster, *Tooth and Nail: A
Novel Approach to the New SAT* (1994)

Sharing

In Literature: "Sharing is a splendid, special
thing . . . That's our magic word!"
—Mal Leicester, *Stories for Classroom and Assembly*
(2003)

Shazam

To rub the golden lamp and say the magic word
'Shazzam!' is to force the genie
to do your bidding.
—Dwight Pryor, "Patterns and Principles of
Jewish Prayer" (2004)

Mystique: Not every magic word comes with
a built-in puff of smoke. With *shazam* comes all
the power of a lightning bolt. When spoken, this
mysterious, musical word takes flight as if blown
by the wind, with a hard *shhh*, then sizzles with
the electrical *zzz* before slamming home with
the final *am*. *Shazam* is an entire special effects
package: a flash of light, a thunderous clap, a bil-
lowing cloud, and ripples of astonishment in its
wake. *Shazam* so captures the sense of astonishment that it's popularly used as an expression of
wonder (much like "holy smoke!"). Rich in history, its evocative Arabian flavor enchants us like
a cloud of swirling incense, sparking our imagination with visions of magic lamps, conjured
genies,[609] and wishes granted. But the word is so
profoundly powerful that it has come to be associated with virtually any act of magic with a "wow"
factor, any truly "electrifying moment."[610] Like
that scent of pine that immediately transports you
back to that cabin in the woods from childhood,[611]
shazam instantly recalls our primal sense of wonder. Indeed, "a magic word—*Shazam!* [might]
cause time to run backwards."[612]

Meanings:

- Aha!
  "'Shazam!' Cullins shouted. His face almost
  touched the computer screen. 'She was hidden in the wrong directory. I don't know
  how that happened, but here it is.'"
  —Ian Smith, *The Blackbird Papers* (2004)

- Appear, materialize
  "He just appeared one day. Shazam. A boy
  from another planet, you know?"
  —Don DeLillo, *Underworld* (1998)

----

609 "[I was] expecting a whole-hog genie to shoot
back out, *shazam*."—Jamie Gilson, *Hello, My Name
is Scrambled Eggs* (1985)
610 Tom Stoppard, *Dogg's Hamlet* (1980). As Margaret
Weis puts its, "The words of magic flame in the
mind" (*Dragons of Autumn Twilight* [1984]).
611 Mari Messer, *Pencil Dancing* (2001)
612 Lucie Armitt, *Contemporary Women's Fiction and the
Fantastic* (2000)

"[T]he decrypted message will suddenly appear. Shazam! That is way too cool."
—Chey Cobb, *Cryptography for Dummies* (2004)

"You'd say a few words, shoot the shit, and shazam! He'd like, materialize."
—G.H. Ephron, *Delusion* (2002)

- Astonishment
"I expect some expression of astonishment—maybe not a Gomer Pyle 'Shazam,' but something—but I should have known better."
—Greg Iles, *Dead Sleep* (2001)

"Shazzam! What an act!"
—John F. Kavanaugh, *The Word Engaged* (1997)

"Shazam! Are you telling me I can sit at my computer, compose verse, and feel meditative effects?"
—Jeffrey P. Davidson, *The Complete Idiot's Guide to Managing Stress* (1999)

"[T]he world looked amazingly brilliant, every line and shape perfectly defined. 'Shazam,' Bobby said, and laughed shakily. 'What just happened?'"
—Stephen King, *Hearts in Atlantis* (1999)

"Wow! Shazam and alakazam!"
—L.D. Brodsky, *Yellow Bricks* (1999)

- Bejesus
"He looks berserk. He's scaring the shazzam out of me."
—Terry Sunbord, *Nebula Express* (2004)

- Change, transform
"[G]ive Uncle Sam time to slip off and shazam himself into the President."
—Robert Coover, *The Public Burning* (1977)

"Shazam! With a wave of her bone she could turn herself into anything she wanted."
—Shelly Jackson, "Bone," *Juncture* (2003)•
Charm, luck

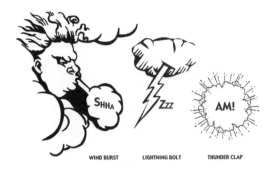

Figure 37. *Shazam* is an entire special effects package.

"[T]he team waited for him to rekindle that spark that'd lit the way all season. . . . Again and again Starks would carefully place his toes on the three-point line, as he always does, and let the ball fly, looking for that magic *shazam*."
—Ethan Hawke, *Ash Wednesday* (2002)

- Confusion
"Clearing their ear, rubbing their eyes, and scratching their heads with confusion, the boys said . . . 'Shazam!'"
—Doug Fields, *Spontaneous Melodramas 2* (2001)

- Conjuring
"Yefim directs a *shazam*-like wave of his hands in her direction. She says the pain is gone."
—Dan Zevin, *The Day I Turned Uncool* (2002)

"Shazam! Conjuring more storage space . . ."
—Lori Baird, *Cut the Clutter and Stow the Stuff* (2002)

- Curse word (euphemism)
"[T]he only way to stem the blurt of bad words is to sterilize your own speech. Before it's too late, get back in touch with 'Drat!' 'Shucks!' 'Shazam!' 'Golly!' 'Fiddlesticks!' and 'Gee-Willikers!'"
—Walter Roark, *Keeping the Baby Alive Till Your Wife Gets Home* (2001)

"I was immediately distracted by my audience scan because, holy shazam, was that Liam standing at the escalator on the second level of the mall in front of The Limited?"
—Rachel Cohn, *Pop Princess* (2004)

"What a shi—shazam of a day."
—Carole Nelson Douglas, *Catnap* (1992)

- Disappear, vanish
"Nobody said, 'Get out of here,' it was just shazam and they were gone."
—Patty Duke, *Call Me Anna* (1988)

"So, with a sick brother, a pigtailed beloved who would have liked to shazam me from the earth's face, a mother distracted by bills and lack of love for her husband, I spent much time alone."
—Geoffrey Wolff, *Duke of Deception* (1979)

"It was like a magician saying 'shazam,' suddenly you disappeared."
—William Coughlin, *Death Penalty* (1992)

"Shazzam! It disappears right before your eyes!"
—Tamson Weston, *Hey, Pancakes!* (2003)

"You want to disappear, Mr. James—shazam. I personally sprinkle you with pixie dust."
—Chuck Logan, *The Big Law* (1998)

"[J]ust like that, poof, click, do you hear me snapping my fingers, shazam, obliteration, nothingness, the void."
—Gerald Locklin, *Candy Bars* (2000)

- Disbelief
"Dex couldn't believe what he was seeing. His jaw dropped. 'Shazam!'"
—Kevin J. Anderson, *Sky Captain and the World of Tomorrow* (2004)

- Eureka
—David T. MacFarland, *Future Radio Programming Strategies* (1997)

"[T]he lucky scientist who finds [a self-replicating molecule in the laboratory]

would be able to cry, 'Shazam! I have created life!'"
—Christopher Wills, *The Spark of Life* (2000)

"Theories abound on how life began, but I cling happily to the one in which a bolt of lightning strikes a soup of chemicals sloshing about in the hollow of a primordial rock. SHAZAM! A microscopic dot of life is created. Call it Elmer."
—Arthur Watterson Hoppe, *Having a Wonderful Time* (1995)

- Explosion, flash of light
"[M]y mate got struck down in a thunderstorm . . . a bizarre accident . . . a bolt from the blue, zig-zagged right on to the perforated snout of his Mickey Mouse gas mask. He was delivering five of them at the bacteriological research children's party—entering into the spirit of it—when, shazam!—it was an electrifying moment, left his nose looking more like Donald Duck and his ears like they popped out of a toaster."
—Tom Stoppard, *Dogg's Hamlet* (1980)

"Shazam! Out of nowhere, just like that: detonation of the dream deferred."
—Kathryn Bertine, *All the Sundays Yet to Come* (2003)

"You will also need changes in a flash, Shazam! or in a shower of sparks!"
—Carol Emshwiller, *Verging on the Pertinent* (1989)

- Flash of insight
"[Creativity is characterized] as the 'shazzam!' or flash of insight that leads to novel and valuable products and services."
—Cameron M. Ford, *Creative Action in Organizations* (1995)

- Inspiration, enlightenment
"[Brian Wilson] was out to move the very soul of teenage America, to create music so passionate, so majestic that when you turned

on your radio—shazam—Instant Epiphany. And inspiration was everywhere."
—Nick Kent, *The Dark Stuff* (1994)

"Shazam! Suddenly, lights go on and bells begin to clang."
—Donald Lussier, *Job Search Secrets* (1998)

- Instantly
"Babadahs puts the mala on you right off and—Shazzam! you're a Swami."
—Michael Aaron Rockland, *A Bliss Case* (1989)

"Then, *shazam*, they put out to sea."
—Tom Clancy, *Executive Orders* (1996)

"[T]hrow a steak in there and, *shazam!* an instant and ferocious fight."
—Raymond Coppinger, *Dogs* (2002)

"Not little by little, but—shazam!—all at once."
—Mari Messer, *Pencil Dancing* (2001)

- Look
"[P]ointing to the right, [he said,] 'Shazam!' He stopped on the shoulder, and we admired the scene. The Humboldt River, blue and full, was flowing toward us, with panes of white ice at its edges, sage and green meadow beside it, and dry russet uplands rising behind."
—John McPhee, *Annals of the Former World* (1981)

- Magic, act of
"Okay—*shazzam*, it's done!"
—Robert L. Voyles, *Ransom for Justice* (2000)

"Five minutes later, shazam! He was system manager."
—Clifford Stoll, *The Cuckoo's Egg* (1989)

- Magical powers
"With practice, he'll soon become a master [at hammering nails]. It's the next best thing to giving him the power of SHAZAM."
—Walter Browder, *101 Secrets a Good Dad Knows* (2000)

- Magic word
"The genie will pop out before you can say 'Shazam.'"
—Dan Anderson and Maggie Berman, *Sex Tips for Straight Women from a Gay Man* (1997)

- Mind-boggling
"[T]he world is going shazam."
—Norman Mailer, *Why Are We in Vietnam? A Novel* (1967)

- Nonsense
"Usually the words were some sort of nonsense like 'Shazam.' My magic words have turned out to be 'I don't know.'"
—Rachel Naomi Remen, *Kitchen Table Wisdom* (1996)

- Revive
"[T]he chairs begin to shake and lightning outside / Shazams you back to life."
—Frederick Seidel, *The Cosmos Trilogy* (2003)

- Solution
"'I need a *shazam*,' Jason said. 'A brilliant way out of my pickle.'"
—Herbert Benson, *The Breakout Principle* (2003)

Origins: This Arabic-sounding word likely dates back to the culture of ancient Egypt.[613]

Facts: Famously, *Shazam* is the trigger to transform the boy Billy Batson into the superhero Captain Marvel, as in the comic books. In the television series (1974–1977), the letters stand for the six elder gods and heroes who grant the powers: Solomon (wisdom), Hercules (strength), Achilles (courage), Zeus (power), Atlas (stamina), and Mercury (speed). However, in the comic book, Shazam is simply the name of a 3000-year-old Egyptian wizard who grants Billy Batson the power to transform. "I am old now," Shazam

613 Barbara Johnstone, *Discourse Analysis* (2002)

says; "You shall be my successor. Merely by speaking my name, you can become the strongest and mightiest man in the world—Captain Marvel!"[614] In the spirit of Captain Marvel, the word *shazam* connotes something coming to fruition or maturation: "Shazam, I'm a man. If not a man, at least a tall boy. Would you accept an enormous child?"[615]

"Shazzam" is the name of professional magician Blair Marshall's revue.

In the film *Bringing Down the House* (2003), when Eugene Levy sees Queen Latifah descending a staircase the only word he can utter is *shazzam*.

"Shazam" is TV character Gomer Pyle's favorite cry at anything out of the ordinary.[616]

In a *Monty Python's Flying Circus* comedy sketch, "Mrs. Shazam" is a character who doesn't realize that "exploding is a perfectly normal medical phenomenon."[617]

Talk show host Oprah Winfrey claims she yells *shazam!* when she is angry.[618]

Common Magician's Applications: Any act of conjuring.

Variations and Incantations:

- Acka shazam
  —Justin Martin, *150 Totally Terrific Writing Prompts* (1999)

- Alley shazam
  "Look! Magic! Alley shazam!"
  —Nevada Barr, *Track of the Cat* (1993)

- Mazam
  —Loris Bree, *Kids' Magic Secrets* (2003)

- Shazaam
  —Kathleen Eagle, *The Last Good Man* (2000)

- Shazaam alakazaam, abracadabra, hocus-pocus
  —Bruce Olds, *Bucking the Tiger* (2001)

- Shazoom
  —Terry Pratchett, "Imaginary Worlds, Real Stories," *Folklore* (2000)

- Shazzam
  —Martin Hegwood, *The Green-Eyed Hurricane* (2000)

In Literature:

- "Revolution reminded him of 'Shazzam,' a magical word."
  —Alan Lelchuk, *Brooklyn Boy* (1990)

- "The name written above the castle, across the sky in electric blue, was Shazzam."
  —Martin Hegwood, *The Green-Eyed Hurricane* (2000)

- "I remember a lightning bolt shooting straight to my crotch. ShaZAM!"
  —Megan McCafferty, *Sloppy Firsts* (2001)

- "Science fiction movies often use the attention-getting command 'Computer!' to wake up a machine so it pays attention to what the human will say next. That's not very smart, because the word 'computer' is part of everyday language. If I'm telling my wife at dinner about a thunderstorm that afternoon and say, 'As soon as the lightning struck, the computer shut down,' my home machine would take note and might faithfully shut down itself and all the other computers in the house! That's why I prefer

614 John Clute, *The Encyclopedia of Fantasy* (1997)

615 Neil Simon, quoted in *Neil Simon: A Casebook* by Gary Konas (1997)

616 Brendon Lemon, *Last Night* (2002)

617 Graham Chapman, *The Complete Monty Python's Flying Circus: All the Words* (1989)

618 James V. O'Connor, *Cuss Control* (2000)

the prompting word 'Shazam,' because it's unlikely to occur in normal conversation."
—Michael L. Dertouzos, *The Unfinished Revolution* (2001)

- From Gregory Corso, "Power," *Mindfield: New and Selected Poems* (1989):

  O but there are times SHAZAM is not enough
  There is a brutality in the rabbit.

- "After all, the Egyptian wizard didn't give Billy Batson a magic word in English or Latin. It was a private word in a private language. . . . Michael knew that the magic word was the same as the name of the wizard: *Shazam!*"
  —Pete Hamill, *Snow in August* (1998)

- "'André, Elise,' he said. 'Hold out one hand and make a wish.' Mr. Balzini moved his hands in quick circles. Then he smacked them together and a stream of glistening salt flowed from his left hand, until he had made a pile in each of our palms. 'Shazam, shazam,' he said and opened the door."
  —Ian Wallace, *The Man Who Walked the Earth* (2003)

- "[O]n a day when no one's around to play with, take a towel, tie it around your neck as a cape, climb up on the roof edge, say the magic word, 'Shazam!' raise your arms and fly off into . . . Better wear your helmet with this one. The landing's a little rough, as I recall."
  —Jerry Flemmons, *Curmudgeon in Corduroy* (2000)

- "Dr. Hartman created a flourish with an imaginary wand, laughing. 'Shazam!'"
  —Tony Hillerman, *Talking God* (1989)

- "At that moment—in a mad flurry of exhilaration—Suzy charged into the room dressed in an angel costume, her hand brandishing a silver, star-shaped wand. She rushed up to Sheila and stood on her tiptoes, waving the staff wildly across her head. 'Shazam! Shazam! Abracadabra!' she yelled. 'I am the Angel Ariah and you will be spared if no more hate or lies spew out of your mouth. So be it!' She finished with a few more twirling maneuvers over the shocked woman's head and ended with, 'Shazam! Shazam! Fini!!'"
  —Marguerite McCall, *Danielle* (2002)

- "[Pete said,] 'I can't move until I hear the magic word. I gritted my teeth. 'Okay, magic word. Abracadabra?' 'Nope. You missed. Try again.' 'Try again, magic word . . . okay, I think I've got it: shazzam.' He shook his head. 'Pete, that's a perfectly good magic word.' 'I know, Hankie, but it's not the right one. Keep trying. I've got all day.'"
  —John R. Erickon, *The Case of the Kidnapped Collie* (1996)

Shazbat Shazoom
(see *shazoom*)

In Literature: "Shazbat shazoom, we enter the room, the last pit stop on the path toward doom."
—Pat Tanzola, "Wednesdays at the Mod," *Freedom is a Cupcake* (2004)

Shazeem

Origins: This magic word is a variation of *shazam*.

Shazoom

Origins: This is a variation of *shazam*.

Facts: In a Captain Marvel parody in *Mad Magazine* #4 (1953), this is the magic word that transforms Billy Spafon into Captain Marbles. The letters of the word are an acronym for: Strength, Health, Aptitude, Zeal, Ox (power of), Ox (power of another), and Money.

Variations and Incantations:

- Shazeem

- Shazoom

- Shazbat shazoom
  —Pat Tanzola, "Wednesdays at the Mod," *Freedom is a Cupcake* (2004)

In Literature:

- "The world is magical, not simply in the sense that people in pointy hats can wave their hands and go 'shazoom!'"
  —Terry Pratchett, "Imaginary Worlds, Real Stories," *Folklore* (2000)

- "KAZAAM! Your kids were never born. SHAZOOM! Your husband never existed, or you never met."
  —Andrea Nemerson, "Oh, Mama!" Alt. sex.column (2003)

- "Then, shazoom! I felt myself become a hostel manager again, and Dianne remembered that she didn't like to be touched by men, and our hands fell apart."
  —Greg Hills, "History" (1994)

Shazza Bowzer Googly Nowzer

Common Magician's Applications: Production.

In Literature: What words would make the dog reappear? 'Shazza Bowzer Googly Nowzer!'"
—Susan Meddaugh, *Lulu's Hat* (2002)

Shibumi

Shibumi, the value of empty space.
—Maribeth Fischer, *The Language of Good-Bye* (2001)

Mystique: "*Shibumi*. This word conjures up an idea of gentle but continuous motion, almost like drifting or floating in a mist free from shocks or sudden changes."[619] *Shibumi* is a magical state of mind in which manifestation automatically follows intention. "It's a kind of subtle power, an effortless authority. In the narrower, intellectual sense, it might be called wisdom."[620] *Shibumi* is related to the Zen Buddhist concept of *Sabi*, an expression of the everyday world "veiled exquisitely with the mist of transcendental inwardness."[621]

Meanings:

- Effortless perfection
  —Trevanian, *Shibumi* (1983)

- Elegant, unpretentious beauty
  —Matsuo Basho, *Narrow Road to the Interior* (1998)

619 Takashi Sawano, *Creating Your Own Japanese Garden* (1999)

620 Barry Eisler, *Rain Fall* (2002)

621 Daisetz Suzuki, *Zen Buddhism* (1956)

- "Carefully restrained grace and form"
  —Keith R. Laux, *The World's Greatest Paper Airplane and Toy Book* (1987)

- Minimalism
  —Lee Wedlake, *Kenpo Karate 101* (2000)

- Serenity, inner peace
  —Wayne W. Dyer, *What Do You Really Want for Your Children?* (2001)

Origins: *Shibumi* is of Japanese origin.

Common Magician's Applications: Levitation.

Shingon

Meanings: Mantra, sacred recitation vehicle

Facts: In the mystical Shingon sect of Buddhism, the name *Shingon* is known as the "True Word" or "Magic Word." Anyone "who knows the Magic Word is able to achieve results by simply thinking or speaking the thought expressed by such words. Thus . . . Shingon is characterized by the words Mystery and Magic, and Shingon priests are past masters in all mystery as to magic words and signs made with the fingers and the hands."[622]

In Literature: "Part of the magic of 'true words' (Shingon) is the look and sound of words in their original language."
—H. Gene Blocker, *Japanese Philosophy* (2001)

Shirak

Meanings:

- Israeli flatbread
  —Paul Gayler, *Mediterranean Cook* (2004)

- Light
  —Paul B. Thompson, *Darkness and Light* (1989)

  "Lorac whispered, 'Shirak!' and a globe of golden light appeared above his head."
  —Nancy Varian Berberick, *Dalamar the Dark* (2000)

- Magic word
  —Margaret Weis, *Dragons of Winter Night* (2000)

- Stand down
  "I said 'Shirak' and the staff broke in two, *hiss-click-hiss-click*, and disappeared. 'Oh, a magic word,' Mara said. 'Not exactly. A real *magic* word would require the speaker to know the mental disciplines. I could write down the words to one of my spells, and teach you the gestures, and it would do nothing for you without the mental disciplines.' . . . 'What was that word again?' 'Shirak. It means *stand down.*' 'Shirak,' she said, and the staff folded and vanished." —Chris Gonnerman, "The Adventures of Solo Jones" (2002)

Origins: The word *shirak* is of Armenian origin.

Facts: *Shirak* is the name of a rugged, "musically fertile"[623] region of northwest Armenia.

As a magic spell, *shirak* tends to be associated with creating illumination, as at the tip of a wand or staff.

---

622 August Karl Reischauer, *Studies in Japanese Buddhism* (2004)

623 V. Danielson, *The Middle East (Garland Encyclopedia of World Music, Volume 6)* (2001)

Variations and Incantations: Talkarpas ang shirak

"He made a quick gesture, then pointed across the black room. 'Talkarpas ang shirak,' he declared. Magic flashed through him, too little and too quick to bring about the euphoria he usually felt."
—Chris Pierson, *Divine Hammer* (2002)

In Literature:

- "Words of the arcane must be penned with precision, exactness, neatness, and care on the scroll, else they would not work. Write the spell word *shirak*, for example, with a wobble in the *a* and a scrunch in the *k*, and the mage who wants light will be left in the dark."
  —Tracy Hickman, *The Soulforge* (1998)

- "Raising his hoopak high, Sindri whispered one of the first spells Maddoc had taught him. '*Shirak.*' As though it had been set aflame, the woven sling at the top of his staff flared with light."
  —Jeff Sampson, *Dragon Spell* (2005)

- "Palin licked dry lips, spoke the first and only magical word that came into his mind. '*Shirak!*'"
  —Margaret Weis, *Dragons of Summer Flame* (1995)

- "'*Shirak!*' The magical light of the staff gleamed."
  —Kevin Stein, *Brothers Majere* (1989)

- "'*Shirak!*' He spoke the magic word to the staff and, instantly the faceted crystal globe on top burst into light."
  —Margaret Weis, *Kender, Gully Dwarves and Gnomes* (1987)

Shubismack

Common Magician's Applications: Mentalism. For example: "When you read the magic word the second time, you will wake from your trance and do exactly what has been instructed. The magic word is . . . 'Shubismack.'"[624]

Shuffle Duffle Muzzle Muff

In Literature: "'Then *I* must think of some magic words!' groaned the King. 'Oh, what are those words my magicians say . . . ? *Shuffle . . . duffle . . . muzzle . . . muff . . .*'"
—Dr. Seuss, *Bartholomew and the Oobleck* (1949)

Sibthorp

Sibthorp—(scintillations fly from our pen as we trace the magic word).
—*Punch*, Aug. 28, 1841

Origins: This magic word derives from the name "Charles De Laet Waldo Sibthorp (Colonel)," a widely lampooned eccentric British Tory politician who served three decades in Parliament (1826–1855).

<Silence>

The potent and magical silence.
—Thomas Wolfe, *Of Time and the River* (1935)

"I must give you one caution," she went on, as they entered the house. "It's the

----

624 Xilan Horidre (2000)

same that the magicians give to those who are present at their incantations. Be careful not to pronounce sacred words."

"But don't they use them?"

"Oh, abundantly; but they know how to use them in a fashion understood only by the initiated, so that they are harmless."
—Arlo Bates, *The Puritans* (1899)

Mystique: "Silence is at once the most harmless and the most awful thing in all nature," said Herman Melville. "It speaks of the Reserved Forces of Fate. Silence is the only Voice of our God. Nor is this so august Silence confined to things simply touching or grand. Like the air, Silence permeates all things, and produces its magical power, as well during that peculiar mood which prevails at a solitary traveler's first setting forth on a journey, as at the unimaginable time when before the world was, Silence brooded on the face of the waters" (*Pierre, Or the Ambiguities* [1852]).

In Literature:

• "He heard something snap loudly in the fiery stillness. She had broken her fan. Two thin pieces of ivory fell, one after another, without a sound, on the thick carpet, and instinctively he stooped to pick them up. While he groped at her feet it occurred to him that the woman there had in her hands an indispensable gift which nothing else on earth could give; and when he stood up he was penetrated by an irresistible belief in an enigma, by the conviction that within his reach and passing away from him was the very secret of existence—its certitude, immaterial and precious! She moved to the door, and he followed at her elbow, casting about for a magic word that would make the enigma clear, that would compel the surrender of the gift. And there is no such word! The enigma is only made clear by sacrifice, and the gift of heaven is in the hands of every man. But they had lived in a world that abhors enigmas, and cares for no gifts but such as can be obtained in the street."
—Joseph Conrad, *Tales of Unrest* (1898)

• "'In the midst of silence a hidden word was spoken to me.' Where is this Silence, and where is the place in which this word is spoken? 'It is in the purest that the soul can produce, in her noblest part, in the Ground, even the Being of the Soul.' So Eckhart: and here he does but subscribe to a universal tradition. The mystics have always insisted that 'Be still, be still, and know' is the condition of man's purest and most direct apprehensions of reality: that he experiences in quiet the truest and deepest activity: and Christianity when she formulated her philosophy made haste to adopt and express this paradox."
—Evelyn Underhill, *Mysticism* (1911)

Sim Sala Bim

Origins: This magic phrase is popularly believed to have originated in Scandinavian folklore.

Sim salabim is spoken by a Turkish alchemist with magical powers in the early medieval folk play entitled *Robyn Hode: A Mummers Play*: "I have here a potion, brought from the east. It is called the golden elixir, and with one drop I will revive Robyn Hode with these magic words: 'Sim Salabim.' Rise up young man and see how your body can walk and sing."[625]

Dr. Herbert H. Nehrlich suggests that *sim sala bim* "is named after Ali Sim-sala-bim, a desert wanderer and—most importantly—a magician."[626]

----

625 Daniel Diehl, *Medieval Celebrations* (2001)

626 "Carpe Diem, Quam Minimum Credula Postero" (2004)

Facts: *Sim sala bim* is "the Swedish equivalent of 'abracadabra,'"[627] and is known in other Scandinavian cultures as well.

These magic words were made popular by the famous professional magician Dante/The Great Jansen. They also served as the name of his famous touring magic show. Professional magician Whit Haydn once used these words in his performances as a tribute to Dante. He explains: "Sim Sala Bim are nonsense syllables from a Danish nursery rhyme. Dante used them in his show, saying they meant 'A thousand thanks.' He said that the more applause, the bigger the bow, and the more thanks that the Sim Sala Bim would mean. Soon after moving to L.A. in the seventies, I bought a set of Dante's rings from Ken Leckvold, who had bought them from Dante's son. I really enjoyed performing with these rings, and eventually added Dante's line as a magic word in my rope routine and silk to egg, sort of a tribute thing. I liked the Ali Baba/Aladdin kind of sound of the words."[628]

After the Second World War, Kalanag, the stage name of professional German magician Helmut Schreiber, "toured the world with his spectacular, colorful illusion show *Sim Sala Bim.* . . . His show is now in the collection of the popular British magician, Paul Daniels."[629]

Sim Sala Bim is the name of a card trick by Kolin Tregaskes.

Professional magician Jade uses the magic phrase *sim sala bim* in Houdin's Light & Heavy Chest illusion: "A box is easy to carry until—ZAP!—the magician Jade says the magic words. Suddenly, the box can't be moved! In the front stage, you are invited to lift Jade's magic chest.

Then, with just the magic words, 'Sim sala bim,' Jade makes the chest too heavy to lift."[630]

Orson Welles uses *Sim Sala Bim* as magic words in the 1967 film *Casino Royale.*

Variations and Incantations:

- Abracadabra-simsalabim
  —Susanne Friedrich (2001)

- Abracadabra, hocus-pocus, sim salabim, OPEN SESAME!
  —Allan Pred, "Re-Presenting the Extended Moment of Danger: A Meditation on Hypermodernity, Identity and the Montage Form," *Space and Social Theory: Interpreting Modernity and Postmodernity* (1997)

- Bimsalabim abrakadabra alakazam
  —*Kaskus.com* (2004)

- Seem salabim
  —Howard Stern, *Private Parts* (1993)

- Sim sala bam

- Simsalabim

- Sim salabim
  —*Robyn Hode: A Mummers Play*

- Simsalabim-salabam-salabim
  This is a German expression, discussed in *Magic and Showmanship: A Handbook for Conjurers* by Henning Nelms (1969).

- Simsalabim bamba sala do saladim
  "You'd never suspect that, if you utter the magic phrase 'Sim sala bim bamba sala do saladim,' a door will appear in the side of this large concrete block, allowing those with a key to gain entrance."
  —Martin Krzywinski, "Port Knocking" (2004)

- Simsalabim-baum
  —Henriette Kress (1995)

---

627 Per Mollerup, *Collapsible: The Genius of Space-Saving Design* (2002)

628 Quoted by Tim Quinlan, "The Whit Haydn Interview," *Inside Magic* (2003). Whit Haydn's website is *WhitHaydn.com.*

629 Bruce Smith, *Great Coin Tricks* (1995)

630 *MagicExhibit.org* (2000)

- Simsalabim, simsalabim, oooh salabim, sim sim sim salabim
  —Bill Hicks, *Love All the People: Letters, Lyrics, Routines* (2004)

- Sim sala dim, bam ba sala du sala dim
  This is from a traditional folksong entitled "Auf einem Baum ein Kuckuk."

- Sim sim alla bim and all that $#¡†
  —Professional magician Frank Cannella ("The Great Frankie Raymond")

- Sim sim sala beem
  "Her words were not familiar to me as she said *sim sim sala beem*. We all repeated, again *sim sim sala beem*. After what seemed like twenty minutes of repeating these odd words and phrases, mom stopped. I felt a cold gust of winter air blow down my spine. I found this unbelievable as it was a hot August evening."
  —*WowEssays.com* (2005)

- Sim sim salabim, sim sim salabim
  —James E. Churches, *Pirates of the Potomac* (2004)

- Zim Salabim
  —Marie-Dominique Crapon, *Sloughi* (2004)

- Zim Za La Bim
  "I've always found 'zim za la bim' an amusing and somewhat magical phrase."
  —Professional magician Fitzgerald, personal correspondence (2005), *FitzgeraldComedy.com*

- Zim Zala Bim, Bombbooz Zala Dim
  —Chautae Repartee, "Harry Potter Goes to Amsterdam" (2001)

In Literature:

- "The water faucet and sink was the other *Zauberei* or magic in our new home. All one had to do was turn the handle, and *Simsalabim!*—abracadabra!—water came rushing out of the pipes."
  —Elizabeth B. Walter, *Barefoot in the Rubble* (1997)

- "Social constructions of difference and Otherness are—abracadabra, hocus-pocus, simsalabim—transformed to appear in the guise of the natural, of the given and immutable, of unquestionable and undeniable facts, of categorical truth(-claim)s that cannot be otherwise."
  —Allan Richard Pred, *Even in Sweden* (2000)

- "'Sim sala bim!' said Beezel [in response to a newspaper's bad review of a magic show]. 'What does it mean, "a faulty start"?'"
  —Pam Smallcomb, *Trimoni Twins and the Changing Coin* (2004)

Simsim

(see also *open sesame* and *sim sala bim*)

Mystique: "Some words are ancient beyond our knowledge. They express our common human heritage. Simsim has a magic power to remove obstacles and open doors."[631]

Origins: *Simsim* is said to be the authentic translation of the magic phrase "open sesame."[632] It is "the modern Arabic form of the Akkadian word for what we call sesame."[633]

---

631 Jonathan Fine, "Formatting SGML Manuscripts" (1995)

632 Donald A. Norman, *The Design of Everyday Things* (1988)

633 Jonathan Fine, "Formatting SGML Manuscripts" (1995)

S 307

Sis Boom Bah

(see also *ali-sis-koombah*)

Variations and Incantations:

- Abner cadaver sis boom bah
  "In the seconds before the explosion Ki-anne screamed the only magic words that came to mind hoping she could maybe bluff him into running away. 'Abner Cadaver Sis Boom Bah!'"
  —Kianne and Theodore Spazmodeous, "Kenders and Towers" (2001)

- Flash bang sis boom bah

- Ha ha sis boom bah

- Hocus-pocus alla-ma-gocus sheeba-shaba-shooby fire-cracker-fire-cracker sis-boom-bah
  —Travis, "Travis Inside Out" (2003)

- Hocus pocus dominocus, sis sis siscumbah, rah rah rah
  —Stephanie Calmenson and Joanna Cole, *Miss Mary Mack* (1990)

- Karaborrah-karaborrah, Sis-boom-bah
  This phrase is from a Scout Patrol yell.

- Rah rah sis boom bah

- Rah rah siskoombah
  This is a phrase from a college fighting shout.

- Sis boom bah
  Johnny Carson, playing the psychic "Carnac the Magnificent" on *The Tonight Show*, predicted "sis boom bah" to be "the sound of a sheep exploding."

- Sis boom bah and al-le-lu-ia
  This is a refrain from the parody song "The Battle Hymn of the Republicans."
  —*PoliticsOL.com* (2000)

- Sis-boom-bah-ta-da
  "I say the magic words, and siss-boom-bah-ta-da!"
  —Esmé Raji Codell, *Diary of a Fairy Godmother* (2005)

- Wa wa sis boom bah

- Yakkity smakkity sis boom bah, rah rah rah
  —*Nwn.Bioware.com* (2003)

- Yaddah yaddah, sis boom bah
  —Bob "Dex" Armstrong, "The Men Who Wore Peacoats" (2005)

Siweklach

Origins: This word is found in an Austrian fairy tale called "The Bird Wehmus" (the word *wehmus* meaning *phoenix*).[634]

In Literature: "If you want me at any time, just clap your hands and say 'Siweklach' (that is just a meaningless spell-word) and I will help you."
—Marie-Louise Von Franz, *Individuation in Fairy Tales* (1977)

Skål

Meanings:

- Bowl, goblet, or other drinking vessel

- Celebration

- Cheers

- Great gray-wolf of the Twilight
  —Dahlov Ipcar, *A Dark Horn Blowing* (1997)

- "To your health"

---

634 Marie-Louise Von Franz, *Individuation in Fairy Tales* (1977)

Origins: *Skål* is of Scandinavian origin.

Facts: In Norse mythology, *Skol* (also spelled *Skoll*) is the "monster wolf-son of the giantess of Iron Wood" who chases the Sun.[635]

In Literature: "One raises one's glass, proclaims the toastee's name, looks into his or her eyes, utters the magic word '*skål*' . . ."
—Richard D. Lewis, *When Cultures Collide* (1999)

Skol
(see also *skål*)

Meaning: Shall; will
—Richard Boudreau, *The Literary Heritage of Wisconsin* (1986)

Slam Bam Alacazam
(see also *alakazam, wam bam alakazam,*
and *wham bam alakazam*)

In Literature: "With the coming of Krupa, it was slam, bam, alacazam, with the rim shots exploding like Roman candles in the skies of the mid-thirties."
—Mel Torme, *Drummin' Men* (1990)

Sleep
(see also *awake*)

The sleep-magician's midnight spell is o'er.
—William Millar, "To Bertha,"
The Fairy Minstrel (1822)

Common Magician's Applications: Hypnotism.

In Literature: "He . . . waved his hands, and chanted the mystic word 'Sleeeeeeep!' Instantly, the three goblins collapsed on the floor and began snoring loudly."
—Roger M. Wilcox, *The Intercontinental Proliferation of Disgusting Characters* (2000)

Slobibble

Facts: "Saying 'Slobibble' makes any object you choose become very, very tiny," according to *Writing Prompts* by Justin McCory Martin (2001).

<Snap of the Fingers>

The tuxedoed stage performer will snap his fingers and something will appear.
—Sidney L. Friedman,
Your Mind Knows More Than You Do (2000)

Meanings: Magic moment
"Then, of course, there's providing a magic moment: Snap your fingers over the deck."
—Tom Ogden, *The Complete Idiot's Guide to Magic Tricks* (1999)
Common Magician's Applications: Triggering. For example: "The magic hasn't even begun to take place yet. Not until . . . now! . . . and you snap your fingers. It happens, at that instant, at the magic moment."[636] Simarily, "[D]on't forget to snap the end of the pack first, that's what works the magic."[637]

---

635 D. J. Conway, *Norse Magic* (1990)

636 Tom Ogden, *The Complete Idiot's Guide to Magic Tricks* (1999)

637 Mark Wilon, *Mark Wilson's Complete Course in Magic* (1975)

In Literature:

- "What, you snap your fingers and poof, it isn't there anymore?"
  —Silver Ravenwolf, *To Stir a Magick Cauldron* (1996)

- "I will snap my fingers twice! That will make this trick twice as snappy. Now, without looking I will tell you the color of this crayon behind my back."
  —Ray Broekel and Laurence B. White Jr., *Abra-ca-dazzle* (1982)

Snarfugeez

Common Magician's Applications: Triggering. For example: "You repeat the trick. This time you say a magic word: SNARFUGEEZ! Like magic, the water stays inside the glass."[638]

Sneezumsnackum

In Literature: "'Of course I can fix him!' said the fairy prince. 'Wait a minute.' So he stood up on one foot, and swung his fish pole around his head three times, so that the line whistled in the wind, and then he pronounced the magical word, 'Sneezumsnackum!' Then he cried: 'You will not be sleepy any more, Possum Pinktoes, except when it's time to go to bed,' and the funny part of it was that Possum Pinktoes wasn't. Now, of course, I'm not saying that if you pronounced the word 'Sneezumsnackum' it would make you so you wouldn't be sleepy, but it will do no harm to try it, anyhow."
—Howard Roger Garis, *Johnnie and Billie Bushytail* (1910)

Snippety-Bobbity-Boo
(see *bibbidy-bobbidy-boo*)

In Literature: *Action Adventure Excitement 9* (2003)

Spiderae Aught Icor Ven

In Literature: R.A. Salvatore, *The Dark Elf Trilogy* (1998)

Squeamish Ossifrage

Meanings:

- Easily nauseated (or disgusted) osprey

- Nonsense
  —Adam Back, "Cyberpunks Write Code!" (2005)

Origins: These magic words were featured in the Rivest-Shamir-Adelman (RSA) public key algorithm challenge of 1977. In 1994, over 600 volunteer cryptographers from around the word,

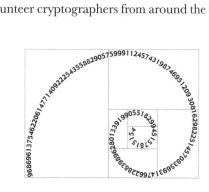

Figure 38. "The magic words are *squeamish ossifrage*" as encoded in the RSA public key algorithm challenge.

---

638 *Ibid.*

using 1500 computers over a period of eight months, managed to break the code of RSA's 129-digit number. The decrypted message read: "The magic words are *squeamish ossifrage.*" Thus began a tradition of using *squeamish ossifrage* in key-breaking challenges.

Facts: *Ossifrage* refers to a "bone-crushing" predatory vulture.

Squeeza-Ma-Jintiun

In Literature: "[There was] an expert fisherman who while his companions caught little would pull up one trout after the other. Of course they were astonished and questioned him about his accomplishment. 'Oh,' he vaguely replied, 'I just put the old squeeza-ma-jintiun (his word for magic) on them.' When asked what he meant he replied, 'I just sit in the boat and mentally picture the fish swimming up to my bait. I picture the fish taking the line, and I just pull 'em in.'"
—Robert Collier, *Prayer Works* (1950)

Sucop Sucoh

Sucop, Sucoh! Hold on tight!
Soon my magic will work right.
—Kemal Kurt,
Mixed-Up Journey to Magic Mountain (2002)

Facts: This magic phrase is *hocus pocus* spelled backwards.

In Literature:

- From *Mixed-Up Journey to Magic Mountain* by Kemal Kurt (2002):

Rabbit's paw, garden snail,
Cat's eye, mouse hair, dragon tail,
Cross your fingers if you dare,
From my hat will hop a hare!
Sucop, Sucoh!
You will see,
My spells are working perfectly!

- "The crowd circles around the old soothsayer with his long white beard and gray tunic. He was casting his wicked incantations upon Anazasi. 'SUCOP . . . SUCOH,' he chanted loudly."
  —Joseph DeMarco, *4 Hundred and 20 Assassins of Emir Abdullah-Harazins* (2004)

Symplocarpus Foetidus

Origins: *Symplocarpus foetidus* is the Latin name for skunk cabbage.

Facts: Skunk cabbage is considered a magical herb. Wrapped in a bay leaf on a Sunday, it "forms a talisman which draws good fortune to the bearer."[639]

In Literature: "'*Symplocarpus foetidus.*' She liked the sound of the words. '*Symplocarpus foetidus,*' she repeated, rolling the syllables off her tongue. . . . 'Do you think the words are magic?' 'Maybe it's a combination—of magic in the words, and naming.'"
—A.C. Lemieux, *The Fairy Lair: A Magic Place* (1998)

---

639 Scott Cunningham, *Cunningham's Encyclopedia of Magical Herbs* (2003)

Syos

Meanings:

- Divine
  —Jacobus de Voragine, *Golden Legend: Readings on the Saints* (1993)

- God or godly
  —Jacobus de Voragine, *Golden Legend: Readings on the Saints* (1993)

- Master (honorific), as in the Pandoran language
  —*Pandoran-English Dictionary 3rd Edition*

Origins: *Syos* is likely derived from the old Greek word *theos*, meaning "to shine" with divine light. *Sios* is the Laconian variant of *theos*.

Magicians living in the 12th and 13th centuries used *Syos* as a magical invocation to the cardinal directions.[640]

In Literature: "Having reached the potter's earth, he plants his heel upon it and turning successively to the East, South, and North, repeats the magic word 'Syos' to each of those cardinal points."
—Lynn Thorndike, *History of Magic and Experimental Science* (1923)

T

Ta-Da

That's what [the words *ta-da*] are—magic.
—Amanda Gore,
"The Benefits of Ta-Da!" (2004)

Meanings:

- Surprise
- Triumphant flourish
- Voilà

Variations and Incantations:

- Tada
- Ta-dah
- Tah-dah
  —Janice Eaton Kilby, *Book of Wizard Magic: In Which the Apprentice Finds Marvelous Magic Tricks, Mystifying Illusions & Astonishing Tales* (2003)

In Literature:

- "TADA! went Jazz's stomach. Open Sesame! went her heart."
  —Melissa Nathan, *Pride, Prejudice and Jasmin Field* (2000)

- "Extending her arms high in the air she sang out: 'TA-DA!'"
  —David E. Leininger, "He Rose Again" (2005)

- "[J]ust as a magician uses the magic words 'TA-DA!', you can magically change your life."
  —T.L. Pakii Pierce, "The Power of Focus" (2004)

- "'Ta-dah!' Cornelius sang out. He held up a box labeled MAGIC ITEMS."
  —Vivian Vande Velde, *User Unfriendly* (1991)

- "I crashed the two circles together, then held them up, now linked together. 'Ta da!'"
  —Jon Scieszka, *Sam Samurai* (2001)

---

640 Lynn Thorndike, *History of Magic and Experimental Science* (1923)

Tahini Cubini, Baffle Houdini

Common Magician's Applications: Tricks involving cube props, as in an optical illusion described in *Origami to Astonish and Amuse* by Jeremy Shafer (2001).

In Literature: "Now let's all say the magic words, *Tahini Cubini, Baffle Houdini!*"
—Jeremy Shafer, *Origami to Astonish and Amuse* (2001)

Talitha, Kum

> "Talitha!" It went to my soul immediately.
> —Walter Wangerin,
> *Ragman and Other Cries of Faith* (2004)

Meanings:

• Arise, daughter

Origins: *Talitha, kum* is an Aramaic phrase used in incantations to raise the dead.

Facts: In the New Testament, Jesus uses the words *Talitha, kum* to resurrect a girl.[641]

Variations and Incantations:

• Talitha, Cum

• Talitha, Cumi

• Talitha, Koum

• Talitha, Kumi

• Talitha, Qumi

In Literature:

• "Those words are the very words of his magic curative power, as he actually spoke them: 'Ephphatha,' the magic word that healed deafness, and 'Talitha, kum!' the magic words that raised the dead."
—Norman Weeks, *The Test of Love* (1992)

• "Mark's recording of the Aramaic words Jesus used, Talitha kum, seem to suggest they have some magical power."
—John P. Keenan, *The Gospel of Mark: A Mahayana Reading* (1995)

Talkarpas Ang Shirak
(see *shirak*)

In Literature: "'*Talkarpas ang shirak*,' he declared. Magic flashed through him, too little and too quick to bring about the euphoria he usually felt. Light spells were parlor tricks, cantrips initiates learned early on."
—Chris Pierson, *Divine Hammer* (2002)

Tamâghis Ba'dân Yaswâdda Waghdâs Nawfanâ Ghâdis

Origins: "These magical words seem to be Aramaic."[642] They are ascribed to "the famous tenth-century Spanish scientist Maslamah b. Ahmad al-Majrîtî."[643]

Facts: This magic phrase is called "the dream word of the perfect nature" and is to be said

----

641 Jaroslav Pelikan, *Jesus through the Centuries: His Place in the History of Culture* (1985)

642 Ibn Khaldun, *Muqaddimah: An Introduction to History* (1967)

643 *Ibid.*

upon falling asleep to clear the way for supernatural perception and wish-fulfillment.[644]

Common Magician's Applications: Hypnotism, levitation.

Tara

Mystique: "Tara is a magical word to all us Irish . . . and a magical place. It was the center of all Ireland, the home of the High Kings. Before there was a Rome, or an Athens, far, far back when the world was young and hopeful, there ruled in Ireland great kings who were as fair and beauteous as the sun. They passed laws of great wisdom and gave shelter and riches to poets. And they were brave giants of men who punished wrong with fearful wrath and fought the enemies of truth and beauty in Ireland with blood-gouted swords and stainless hearts. For hundreds and thousands of years they ruled their sweet green island, and there was music throughout the land. Five roads led to the hill of Tara from every corner of the country, and every third year did all the people come to feast in the banquet hall and hear the poets sing. This is not a story only, but a great truth, for all the histories of other lands record it, and the sad words of the end are written in the great books of the monasteries. 'In the Year of Our Lord five hundred fifty and four was held the last feast of Tara.'"[645] The Arch-Druid of Tara is depicted as "a leaping juggler with ear-clasps of gold, and a speckled cloak; he tosses swords and balls into the air, and like the buzzing of bees on a beautiful day is the motion of each passing the other."[646]

Facts: "In Hindu mythology, Tara is a star goddess who encompasses all time and the spark of life."[647]

Tara is a beloved mother goddess in Tibetan Buddhism.

Ta-Ra-Ra-Boom-Di-Ay

Origins: *Ta-ra-ra-boom-di-ay* is a bawdy song written in 1891 by Henry J. Sayers and made famous by singer Lottie Collins.

Facts: This magic word is featured in the role-playing campaign *The Ripper Game*, "combining various genres of horror and mysticism from late Victorian England" and played in Chicago, Illinois from 1996 to 1997.[648] One of the characters in the game, Frederick Bailey Deeming, uses the magic word *Ta-ra-ra-boom-di-ay*. He is described as "A lunatic murderer who aimed to be Jack the Ripper. He was a rough, tanned fellow—nevertheless well-dressed in a shabby genteel. A bit foreign-looking, [he had] dark hair and a mustache. He was encountered by the company in Nether-London, where he demanded Hamilton's notes of the party. When they resisted, he all but slaughtered the company after using the magic word: 'Ta-ra-ra-boom-di-ay.'"[649]

Common Magician's Applications: Animation. For example, the phrase *Ta-ra-ra-boom-di-ay* was used by magician William Larsen Sr. in a handkerchief routine he devised. He would say: "Many of you wonder how I accomplish these things [with the handkerchief]. Actually, I have an invisible assistant, Fatima. Hers is the power that permits miracles." Larsen would tie the handkerchief to create the form of a body, with a knotted head and two legs made from twisted corners. When Fatima

----

644 *Ibid.*

645 Alexandra Ripley, *Scarlett* (1991)

646 James Bonwick, *Irish Druids and Old Irish Religions* (1894)

647 Patricia Telesco, *365 Goddess* (1998)

648 John H. Kim, *Darkshire.net* (2005)

649 *Ibid.*

began to magically animate the handkerchief, Larsen would recite the following verse:

> *Fatima was a dancer gay.*
> *For fifty cents she'd dance this way.*
> *But if one dollar you would pay,*
> *She'd do the ta ra ra boom de aye.*

On the last line of the stanza, the handkerchief figure would kick her leg like a Vaudeville dancer.[650]

Variations and Incantations:

- Ta rah rah boom dee re
  —Steve Martin, *Picasso at the Lapin Agile* (1996)

- Ta-ra-la-boom-de-ay

- Ta-ra-ra-boom-de-ay

- Ta ra ra boom de-aye
  —William Larsen Sr., quoted in *Self-Working Handkerchief Magic* by Karl Fulves (1988)

- Ta-ra-ra boom dee eh

- Ta ra ra boom der re
  —Paul Oliver, *Songsters and Saints* (1984)

- Ta ra ra boom tee ay
  —T.F. Curley, *Tristan: A Romance of the Sixties* (1999)

Tarkemelhion

Facts: *Tarkemelhion* is a dragon's name.

In Literature: "Tarkemelhion . . . there was magic fueling the word — powerful magic that called to him and which he could not disobey."
—Tim Waggoner, *Temple of the Dragonslayer* (2004)

Tartshoh Nerokregeſp

Common Magician's Applications: Levitation.

In Literature: Roland H. Bainton, *Here I Stand: A Life of Martin Luther* (1995)

Teeny-Weeny Houdini

Facts: These are magic words used by professional magician Steve Charney.[651]

Teetum waggle bari se nee

In Literature: "The children who live in the clouds had seen him falling and said some magic words. They either said, 'Fumble gralley goggle ho hee,' or 'Teetum waggle bari se nee,' or was it 'Gargle giggle fiddle num dee?'"
—John Burningham, *Cloudland* (1999)

Tetragrammaton

The most important of all the Names of God used in Cabalistic magic is the Tetragrammaton, the Name of Four Letters.
—John Michael Greer, *Circles of Power* (1997)

Mystique: "Truly ambitious sorcerers . . . sought the true name of God, the most powerful magic word imaginable. The search for God's true name took on epic proportions during the middle ages. The name was referred to as the

---

650 Karl Fulves, *Self-Working Handkerchief Magic* (1988)

651 *Hocus Jokus: 50 Funny Magic Tricks Complete with Jokes* (2003)

Tetragrammaton, because it was believed to have four letters."[652]

P.D. Ouspensky explains that Kabalist philosophers study the four letters of the Tetragrammaton as "a powerful means of widening consciousness. This idea is perfectly clear, for if the Name of God be really in all (if God be present in all), all should be analogous to each other—the smallest particle analogous to the whole, the speck of dust analogous to the universe, and all analogous to God. The Name of God, the Word or Logos is the origin of the world. Logos also means Reason; the Word is the Logos, the Reason of everything. There is a complete correspondence between the Kabala and Alchemy and Magic. In Alchemy the four elements which constitute the real world are called fire, water, air and earth; these fully correspond in significance with the four kabalistic letters. In Magic they are

Figure 39. This depiction of *Tetragrammaton* is based upon the work of occult scholar Éliphas Lévi in *Transcendental Magic* (1896). Lévi explains: "The Pentagram is the Star of the Epiphany. . . . This Star which the Magi saw in the East, this Star of the Absolute and the universal synthesis . . . opens to human aspirations the fifty gates of knowledge."

expressed as the four classes of spirits: elves (or salamanders), undines, sylphs and gnomes."[653]

Meanings: Literally meaning "the four letters" in Greek, the sacred *Tetragrammaton* is comprised of four Hebrew letters (*Yod, He, Waw,* and *He*), spelling the unpronounceable name of the Hebrew God but often transliterated as "Yahweh" or "Jehovah."

Facts: "According to the Qabalistic traditions, the world came into existence through the utterance of the sacred name of God, the Tetragrammaton YHVH."[654]

Thank You
(see also *please*)

I urge you with . . . passion to use the magic words 'thank you' every chance you get.
—Hal Urban, *Life's Greatest Lessons* (2002)

Facts: "Belief in the power of magic words has really not diminished much over the centuries. The notion that 'please' and 'thank you' will bring magical results is still taught to children (at least by some folks) and still works."[655]

In Literature:

- "'Maybe you should try the magic words,' he said. 'Hocus pocus?' Elvis asked. '*Please* and *thank you*,' said Cluck."
  —Denys Cazet, *Elvis the Rooster and the Magic Words* (2004)

- "My favorite philosopher, Dennis the Menace, all dressed up in his magician's suit, said he could do only two magic tricks because

652 "Kabbalah," *Rotten.com* (2005)

653 *The Symbolism of the Tarot* (1913)

654 Ted Andrews, *Simplified Qabala Magic* (2003)

655 Allan Zola Kronzek, *The Sorcerer's Companion* (2001)

he knew only two magic words, *please* and *thank you*."
—Zig Ziglar, *Over the Top* (1994)

- "Use the magic words: *please, thank you*, and *you're welcome*."
—Michael Jay Goldberh, *The 9 Ways of Working* (1996)

Therefore

In Literature: "'Therefore,' approximately in the sense of 'Abracadabra' or 'Open Sesame.'"
—Roger Kimball, *The Rape of the Masters* (2004)

There's No Place Like Home
(see also *home*)

Dorothy returns to Kansas by repeating a magical phrase: "There's no place like home."
— "L. Frank Baum," *TheFreeLibrary.com* (2004)

Mystique: "Jesse Stewart, author of *Secrets of the Yellow Brick Road* feels [*There's no place like home*] is a difficult phrase to describe or understand with our limited vocabulary. It points to something that transcends ordinary experience so that it can only be alluded to with words, yet not fully recognized until experienced, unless you are already there."[656]

Meanings: The "magical incantation"[657] *There's no place like home*, chanted "three times while she clicks together heels gripped by hard-won ruby slippers, returns Dorothy home from her nightmare-dream in the land of Oz. On its face, the phrase expresses a heartfelt home-yearning, as in 'There's *no* place like home, [sigh].' Here the phrase suggests that home is so unique, wonderful, and irreplaceable a place (a 'place where people know me, where I can just be,' in Minnie Bruce Pratt's phrasing), that no other place ever lives up to it. However, the selfsame phrase unmasks this yearning for home as a fantasy. Switch the emphasis to 'There's no place *like* home,' and the phrase now seems to suggest that there is no place as wonderful as home is mythologized to be, and that includes home itself. The uncanny, punlike character of the phrase combines an unrelenting yearning for home together with an awareness that the home so yearned for is a fantasy."[658]

Origins: *There's No Place Like Home* was coined by playwright John Howard Payne (d. 1852) in his song "Home Sweet Home." The song's "best-known phrase, 'There's no place like home,' served as a talisman for Dorothy in *The Wizard of Oz*. Perhaps Americans were so sentimental about home because of their heritage as immigrants, pioneers, and frontiersmen, a people with shallow roots."[659]

In Literature:

- L. Frank Baum, *The Wizard of Oz* (1900)

- "What do I have to do, close my eyes and click my heels three times while I repeat the magic words—there's no place like home, there's no place like home. . ."
—Lisa Kaniut Cobb, *Some Luck* (2004)

----

656 Judy Kennedy, *Beyond the Rainbow* (2004)
657 Lizbeth Goodman, *Literature and Gender* (1996)
658 Bonnie Honig, *Democracy and the Foreigner* (2001)
659 Diane Ravitch, *The American Reader* (2000)

They Lived Happily Ever After

(see also *once upon a time*)

Facts: "They Lived Happily Ever After" is an English "closing formula"[660] for fables, magic tales, and "any tall story told to amuse, deceive, or console."[661] Such formulae draw "the listener into the realm of magic."[662]

Variations and Incantations: They lived well, we even better
—Margaret Alexiou, *After Antiquity: Greek Language, Myth, and Metaphor* (2002)

Thick, Brick, Fiddlestick, Tickle, Pickle, Limerick, Magic Words Do the Trick

In Literature: "With a very grand voice, he said, 'And now I, Lioneldini, super escape artist, will escape. Could you close the door, please?' Leona knew a few things about magic tricks, too. 'Wait a minute!' she said. 'Magic words! Do you know Houdini's magic words?' 'No,' said Lionel. 'Houdini didn't use magic words! It takes skill to do a trick, not magic words! Now close the door—I'm escaping!' But Leona still wanted to help Lionel get out, so Click helped her pick some magic words. 'Thick, brick, fiddlestick, tickle, pickle, limerick, magic words do the trick!' said Click. Back at the closet, Leona spoke the magic words. 'Thick, brick, fiddlestick, tickle, pickle, limerick,

---

660 William F. Hansen, *Ariadne's Thread: A Guide to International Tales Found in Classical Literature* (2002)

661 Margaret Alexiou, *After Antiquity: Greek Language, Myth, and Metaphor* (2002)

662 *Ibid.*

magic words do the trick!' She opened the door and . . . Lionel was gone!"
—"Lionel's Great Escape Trick," *PBSkids.org* (2002)

Thirteen Uncles, Eighteen Nieces, Waggle Wag Your Tail to Pieces

Facts: This is a magic spell to cause inanimate objects to move in the *Bewitched* television series.

Thohay

Origin: *Thohay* is a Navajo word meaning "stay," and is used in ceremonial acts.

In Literature: "Several acts of magic came along after midnight. First the dance of the arcs. A chorus came in followed by eight men bearing the arcs: slender wands arching from one hand to the other, which held bunches of piñon needles. They danced round the fire, dipping the arcs toward it, went through a stately dance, and finally produced their magic. The dancers knelt in two facing rows; each dancer held his head very steady while his vis-à-vis placed the arc over it, where it stood without touching, except as the bunches of piñon came close to the ears. All the time they called: 'Thohay, thohay (Stay, stay),' the magic word which held the arcs. The string which rested on the man's head was quite invisible in the firelight. Then they rose and, holding backs and necks in frozen erectness, they danced slowly out of the circle. This act was well done and it brought approving murmurs from all our Navajo neighbors."
—Erna Fergusson, *Dancing Gods* (1931)

Tho-Nya-Cht-Tur

In forceful tones say: "THO-NYA-CHT-TUR."
—*The-Spoiler.com* (2005)

Facts: These are magic words featured in the computer game "Shadow of the Comet" (1994).

Three

Mystique: The number three is lucky—we say that "the third time's a charm." Three is the number associated with a genie's wishes, and it's three cheers when we say "Hip, Hip, Horray!" On your mark, get set, go! *Three* is what moves us.

Facts: Magicians often speak magic words in three-part incantations, such as *"abracadabra, alakazam, hocus pocus"* or *"wikki wikki wikki."* Professor Alan Dundes of Berkeley University has made an interesting study of trichotomic patterns in American culture as evidenced in folk speech. To cite just a few of his examples:

> The model for America's rhetorical heritage includes such triple constructions as veni, vidi, vici (and it was surely no accident that all Gaul was divided into three parts) or liberté, égalité, fraternité. Small wonder that American political style favors: life, liberty, and the pursuit of happiness; a government of the people, by the people, and for the people. Political slogans likewise may consist of three words: I Like Ike; We Shall Overcome. But nonpolitical folk expressions are equally three-structured: beg, borrow, or steal; bell, book, and candle; blood, sweat, and tears; cool, calm, and collected; fat, dumb, and happy; hither, thither, and yon; hook, line, and sinker; hop, skip, and jump; lock, stock, and barrel; me, myself, and I; men, women, and children; ready, willing, and able; signed, sealed, and delivered; tall, dark, and handsome; Tom, Dick, and Harry; and wine, women, and song. Railroad crossing signs warn motorists to "stop, look, and listen." Advertising clichés manifest the same structure. A skin cream advertisement maintains: "she's lovely, she's engaged, she uses Pond's"; the breakfast cereal Rice Krispies is represented by "Snap, Crackle, and Pop." . . . Superman, a mass media folk hero for American children, is introduced in threes: "Faster than a speeding bullet, more powerful than a locomotive, able to leap tall buildings at a single bound. It's a bird! It's a plane! It's Superman!" Superman's own formula is "Up, up, and away."
>
> Many American verbal rituals are in the same tradition. The various countdowns prior to the starting point of events may be in threes: ready, set, go; or ready, aim, fire. The auctioneers phrase—going once, going twice, sold; or going, going, gone—is an example. There is also the barker's cry: "Hurry, hurry, hurry," often followed by "Step right up." American judicial rituals also provide illustrations. The cry of "hearye" or "oyez" repeated three times is one, while the oath sworn by a witness is another. A witness is sworn by asking him to repeat "truth" three times, as he must do when he swears to "tell the truth, the whole truth, and nothing but the truth." Similarly, in wedding ritual, there is the promise to "love, honor, and obey."[663]

---

663 "The Number Three in American Culture" (1968)

Variations and Incantations: One, two, three, poof
This is a magic phrase attributed to magician Terry Collins (Emazdad, *TheMagicCafe.com* [2003]).

In Literature: "Think of me as a magician. I count three, and when I reach it . . . you are gone."
—Stephen Hunter, *Havana* (2003)

Thrummular, Thrummular Thrilp, Hum Lipsible, Lipsible Lilp; Dim Thricken Mithrummy, Lumgumptulous Hummy, Stormgurgle Umbumdular Bilp

Facts: This "meaningless" magic phrase by philosopher Alan Watts represents "dancing patterns of light and sound, water and fire, rhythm and vibration, electricity and spacetime."[664]

Thunder Dunder, Seven Day Wonder

Facts: This phrase for dispelling is from the *Bewitched* television series.

Thunderbolt, Zazoom

In Literature: "On many occasions, I had to hold on tight to keep myself from falling, so excited was I by that moment when Captain Thunder transformed himself from a timid professor to a high voltage crime fighter by uttering the magic words 'Thunderbolt, Zazoom!'"
—Antonio Hernandez, *Merchant of Illusion* (2002)

Tiba Diba Riba

Facts: This is a magic phrase for materializing a red hawk in *Oral Storytelling and Teaching Mathematics* by Michael Schiro (2004).

Tien Ling Ling, Dee Ling Ling, Bien

Meanings: *Tien* is Chinese for "celestial" or "heavenly." *Ling* is the magical power . . . of uncanny intelligence . . . an attribute of the cosmological interplay between order and disorder."[665] *Dee* (or *di*) means "God" or "Lord on High". *Bien* (or *bian*) can mean "expedient."

Origins: This magic phrase originated in China and may be transcribed as shown on the next page.

----

664 *The Book: On the Taboo Against Knowing Who You Are* (1966)

665 Stephan Feuchtwang, "Chinese Religions," *Religion in the Modern World*, edited by Linda Woodhead (2001)

In Literature: Henning Nelms, *Magic and Showmanship: A Handbook for Conjurers* (1969).

天令令弟令令便

Time Flies

Common Magician's Applications: Vanishing. For example: "The spectator puts the watch into the box and closes the drawer. Say the magic words, 'Time Flies,' and when you open the box the watch has disappeared!"[666]

Time for Supper

Facts: This is a magic phrase recommended by professional magician Karl Fulves for tricks that awaken or animate an inanimate object.[667]

Tinkie Winkie, Dipsy, La La, Po

Origins: This phrase lists the names of the characters from the *Teletubbies* television series (1997).

In Literature: "Mr. Parsons said he would only keep me on if I had a spectacular trick. I've been practising this one for weeks and it works, most of the time. Now, as you can see, this is an ordinary scarf, I put it over the phone, then I say the magic words, 'Tinkie Winkie, Dipsy, La La and Po,' and then, Hey Presto! (He hits the cloth with a hammer and there is a loud smash. When he lifts the cloth away, the phone has disappeared!)"
—Kim Fuller, "S Club Party" (2005)

Tirratarratorra-tarratirratum

Mystique: "[T]he long strings of formidable words which roar and moan through so many conjurations have a real effect in exalting the consciousness of the magician—that they should do so is no more extraordinary than music of any kind should do so."[668]

In Literature: "And he spoke the magic word, which must never be spoken except on Friday nights, so if you read this on any night but Friday you must skip it, and wait. The word is (Tirratarratorratarratirratarratum), and I put it in brackets, so there would be no mistake. Well, all of a sudden, after the magic word was spoken, if Sammie's ball didn't come bounding up out of that water, and it was as dry as a bone, and it had a nice, new, clean, white cover on."
—Howard R. Garis, *Sammie and Susie Littletail* (1910)

---

666 Bob Solari Magic Company
667 *Self-Working Paper Magic* (1985)
668 Aleister Crowley, *Magick in Theory and Practice* (1913)

Tokoro Ga

Meanings:

- "As for the matter at hand"
- However
- On the contrary

Origins: This phrase is of Japanese origin.

In Literature: "Eventually, he took a sip of tea and mouthed the magic words 'tokoro ga.' This phrase—it means 'as for the matter at hand'—marks the pivotal moment in a Japanese conversation."
—T. R. Reid, *Confucius Lives Next Door* (2000)

Topsy-Turvy, Rickets Scurvy, Barley Rye and Wheatly, Backwards Power, Sweet and Sour, Reverse This Scene Completely

In Literature: John R. Erickson, *Lost in the Dark Unchanted Forest* (1998)

Treasure
(see also *gold*, *fortune*, and *money*)

In Literature:

- "[Treasure] is a magic word, conjuring 'riches beyond measure,' troves of wealth, chests of gold coins, hoards of precious stones, jewel-encrusted reliquaries, crowns and crucifixes, sovereigns and states, pirates and plunder.

The word arrived on the shores of the islands of New Zealand in 1840 with centuries of English history behind it and millennia of Mediterranean history behind that."
—Malcom McKinnon, *A History of the New Zealand Treasury* (2003)

- "During a conversation over several rounds of iced rum, Caesar spoke the magic word that has fired the human mind into insanity for five thousand years and probably caused more grief than half the wars: *treasure*."
—Clive Cussler, *Cyclops* (1986)

- "'It's as if—as if the key to the treasure *is* the treasure!' As soon as she spoke these last words, a genie appeared from nowhere right there in our library-stacks."
—John Barth, *Chimera* (1972)

Trochtie, Bedochtie, Bedochtie, Bedoch! Snip Snap Snoorah, Foorah, BAZÎLOORA!!!

Origins: Magician Leslie Melville recalls, "These words were taught to me in 1981 by a Russian Ship's Purser. He said that they came from a popular Russian children's book. The story was about a boy who found a bottle on a beach and released a Djinn. The Djinn had a long white beard and whenever he cast his spells, he would take one of the hairs of his beard and split the hair with his thumb nail as he muttered the above incantation. I have regularly used the spell ever since!"[669]

---

669 *Shadow Digest*, vol. 10, #200

Trojan, Ramses, Magnum, Sheik

Facts: This is a spell to get rid of zombies (actually names of condom brands), chanted by cartoon character Bart Simpson in the episode "Dial Z For Zombies" of *The Simpsons* television series.

Truth

In Literature: "Tristan . . . found within the book the mastery of magic, his own heritage, which had eluded him. . . . [He] rode with a sword graven with magical words of *Truth* and *Illusion*, cleaving one from the other, and wielded that weapon against the Shadow of shadows."
—C.J. Cherryh, *Fortress of Eagles* (1998)

Try

Meaning: An attempt

Origins: *Try* is of Middle English origin.

In Literature: "Wake not to the external life, but in thy slumber seize on the word I whisper in thine ears; it is a magic word—a mighty talisman, more potent than the seal of Solomon—more powerful than the Chaldean's wand—but it is potential for ill as for Good. See to it, therefore, that it is wisely used. The word is, 'TRY!' As though shalt avail thyself of its power, so be it unto thee. I now leave thee to thy fate, and the fortunes that may befall thee."
—R. Swinburne Clymer, *Dr. Paschal Beverly Randolph and the Supreme Grand Dome of the Rosicrucians in France 1928–1929* (2003)

Tsi-Nan-Fu

Origins: *Tsi-Nan-Fu* is the capital of Shantung Province in China.

Facts: This haunting magical phrase is both spoken and seen to glimmer in the Fritz Lang film *Dr. Mabuse: The Gambler* (1922): "[V]on Wenk reaches to turns his cards over, but beneath them the magical words *Tsi-Nan-Fu* sparkle."[670]

Variations and Incantations: Chi-Nan-Fu

Turius Und Shurius Inturius

Origins: This phrase originated in Amsterdam, the Netherlands, in the late sixteenth century.

Facts: This magic phrase figured into the witchcraft trials of the 1700s. In Amsterdam "a crazy girl confessed that she could cause sterility in cattle, and bewitch pigs and poultry by merely repeating the magic words Turius und Shurius Inturius! She was hanged and burned."[671]

Common Magician's Applications: Enchanting animals.

In Literature: Andrew Tobias, *Extraordinary Popular Delusions & the Madness of Crowds* (1995)

---

670 Tom Gunning, *The Films of Fritz Lang: Allegories of Vision and Modernity* (2000)

671 Charles Mackay, *Memoirs of Extraordinary Popular Delusions and the Madness of Crowds* (1841)

Twinkle Twankle Twinkle

Facts: This is a magic phrase used in conjunction with clapping three times for materializing a halo of stars, allowing one to see in the dark in *Oral Storytelling and Teaching Mathematics* by Michael Schiro (2004).

U

Ubos Chontillo Cumaseba

Origins: *Ubos* is the name of a tree native to the Peruvian Amazon. *Chontillo* and *Cumaseba* are names of Amazonian lakes.

Common Magician's Applications: Restoration. For example: "In an attempt to recover my dignity, I took out a three-foot length of sash cord I had brought along and set out to demonstrate my powers of magic. I was standing at ground level. My audience consisting of Moico, Roy, the fisherman, the wizened old woman and the young boy who were seated, facing me, with their legs dangling from the edge of the second floor of the hut. I doubled the rope into a hair pin in my left hand. I handed the fisherman my Swiss army knife and asked him to cut the exposed loop. I then tied the cut ends together and demonstrated by tugging on the loose ends that I now had a repaired rope with a knot in the middle of its length. There were polite smiles that conveyed a message of 'dumb trick, gringo.' The smiles turned to looks of amazement and disbelief as I covered the knot with my left hand, uttered the magic words, 'Ubos, Chontillo, Cumaseba,' and pulled a complete, uncut original length of rope from my left hand."[672]

Uguh Buguh Alacazam
(see also *ooga-booga*)

In Literature:

- Brian Hill, *Cisco: The Complete Reference* (2002)

Uju Buju Suck Another Juju

Facts: These are magic words used by professional magician Ali Bongo. *Juju* refers to a hard candy.

Umajo Danu

Facts: *Umajo Danu* is a magic phrase from the role-playing computer game "Albion" (1995).

Umpah Umpah

Facts: This is a favorite magic phrase of magician Nicholas J. Johnson.[673]

Until

In Literature: "[T]hat is really the magic word—'until.' There is nothing that is impossible for the man or woman who says, 'I will not quit until I succeed.' And the good news is that we were all born with this 'never say die' spirit." —Eric Aronson, *Dash* (2003)

672 Marcus P. Borom, "Amazon Adventures" (1993)

673 *TheMagicCafe.com* (2005)

Urza

In Literature: "'Speak the magic word and the gates to the treasure swing open,' she said to herself, thinking of an old Fallaji legend, 'And the second word is *Urza*.'"
—Jeff Grubb, *The Brothers of War* (1998)

Uuuhhh Uuuhhh

I bellowed the magic words,
"Uuuhhh, Uuuhhh."
—Raymond W. Baker,
Capitalism's Achilles Heel (2005)

Meanings:

- Attention!

- "The time is now"

Facts: *Uuuhhh Uuuhhh* is a primal grunt used by alligator caretakers to signal feeding time.[674]

V

Vacation

Mystique: "We get mesmerized by magic words," says Dale Mathers,[675] and the word *vacation* is mesmerizing indeed. "'Vacation' is a magic word. Use it in a conversation and people are likely to momentarily spirit off to their private bit of paradise, disappear to somewhere that exists be-

tween fantasy and the world-as-we-know-it."[676] The inclusion of the word *vacation* in a magician's patter is a guaranteed distraction.

Vamoose

Vanish, vamoose.
—Bob Levy, *Broken Hearts* (2000)

Meanings: Leave quickly, go away

Origins: This is a slang form of *vamos*, a Spanish word meaning "let's go."

Common Magician's Applications: Vanishing. For example, the "Triple Vamoose" is a coin vanishing trick performed by professional magician Barry Taylor.

In Literature: "'Vamoose!' Wizard yelled. 'That's a magic word, when you need to hurry!'"
—Janice Lee Smith, *Wizard and Wart* (1995)

Vê, Não Vê
(see *now you see it, now you don't*)

Origins: Of Portuguese origin, this is an expression from the Amazon equivalent to *now you see it, now you don't*.[677]

In Literature: Candace Slater, *Entangled Edens: Visions of the Amazon* (2002)

---

674 Raymond W. Baker, *Capitalism's Achilles Heel* (2005)
675 *An Introduction to Meaning and Purpose in Analytical Psychology* (2002)
676 Scott Rains, "The Six Knows to Preparing to Travel" (2004)
677 Candace Slater, *Entangled Edens: Visions of the Amazon* (2002)

Voilà

Voila, bewildered and hypnotized I had fallen
for your magic and tricks.
—Sorana Salomeia, "Simsalabim" (2004)

Meanings:

- Behold!

- Magic word
  "[V]eil or no veil, I was readying myself to
  'voilà!' at any moment . . ."
  —Wesley Stace, *Misfortune* (2005)

- There it is!
  "Intuition often speaks to us in dreams,
  when the conscious mind is asleep. We'll go
  to sleep within an insurmountable problem,
  and in the morning—*voilà!*—like magic, we
  have an answer."
  —Craig Karges, *The Wizard's Legacy* (2002)

Origins: *Voilà* is a French word.

Common Magician's Applications: Production. For example: "Charlotte made a sweeping
motion, and just like that, the old coin was gone.
'Et voilà!' said Charlotte in her best Parisian
accent."[678]

In Literature:

- Jennifer Finney Boylan, *She's Not There: A Life
  in Two Genders* (2003)

- "The magician . . . takes on a voice somewhat mystically transformed: 'Voilà now,
  and with a flourish of the scarf!'"
  —R.K. Puma, "The Magician," *RKPuma.com*
  (2003)

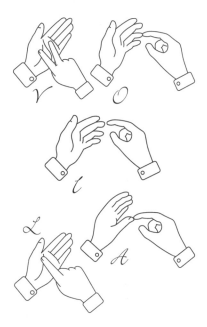

Figure 40. Before producing a coin, a sleight-of-hand
magician can sign a magic word like *voilà* using the two-handed manual alphabet. Such finger movements add
mystique and meaning to even the simplest production
routine. For a guide to the two-handed manual alphabet, see *Deafblind.com*.

- "[He might] pull the papers from his shirt
  like a magician: 'Voilà! I have these secret
  documents from the homes of enemies of
  the state."
  —Margaret Peterson Haddix, *Among the Brave*
  (2004)

- "She waved her arms and snapped her fingers like a magician's. '. . . voilà.'"
  —Claire Daniels, *Body of Intuition* (2002)

- "'Voilà!' He clasped the rough-edged object
  in his hand. He brought it carefully to the
  surface. It glowed a shiny yellow in the afternoon sunlight, its magic qualities hidden
  cleverly beneath its smooth golden surface."
  —Beverly S. Adam, *Irish Magic* (2003)

---

678 Annie Bryant, *Out of Bounds* (2005)

W

Waka Waka Wow

In Literature: From John Lindsey, "Love!" (2004):

> *So I caught that bird*
> *And tied it to the cow*
> *And said the magic word*
> *"Waka Waka Wow!"*

Wam Bam Alakazam
(see *wham bam alakazam*)

In Literature: "Wam! Bam! Alakazam! Bill's hands flew off the lamp and over his head." —Penn Jillette and Teller, *Penn & Teller's How to Play in Traffic* (1997)

Wam Bam Diddly Doody Do Mam

Variations and Incantations: Bam wham ham flam jamb cram alla kazam slam! —Linda Varsell Smith, *The Rainbow Redemption* (2003)

In Literature: "[S]tand on one leg . . . say the magic word 'wam bam diddly doody do mam' and stick out your tongue." —Mark Barton, "Missive 47," *Losing Today* (2004)

Want To See Something?
(see also *watch* and *what if*)

Common Magician's Applications: "[Professional magician David Blaine] doesn't say a lot. He doesn't jump up and down and wave his arms . . . but he reacts as if what he's doing is *real magic*. . . . You have to ask yourself the two words . . . 'what if?' What if I really could do magic? Would I be telling a big long story with the trick? Or would I just walk up to someone and say, 'want to see something?'" —*Ellusionist.com* (2004)

Watch
(see also *look, look* and *want to see something?*)

Facts: Professional magician Criss Angel uses the magic word *watch* during his bar room magic. *Watch* is the favorite magic word of professional magician Seth Garrison Grabel, "to let the audience know you are about to do something spectacular."[679]

Variations and Incantations:

- Watch this, kiddo!
  This is a magic phrase used by professional magician Al Flosso.

- Watch, watch
  This is a magic phrase used by professional magician David Blaine.

We Love All, We Serve All

Facts: These are professional magician Prof. B. Kamesh's magic words, part of his Indian culture and spirituality magic show.

Weebus Warbus

Facts: These are magic words for taking flight in the *Bewitched* television series.

- -

Wham Bam Alakazam

(see also *alakazam, wam bam alakazam*)

Meanings:

- Like magic
"Wham! Bam! AlakaZam! The old gal was her old self again."
—Dave Galey, *The Joys of Busing* (1996)

- Suddenly
"That's when it hit her—wham bam alakazam."
—Nancy Moser, *Time Lottery* (2002)

Variations and Incantations:

- Bam wham ham flam jamb cram alla kazam slam!
—Linda Varsell Smith, *The Rainbow Redemption* (2003)

- Wam bam alakazam
—Penn Jillette and Teller, *Penn & Teller's How to Play in Traffic* (1997)

- Wham-zam, alakazam
—Matthew Kinne, *FirstFiction.net* (2004)

- Zam Zam Alakazam

In Literature: Nancy Moser, *Time Lottery* (2002)

Whammy

He hit her with some kind of mind-magic hypnosis whammy, and zoned her out entirely.
—Jim Butcher, *Blood Rites* (2004)

Meanings:

- Catch, deception, string attached
"And here's the real whammy . . ."
—Elizabeth Warren, *All Your Worth* (2005)

- Enchanting
"Yeah, she's really spiritual. You know how she looks at you with those whammy eyes. There is DEFINITELY something greater than we are, oh golly, there's a MUCH greater power out there."
—Stephen Goodwin, *Breaking Her Fall* (2003)

- Evil eye, jinx
"What happened? Senna put the whammy on David? Cast a voodoo spell?"
—K.A. Applegate, *Land of Loss* (1999)
  "[W]hen they were left unhypnotized for a few days, they were afflicted with more than the usual number of hexes and whammies and practiced all sorts of magic to undo them."
—Bernard Malamud, *The Natural* (1952)
  "[O]ne could very well imagine that the whammies and the jinxes, too, seeped in from the dark gap between the buildings."
—Orhan Pamuk, *The Black Book* (1994)

- Flare, spark, drama
"[T]he fireworks, the whammy, the zing is what makes people chatter about what rattled their saddles last night."
—Marc Kelly Smith, *Complete Idiot's Guide to Slam Poetry* (2004)

- Impact
This sense of the word is often intensified: "double-whammy," "triple-whammy."

- Magic spell

  "[W]ith the right magic whammy, he wouldn't need any aliases."
  —John Passarella, *Monolith* (2004)

      "Lewis told me that some wizard put a magical whammy on the bridge."
  —Brad Strickland, *The Beast Under the Wizard's Bridge* (2002)

- Voilà

  "You get a wolf-hide belt, put it on, say the magic words, and whammy, you're a wolf. A Hexenwolf."
  —Jim Butcher, *Full Moon* (2001)

Variations and Incantations: Whim-whammy ."I don't suppose you can use your whim-whammies to conjure up a cold six-pack, can you?"
—K.A. Applegate, *Everworld 4* (1999)

What If
(see also *if*)

Be a magician: ask "what if."
—Roger von Oech,
*A Whack On the Side of the Head:
How to Unlock Your Mind for Innovation* (1983)

Mystique: "'What if . . .' The room fell quiet. Those two magic words can instantly rivet the attention of an entire room."[680] The words *what if* are an "open sesame" to a world where anything is possible. They ignite suspended disbelief, allowing our eyes to be deceived. *What if* calls upon us to question the rational and expand the limits of what is possible. Like a poet who lets his imagination flow and creates miracles on paper,

the magician asks "What if? What if this could happen—or this? And then it happens, because [he] lets the magic flow."[681]

In Literature: "What if, what if, what if, what if? The world can change in a minute."
—Kevin Henkes, *Olive's Ocean* (2005)

Whatever Happens

Mystique: *Whatever happens* is a mantra, of sorts, embracing the whims of the Foruna, the goddess of luck or chance.

In Literature: "As her mind gradually cleared, she became aware of the two words that seemed to stand before her mental vision in letters of fire: 'Whatever happens!' Was it comprehensible? Was it possible that this mysterious behest could apply to the terrible event that had just taken place? 'Whatever happens!' the behest had gone on to say, 'do not lose your faith or your trust in those who have pledged their honour to save you, and who have never failed to keep their word.' Eve had obeyed the command to destroy the missive as soon as read. But she had committed every word to memory. Until a few hours ago these words had been to her like a profession of faith and of hope. She had sworn before God that she would never lose her faith. But now that faith began to waver, and hope to recede into clouds of despair, she recited them sotto voce over and over again forcing hope to return to her, and faith to revive. 'Whatever happens' was comprehensive, she kept on reiterating to her-

----

680 *The Imagineering Way* (2003)

681 Robert Currie, quoted in *The Place My Words Are Looking For: What Poets Say About and Through Their Work* by Paul B. Janeczko (1990)

self, forcing herself with all the will-power she possessed to trust and to believe. Whatever happens! The words at the close of the missive had been underlined. Whatever happens, her arrest and that of her children, the terror, the humiliation, the terrible predicament in which she now was, being driven along, whither she knew not, guarded by a posse of soldiers who of a surety would never allow her to escape—were all these horrors hinted at in the magic word: 'Whatever'? . . . In vain did she try and infuse hope into her stricken soul. In vain did she make brave efforts to keep two magic words before her mind: "Whatever happens . . ."
—Baroness Orczy, *Mam'zelle Guillotine* (1940)

Whiz Bang

Whiz, bang, wave of hands.
—Donald A. Norman,
The Design of Everyday Things (2002)

Variations and Incantations: Whiz Bang Fu Man Chu
This phrase is featured in the virtual world "LegendMUD" (2001).

In Literature: "My mom had some chairs dipped and all the paint came off, whiz bang, like magic."
—Judy Delton, *Angel's Mother's Wedding* (1987)

Whoopi-Ti-Yi-Yo

Facts: Whoopi-Ti-Yi-Yo is associated with a cowboy's lament.

Variations and Incantations:

- Whoopee Ki Yi Yo
  —Douglas Preston, *Mount Dragon* (1997)

- Whoopee Ti Yi Yo

- Yipee Ti Yi Yo

In Literature: "Never knew 'Whoopti-ti-yi-yo' qualified as magic words."
—Christopher Stasheff, *The Secular Wizard* (1995)

Whooshsky-Cadabra

In Literature: "Everything away! Whooshsky-cadabra!"
—Jan Dean, *Funny Poems* (2003)

Wibbly Wobbly

Facts: These are magic words featured in performances by Zappo the Magician.

In the Summer of 2004, Irish candy maker Chivers Jelly launched "a promotion for all budding young magicians, where children get a chance to win a day at the Chivers Jelly Wibbly Wobbly Magic School. Three lucky winners and their guardians will be whisked off by helicopter to the Chivers Jelly Magic Castle in a mystery location in Ireland. Mr. Jolly, one of Ireland's most talented and entertaining magicians, will be there to meet the young magicians and will intrigue them with his tricks and illusions."[682]

Common Magician's Applications: Triggering. For example: "As the children helped with the magic words 'Wibbly Wobbly,' balls multiplied and then joined together, separate coloured silk handkerchiefs melded into a multicoloured silk scarf and Zappo's uncontrollable wand tried

682 *Checkout* (2004)

to stick itself into his ears and up his nose much to everyone's amusement."[683]

Wiggle Your Fingers, Wiggle Your Thumbs, That's the Way the Magic Comes

Facts: This is a traditional magic phrase used by magician and storyteller Uncle Michael.[684]

Wiggly Woggly

Facts: This is a favorite magic phrase of magician Phillip B. Jones, who explains that it gets some giggles from the audience. "I shout 'wiggly,' the kids shout 'woggly.'"[685]

Wiki Wiki

Meanings: Quickly, in a hurry
—Carolyn Keene, *The Secret of the Golden Pavilion* (1959)

Origins: *Wiki wiki* is a Hawaiian phrase.

Facts: *Wiki wiki* is equivalent to *presto*, as it conjures a quick change.

Common Magician's Applications: Card forcing. For example, these magic words are used by professional magician The Amazing John Pas-

saniti: "I see the image of the card in your mind. Now I simply wave my hand over the cards and, say the magic words, 'Wiki Wiki.' Tell me, was *this* your card?!"

Variations and Incantations:

- Wiki-wiki, chop-chop
  —James Jones, *From Here to Eternity* (1951)

- Wicky wocky
  —Marlene Karkoska, "The Knight and the Wizard" (2005)

Wingardium Leviosa

Origins: *Wingardium* is derived from the English word "wing" and the Latin word meaning "steep" (*arduus*). *Leviosa* is from the Latin word meaning "to lift" (*levo*).

In Literature: *Wingardium Leviosa* is a levitation spell in *Harry Potter and the Philosopher's Stone* by J.K. Rowling (1997).

Winko

Presto, Chango that's a thing of the past
Winko, Winko works twice as fast
—John Marion Gart and John Redmond,
"Winky Dink" (1953)

In Literature: "The highlight of the convention for me was [seeing] . . . a tape of one of the greatest TV shows of all time: 'Winky Dink.' This was the first 'interactive' TV show. You, the viewer, sent 50 cents to Box 5, New York 19, New York, and you got back a Magic Window, which was a piece of transparent plastic that you put on your TV screen. Then, under the direction of your host, Jack Barry, you used special crayons to draw

683 *Library.org.nz* (2005)

684 *Prestbury.net* (2004)

685 *TheMagicCafe.com* (2003)

lines on the plastic. (Or, if you were my sister and I, and you didn't have a Magic Window, you drew right on the TV screen and interacted with your parents later.) After the lines were drawn, you and Jack Barry said the Magic Word 'WINKO!' and the lines became part of, say, a bridge, which Winky Dink would use to get across a river. . . . As part of a nostalgia display, NATPE had a TV set up on the convention floor, playing old Winky Dink shows. Mike put a piece of plastic on the screen and gave me a marker. I drew the lines where Jack Barry told me to, producing a vaguely round object. 'OK, kids,' said Jack Barry. 'Let's say the magic word! One, two, three . . .' 'WINKO!!' yelled Mike and I, causing startled TV executives to whirl around and stare at us. Inside the circle I had drawn, goldfish appeared. It was a fish bowl! You don't get quality entertainment like that anymore."
—Dave Barry, "The Idiot Box" (1994)

Wish Hug Believe

In Literature: "She held Stormy close and squeezed Skippy while barely whispering the three magic words, 'WISH HUG BELIEVE!' As Windy gasped the last magical word, she looked into her arms for her friends and saw nothing but darkness everywhere except for one glowing, bright red eye."
—R. Frie and K. Zahradnik, *Windy Wildwood* (2004)

Wishka, Washka, Wushka

In Literature: "[T]he fairy jumped up and down in front of the old lady squirrel three times, and said: 'Wishka, Washka, Wushka!' which is magical, you know, and then she added: 'Look at your tail!' and believe me, if grandma's tail hadn't turned silver-gray, just like grandpa's,

and she felt ever so much better. Then the fairy jumped out of the window and disappeared, after saying good-bye."
—Howard Roger Garis, *Johnnie and Billie Bushytail* (1910)

Wishy Washy Washy Wish

Facts: This is a magic phrase attributed to magician David Holloway.[686]

Wishy Washy's Wish is the name of a novel by Walter H. Barkas.

Wonder

I insist upon the word 'wonders.' Oh, you are a magician! We know your power; we know that you could find gold, even were there none in the world. And, in fact, people say you make it.
—Alexandre Dumas,
The Man in the Iron Mask (1850)

Mystique: "Wonder is our response to something we experience or encounter that literally takes our breath away."[687] "*Wonder* is a word to wonder about," wrote Dr. Lewis Thomas. "It contains a mixture of messages: something marvelous and miraculous, surprising, raising unanswerable questions about itself, making the observer wonder, even raising skeptical questions like 'I wonder about that.' Miraculous and marvelous are clues; both come from an ancient Indo-European root meaning simply to smile or laugh. Anything wonderful is something to smile in the presence of, in admiration (which, by the

---

686 Emazdad, *TheMagicCafe.com* (2003)

687 Msgr. Jim Lisante, "Wonder Lets Life's Magic Trickle In" (2002)

way, comes from the same root, along with, of all telling words, mirror).”[688]

Facts: *Wonder* is professional magician Bill Wisch's favorite magic word. He explains: “A while back I gave a lot of thought to what makes magic different from any other performing art. Even though the word *wonder* can certainly be applied to any art or many situations for that matter, for obvious reasons I still find it hard to come up with a better one word definition of magic . . . *wonder*.”[689]

In Literature: “‘The man who has lost his power of wonder,’ wrote the scientist Albert Einstein, ‘is a dead man.’ Perhaps the nearest things to magic, in this sense, are dreams and fairy tales.”
—Eugene Burger, *Magic and Meaning* (1995)

Woo Woo Woo

Facts: Woo Woo Woo is the “magic sound” that professional magician Terry Lunceford suggests to his volunteers to utter during stage shows.[690]

Wooga-Wooga-Wooga

Mystique: “The magical word is the chanted word,” said the poet W.B. Yeats.[691] The magical incantation *wooga-wooga-wooga* captures the spirit of a chanted ritual held around a bonfire.[692]

Meanings:

- Crazy

- Mumbo-jumbo

- Spooky
  “It's not even spooky booga-wooga wooga. It's just everyday real.”
  —*TalkAboutRecovery.com* (2003)

- Unscientific, superstitious
  “[H]ypnosis is still considered to be pretty wooga wooga by many people, even though it has research to back it up.”
  —Stephanie J. Buehler (2005)

Facts: Susan Finger, an instructor at Carnegie Mellon University, recommends “Wooga wooga wooga” to be said when tossing an imaginary ball.

“Wooga-wooga” is the flapping sound of papers being waved in the air.[693]

“Wooga-wooga” is an electric life energy that pulls one forward, like an invisible thread. Wavy Gravy, the founder of the original Hog Farm Commune in Tujunga, California, describes “some kind of spiritual wooga-wooga that I'm entitled to spend my days in quest of.”[694]

“Wooga Wooga” is “a café in the astral dimension where Charlie Parker jams every Saturday night.”[695]

688 Lewis Thomas, “Seven Wonders” (1983)
689 Personal correspondence (2005), *Wisch-Craft.com*
690 As observed in his October 2005 appearance at Hollywood's Magic Castle
691 Quoted in *The Life of W.B. Yeats* by Terence Brown (1999)
692 Dave Smith (2002)
693 G.M. Ford, *Slow Burn* (1998)
694 Quoted in *Interviews with Icons* by Lisa Law (2000)
695 Tom Robbins, *Even Cowgirls Get the Blues* (1976)

Variations and Incantations:

- Booga-wooga wooga
  —*TalkAboutRecovery.com* (2003)
- Booga-wooga-wooga-wooga
  —Majority Report Radio (2004)
- Booga wooga wooga wooga wooga
  —*SpongeBob SquarePants* (1999)
- Wooga-wooga-wooga-wooga-wooga
  —*Deconstruction.f9.co.uk* (2005)

In Literature:

- Cheryl Charming, *Be a Star Magician!* (2002)
- Christopher Durang, *Naomi in the Living Room and Other Short Plays* (1998)

Woogie

Facts: This is a magic word featured in the Valu-Soft computer game "Blue's Room: Blue Talks" (2004), spoken by a talking jukebox named Boogie Woogie.

Work

Mystique: "Though a little one, the master-word looms large in meaning. It is the open sesame to every portal, the great equalizer in the world, the true philosopher's stone, which transmutes all the base metal of humanity into gold. . . . With the magic word in your heart all things are possible, and without it all study is vanity and vexation. The miracles of life are with it . . . Not only has it been the touchstone of progress, but it is the measure of success in every-day life. . . . And the master-word is *Work*, a little one . . . but fraught with momentous sequences if you can but write it on the tablets of your hearts, and bind it upon your foreheads."[696]

Wow

What is *wow?* Is it filled with magic, too . . . ?
Is it a magic word?
—Tom Birdseye, *The Eye of the Stone* (2003)

Mystique: *Wow* is the ultimate expression of surprise and wonder, of enthusiasm, of a thrill. As an exclamation, it often seems involuntary, as if it is the voice of Awe-itself channeling through. When spoken slowly, it sounds like a holy mantra, and indeed the word has a sacred quality to it. With a slight change in pronunciation, *wow* becomes another popular expression of wonderment: *whoa.* When a magician says "wow" as a magic word, he serves a double purpose: to express proper respect for a marvel taking place (the sense of *wow* as a noun), and to subtly command his spectators to be amazed (the sense of *wow* as a verb). When a magician appears to be personally moved by a magical effect, he communicates a dignified modesty while retaining the respect of the audience for having manifested the illusion.

In Literature: "One participant summed it up in three magic words: 'I was wowed!'"
—T. Scott Gross, *Why Service Stinks* (2003)

---

696 William Osler, *Osler's "A Way of Life" and Other Addresses* (2001)

X

Xatanitos

Origins: *Xatanitos* is an antiquated magic word for use during card shuffling and for luck involving five cards. This word comes from an Egyptian book of magical talismans entitled *Treasure of the Old Man of the Pyramids*, "translated from the Language of the Magi" in the eighteenth century.[697]

Figure 41. Emblazoned with mysterious symbols, this good luck charm is a "Five Card Stud" talisman. It is based upon the research of Arthur Edward Waite in *The Book of Ceremonial Magic* (1913).

Facts: The original manuscript recommends making a talisman of the magic word and binding it upon one's left arm with a white ribbon. The word should be spoken "when shuffling for self or partner. Before beginning, touch your left arm with your right hand in the neighborhood of the talisman."[698]

Common Magician's Applications: Card tricks, particularly the "Five Card Stud" routine. When a magician incorporates a "good luck" talisman and intones the mysterious word *Xatanitos*, he can color his card routine with an ancient Egyptian mystique.

Xor-thax Teray

In Literature: "Alexei fastened his eyes to that rampart as he began to cast a spell. '*Xor-thax, teray.*' In the blink of an eye, Alexei teleported to the center of the ramp, materializing in one place as he vanished from the other."
—Douglas Niles, *Black Wizards* (2004)

Xum

Origins: *Xum* is the name for the North Wind in the language of the Tlingit Indians of the Pacific Northwest Coast.[699]

In Literature: "The magical word XUM [pronounced 'etz-oom'] corresponds to the Root Center (the *Muladhara chakra* of Kundalini yoga) . . ."
—Gerald Schueler, *The Angels' Message to Humanity: Ascension to Divine Union: Powerful Enochian Magic* (1996)

Xyzzy

A note on the wall says: "Magic word XYZZY."
—Susan Holtzer, *The Wedding Game* (2001)

Origins: *Xyzzy* is "a mnemonic device to remember how to do cross products" in math, the

---

697 Arthur Edward Waite, *The Book of Ceremonial Magic* (1913)

698 *Ibid.*

699 Frank Caldwell, *Land of the Ocean Mists* (1986)

letters consisting of the subscripts in an equation.[700]

Facts: This magic word is pronounced "exs-wie-zee-zee-wie"[701]

Xyzzy is featured in early "interactive fiction" computer games such as "Adventure" and "Colossal Cave." Game analyst Graham Nelson explains that "[T]he traditional magic word 'xyzzy,' written on the cave's walls, is in keeping with the centuries of initials carved by the first explorers of the Mammoth cave."[702]

Popularized by computer gaming, *xyzzy* is a commonly-used computer password.

In the abbreviated signoffs of computer messages, *XYZZY* means "a kiss that moves you."[703]

In Literature: "As he stepped through [the door], he turned and said 'Xyzzy.' A small garden gnome fell off the shelf, narrowly missing his nose, and shattered on the floor in front of him." —Robert G. Ferrell, *Tangent* (2004)

Y

Ya Ali

(see also *ala*)

Meanings:

- Invocation for help
  Literally, "Ali is our help."
  —Stanley J. Tambiah, *Leveling Crowds* (1996)

- Magic phrase
  —M. Gonzalez-Wippler, *Complete Book of Spells, Ceremonies and Magic* (1978)

Origins: *Ya Ali* is of Arabic origin.[704] *Ali* is an Arabic word meaning "by the most high." Similarly, *Ali'i* is a Hawaiian word meaning "chief."

Yabba-Dabba-Doo

I want some silly words, some happy words . . .
And if you have any magic words,
I want them too.
—Monalisa DeGross,
Donavan's Word Jar (1998)

Meanings:

- Comic war cry
  —Steve Rivkin, *The Making of a Name* (2004)

- Excitement
  "[G]ulping down hard on the yabba-dabba-doo rising up his throat . . ."
  —Glenn Stout, *Chasing Tiger* (2002)

- Hooray!
  "Geppetto bolted up, clicked his heels, and shouted, 'Yabba-dabba-doo!' (Italian for Hooray!)"
  —A.J. Jacobs, *Fractured Fairy Tales* (1999)

- Magic words
  "There's no hocus-pocus, abracadabra, or yabba-dabba-doo to being saved."
  —D.A. Carson, *Sunsets* (2005)

Origins: *Yabba-dabba-doo* is an Italian phrase.[705]

700 Ron Hunsinger, quoted in "Everything You Ever Wanted to Know About the Magic Word XYZZY," *RickAdams.org*

701 The Jargon File (1990)

702 "The Craft of Adventure" (1995)

703 Brad Templeton, *The Internet Joke Book* (1995)

704 Migene Gonzalez-Wippler, *The Complete Book of Spells, Ceremonies and Magic* (1978)

705 A.J. Jacobs, *Fractured Fairy Tales* (1999)

Facts: *Yabba-dabba-doo* became a national catch-phrase through the animated television series *The Flintstones*.[706]

This phrase has been called "English gibberish"—that is, nonsense, but in the English language—by Distinguished Arts and Science Professor Daniel C. Dennett.[707]

Variations and Incantations:

- Abba-dabba-do
  —Steve Rivkin, *The Making of a Name* (2004)

- Abba-dabba-ooga-booga-hoojee-goojee-yabba-dabba-doo
  —Edward Allen, *Mustang Sally* (1992)

- Yabba-dabba-doo-fiddledy-dee-tiddly-pom-fi-fi-fo-fum
  —Daniel C. Dennett, *Consciousness Explained* (1991)

In Literature: D.A. Carson, *Sunsets: Reflections for Life's Final Journey* (2005)

Yagazuzi, Yagazuzi, Yagazuzi, Zim Zoomazoozi, Zoomazoozi, Zoomazoozi, Bim Zuzzi, Hi! Zuma Huga Pits

Facts: In the *Bewitched* episode "The Joker is a Card" (1965), warlock Uncle Arthur convinces Darrin he can protect himself from the wrath of the witch Endora by saying "Yagazuzi, yagazuzi, yagazuzi, zim [sound of cowbell, and a duck call]; Zoomazoozi, zoomazoozi, zoomazoozi, bim [cowbell, duck call repeated]; Zuzzi, hi! Zuma Huga Pits."

Yaldabaoth

Meanings:

- Demi-Urge
  —Scott A. Leonard, *Myth and Knowing* (2003)

- Ruler of Darkness and Evil
  —Victor Paul Furnish, *II Corinthians* (1984)

- Son of chaos
  —Yuri Stoyanov, *The Other God* (2000)

- Yahweh, the "blind," "jealous" god
  —Alan H. Hauser, *A History of Biblical Interpretation* (2003)

Facts: "The magic word Yaldabaoth [has been] found in many of [the Hellenistic-Egyptian amulets and] ancient spells . . . suggesting that the sacred pronunciation [of the Tetragrammaton] was indeed well known at [that] time to religious cognoscenti and magicians."[708]

Yaldabaoth (also called *Samael*) is "a name reminiscent of 'Yahweh, Lord of Sabbaths,' from the Old Testament."[709] In *The Apocryphon of John*, "an important work of mythological Gnosticism," the light-being Sophia (an emanation of the supreme deity) "desires to bring forth a being without the approval of the great Spirit or her consort. Consequently, she produces the monstrous creator-god Yaldabaoth, who still

706 Michael Mallory, *Hanna-Barbera Cartoons* (1998)

707 *Consciousness Explained* (1991)

708 Mark Belletini, "Arius in the Mirror" (2003)

709 Bart D. Ehrman, *The Lost Christianities* (2003)

possesses some of the light-power of his mother. Yaldabaoth creates angels to rule over the world and aid in the creation of man; man himself is fashioned after the perfect Father's image, which was mirrored on the water. Man comes to life when Yaldabaoth is tricked into breathing light-power into him. Thus begins a continuous struggle between the powers of light and the powers of darkness for the possession of the divine particles in man."[710]

The Gnostics identified the "quality of evil" and "called it *Yaldabaoth*, a being with the head of a lion and the body of a serpent."[711]

Yantru-Mantru-Jãlajãla-Tantru

Mystique: The sounds of *yantru*, *mantru*, *jala*, and *tantru* evoke the Hindu words *yantra* ("instrument"), *mantra* ("formula"), *jala* ("net"), and *tantra* ("expansion"), as if to form the mystical sentence "With the proper instrument and formula, one nets liberation through expansion."

Origins: This magic phrase comes from the itinerant street conjurers of India, who have an interesting origin of their own:

[These conjurers] evolved out of the magician-priest, the court figure who, in ancient India, was responsible for casting curses and binding spells, performing exorcisms and divinations, curing illnesses and warding off other evils, paralyzing enemy armies and entrancing women desired by the ruler. Apotropaic rituals were transformed into amusing skits; the magician-entertainer emerged, and magic shows became a fashionable courtly diversion in both classical and Moghul India. The magician, traveling from court to court, carrying a peacock-feather wand and a skull, earned his livelihood by performing both theatrical illusions and close-up sleights of hand.

Bound together by a secret language and secrecy itself, [modern day magicians] are trained in a tradition of magic from infancy. The boys perform with their fathers until they are old enough to go out on their own. The girls perform—handle the snakes, are stuffed into baskets, have swords passed through their necks—until they are women. Then they are expected to bear new conjurers, to nourish them and teach them the ancient secrets of magic.[712]

Facts: *Yantru* and *Mantru* are proper names.

Common Magician's Applications: Restorations. For example: "[A] shawl, borrowed from an uneasy member of the crowd, is cut into shreds and then, after the wave of a magic wand, a puff of magic breath, and the muttering of magic words—'gilli-gilli-gilli' or 'yantru-mantru-jãlajãla-tantru'—it is whole again."[713]

Yardegar

Origins: This magic phrase originated in Iran.[714]

710 James M. Robinson, *The Nag Hammadi Library in English* (1978)

711 Darlene L'Orange, *Ancient Roots, Many Branches* (2002)

712 Margaret A. Mills, *South Asian Folklore: An Encyclopedia* (2003)

713 *Ibid.*

714 Henning Nelms, *Magic and Showmanship: A Handbook for Conjurers* (1969)

In Literature: Henning Nelms, *Magic and Show-manship: A Handbook for Conjurers* (1969)

Yazam

Origin: *Yazam* is a Hebrew word meaning "entre-preneur."[715]

In Literature: This magic word was coined by author Robert D. San Souci for a story about a bumbling magician named "The Great Yami Yogurt."[716]

Ye Ye Ye Woopy A Ɛ ῑ O U Bang Bang Fling Flang
(see also *aeeiouo*)

Facts: This phrase features the vowels *A, E, I, O,* and *U.* Throughout the evolution of alphabets around the world, vowels have been considered to possess "energetic qualities which were either life-giving and vital, or deadly and suppressive."[717]

In Literature: Raymond Federman, *Take It or Leave It* (1976)

Yes

"Yes" is a magic word.
—William Ury, *Getting Past No* (1991)

"Yes," that magic word, like "Open Sesame."
—*Princeton.edu* (1965)

Variations and Incantations:

- Certainly
  "He . . . spoke one word that was magic to my ears: 'Certainly.'"
  —Frank Voehl, *Deming* (1995)

In Literature:

- "Accumulate yeses. Yes is a magical word and a powerful tool for bringing people closer."
  —James M. Kouzes and Barry Z. Posner, *The Leadership Challenge* (2003)

- "I remember my 'magic moment'—that instant when a 'yes' or a 'no' can change one's life forever."
  —Paulo Coelho, *By the River Piedra I Sat Down and Wept* (1994)

- "Yes is the magic word."
  —Chris Glaser, *Come Home!* (1990)

Ylufgzh Qhqfcfhuzar
(see also *qmfbtf*)

In Literature: Balanced Alternative Technologies Multi-User Dimension, *Bat.org* (2004)

Yobo Sao

Origins: This magic phrase originated in Korea.[718]

In Literature: Henning Nelms, *Magic and Show-manship: A Handbook for Conjurers* (1969)

---

715 Carter Dougherty, "The Israeli Connection," *VirtualCXO.net* (2007)

716 "Sharing My Story," *Appleseeds* (2001)

717 A.T. Mann, *Sacred Architecture* (2002)

718 Henning Nelms, *Magic and Showmanship: A Handbook for Conjurers* (1969)

Yogi Yogi

Meanings:

- Ascetic

- One who practices yoga

- Union

In Literature: "The hallway was lined on the left side with all kinds of magic posters some bearing pictures of imps and devils, along with famous magicians. As I crossed the threshold of the magic shop [Baltimore's Yogi Magic Mart, in 1956] a loud bell announced my entrance into a world that would change my life forever. I realized I was entering into a different world, one of mystery and intrigue, where miracles happened with the muttering of a few magic words, like 'Yogi, Yogi' and 'Sim Sala Bim.' This was a 'real' magic shop. There were no costumes, wigs or masks, only magic. Directly in front and to the right side of me were old glass cases overflowing with hundreds of props and tricks. Brass bowls, feather flowers, spring flowers, coins, cards, mysterious boxes and tubes of metal with 'ancient' Chinese symbols, steel rings and ropes and fabulous silk scarves with incredible designs on them. Everywhere you looked there was magic!"
—Barry Gibbs, "In the Beginning," *Inside Magic* (2003)

Yoho

Facts: "Scott Adams . . . used to run a rather profitable business selling software for home computers before the IBM PC came out. One of his most successful lines were the text-based adventure games he wrote himself. His second adventure game, 'Pirate's Adventure,' featured the magic word YOHO, which when uttered would teleport you to another room. The description that accompanied this teleportation was, 'Everything spins around and suddenly I'm elsewhere.'"[719]

Yoom

Origins: *Yoom* is a mantra of Hindu origin. This magical syllable is repeated sixteen times by magicians performing dematerialization rites.[720]

You

Mystique: *You* "is a magical word, because it is infinitely singular and/or infinitely plural, depending on the perspective of the reader. The relationship of the one to the many, the part to the whole, is a matter of current concern to both science and metaphysics, so that one can deeply appreciate not only the influence of the collective state of consciousness upon the individual, but also the effect of an individual's transformation upon the collective state of consciousness."[721]

719 Roger M. Wilcox, "Cutsey, Kitschy References in the Disgusting Characters Stories" (2003)

720 M. Gonzalez-Wippler, *Complete Book of Spells, Ceremonies and Magic* (1978)

721 W. Brugh Joy, *Joy's Way* (1979)

Z

Za Za

Origins: *Za Za* (or *Za*) is a magic name of Hebrew origin, mentioned in *Magic Spells and Formulae by* Joseph Naveh and Shaul Shaked (1993).

Facts: *Za Za* is part of a Runic chant discussed in *The Runes Workbook* by Leo D. Wild (2004).

Zabar, Kresge, Caldor, Wal-Mart

Facts: This is a spell that conjures zombies (actually names of discount retail markets), chanted by cartoon character Bart Simpson in the episode "Dial Z For Zombies"[722] of *The Simpsons* television series.

Zabba

Facts: *Zabba* is another name for Zenobia, a legendary queen of Arabia.[723]

As a magic word, *zabba* is used as a variation of *abba*.

Zam-Zam Alacazam
(see also *alacazam*)

Variations and Incantations:

- Twiddlelaayeehoo—zam zam alakazam
  —DaRoyalQueen Thumbelina, *Blogger.com* (2004)

- Wham-zam, alakazam
  —Matthew Kinne, *FirstFiction.net* (2004)

- Zam Zam Ala Kazam

- Zam zam ala-kazam

In Literature:

- "As Sinbad on his magic carpet, the nursling simply forms a whimper and a wish and 'zam-zam alacazam,' a Shangri-La of nurturance and affection quickly unfolds."
  —Harvey Milkman, *Craving for Ecstasy* (1987)

- "Zam zam ala-kazam, magic carpets and genies would by no means pass these chaps."
  —*Ameerzulkifli.com* (2004)

Zanzibar

Mystique: "Zanzibar is one of those names that possess a peculiar, singing magic in every syllable; like Samarkand or Rajasthan, or Kilimanjaro."[724]

Facts: *Zanzibar* is an archipelago off the coast of Tanzania. It is "a hotbed of magic"[725] and mystical belief systems.

Zanzibar is the name of a *Mystery Men* comic book character, "a stage magician who uses his mental powers to fight crime. He's got telekinesis,

---

722 Season 4, Episode 64, Oct. 29, 1992

723 Robert G. Hoyland, *Arabia and the Arabs* (2001)

724 M.M. Kaye, *Death in Zanzibar* (1959)

725 Toby Green, *Meeting the Invisible Man* (2004)

mentally-powered superstrength, and hypnosis/mind-control."[726]

"The Mysterious Floating Orb of Zanzibar" is an illusion performed by professional magician Simon Lovell.

Zanzib is the name of a town where magic carpets are sold in the novel *Castle in the Air* by Diana Wynne Jones (1990).

Variations and Incantations: Zanzabar "I headed home to watch *The Seven Tongues of Mr. Mystero* . . . Mr. Mystero was a big hairy dude who could sprout six extra tongues when he said the magic word. The magic word was 'Zanzabar.'" —Steve Kedrowski, "Dirty Movies" (2004)

Zap

Zap! There's the magick! —Patricia Telesco, *Exploring Candle Magick* (2001)

Mystique: "[I]t's when the magic . . . zaps you, captures you, sits you right down and makes you its own. You become a part of it and it a part of you."[727]

Zap is a surge of directed energy. It's also a direct hit.[728] "ZAP! You are under my spell!"[729]

Variations and Incantations:

- •Www-zap
  —*W.I.T.C.H.: Out of the Dark* (2004)

- • Zappo Zingo
  —David Greenberg, *Slugs* (1983)

In Literature: "I hope my magic works now! Zap!" —Grace Maccarone, *Magic Matt and the Jack-o'-Lantern* (2003)

Zapazoyd

In Literature: "To make them disappear use the magic word 'Zapazoyd.'" —Jennifer McCarthy, "Sarah's Journey" (2000)

Zara

Zara, enchanted by your powerful magic. —John Lord Campbell, *The Lives of the Lord Chancellors and Keepers of the Great Seal of England Vol. 4* (1851)

Mystique: *Zara* recalls *Zarathustra* (also known as Zoroaster), the ancient Persian prophet.

Meanings: The root of *Zara* is *zar*, meaning "gold."

Origins: *Zara* is of Persian origin.

In Literature:

- • "Across the table, he leaned forward and, in a husky whisper, pronounced the magic word: 'Zara!'"
  —Jacqueline Park, *The Secret Book of Grazia Dei Rossi* (1997)

- • "[I said] a magic word. . . . Her name. Zara [the Queen of Light]."
  —Tony Abbott, *The Knights of Silversnow* (2002)

726 Jess Nevins, "The Golden Age Heroes Directory" (2004)

727 Ann Hazard, *Cooking With Baja Magic* (1997)

728 Nina Bernstein, *Magic by the Book* (2005)

729 Laurence B. White, *Shazam! Simple Science Magic* (1991)

Zatara

Facts: *Zatara* is the name of an *Action Comics* hero, "a famous stage magician who actually has magical powers. Speaking his backwards spells, he travels the world, fighting evil and wicked magicians wherever he finds them, including his 'loving enemy' the Tigress. His power is his magical ability; he can do anything with his spells."[730]

Zatza Lepus Wagra Doozie

Common Magician's Applications: Production. For example: "You say the magic words. *Zatza Lepus Wagra Doozie.* You put your hand in the hat. You pull out a rabbit."[731]

In Literature: Susan Meddaugh, *Lulu's Hat* (2002)

Zauberwort

Origins: *Zauberwort* is a German word meaning "magic formula."

Zazar

Origins: *Zazar* is a magic word from the *Gremoire du Pape Honorius* (1800).

Facts: In Alchemy, *zazar* means *sugar.*[732]

A guardian named *Zazar* is the "great Wy-sen-wyf of the Bale Bog" in *Knight or Knave* by Andre Norton (2001).

In Literature: "Zazar spoke alone. 'I am the Eldest. I am the Power of Earth Magic.'" —Andre Norton, *A Crown Disowned* (2002)

Zblrt-Tbpttpt
(see also *qmfbtf*)

What are magic spells but magic spellings?
—Morris Bishop,
"Good Usage, Bad Usage, and Usage" (1969)

Facts: This is a magic phrase for conjuring blurred vision.

In Literature: Balanced Alternative Technologies Multi-User Dimension, *Bat.org* (2004)

Zengawii

Origins: *Zengawii* is a nonsense word meant to capture the mystique of African tribal rituals. It appears in several novels for young adults by Henry Winkler.

Common Magician's Applications: Restoration. For example: "There's this one trick Frankie does where he cuts a rope in two pieces and drops it into a top hat. He waves a magic wand over the hat and says, '*Zengawii*,' which is his magic word he learned in Zimbabwe. When he pulls the rope out of the hat, it's back in one piece!"[733]

In Literature: Henry Winkler, *Niagara Falls, Or Does It?* (2003), *I Got a D in Salami* (2003), *The*

730 *Ibid.*
731 Susan Meddaugh, *Lulu's Hat* (2002)
732 Martinus Rulandus, *Lexicon of Alchemy* (1612)
733 Henry Winkler, *The Night I Flunked My Field Trip* (2004)

Night I Flunked My Field Trip (2004), and *Day of the Iguana* (2003)

Zeph-a-ni-ah

Origins: *Zephaniah* means "'the Lord conceals,' 'the Lord protects,' or, possibly, 'God of darkness.'"[734]

Facts: This word is equivalent to *open sesame.*

In Literature: "She could . . . tell you the essential words needed to get you through magic doors and portals. But it was up to you to spell them correctly or you could not enter. . . . Zoe said the magic word 'Zeph-a-ni-ah.' Luke then had to spell it; his first couple of times were wrong. Then finally he got it right, 'Z-e-p-h-a-n-i-a-h.' Within a second after the spelling, they were safely through the portal."
—Ted Lazaris, *Dragon Man: The Adventures of Luke Starr* (2002)

Zi-Ana

Meanings:

- Heavenly life

- Spirit of the Heavens
  —George Stephen Goodspeed, *A History of the Babylonians and Assyrians* (1902)

- Supreme Being

Origins: *Zi-Ana* is of ancient Sumerian origin.

Facts: *Zi-Ana* was "frequently invoked in the magical texts"[735] and uttered by Incan priests in their incantations to invoke the divine.[736]

In Literature: "In the Way of Zi-Ana you shall attain freedom, from the lies of all gods and Sephirotic veils of illusion."
—Uriah, *Ziana* (2006)

Zigazak

Origins: The magic word *zigazak* originated in a Jewish fable.

In Literature: Eric Kimmel, *Zigazak! A Magical Hanukkah Night* (2001)

Zim Salabim
(see also *sim sala bim*)

In Literature: Marie-Dominique Crapon, *Sloughi* (2004)

Zim Zala Bim
(see also *sim salabim*)

Facts: *Zim Zala Bim* is the name of a Commodore64 computer game (1984).

Variations and Incantations:

- Abrakadabra zim zala bim
  —Anonymous, "Earth Dream" (2000)

735 Claude Reignier Conder, *Altaic Hieroglyphs and Hittite Inscriptions* (1887)
736 Robert Brown, *The Hall of Seb: A Study of the Origin of the Idea of Time* (1895)

734 *Wikipedia.com* (2007)

- Zim Zala Bim, Bombbooz Zala Dim
  —Chautae Repartee, "Harry Potter Goes to Amsterdam" (2001)

- Zim-zala, dim-zala, zim-zala, do-zalza, day
  From a German nursey song, quoted in *Human Values.net* (2004)

- Zim Zala Pim, Pipiti Popiti Pù
  —*Digilander.libero.it/ludozone* (2004)

Zimmity Zammity Zoo

Origins: *Zammit* is a Maltese surname derived from the Hebrew *Shemuel* meaning 'peace.' "The 'it' may reflect the Hebrew adjectival ending and thus the name may also signify 'pertaining to peace' and perhaps indicating one of a peaceful nature. Zammit may also be derived from the Semitic (Arabic and Hebrew) 'sami' meaning 'to hear' and in fact the root word of the personal name Simon."[737]

Variations and Incantations: Abracadabra-zimmity-ZAM
"She poked her fingers at the street. 'Abracadabra-zimmity-ZAM! How's *that?*'"
—Ray Bradbury, *Dandelion Wine* (1946)

In Literature: "After I made my wishes I said my magic words 'zimmity, zammity, zoo.' I discreetly waved my wand so Jimmy wouldn't see me. My magic was done."
—Amy Graham, "Josh the Great," *The Palimpsest Review* (2000)

Zing
(see also *zingo*)

There was the sudden zip and zing of magic.
—Terry Pratchett, *The Light Fantastic* (2000)

Mystique: *Zing* is a little bolt of flowing energy, a "tiny shock."[738] It whizzes past and bounces up, glittering all the way. *Zing* is something we add, to get things energized and moving. *Zing* is also associated with release, as in the saying, "Zing went the strings of my heart."

Meanings:

- Amazement
  "[W]ow, zing and magic . . ."
  —Seth Godin, *Unleashing the Ideavirus* (2001)

- Bounce
  "[P]erhaps a little too much zing in my step ."
  —Garth Nix, *Lirael* (2001)

- Brightness

- Dazzling flash
  "ZING!—A shimmering ray of sunlight, powerful as a laser beam, flashed."
  —Roger George Clark, *The Magic Statue* (2004)

- Electricity
  "He felt a zing like a static shock."
  —Jennifer Stevenson, *Trash Sex Magic* (2004)

- Go up
  —Linda Varsell Smith, *The Rainbow Rescue* (2003)

- Instantaneous
  —D.J. MacHale, *Black Water* (2004)

- Magic
  "There was the sudden zip and zing of magic."

---

737 Vincent Zammit, "History of Zammit," *Search Malta.com* (2007)

738 Diana G. Gallagher, *Showdown at the Mall* (1997)

—Terry Pratchett, *The Light Fantastic* (2000)

- Pizzazz
—Laurie Notaro, *We Thought You Would Be Prettier* (2005)

- Sparkle
"All the stars zing."
—Margo Lanagan, *Black Juice* (2005)

- Vibrate
"She gave him a look with those blue eyes of hers that made him zing like one of the strings she was strumming."
—Katherine Paterson, *Bridge to Terabithia* (1977)

- Whizzing past
—K.A. Applegate, *The Exposed* (1999)

- Zigzag
"Icefire felt the euphoria of magic zing through his body."
—Christina Woods, *Wizard's Curse* (2005)

Common Magician's Applications: Mentalism. For example: "Explain that on the word 'Zing' (or other suitable word, Abracadabra, Shazzam, etc.) a magic spell will take hold of the group. The effect of the spell is that one member will become a frozen 'statue' but the other person will have the power to free their partner."[739]

Variations and Incantations:

- Abracadabra, fling, zing
—Peter Lerangis, *Zap! Science Fair Surprise!* (2002)

- Ka-zing

- K-k-k-zing
—Tony Abbott, *Quest for the Queen* (2000)

In Literature: "'So what about the Zing?' 'Ahhh, the Zing,' she says like she is the high priestess of Zing, about to reveal one of life's great mysteries."
—Christine Walker Bos, *The Magical Man List* (2003)

Zingo
(see also *bingo* and *zing*)

Zingo! Her jaw dropped. Her eyes widened.
—Ray Kroc, *Grinding It Out* (1992)

Mystique: *Zingo* has all the punch of *bingo*, but with an electric zap.

Meanings:

- All of a sudden
"[T]hen—zingo!—he was in the air . . ."
—Creative Publishing International, *Outdoor Life: If Nature Calls . . . Hang Up!* (1999)
"[Z]ingo, right through the fingers."
—James Kirkwood, *P.S. Your Cat is Dead* (1972)

- Energy, electricity
—Henry Jenkins, *What Made Pistachio Nuts?* (1992)

- Exactly
—Arnold B. Kanter, *The Ins and Outs of Law Firm Mismanagement* (1994)

- Great idea
—Arnold B. Kanter, *The Ins and Outs of Law Firm Mismanagement* (1994)

Facts: This magic word is recommended for magician Art Kahn's "Enchanted Glass" trick.[740]

739 Bernie Warren, *Using the Creative Arts in Therapy* (1984)

740 Bob Gibbons, *BobGibbonsMagic.com* (2005)

Variations and Incantations:

- Zappo Zingo
  —David Greenberg, *Slugs* (1983)

- Zingo bingo bang
  —Tim O'Brien, *Going After Cacciato* (1999)

- Zingo Zango
  —James Joyce, *Finnegans Wake* (1939)

- Zingo Zip
  —John A. Schindler, *How to Live 365 Days a Year* (1954)

- Zip-Zap-Zingo
  —Barry L. Dordick, *Macaroni on the Moon* (2003)

Zippity Doo Daa, Zippity Yeah

Origins: A George Washington Dixon minstrel song entitled "Zip Coon" (1834) featured this lyric: "Zip a duden duden duden zip a duden day." It was sung to an Irish or Scottish melody later rearranged as "Turkey in the Straw."[741] The words were adapted into lyrics for "Zip-a-dee Doo-Dah," a song in the Walt Disney film *Song of the South* (1946).

Facts: *Zippity doo daa, zippity yeah* are magic words for reversing an effect in the *Bewitched* television series.

Variations and Incantations:

- Flip-a-dee-doodle, flip-a-dee-ay
  —Jig Star, *High School Soap Opera* (2002)

- Razzamatazz hocus pocus zippity-doo-dah
  —Ntozake Shange, "Spell #7," *Honey, Hush!* (1998)

- Zippity doo da
  —Kenneth Wapnick, *Absence from Felicity* (1991)

- Zippity doo-dah ding dong derry day
  —Steven Curtis Lance, "Hosed," *New Poems* (2005)

- Zippity doo dah, zippity aye
  —Eric Hansen, *Stranger in the Forest* (2000)

- Zippity doo dah, zippity day
  —Loren W. Christensen, *Skid Row Beat* (1999)

Zolda Pranken Kopeck Lum

Facts: These are the magic words the character Uncle Arthur teaches Darrin Stephens in the television series *Bewitched*, when Darrin is convinced he's been turned into a Warlock.[742]

Zorami Zaitux Elastot

Origins: *Zorami Zaitux Elastot* are antiquated magical words for instant success from an Egyptian book of magical talismans entitled *Treasure of the Old Man of the Pyramids*, "translated from the Language of the Magi" in the eighteenth century.[743]

----

741 Larry Starr, *American Popular Music* (2003)

742 *EyeOnSoaps.com/whoiscrone.htm*

743 Arthur Edward Waite, *The Book of Ceremonial Magic* (1913)

ZORAMI ZAITUX ELASTOT

Figure 42. This "immediate achievement" talisman has an occult appearance but not an infernal purpose. It is based upon the research of Arthur Edward Waite in *The Book of Ceremonial Magic* (1913).

Facts: These magic words were believed to call upon the assistance of "enough genii for the immediate achievement" of any undertaking. The words were to be embroidered in silk.[744]

Common Magician's Applications: Silk animation. When printed onto a silk in the form of an ancient talisman, *Zorami Zaitux Elastot* can lend an ancient Egyptian mystique to the routine.

Zot Mar Nak Grttzt
(see also *qmfbtf*)

In Literature: Balanced Alternative Technologies Multi-User Dimension, *Bat.org* (2004)

Zxcvbnm
(see *qwertyuiop asdfghjkl zxcvbnm*)

Figure 43. *Zxcvbnm* depicted in the form of a sigil, a graphic representation meant to capture the "essence" of the word and channel its magical energy like a circuit board.

Zymeloz

Origins: *Zymeloz* is an angelic name found in the *Lemegeton Clavicula Salomonis or The Lesser Key of Solomon* (17th century).

Zzzz

Mystique: *Zzzz* is the electrical zap of pure, focused energy.

Facts: The evil magician in Doug Henning's musical *The Magic Show* (1981) uses the magic trigger word *zzzz* over and over again during his act.

---

744 *Ibid.*

APPENDIX

Magic words mean quite different
hings to different audiences.
—Joseph J. Ellis,
What Did the Declaration Declare? (1999)

The following list features magic words of special relevance to specialized audiences. A professional magician entertaining such groups might
consider incorporating the appropriate magic
words to demonstrate that he's "in tune" with the
audience as well as to get a few laughs.

ACTORS AND MOVIE DIRECTORS

- *action!*
  —Edward Jay Epstein, *The Big Picture: The
  New Logic of Money and Power in Hollywood*
  (2005)

ADVERTISERS

- *breakthrough, secret, revealed, new, first, best, im-
  proved, bargain, sensational, easy, remarkable, genuine, popular, limited, proven, classic*
  —David Taylor, *The Freelance Success Book*
  (2003)

AIR TRAFFIC CONTROLLERS

- *cleared for the approach*
  "[T]he magic words, 'Cleared for the approach . . .'"
  —Steven Cushing, *Fatal Words: Communication Clashes and Aircraft Crashes* (1994)

ANIMAL TRAINERS

- *consistency*
  —Charles Wilhelm, *Building Your Dream Horse*
  (2005)

ARMED FORCES

- *duty, honor, country*
  "Duty, honor, country: Those three hallowed words reverently dictate what you
  ought to be, what you can be, what you will
  be. They are your rallying point to build
  courage when courage seems to fail, to re-
  gain faith when there seems to be little cause
  for faith, to create hope when hope becomes
  forlorn."
  —General Douglas MacArthur, Thayer
  Award Speech (1962)

- *home*
  —Gordon Sullivan, *This Kind of War: The
  Classic Korean War History* (2000)

- *liberty*
  —Todd Hansen, *The Alamo Reader* (2003)

ASTROLOGERS

- *integration*
  "The single most magical word in astrologi-
  cal interpretation is integration."
  —Steven Forrest, *The Changing Sky* (1999)

ATTORNEYS

- *lawyer*
  "She left with a few insults and five thousand
  dollars in compensation—a sum of money
  beyond her wildest dreams—and all because
  of that magic word 'lawyer.'"
  —Paul Coelho, *Eleven Minutes* (2004)

Appendix

AUTOBIOGRAPHERS

- *I imagine*
  "'I imagine' is an instant disclaimer you can give yourself at any point with a work, two magic words that many autobiographic writers forget they can use."
  —Tristine Rainer, *Your Life As Story* (1998)

BOARD MEMBERS

- *meeting adjourned*
  —C. Alan Jennings, *Robert's Rules for Dummies* (2004)

BUDDHISTS

- *emptiness*
  "'Emptiness' is the magic word that names the essence of the universe."
  —Stephan Beyer, *Cult of Tara: Magic and Ritual in Tibet* (1978)

BUSINESS PEOPLE

- *funding*
  —Tom Clancy, *Rainbow Six* (2004)

- *opportunity, enterprise, prosperity, success*
  "[The skyscrapers] were materialized by those hard, cold, magic words—opportunity, enterprise, prosperity, success—just business words out of world-wide commerce from a land rich in natural resource."
  —Younghill Kang, "A Korean Discovers New York," *The American Reader: Words That Moved a Nation* (2000)

- *import-export*
  —Elie Wiesel, *All Rivers Run to the Sea: A Memoir* (1995)

CATERERS

- *refreshment*
  "At that magic word *refreshment* the whole crowd formed up in procession and silently awaited the signal to start."
  —Kenneth Grahame, *The Reluctant Dragon* (1983)

CHEFS

- *al dente*
  —Mark Bittman, *How to Cook Everything* (1998)

CHILDREN

- *once upon a time*
  "'Once upon a time' are the magic words that open the floodgates of a child's imagination."
  —Dale Carnegie, *The Quick and Easy Way to Effective Speaking* (1990)

COMPUTER PROGRAMMERS

- *troubleshoot*
  —Dan Bobola, *Complete Idiot's Guide to Microsoft Word 2000* (1999)

DIETERS

- *willpower, fortitude, moral fiber, resolution*
  —Geneen Roth, *Feeding the Hungry Heart* (1993)

DIETICIANS

- *low fat, fat free*
  —Susan Love, *Dr. Susan Love's Menopause and Hormone Book: Making Informed Choices* (2003)

GOLFERS

- *the short game*
  "*The short game.* Those are the magic words."
  —Harvey Penick, *Harvey Penick's Little Red Book* (1999)

HALLOWEEN CELEBRANTS

- *trick or treat*
  —Abraham Verghese, *The Tennis Partner* (1999)

INVESTORS

- *cash flow*
  —Robert T. Kiyosaki, *Rich Dad's Guide to Investing* (2000)

- *growth*
  —Burton G. Malkiel, *A Random Walk Down Wall Street* (2004)

- *enough*
  —Joe Dominguez, *Your Money or Your Life* (1999)

- *all the money you need*
  —Andy Kessler, *Running Money* (2004)

MANAGERS

- *we are all in this together*
  "No operation is being singled out, no one is being fingered. 'We are all in this together.' What magic words."
  —Philip B. Crosby, *Quality is Free* (1980)

- *we, us, our*
  —Leil Lowndes, *Talking the Winner's Way* (1999)

MARKETERS

- *go wide fast*
  —Mark Yarnell, *Your First Year in Network Marketing* (1998)

MARRIAGE COUNSELORS

- *compromise*
  —David Niven, *100 Simple Secrets of Great Relationships* (2003)

- *sharing, openness*
  —Joan Gould, *Spinning Straw into Gold* (2005)

MOTIVATORS

- *now*
  "*Now* is the magic word of success."
  —David Schwartz, *The Magic of Thinking Big* (1987)

- *great job*
  "'You're doing a great job,' magic words that can make a person's day."
  —Judith Orloff, *Positive Energy* (2004)

- *do what you can*
  —Cindy Glovinsky, *Making Peace With the Things in Your Life* (2002)

- *triumph*
  —Keith Harrell, *Attitude is Everything* (2002)

MOTORCYCLISTS

- *counter steering*
  —Keith Code, *A Twist of the Wrist 2* (1997)

NEGOTIATORS

- *I'm sorry*
  —William Ury, *Getting Past No* (1993)

NOVELISTS

- *what if*
  —Lou W. Stanek, *Writing Your Life* (1971)

NUTRITIONISTS

- *calcium added*
  —Harvy Diamond, *Fit For Life II* (1989)

PARENTS

- *discipline*
  "Discipline—that magic word you've been waiting for."
  —James Sears, *The Baby Book* (2003)

- *wait*
  —Stanley Greenspan, *Building Healthy Minds* (2000)

PHARMACEUTICAL WORKERS

- *research, innovation, American*
  —Marcia Angell, *The Truth About the Drug Companies* (2004)

- *prescription*
  —Al Ries, *Focus: The Future of Your Company Depends on It* (1997)

PHOTOGRAPHERS

- *cheese*
  —*broward.org* (2005)

PHYSICIANS

- *you're the doctor*
  "'You're the doctor.' Those magic words."
  —Carl Hiaasen, *Skin Tight* (2002)

POETS

- *wit*
  "No one was ready to give up the magic word *wit*."
  —C.S. Lewis, *Studies in Words* (1960)

POLITICIANS

- *mainstream*
  "The magic word—always had been, always would be—was 'mainstream.'"
  —George W.S. Trow, *Within the Context of No Context* (1997)

- *confidence, growth*
  —"Global Roulette: In a Volatile World Economy, Can Everyone Lose?" *Harpers Magazine*, (June 1, 1998)

PROCRASTINATORS

- *mañana*
  —Linda Dillow, *Intimate Issues: 21 Questions Christian Women Ask About Sex* (1999)

PROVENÇAL FRENCH BUILDERS

- *normalement*
  "[U]nspoken disclaimers... are occasionally reinforced by the magic word *normalement*, a supremely versatile escape clause worthy of an insurance policy. *Normalement*—providing it doesn't rain, providing the truck hasn't broken down, providing the brother-in-law hasn't borrowed the tool box—is the Provençal builder's equivalent of the fine print in a contract."
  —Peter Mayle, *A Year in Provence* (1991)

REALTORS

- *independent contractor*
  "You are—magic words coming up here—an 'independent contractor.'"
  —Frank Cook, *21 Things I Wish My Broker Had Told Me* (2002)

R.V.-ERS

- *inexpensive and lightweight*
  —Brent Peterson, *The Complete Idiot's Guide to RVing* (2001)

SALESMEN

- *I did it!*
  "[W]hen you get to the top of the mountain—when you achieve what you've been working for—at last you can say the magic words. Scream them—I DID IT!"
  —Jeffrey Gitomer, *The Sales Bible* (2003)

SOCIOLOGISTS

- *statistics, inference, quantitative, systematic, objective*
  —Roberto Franzosi, *From Words to Numbers* (2004)

STAR TREK FANS

- *beam me up*
  "Beam me up, beam me up. Magic words. Need I say more?"
  —Jack Dann, *Dreaming Down-Under* (2002)

TRAVEL AGENTS

- *adventure*
  —Tony Abbott, *The Magic Escapes* (2002)

TRAVELERS

- *wardrobe*
  "[W]ardrobe, that magical word that is itself the start of a trip."
  —Manu Dibango, *Three Kilos of Coffee* (1994)

TYPESETTERS

- *folio*
  —Ann Longknife, *The Art of Styling Sentences* (2002)

WEBMASTERS

- *free*
  "On the Web the magic word is 'free.'"
  —Rachel McAlpine, *Web Word Wizardry* (2001)

- *bandwidth*
  —Bharati Mukherjee, *Desirable Daughters* (2003)

WELDERS

- *Magnaflux*
  "Magnaflux—a magic word in the welding or metallurgy business."
  —Richard Finch, *Welder's Handbook* (1997)

WINE CONNOISSEURS

- *Chardonnay*
  "[F]ull-bodied white wines with the magic word Chardonnay on the label."
  —Jancis Robinson, *The Oxford Companion to Wine* (1999)

WOMEN

- *forever*
  —Thomas Ellis, *The Rantings of a Single Male* (2005)

WRITERS

- *the end*
  —Carolyn Wheat, *How to Write Killer Fiction* (2003)

ABOUT THE AUTHOR

Craig Conley has been called a "language fanatic" by gossip columnist Cindy Adams, and "cult hero" by *Publisher's Weekly.* His eccentric research has led him to compile *Magic Words: A Dictionary* and *One-Letter Words: A Dictionary,* among other strange and unusual lexicons. Craig splits his time between Florida and Wales, UK.

TO OUR READERS

Weiser Books, an imprint of Red Wheel/Weiser, publishes books across the entire spectrum of occult and esoteric subjects. Our mission is to publish quality books that will make a difference in people's lives without advocating any one particular path or field of study. We value the integrity, originality, and depth of knowledge of our authors.

Our readers are our most important resource, and we appreciate your input, suggestions, and ideas about what you would like to see published. Please feel free to contact us, to request our latest book catalog, or to be added to our mailing list.

Red Wheel/Weiser, LLC
500 Third Street, Suite 230
San Francisco, CA 94107
www.redwheelweiser.com